The Ottoman Empire: Conquest, Organization and Economy

Variorum Revised Editions:

M.-M. ALEXANDRESCU-DERSCA
La campagne de Timur en Anatolie (1402)

DENIS A. ZAKYTHINOS
Le Despotat grec de Morée. Histoire politique
Le Despotat grec de Morée. Vie et institutions

Variorum Reprints:

NICOLAS IORGA
Philippe de Mézières (1327-1405) et la croisade au XIVe siècle
Paris 1896 edition

RUY GONZALES DE CLAVIJO
The Spanish Embassy to Samarkand 1403-1406
ed. I. Sreznevsky. St. Petersburg 1881

In the Collected Studies Series:

VLADIMIR MINORSKY
The Turks, Iran and the Caucasus in the Middle Ages

BERNARD LEWIS
Studies in Classical and Ottoman Islam (7th-16th Centuries)

CLAUDE CAHEN
Turcobyzantina et Oriens Christianus

NIKOLAI TODOROV
La ville balkanique sous les Ottomans (XVe-XIXe. s.)

NICOARA BELDICEANU
Le monde ottoman des Balkans (1402-1566)

PETER TOPPING
Studies on Latin Greece A.D. 1205-1715

HELENE AHRWEILER
Byzance: les pays et les territoires

ANTHONY LUTTRELL
The Hospitallers in Cyprus, Rhodes, Greece and the West (1291-1440)

ELIYAHU ASHTOR
Studies on the Levantine Trade in the Middle Ages

Halil İnalcık

The Ottoman Empire: Conquest, Organization and Economy

Collected Studies

VARIORUM REPRINTS
London 1978

British Library CIP data

Inalcik, Halil
The Ottoman Empire. – (Collected studies series; CS87).
1. Turkey – History – Ottoman Empire, 1288-1918 – Collected works
I. Title
949.6′008 DR440

ISBN 0-86078-032-5

Published in Great Britain by Variorum Reprints
21a Pembridge Mews London W11 3EQ

Printed in Great Britain by Kingprint Ltd
Richmond Surrey TW9 4PD

VARIORUM REPRINT CS87

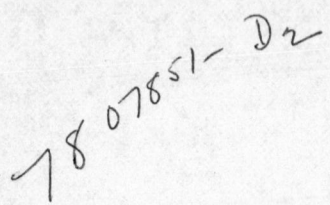

CONTENTS

This volume contains a total of 362 pages

PREFACE

Whether one is dealing with Byzantine and Balkan history in the late Middle Ages, or with the fundamental changes in the Islamic world in modern times, or with the resurgence of the Mediterranean as the center of world history in the sixteenth century, or even with such crucial developments as the rise of nation-states and of capitalism in Europe, one is inevitably confronted with that colossus called the Ottoman Empire. In one way or another for six centuries down to the first world war, the Ottoman Empire remained a major problem for Europe, symbolizing the challenge of Islam first in the face of crusade and then of colonialism. It was commonly envisaged in the West as the Antichrist, a threat to every value of Western culture, an anachronism that stood in the way of the "normal course" of history and had to be eliminated. These images were embedded in the Western mind and became part of its cultural tradition. They also became, understandably, an integral part of the set of unquestioned assumptions that determined the outlook of European historians, despite the insights given by a few dissident historians, such as Nicola Jorga, Paul Wittek and Fernand Braudel. It is indeed difficult to explain how some distinguished historians in the fields of European or Byzantine history can have been so simplistic in their interpretations when it came to the Ottomans.

However, thanks to the rediscovery and opening to study of the Ottoman archives, an unusually rich source for the political, socio-economic and demographic history of the whole Middle East and the Balkans in modern times, studies on the Ottoman Empire, that "zone of formidable uncertainty" as Braudel put it, have made tremendous progress in past decades. One can now say that we are beginning to discern more clearly the real place of the Ottoman

Empire in world history, and to understand the whole historical process in this central region. Born out of Islam's reaction to an expanding Europe in the Eastern Mediterranean during the fourteenth and fifteenth centuries, the Ottoman Empire, despite the borrowing of many Western techniques, represents the strongest and most successful resistance to Europe by any non-Western culture; this challenge, in turn, seems to have contributed significantly to the moulding of what we consider modern Europe. Thus, the story of the Ottomans also becomes of interest to those concerned with the most significant historical process of modern times in one of its crucial stages: that is the development of the technological supremacy of Western Europe over the other cultures of the world.

The papers selected here are designed to present in one volume the results of research in the Ottoman archives on such questions as how the Ottomans made and organized their conquests to build up one of the longest living empires in world history; what were the characteristics of its socio-economic structure; and how, as a result of the military and economic impact of its unyielding rival, Christian Europe, this basically medieval Islamic structure began to disintegrate.

The papers collected here were published between 1954 and 1974. The transliteration of names of Arabic, Persian and Slavic origin is not consistent. We have tried to remedy this by cross-referencing in the index, and to correct some errors or misprints of importance.

H. İNALCIK

University of Chicago
May 1978

CONQUEST AND ORGANIZATION

I

OTTOMAN METHODS OF CONQUEST (*)

(1) *The Method of Gradual Conquest.*

It appears that in the Ottoman conquests there were two distinct stages that were applied almost systematically. The Ottomans first sought to establish some sort of suzerainty over the neighbouring states. They then sought direct control over these countries by the elimination of the native dynasties. Direct control by the Ottomans meant basically the application of the *timar* system which was based upon a methodical recording of the population and resources of the countries in the *defters* (official registers). The establishment of the *timar* system did not necessarily mean a revolutionary change in the former social and economic order. It was in fact a conservative reconciliation of local conditions and classes with Ottoman institutions which aimed at gradual assimilation.

The use of these two stages in the gradual achievement of the Ottoman conquests can be detected from the beginning of Ottoman history. For example, the relationship of Osman Gâzî, the founder of the dynasty, with Köse Mihal (Koze Michael) the local lord of Harmankaya (Chirmenkia), with Samsama Chawush and other *tekviours* appears first to have been in the nature of an alliance, then of a vassalage [1]. This was most probably due to the particular military organization in the

(*) I wish to express my thanks to Mr. D. Sherinian and Mr. Th. Buchanan for the help they gave me in translating this paper from the Turkish.

(1) See my *Stefan Duşandan Osmanli Imparatorluğuna*, in *Mélanges Fuad Köprülü*, Istanbul, 1953, pp. 211-212.

uc, borderlands in which there were overlords *(uc-emîri)* and vassal lords *(bey)* (1). At any rate, in the 14 th century we see many small states being incorporated into the Ottoman state after a more or less long period of vassalage. When Bayezid I (1389-1403) became Sultan on the battlefield of Kossovo there were many vassal rulers such as the Byzantine Emperor (vassal since 1373), the Bulgarian princes (vassals since 1371), the Serbian princes in Serbia and in Macedonia (vassals since 1372), and the local lords in Albania (vassals since 1385), in Greece and in the Aegean islands. In Anatolia, not only the *gâzî* principalities in the West but also the Karamanids in Konya were Ottoman vassals.

Sultan Bayezid I inaugurated a new policy by establishing direct control over these vassal countries in a number of swift military expeditions. He was afforded the opportunity to achieve this by the revolt of the Anatolian principalities at his accession to the throne and the cooperation of the vassal Bulgarian king with the enemy Hungarians. He drove out the local dynasties and brought these countries under direct rule. It is interesting to note that at the famous meeting of Serres, when Bayezid gathered together most of the vassal Balkan princes, there were rumours that for a moment he considered executing them (2). Bayezid also saw the importance of the imperial city of Constantinople in building a unified empire from the Danube to the Euphrates. Thus he erected the Castle of Akcha-hisar *(Anadolu-hisari)* on the Bosphorus and attempted a conquest of the city (3). What is particularly interesting for us is the reaction that showed itself, not only in the conquered lands but also in the Ottoman state itself, against this violent and hasty policy of annexation during and after Bayezid's reign. This policy was considered as being against the good Ottoman tradition. The two points of view, that of hasty and that of gradual expansion, are apparent in Bayezid's time in the differences between Chan-

(1) See F. Köprülü, *Les Origines de l'Empire Ottoman*, Paris 1935, p. 89.
(2) See Zakythinos, *Le despotat grec de Morée*, Paris 1932.
(3) See my *Fatih Devri Üzerinde Tedkikler ve Vesikalar*, Ankara 1954, p. 122.

darli Ali Pasha and Hodja Firuz Pasha. About half a century later, Chandarli Halil Pasha still criticised in the strongest terms Hodja Firuz's policy of unscrupulous war. The popular Ottoman tradition which criticised Bayezid's government also complained bitterly of his introduction into the Ottoman administrative system of the new fiscal method of a central government using *defters*. We shall see that the *defter* was the basic tool of the Ottoman government. Bayezid also attempted to make radical changes in the newly conquered lands in Anatolia, replacing the native aristocracy by his slaves *(gulâm)* (1). His forceful policy of unification, which caused this vigorous reaction, was the real cause of the subsequent collapse of his empire in 1402. In fact, adopting fully the old Islamic and Ilkhanid methods of administration Bayezid was responsible for the development of the semi-feudal state of Osman Gâzî and Orhan Gâzî with its vassals and powerful *uc-beyis* (chiefs in the military frontier-zone), into a real Islamic Sultanate with traditional institutions. It was during the same period that "the army of the Porte" *(Kapi-kulu)*, the instrument of central power, was strengthened and gained significance in the state (2). After the destruction of Bayezid's empire by Timur in 1402 the remnants of his system of government contributed most significantly to the restoration of the empire. Let me only mention the existence of *defters* of *timars* in the Ottoman capital which guaranteed the legal titles to them, and, thus, the *timar*-holders who had obtained them from Bayezid in the newly conquered lands were most interested in the reunification of these lands under the Ottoman Sultan. Thus, it is seen that Bayezid's efforts were not all in vain (3).

Bayezid's successors, Süleyman I, Mehmed I and Murad II, resumed the conservative policy and respected the existence

(1) See below, pp. 120-122.

(2) See Ashik Pashazâde, ed. Ali, Istanbul 1332, p. 78.

(3) P. Wittek (*De la défaite d'Ankara à la prise de Constantinople*, REI, 1938), too, considered the premature character of Bayezid's empire as a cause of its fall.

of the restored principalities in old Turkish Anatolia (1) and of the small states in the Balkans. When the Ottomans found it necessary to act against these Moslem states, they did their best to justify such actions in the eyes of the Islamic world. There were several good reasons for this conservative policy, such as the existence of Ottoman pretenders to the throne in Constantinople (2), the threat of a new invasion from the East, and the fear of a crusade from the west. The Chandarlis, an old Ottoman family of Vizirs who had acquired an absolute authority in state affairs, were primarily responsible for this policy, the Grand Vizir Chandarli Halil Pasha (1429-1453) being a particularly strong advocate of it. The restoration of Serbia in 1444 and the maintenance of peace with Byzantium demonstrated strikingly Chandarli Halil Pasha's policy. In order to promote this policy of peace and reconciliation he was forced to struggle against a new military group which gathered around the young Sultan Mehmed II in 1444. After the success of this military group with the conquest of Constantinople in 1453, Chandarli Halil was eliminated, and the policy of unification by conquest prevailed once more. It appears that the conditions at the time justified such a policy. The period after the conclusion of Union between Rome and Constantinople in 1439 was critical. Mehmed II having been deposed in 1446 and his warlike advisers having been eliminated from the government, it was evident to him upon his second accession to the throne in 1451 that the conquest was a necessity for the firm establishment of his own position as well as for the future of the Ottoman Empire (3).

(1) Divided again into the former principalities under their old dynasties, Western Anatolia no longer enjoyed the benefits of safety and large-scale *gâzî* activities which it had known under Ottoman rule. Therefore Murad II reconquered these principalities without great difficulty (1423). The Ottoman Sultans as the real successors of the ancient *uc-emîris* could easily claim the areas beyond the historical boundaries of the former Seldjuk state, which had been conquered by the *gâzîs*, the frontier warriors.

(2) First, Mustafa, Bayezid's son, attempted to seize the throne in 1416 and in 1421. Then Orhan Chelebi, most likely a grandson of Bayezid I, became active in Indjegiz and Dobrudja in 1444. It would be safe to say that the struggle for the throne among the descendants of Bayezid I ended only after the conquest of Constantinople (see my *Fatih devri*, pp. 69-70).

(3) See for all these developments in 1443-1453 my *Fatih Devri*.

We have seen that the Ottoman conquest in two stages was essentially a product of historical conditions. The tradition survived even beyond the Conqueror's successful activity of unification, which was achieved by an uninterrupted series of expeditions. Let us note, for example, Sultan Süleyman's policy toward Hungary. On the other hand, a policy of gradual incorporation continued even after the establishment of direct rule. This will be dealt with subsequently.

(2) *The Statistical Survey of the Conquered Lands.*

Before the army of conquest was withdrawn, small garrisons were immediately placed in several fortresses of strategic importance. Then the remaining fortresses were often demolished by special order of the Sultan. This measure, which was often applied by the Ottomans, was taken firstly in order to avoid the necessity of maintaining forces in them, and secondly in order to prevent a reemergence of centres of resistance under local lords. Then as a rule *sipâhîs* (cavalrymen) who composed the main force of the Ottoman army were given *timars* in the villages throughout the newly conquered country. Some of these, with the name *hisar-eri* or *kale-eri*, were stationed in the fortresses as well. These *hisar-eris* constituted the real military force in most of the fortresses in the 15 th Century. Apparently as a security measure these regular forces were recruited from distant parts of the Empire. According to the record-books the majority of *hisar-eris* in Anatolia came from Rum-ili (the Balkans), and in Rum-ili from Anatolia.

Even with a limited number of fortified places the Ottomans found it necessary to employ the native population as auxiliary forces, otherwise a large part of the Ottoman army would have had to remain inactive in hundreds of fortresses throughout the Empire. The faithfulness of these native forces was encouraged by special privileges, such as exemption from certain taxes. Such privileges, however, were not granted permanently and could be withdrawn at the pleasure of the Sultan [1]. Furthermore, the auxiliary forces in the fortresses were, as we saw, always accompanied by regular Ottoman soldiers. In some special cases the population of a whole town was given exemption from taxes to insure continued faithfulness. For instance, in the record-books of Konya and Kayseri [2] it is stated that the population of these cities was exempt from taxes altogether, "on account of the faithfulness which they had shown during the wars with Uzun Hasan", and indeed it was by such favours that the Ottomans kept these important cities in their hands. The population of Akchahisar (Croïa) in Albania enjoyed exemption from tax before the invasion by Iskender Bey, in return for the guardianship of the fortress [3].

The conquered lands which were usually preserved in their pre-Ottoman administrative boundaries [4], were entrusted to one or several *sancak beyis*, according to the size of these territories. A *sancak* was the real administrative and military unit of the empire, and the *sancak beyi* was primarily the commander of the *timar*-holders in his *sancak*. His main responsibilities were to lead his timariots in war, to secure public order, and to execute legal and governmental decisions. Decisions on all legal affairs in the sanjak, including those concerning the military (*'askerî)*, were the exclusive responsibility of the kâdîs who were independent from the *sancak beyis*. The *sancak* was divided into *vilâyets* under a *subashi* who was a subordinate of the *sancak beyi*, with the same responsibilities. In Ashik Pashazâde [5], whose source was written toward the end of the 14th century, we find statements about Osman Gâzî appointing kâdîs and subashis in the newly conquered towns. In fact, according to the defter of Albania of 1431, every town had a kâdî and a *subashi*. What is interesting to note is that the

(1) See *Fatih Devri*, p. 163, 180.

(2) Istanbul Başvekâlet Arşiv Umum Müdürlüğü, Tapu defterleri N° 40 (Konya), N° 33 (Kayseri).

(3) See *Arvanid Sancaği Defteri*, my edition, Ankara 1954, p. 103.

(4) See *Fatih Devri*, p. 181.

(5) Ali's edition, Istanbul 1332, pp. 18-20.

kâdîs in the same defter were granted *timars* as a salary, which indicates further the significance of the *timar* system in the provincial administration during this period.

The *vilâyet tahrîri* was the basis of Ottoman administration. It consisted of assessing all taxable resources on the spot and of recording the data in record books called *defter-i hâkâni* (Imperial Register). These *defters* were then used in appropriating certain districts to the military for the collection of taxes which were to be their pay. Not only did the *defters* determine the amount of taxes due from the individual peasants, they were also used as official land records which established legal claims to land.

The oldest available *defters* of this kind in the Turkish archives are those relating to Albania, dated 835 A. H. (1431-1432) (1). The records in the defter of Premedi-Görice (Koritsa) indicate clearly that an earlier record of this area was made in the time of Bayezid I (1389-1403), whereas the area north of it appears to have been assessed only in the time of Mehmed I (1413-1421). These earlier assessments must have been made almost immediately after the respective conquests of these areas by the Ottomans (2). There are also indications in a *defter* of Ankara dated 868 A. H. (3), concerning an assessment of this province made by Timurtash Pasha who was, we know, its governor at about 1396. The old anonymous popular chronicles criticised the ulemâ severely for their introduction of the *defter* system into the Ottoman dominion (4). Taken together with the accounts in the defters which I have mentioned, this indirect allusion might be considered as additional evidence concerning the real beginning of the *tahrîr* system in the Ottoman state. On the other hand, the chronicler Ashik Pashazâde refers to a *tahrîr* of Karasi after its conquest in the time of Orhan Gâzî (1326 ?-1361) (5). This by itself is not adequate

(1) See my *Arvanid Defteri*, Giriş, p. I.
(2) *Ibid.*, pp. III-V.
(3) Başvekâlet Archives, Maliye def. N° 9.
(4) *Tevârih-i Al-i Osman*, ed. I. H. Ertaylan, p. 47.
(5) Ali's edition, p. 45.

evidence for concluding that the system exsisted in this period ; but we find well developed Turkish formulas and terminology in the *defters* of 1431, which were the same even two centuries later. This might indicate that the *tahrîr* system had been used over a long period of time before Bayezid I. We know, moreover, the exsistence of a highly developed Ottoman chancery even in the time of Orhan Gâzî (1). Lastly in the *defters* of 1431 occur many formulas in Persian that might indicate a Persian-Ilkhanid or Seldjukid origin of the system.

We have two decrees dated 983 A. H. (1575 A. D.), containing instructions to the officials in charge of a *tahrîr* of the Eastern provinces in Anatolia (2) which had been conquered about sixty years earlier. These decrees which give us a perfect idea of how the *tahrîrs* were carried out, can be summarized as follows : 1. An *emîn* was appointed for the task. He was assisted by a clerk *(kâtib)* who was under his authority and who drew up the records and recorded the data in the *defter*. Each of them was authorized to collect one *akcha* per household in the districts recorded in order to meet their expenses during the *tahrîr*. 2. The *emîn* collected data on population, land under cultivation, vineyards, orchards, etc., in short all the data upon which taxation was based. He was to be assisted and supervised in each district by the local kâdî. 3. Before beginning the assessment of a particular district the *emîn* gathered together all the *timar*-holders or their trustees and instructed them to hand him various legal documents in their possession, i. e. *berâts* (imperial decrees acknowledging their title to *timars* or to tax exemption), *sûret -i defters* (official copies of the record of their *timars* in a previous register), *temessüks* (documents given by the public authorities concerning *timars* or tax exemptions), and *mahsulât defteris* (documents stating the amounts of specific taxes). 4. Then the *emîn*, going from village to village, began his inspection on the spot, comparing the current data with the pre-

(1) See the *mülknâme* of Orhan Gâzî, *Arşiv Klavuzu*, I. p. 277.

(2) *Münshe'ât*, British Museum, Rieu, Or. 9503, pp. 36-41, 46-51 ; cf. Ö. L. Barkan, *Iktisat Fakültesi Mecmuasi*, II, 1, pp. 39-44.

vious records. 5. Every *timar*-holder was instructed to bring all the adults in his *timar* before the *emîn* who was to record their names. The result of this survey, compiled in the form of a book *(defter)*, was to be submitted to the Sultan who confirmed it after examination. 5. The *defters of Cizye* (capitation paid only by adult non-Muslims) and of *'avâriz* (an emergency tax) were to be drawn up separately by the kâdîs and to be submitted to the Sultan. 7. The *emîn* was also charged with reporting all particular local practices of taxation with special regard to differences in rates. These local practices, after examination and confirmation by the Sultan, were recorded on the first page of the defter as the *kanûnnâme* (the fiscal law) of the *sancak* concerned. 8. The *emîn* was instructed also to make a report of all *timar*-holders and their retainers *(cebelu)* in the *sancak*. Then a redistribution of timars was to be made according to their titles, and compiled in a separate *defter*.

This description of a *tahrîr* made in the the 16th century appears to be the same as that used in the 15th century according to the evidence provided by the *defters* of 1431 (1). Also the first *tahrîr* of a country after its conquest must have been made in the same manner. This is substantiated by the *defters* we have today of Eastern Anatolia and Cyprus, made immediately after their conquests in 1518 and 1572 respectively.

It is reasonable to expect that for the first *tahrîr* of a country after its conquest the *emîn* was assisted by the military occupying the country as well as by the natives. It is well known that in the 15th Century there were Christians or converts employed as *kâtibs*, such as Dimo, Yorgi, and Zaganuz son of Mankole, in the *defter* of Albania of 1431 (2).

The *tahrîrs* were on rare occasions disturbed by native opposition as seen in Albania and in Zulkadriye (3). In both cases the semi-nomadic and feudal organization of the country was principally responsible for the disturbances, and it is to be

(1) *Arvanid defteri*, p. XII.
(2) *Ibid.*, p. VII.
(3) Kemâl Pashazâde.

noted that the *tahrîr* of 1431 in Albania was the real start of the long struggle of the mountaineers under native feudal chiefs such as Araniti and Thopia Zenebissi first, and then Iskender Bey Kastriota (1).

(3) *Assimilation and Creation of the Empire.*

We have seen that two kinds of defters were compiled after the *tahrîr*. The first indicated the taxes, specifying their sources in detail *(mufassal defter)*. The second indicated the distribution of the revenue among the military class *(icmâl defteri)*. This distinction corresponded to a fundamental principle of the Ottoman state.

In the Empire there were two principal classes : the *re'âyâ* (subjects), and the *'askerî* (the military). In principle the *'askerî* included not only the army, but also all public servants and the members of their households. They were paid by the Sultan and exempt from taxation. Thus, the ruled were sharply distinguished from the rulers and it is little wonder if most twentieth century minds find it difficult to grasp this peculiar concept of state based principally on the idea of conquest. It must be immediately added that the *'askerî* were not an aristocratic class with historically established rights, but membership of it was contingent upon the will of the Sultan. We will see, however, that this did not prevent the Ottoman sultans from adopting in the beginning a conciliatory conservative policy toward the pre-conquest aristocratic groups.

According to Ottoman theory all subjects and lands within the realm belonged to the Sultan. This principle abolished all local and inherited rights and privileges in the Empire, and it was formulated essentially in order to confirm the Sultan's absolute authority and to show that all rights stem from his will. Only the Sultan's special decrees, called *berât*, established

(1) See my *Timariotes chrétiens en Albanie au* XVe *siècle*, in *Mitt. d. Österr. Staatsarchivs*, Bd. IV, 1952, 120-128.

rights not only to official commissions, but also to all land titles including endowments *(wakfs)*. All commissions and rights became invalid at the death of the reigning Sultan. There was real meaning in the expression : "the Sultan was the state itself".

Thus, the absolute power of the Sultan called for an executive body with absolute fidelity to him. The only source of authority was his will and delegation. Consequently, those who were in the service of the Sultan or who exercised authority in his name, the *'askerî*, were considered a separate and distinct group above the rest of the population. Although the civil and penal laws, based on Islamic law, were essentially the same for the *reâyä* and the *'askerî*, the latter were subject to a special law, *kanûn-i sipâhiyân*, created by the Sultan's will. The rule that a *ra'iyyet* (subject) could not be admitted directly into the *'askerî* was considered one of the organic laws of the Empire. However, the Sultan could by decree elevate a *ra'iyyet* into the *'askerî* class if he fulfilled certain qualifications, such as the performance of an outstanding military deed. Similarly the Sultan could deprive an *'askerî* of his status by an edict. The class nature of the *'askerî* was further demonstrated by the fact that when an *'askerî* was merely dismissed from his post he continued to belong to the *'askerî* and as such was eligible for an office at any future time. Only if upon dismissal he adopted a non-governmental occupation, was he definitely deprived of his *'askerî* status. Also any bey or pasha who was dismissed from his position received compensation until he was appointed to a new post. It is noteworthy that when under certain circumstances the sons of *'askerî* were included in the record books as *re'âyâ*, they were listed in a separate category indicating their military origin.

The Ottoman record-books of the 15th Century show that not only many Ottoman Beys in the government of the provinces but also a considerable number of timariots in the main Ottoman army during the 15th Century were direct descendants of the pre-Ottoman local military classes or nobility. It is rather surprising to find that in some areas in the 15th century approximately half of the timariots were Christians : 62 timariots out of a total of 125 in the district of Branicheva in 1468, 60 timariots out of a total 335 in Albania in 1431, and 36 out of 182 in the province of Tirhala (in Thessaly) in 1455 were Christians (1). These proportions were no doubt higher in these areas in the first years after the conquest. An especially illustrative record concerning such a timar is the following : "Because the sancakbeyi reported that the rights to the *hisse* (portion) of a *timar* belonging to the aforesaid Mehmed have been revoked, they were given to the Christian Ivradko, for he was originally, it is said, a *sipâhî* and proved himself devoted in the service of the Sultan" (2). For a Christian to be eligible to hold a *timar* we find here two clearly expressed qualifications : firstly, he must be of military origin, and secondly, he must have proved himself loyal to the Sultan. It should be noted that all these Christian timariots belonged originally to the military gentry of the previous Balkan states (3).

During the same period and until the 16th century the Christian *voynuks* in Bosnia, Serbia, Macedonia, Albania, Thessaly and Bulgaria were also incorporated into the Ottoman army, with the status of *'askerî* (military), in great numbers. For instance, in the district of Branicheva (Serbia) there were 217 *voynuks,* 503 *yamaks* (reserve candidates) and 61 *lagators* (officers), and in Tirhala, 103 *voynuks* and 203 *yamaks*. They were originally the Serbian *voynici* who had formed the numerous lesser nobility with their small properties (*bashtina*) in the empire of Stephan Dushan (1333-1355) (4). The following document, one of the oldest and most interesting indications of their position in the Ottoman state, reads : "*Voynuk*: Nikola, son of Dushik ; *Yamaks* : Gin and Milan and Dimitri ; as they were

(1) See *Stefan Duşandan...*, p. 230.
(2) *Ibid.*, p. 232.
(3) *Ibid.*, pp. 231-235.
(4) *Ibid.*, pp. 237-241.

the sons of former *sipâhîs* (1) they are registered as *voynuks* with the properties, vineyards and lands which are now in their possession. Recorded in Muharrem of the year 858 in Adrianople" (2).

It should be noted that the incorporation of the Christian military groups into the Ottoman *'askerî* class was facilitated, no doubt, by their previous experience as auxiliary forces of the Ottoman army during the vassalage of their countries. Seeing that their position and lands were effectively guaranteed by the strong Ottoman administration, the majority of these Christian soldiers must not have been averse to the change. No wonder that many Christian garrisons surrendered their castles without resistance and joined the Ottoman ranks. The conservative Ottoman policy and promise of *timars* surely attracted many of them. This is one explanation of the comparatively rapid expansion of Ottoman rule in the Balkans.

It is noteworthy that by the Sultan's decrees the Christian timariots and *voynuks* often maintained a position in the Ottoman state commensurate with their former social status. The Ottomans preserved to a great extent the land-holding rights of these people in the form of *timar* or *bashtina*. Thus, the great families (seigneurs, voyvods) frequently retained the greater part of their patrimonies as great Ottoman *timar*-holders, and when they adopted Islam they took the title of bey and were eligible for attaining the highest administrative posts. In a record book of about 1448 I came across one instance of a Christian, named Gergi Istepan, who had attained the position of *subashi* (the military and administrative head of a county) (3). Although there were no Christian *sancak-beyis* (governors of provinces), we find many *sancak-beyis* from local Christian great families who were converts to Islam, such as Yakub Bey and Hamza Bey, governors of Albania in the time of Murad II

(1) This term should be translated here as military rather than as cavalryman.

(2) Başvekâlet Archives, Maliye deft. N° 303, Kircheva Defteri.

(3) All *subashis* bore the title of bey in the 15th century. As a rule, *timar*-holders below the rank of *subashi* were not allowed to use this title.

(1421-1451). Hamza Bey and Yakub Bey descended from the famous Albanian dynasties of Castriota and Muzaki respectively (1). Christian *timar*-holders and their islamized descendants, although generally left on their inherited lands, were obliged to abandon part of their lands and their special feudal rights under the new Ottoman timar regime, the greatest families sustaining the greatest loss. These losses promoted some local resistance. It is apparent that the prolonged opposition of the Albanian chiefs led by Iskender Bey (Scanderbeg) was principally due to this (2).

The noble families in the Balkan countries were assimilated to the mass of Ottoman timariots and became Muslim. Islamization was actually a psycho-social phenomenon among the Christian *sipâhîs*, who were definitely the first converts in the Empire (3). The state did not as a rule seek their conversion to Islam as a necessary prerequisite to enrolment in the Ottoman *'askerî* class, and it did not even attempt to achieve such conversion by indirect methods. Thus, we find *timar* assignments to Christian soldiers even in the time of Bayezid II (1481-1512). But in the 16th century Christian timariots were rarely found in the same areas ; what is more, in this century the existence of Christian timariots shocked the people and caused a special inquiry into their origin (4). The previous Christian timariots had gradually adopted Islam and disappeared by the 16th century. In fact, the Christian origin of some of the timariots is only revealed by their rarely used family names such as Kurtik Mustafa in Albania, who was undoubtedly a descendant of the famous Slavo-Albanian lord, Pavlo Kurtik (Kurtić)(5).

Bosnia presents a special case. The Ottomans maintained the old Bosnian nobility on their hereditary lands (*bashtina*), confirming their property rights which had been previously granted

(1) See my *Arnavudluk'ta Osmanli Hakimiyetinin Yerleşmesi*, in Istanbul ve Fatih, II (1953).

(2) *Ibid.*

(3) See *Stefan Duşandan...*, pp. 231-233.; P. Wittek, *Yazijioghlu..*, *BSOAS*, *XIV*-3.

(4) *Stefan..*, p. 247, note 190.

(5) *Ibid.*, p. 226.

by the Bosnian kings. Thus, in Bosnia the old nobility which gradually adopted Islam maintained themselves on their own hereditary lands until the 20th Century. That there was no pressure to adopt Islam, as a condition of having titles to land confirmed, has been shown convincingly in a study by C. Truhelka (1) and recently corroborated by Turkish documents (2). It appears that the different developments in Serbia and Macedonia also came from pre-Ottoman conditions. In Serbia and Macedonia, part of the nobles did not possess *bashtinas* of the same type as in Bosnia. In Serbia and Macedonia the lands which the great nobles (*vlastelin*) possessed were of the nature of Byzantine fiefs (*pronija*). These were easily converted into ordinary *timar* lands by the Ottomans, and therefore they were subject to the general rules concerning *timar* (3).

As to the *voynuks*, because of their special status they were not exposed to the same social influences as were the Christian timariots, and therefore they preserved their Christian faith. When the *voynuks* in the Ottoman army lost their military importance in the 16th century, they were reduced to the status of *re'âyâ* together with the similar Muslim military groups of *yaya* and *musellems*. Yet toward the end of the 15th century the famous historian Idrîs-i Bidlîsî mentions them as Christian soldiers forming an important part of the Ottoman army (4). Later they survived in Bulgaria as Christian grooms in the service of the Imperial Stable (5).

It is not necessary here to discuss other Christian soldiers of non-*'askerî* status such as *cerehors* who were occasional levies from the Christian population, or the Christian guardians in the fortresses and passes who were granted tax exemption. Actually, these groups enjoyed a special position between *re'âyâ* and *'askerî*.

(1) *Die Geschichtliche Grundlage der Bosnischen Agrarfrage*, Sarajevo 1911.
(2) See *Stefan Duşandan...*, pp. 236-240.
(3) See my *Timariotes*. pp. 130-131.
(4) See *Fatih Devri Üzerinde Tedkikler ve Vesikalar*, p. 177.
(5) *Ibid.*, p. 152.

Not only in the Balkans but also in Anatolia the same conservative policy was applied by the Ottomans. For example, according to the *defters* of the province of Karaman ([1]) which were compiled after the annexation of that principality, the great majority of the native aristocracy were maintained in their positions, often with their previous land rights. In the *defter* of 929 A. H. (1519 A. D.) mention is made of the old families of Karaman under this heading : "those *timar*-holders whose fathers where once the notables of Karaman...". Such people formed the majority of the *timar*-holders in this province. Here, too, the grandees took larger timars or *ze'âmets* with the title of bey, and their children also were given large *timars* in various parts of the province. These principal families were Turgud, Kögez, Teke, Bozdogan, Samagar, Yapa, Egdir, Emeleddin, Bulgar, Adalibey, Uchari, Yasavul Musa, Bozkir, and others ([2]). Most of these families provided the chiefs of the tribes in this area. We know that those tribes which were partially settled before the Ottoman conquest had formed the main force of the Karamanid army against the Ottomans. Now, the taxes of the several groups of the Yapalu tribe, which was undoubtedly a new tribal formation around a certain Yapa Bey within the larger tribal organization of Turgud, were granted as *timars* to the descendants of Yapa. Likewise the taxes of the tribes of Bektashlu became the *timars* of the descendants of a certain Bektash. Thus the chiefs were granted the taxes of their tribes as *timars* ; in other words the existing situation was merely confirmed as a peculiar variety of the *timar* system. This appeared to be the only way of establishing Ottoman rule in this area, because the native aristocracy had strong tribal ties and was always inclined to escape from Ottoman centralist administration. More than once they made common cause with the Karaman or Ottoman pretenders or even foreign powers such as the Mamelûks of Egypt or the Shahs of Iran. Shah Ismail (1500-1524)

(1) Başvekâlet Archives, Tapu Defterleri N° 40, 32, 58, 63, 119, 392, Maliye Deft. N° 567.

(2) Some of these families are to be found in the semi-legendary history of Karaman by Shikârî.

became very powerful against the Ottomans in Anatolia by supporting these tribal organizations. The Ottoman government eventually overcame the rebellious attitude of the Karaman tribal aristocracy not by deportation or suppression, but by adjusting its system to the conditions. Time worked in favour of the Ottomans. The descendants of local *timar*-holders were granted new *timars* in the newly conquered lands in the neighbouring countries. In Zulkadriye province, annexed definitely in the first years of Süleyman the Magnificient, we find 35 timariots from Karaman and 6 from Ich-ili, as against 73 native timariots and 41 of unspecified origin. (1) Likewise, a number of timariots of Bosnian and Serbian origin were given *timars* in Hungary after its conquest. Thus, the new generations lost their local connexions and were assimilated into the vast army of timariots by further assignments. Incidentally, it should be added that this process of assimilation was accompanied by a gradual substitution of the native laws and customs by the Ottoman law and system of taxation (2).

Finally, one might think that this Ottoman principle of absorbing into the *ʿaskerî* class only people of military or aristocratic origin might be connected with the *gâzî* origin of the Ottomans. It is known that the *gâzîs* formed a military organization of warriors of the faith in the borderlands, and the members of this organization were given special status by the Seldjukid Sultans. Moreover, they received a religious sanction from the holiest men of the time (3). As has been pointed out, Osman

(1) Tapu Deft. N° 392.

(2) See Ö. L. Barkan, *Kanûnlar*, Istanbul 1943, pp. LXII-LXX ; my *Stefan Duşandan...*, pp. 241-242 ; W. Hinz, *Das Steuerwesen Ostanatoliens im* 15 *und* 16 *Jahrh.*, *ZDMG*, Bd 100-1.

(3) See P. Wittek, *The Rise of the Ottoman Empire*, London 1938, pp. 33-51. Wittek was the first to stress the *gâzî* origin of the Ottoman dynasty, but he denied their tribal origin, while F. Köprülü tried to show their connection with the Kayi tribe (*Belleten* 28, pp. 219-313). Whatever specific tribe its origin might be, Osman's familiy seems to belong to a tribe in the *uc*, the borderland, which does not exclude the possibility of its belonging to the organization of *gâzî*. We have not sufficient evidence to reject altogether the detailed account of Osman's semi-nomadic life as given by the old tradition. Similarly the *gâzî* chiefs of tribal origin in the Ottoman borderland in the 14 th and 15 th centuries, such as Pasha-yigit or Minnetoglu Mehmed Bey or perhaps Evrenos Bey, soon settled in the *uc* towns and became free from tribal ties. In Eastern Anatolia and Iran, chiefs of tribes founded strong states in the 15th Century.

Gâzî's first allies who later became his vassals, were local lords or military chiefs, Christian or Muslim (1). In any case, the first Ottomans were a distinct group with a military tradition.

However, the local gentry was not the only source of the Ottoman ruling class even in the first period of Ottoman history Another fundamental principle of the Ottoman government, which enabled the clients of the military class to obtain *timars* and offices, prevented it from becoming a caste based on blood relationship. As I have already pointed out, the Ottoman Sultans created an administrative organization which was to be totally devoted to the person of the Sultan. The Sultan's household and army in the capital consisted almost entirely of men of servile origin (*kuls*), who were sometimes given *timars* in the provinces ; and the Sultan's personal servants were often appointed as governors. This system was believed to guarantee the absolute power of the Sultan (2). By using the *defters* we are able to trace this system at least as far back as the reign of Bayezid I (1389-1403), and no doubt it existed even earlier. The *kul* system existed also among the *timar*-holders in the provinces where the beys had a retinue of slaves with military func-

(1) See *Stefan Duşandan...*, pp. 219-213. According to a *defter* of Sultan-öyügü of 1467 in the Başvekâlet Archives (Maliye def. N° 8), Mihal Bey possessed Harman-kaya and its neighbouring villages as *timar* or property (*mülk*).

(2) This fundamental institution of the Ottoman empire is adequately emphasized for the 16th century by A. H. Lybyer (*The Government of the Ottoman Empire in the Time of Suleiman the Magnificent*, Cambridge Mass. 1913), who used the contemporary Venetian accounts. The system of *gulâm* or *kul* as such existed before the Ottomans among the Seldjukids of Anatolia, the Mamlûks of Egypt and in the earlier Muslim states. The general practice of this system was as follows : The slaves who were captured in war or bought by the Sultan or the military chiefs were trained as retainers in absolute devotion to the Sultan or the grandees. Even though they were all converted to Islam, they remained bound to their masters. The Ottoman Sultans also recruited children of their Christian subjects for the same purpose. These *kuls* were entrusted with important military and administrative posts and shared governmental responsibilities and authority with their masters who could be certain of their faithfulness. In other words, they became in turn masters themselves. After the Mongol invasion of the Near East the Mongol institution of *nökör* (*nöker*) seems to have influenced the old system of *gulâm* in Central Anatolia. The Yapa family (see above p. 118) had its nomad *nökers* in the 16th century. The word *nöker* is used by the Ottomans as synonymous with *gulâm* in Albania in 1431. At any rate, the *kul* system cannot be explained only by the Islamic institution of *walâ*. The personal attachment of the *kul* was nearer to that of the Mongol *nökör* than to that of the Islamic *mawlâ*.

tions. The beys' servants and *kuls* (in Persian *gulâm*, in Arabic *mamlûk*) could obtain *timars* (1).

On the other hand, the timariots had to maintain and train *cebelûs*, *kuls*, or *nökers*. It is well known that a great many timariots who possessed comparatively large *timars* were required to provide the army with fixed numbers of fully armed cavalrymen, called *cebelû*, whose number varied according to the rank of the timariot and the amount of his timar (2). A *timar*-holder had to furnish a *gulâm* for a part of a *timar* which was smaller than that required for a *cebelû*. In this case the *kul* appears to be a simple valet. In fact the difference between *kul* and *cebelû* seemed to lie in their arms and equipment. Both were entitled to obtain *timars* if opportunity arose. At any rate every *timar*-holder from the simple *sipâhî* to the *pasha* in the *Porte* had their own retainers, as in a feudal army. The *kuls* seemed to be directly under their master's command until they were made timariots by the Sultan. Some great Ottoman *uc-beyis* in the distant border zones such as Evrenos Bey, Turahan Bey, Ishak Bey of Usküp (Skoplje) and later their sons had hundreds of *kuls*, and the *timar*-holders in their provinces were much more dependant on them than those in other provinces of the Empire (3). In fact the powerful *uc-beyis* in the Balkans acted somewhat independently and played a major role in the struggle for the throne between Bayezid I's sons and grandsons until the conquest of Constantinople (4). However, because all the timars were given directly by the Sultan, these beys were prevented from becoming feudal lords with truly private armies. On the other hand, having the largest group of *kuls*, the Sultan was actually able to check the beys' power. Under Mehmed II the Sultan's

(1) According to the *defter* of Albania of 1431 the *kuls* possessing *timars* outnumbered other groups of timariots.

(2) In the Kanûnnâme of Süleyman I the numbers of *cebelûs* and *gulâms* and their equipment are laid down in detail. The uncritical edition by Arif Bey in TOEM contains many omissions and mistakes, and is unreliable.

(3) In 1455 in the *uc* province of Üsküp about 160 out of a total of 189 timar-holders were the former servants or *kuls* of Ishak Bey and of his son and successor in the governorship, Isa Bey. See *Fatih Devri üzerinde Tedkikler ve Vesikalar*, p. 149.

(4) *Ibid.*, p. 69.

I

kuls became absolutely predominant all over the empire and the old aristocratic groups as well as the powerful families in the *uc* lost their importance to a large extent. It is also noteworthy that in contrast to the situation before the conquest of Constantinople most of the grand vizirs of Mehmed II were of *kul* origin. In short, the *timar system* and the *kul system*, which was actually a part of the former, enabled the Sultans eventually to prevent the old feudal and aristocratic elements from dominating the Empire at the expense of the central government. This, too, was achieved gradually and completed the slow process of integration of the different elements in the conquered lands by one unified centralist administration under an absolute ruler.

(4) *Deportation and Emigration as a Tool of Reorganization.*

In order to make their new conquest secure the Ottomans used an elaborate system of colonization and mass deportation *(sürgün)*. The turbulent nomads or the rebellious population of a village and even of a town which had caused or might cause trouble were shifted to a distant part of the Empire. The Ottoman state was also greatly concerned with the settlement of Turkish people in conquered lands.

In the old Ottoman chronicles the account of the first conquests in the Gallipoli peninsula reads : "(Süleyman Pasha, son of Orhan Gâzî, informed his father) that a large Moslem population was needed in these conquered lands and fortresses. He also asked him to send valiant *gâzîs*. Orhan approved and deported to Rum-ili the nomads called Kara Arabs who had come into his territory. New families arrived every day from Karasi. These newcomers settled down and started the *gazâ* (holy war) [1]". We also read : "Süleyman Pasha ordered : Take the Christian military men out of these fortresses (in Europe) and send them to

(1) **Ashik Pashazâde, pp. 49-50.**

Karasi (in Anatolia) so that they can not give us trouble in the future. And so they were sent" (1).

Such examples of deportation recorded in the chronicles are numerous. Evidently mass deportation was practised by the Ottoman state from the earliest time.

The documents of later periods confirm this old tradition of mass deportation and give interesting details. According to an imperial decree of deportation dated 13 Djumâda I, 980 (24 September 1572) (2) one family out of every ten in the provinces of Anatolia, Rum (Sivas), Karaman and Zulkadriye were to be sent to newly conquered Cyprus. The expressed motives for this particular deportation were the rehabilitation and security of the island. The settlers were to be chosen from every level of the society, peasantry, craftsmen, etc. However, the first people to be sent to the island were peasants with insufficient or unfertile lands, the poor, the idlers and the nomads. These people equipped with their implements were to be registered in the *defters* and transferred to the island. These deportees were given a special exemption from taxation in their new homes for a period of two years. As these people did not usually like to abandon their homes, the officials concerned were ordered to carry out these measures with firmness. At a later date, convicted usurers and criminals were sent to Cyprus as a punishment for their crimes.

The mass deportations by Mehmed II (1451-1481) from Serbia, Albania, Morea and Caffa to Istanbul are well known. Their chief object was to secure the prosperity of the new capital. A great part of those deported were prisoners of war and were settled in the villages around Constantinople as peasant slaves of the Sultan (3).

An interesting example of mass deportation to a Christian country is the settlement of a large group (1025 families) of

(1) *Ibid.*, p. 49.

(2) See Barkan, *Les déportations comme méthode de peuplement et de colonisation dans l'empire Ottoman* ; *Revue de la Fac. des Sc. Econ. Istanbul* XI, 91.

(3) For the slave peasantry and their status see Barkan, in *Revue de la Fac. des Sc. Econ. Istanbul*, N° 1-3 (1939).

Moslem *re'âyâ* from Anatolia in the Bulgarian district of Pravadi. These people were given the special status of *sürgün* (deportees) and formed an independent administrative unit under an officer called *sürgün subashisi*. These people remained distinct until the middle of the 16th century when they appear to have become assimilated to the local *re'âyâ*. An example of deportation to Anatolia (Trebizond) is the forced settlement of a group of Albanians, probably rebellious, in the 15th century. In short, the examples from Ottoman archives corroborate earlier accounts in the chronicles which illustrate the use of mass deportation by the Ottomans as a tool in organizing newly conquered lands.

As has been seen, the status of the resettled population varied according to circumstances. In the first century of their conquests the Ottomans seemed to be interested rather in using deportation for military purposes. During this period a number of nomadic people in Anatolia who had proved troublesome were transferred to the Balkans, and having been settled in the border zones were given a special military status (1). According to the map drawn up by Barkan, who obtained his information from the early 16th century *defters*, these Turkish nomads, militarily organized under the name *yürük*, were found primarily in Thrace, in the Rhodopes and on the Southern slopes of the Balkan mountains (2), in Macedonia and in Dobrudga, all of which were conquered in the second half of the 14th century. Meanwhile, according to the *defter* of Albania, many deportees from several parts of Asia Minor such as Saruhan, Djanik, Paphlagonia, Tarakliborlu (Bolu) and from Vize (in Thrace) were given *timars* in Albania between 1415 and 1430. These deportations undoubtedly were related to the disorders which occured in Saruhan and Djanik during this period (Sheyh Bedreddin's insurrection and the struggle of Yörgüç Pasha

(1) See, *Sultan Süleyman Kanûnnâmesi*, ed. TOEM, and Barkan, *Osmanli Imperatorluğunda Ziraî Ekonominin Hukukî ve Malî Esaslari*, Istanbul 1943, pp. 260-269. For the Turkish nomads who settled in villages as *re'âyâ* see further below, p. 125.

(2) Barkan, *Les déportations*, pp. 108-119 and map ; cf. C. Truhelka *Uber die Balkan-Yürüken*, in *Rev. Int. des Etudes Balcaniques*, I, 89-99.

against the nomads in Djanik). Considering also the fact that « the Turkish emigrants from Anatolia who accompanied Evrenos Bey and Turahan Bey » (1), as well as the men led by the famous *uc-beyi* of Üsküp, Pasha-yigit Bey, who had been transferred to Üsküp at the head of the troublesome nomads from Saruhan(2), had been granted *timars* in the conquered lands, we come to the conclusion that in the frontier districts the deportees as warriors were treated in an exceptionally generous way (3).

So far we have tried to show how widely deportation was used by the Ottomans in the organization of the empire. In this connection mention must be made of voluntary emigration to the Balkans. In Ö. L. Barkan's map (4), showing the approximate number and location of Turkish elements, settled or nomadic, on the Balkan peninsula in the 16th century, the Muslims constituted about one fourth of the whole population. Apart from the islamized native Slavs in Bosnia and the Muslim communities centered in and around the fortified towns of the *uc*, such as Nigebolu (Nicopolis), Küstendil, Tirhala, Üsküp (Skoplje), Vidin and Silistre, the Muslim Turks were an overwhelming majority in both Thrace and the region south of the Balkan range. They were settled densely along the two great historical routes of the Peninsula, one going through Thrace and Macedonia to the Adriatic and the other passing through the Maritza and Tundja valleys to the Danube. The *yürüks* were settled mostly in the mountainous parts of that area. We can assert on the strength of the material provided by the *defters* of the 15th century that this situation already prevailed in its first half. The village names indicate to some extent the character of the settlements. The names of some villages of the Maritza valley classified in terms of their origins are : 1. Villages named after Turkish nomadic groups such as Kayi, Salurlu,

(1) See *Stefan Duşandan...*, p. 215. The quotation is from the record-book of Tirhala (Thessaly).

(2) See Barkan, *Les déportations*, p. 112.

(3) Under the *timar* system all those who performed conspicuous deeds of war were entitled to receive *timars*.

(4) See above, p. 123 note 2.

Türkmen, Akcakoyunlu. 2. Village names indicating a connexion with districts in Anatolia, such as Saruhanlu, Meteşelü, Simavlu, Hamidlü, Efluganlu. Most of the settlers in these villages must also have been of nomadic origin, as the nomadic groups from a certain area were in general named in the same fashion. 3. A great part of the village names in the Maritza valley and Thrace were derived from the names of famous personalities such as Davud Bey (the village : Davud-Beylü), Turahan Bey (the village : Turahanlu), or Mezîd Bey. 4. Many other villages were named after official titles such as Doganci, Turnaci, Chavush, Damgaci, Müderris, Kadi, Sekban, etc. These villages may have been held as *timars* by officials with such titles. 5. Certain villages bore the names of certain persons such as Karaca Resul, Haci Timurhan, Ibrahim Danishmend, Saru Ömer. This group of villages which may have taken their names from their founders or first settlers constituted the majority. 6. Many other villages developed around a *zâviye* (kind of hostel maintained by a dervish) or a pious foundation. These institutions enjoyed certain financial priviledges which encouraged the formation of villages in their vicinity. In an important study (1) Barkan has mentioned hundreds of such villages and tried to ascertain the nature of their establishment. 7. Finally, we find many villages with Turkish names referring to natural features or economic functions such as Kayacik, Ada, Hisarlu, Yaycilar, Bazarlu, Çömlekci, Gemici, Eskice-bazar, Balci. 8. Villages with Christian names such as Mavri, Makri, Karli, Anahorya, Karbuna, Ostrovica, in districts such as Ipsala, Dimetoka, Gömülcine, Yanbolu, are few in number in the *defters* of the 15th century.

This is not the place to explain the process by which these Turkish villages were established. It should be mentioned, however, that the Turks from Anatolia established separate villages in their new lands and did not usually mix with the native Christian population. According to the census made in

(1) *Istilâ Devrinin Kolonizatör Türk Dervişleri*, in *Vakiflar Dergisi* II, Ankara 1942.

the 15th Century which gives us the names of the people in the towns and villages, the population in these new villages was exclusively Muslim. Even in the cities such as Gallipoli, Adrianople (Edrine), Üsküp, Tirhala, Serez (Serres) which were considerably enlarged by new Turkish arrivals, the Christians were confined to their own separate quarters (1). The few Muslims found in the Christian villages or districts were probably converts. Moreover in the Balkans new towns with an entirely Turkish population, for instance Yenishehir (New-town) in Thessaly, were established.

This pattern of settlement leads us to think that the Muslim population of these areas consisted of Turkish emigrants from Anatolia rather than of native converts. There was apparently a comparative over-population in Western Anatolia about the 14th century, and the rich lands in the West attracted emigrants from the Asiatic hinterland where anarchy had prevailed after the decline of the Ilkhanid domination (2). That Western Anatolia, which had been conquered by the *gâzî* principalities approximately between 1270 and 1330, (3) had an overwhelming Turkish majority in the 14th century is confirmed by an Ottoman *defter* of 1455 (4). (It appears that the Turkicising of Western Anatolia had followed the same process as that of the Balkans in the 15th century, and was due not to a mass conversion to Islam but rather to large-scale Turkish settlement). Now it is generally admitted that this movement extended over Thrace following the Ottoman conquests. This assertion is

(1) According to the *defter* of Üsküp dated 1455, there were 8 Christian and 22 Moslem districts in the city (Başvekâlet Archives, Maliye def. N° 12).

(2) See F. Köprülü, *Les Origines de l'Empire Ottoman*, p. 33-78, and Z. V. Togan, *Umumi Türk Tarihine Giriş*, Istanbul 1946.

(3) These *gâzî* states in Western Anatolia, the last of which was the Ottoman state, are masterly described by P. Wittek in his study *Das Fürstentum Mentesche, Studie zur Geschichte Westkleinasiens im 13-15 Jahrh.*, Istanbul 1934, and in his *Rise of the Ottoman Empire*. F. Köprülü in his various studies has thrown light on the internal factors in the Turkish hinterland (a summary of these studies is found in his *Origines de l'Empire Ottoman*). Both authors stress the emigration and the overpopulation on the Seldjukid-Byzantine frontier zones as a major cause of the Turkish invasion of Western Anatolia. The contemporary author Gregoras (I, 137) emphasized this.

(4) Başvekâlet Archives, Tapu def. N° 1, Aydin.

confirmed to some extent by the records on deportees which I have mentioned. But the extensive Turkish colonization in Thrace and the Maritza valley can be explained only by a spontaneous emigration from Anatolia and not by a mass deportation. The oldest Ottoman tradition records (1) that Timur's invasion of Anatolia in 1402 caused a new influx of Turkish population into the Balkans ; it states explicitly : "Then a great number of people belonging to the Arabs, Kurds and Türkmen (nomads), and from (the settled population of) Anatolia spread over Rum-ili... it is true that the (Muslim) population of Rum-ili came originally from Anatolia".

In the first decades of their conquests the Ottomans undoubtedly encouraged voluntary emigration into the Balkans of the people who were daily coming in increasing numbers into their territories from all parts of Anatolia and the rest of the Islamic world. Military and financial considerations (2) as well as the obligation of settling surplus population made necessary a policy of colonization. In this connection emphasis must be put on the military importance of the Turkish population in that first period of the Ottoman state when a great part of the army was recruited among the Turks in towns as well as villages under the names of *'azab* and *yaya*, respectively. These Turkish soldiers continued to play an important part in the Ottoman army until the 16th century. The documents from the Ottoman archives show that only in the areas ruled by the Ottomans in the 14th Century was the *yaya* military organization extensively established, and the most important area was Eastern Thrace and the Maritza Valley where in Chirmen (Cher-

(1) *Tevârih-i Al-i Osmân*, ed. Fr. Giese (Breslau 1922), text, pp. 45-46 ; another version, edited by I. H. Ertaylan (Istanbul 1946), p. 70.

(2) The Ottoman government was most concerned with the extension of cultivated lands and the establishing of new villages in order to increase the state revenues and thus be able to create new *timars*. (See my *Stefan Duşandan...*, p. 239, note 121). The essential duty of the *tahrîr emîni* was to find or to create such sources of revenue (*ifrâzât* and *şenletme*). The emîns of Mehmed II and Süleyman the Magnificent were particularly active in increasing this type of additional revenue which corresponded to the great extension of the timariot army in the provinces.

manon) a commander-in-chief of these Turkish *yaya* was posted ([1]).

It is also interesting to note that this spontaneous emigration of Turkish masses into the Balkans slackened toward the middle of the 15th century, and Turkish colonization beyond the Rhodope and Balkan ranges was confined to some military centres of the *uc* and composed mostly of populations deported by the state.

(Ankara)

(1) See my *Arvanid Defteri*, p. VI.

II

THE PROBLEM OF THE RELATIONSHIP BETWEEN BYZANTINE AND OTTOMAN TAXATION

Criticising the somewhat hasty conclusion of Professor Sokolov, Fuat Köprülü pointed out in his study on the relationship between Byzantine and Ottoman institutions that Byzantine influence on Ottoman taxation can be found in Western Anatolia and Rumelia and that we have to make our comparisons not on the basis of general similarities but of specific points established firmly from original sources.

During the last ten or fifteen years our knowledge of Byzantine taxation has been particularly enlarged by the important studies of Dölger, Ostrogorskij, Charanis and others. But as will be seen from the latest publications of Professor G. Ostrogorskij, we are still at the stage of hypotheses in many essential points mainly because of the limitation of the available documents. On the Ottoman side, however, recent preliminary studies on the rich material from the fifteenth century Ottoman registers of land, population and taxes enable us to have a good idea of the nature of early Ottoman taxation and to interpret properly the early legislation preserved in the law-books of Mehmed The Conqueror. Moreover our knowledge of such legislation has increased during the last fifteen years by discoveries of new laws in the records of the Ottoman judges of this reign and of a manuscript containing a rich collection of laws of this period. It must also be noted that although the Conqueror was responsible for new legislation in his own reign the greater part of the laws which he collected in two famous codes bearing his name as well as the whole system of taxation and landownership found in the registers were simply the product of the previous reigns. Furthermore the Turkish archives contain some land and tax registers going back to 1430, when the Byzantine state was still in existence. Here it is particularly important to point out that in these registers which were for the most part composed immediately after the conquest, the Ottoman commissioners with the assistance of the natives carefully recorded on the spot the local taxes and practices and that these were made laws of the Ottoman state after the official confirmation of the Sultan. We have indications of this method going as far back as the second half of the fourteenth century. Only laws too obviously contrary to the Ottoman religious and administrative principles were abolished. But in view of the interests of the treasury the Ottoman administration followed a very liberal policy in maintaining local taxes especially in the first centuries of its history. Tax legislation based on local practices was considered legally as deriving from the personal authority of the Sultan and was called *'urfî* as independent from the *Shar'ia*, the Holy Law. On the other hand the Ottoman government was then following the general policy of maintaining the status quo of social groups in the conquered lands with only those changes necessary for its own administration. Thus as I showed in my article on the Christian timar-holders in Rumelia, a number of the local aristocracies were granted timars on their former *pronoias* or domains. Naturally these could not abandon the old practices to which they had been accustomed for generations. It becomes apparent that the Ottoman law system as well as these local elements became the main instruments in the survival of the Byzantine institutions under the Ottoman regime.

In the Ottoman registers, the peasantry, Muslim or Christian, were divided into various categories such as *Chift*, *Nîm-Chift*, *Bennak* or *Benlak*, *Jaba* or *Mücerred*. There were, of course, differences from one province to another. For example in a register of Eastern Thrace dated 1455 we find a simpler division consisting of *Chiftlü* and *Bennak* whereas in a register of Aydın, ancient Ionia, of the same date, there is a more complicated classification as *Chiftlü*, *Nîm-Chiftlü*, *Chiftlü-kara*, *Jaba-kara* and *Kara*. *Chift* means in Turkish simply a pair or a pair of oxen yoked to a plough or as it is defined in the Ottoman law-books a farm of a size that could be worked by a pair of oxen. We find other definitions in the law-books. According to one of them one *Chift* is a lot varying from 60 to 150 dönüm (one dönüm is approximately one thousand square meters) depending on the productivity of the land which was thought to be enough to sustain a peasant family. On the other hand the size of a *Chift* is defined in the law book of the Conqueror as a plot of land sufficiently large for the cultivation of four *mud* (*modioi*) of seed. Now peasants possessing a *Chift* are called *Chiftlü* or simply *Chift*. One *Chift* was considered the normal agricultural unit in the empire and as cultivated lands were in principle under state proprietorship the central government was able to prevent the formation of farm units larger than one *Chift*. Each Chift paid yearly *Chift-resmi*, a fixed tax in the amount of 22 *Akcha* (asper) (30 or 33 in some areas later on). This was an *örfi* tax, that is to say it was assessed by the Sultan independently from the religious law and this characteristic is an indication of its local origin. The second category of peasants were *Nîm-chifts* that is half Chifts who possessed lands of the size of half a Chift and accordingly paid half of the *Chift-resmi* that is 11 Akcha. The third category consisted of peasants with a family who either possessed a plot less than half a Chift or no land. The former were called *Chiftlü-bennak*, married peasants with some land, and paid 6 Akcha (or 9). Here we find a new element, namely marriage which interfered with the rate of the tax. Finally another category included bachelors, *mücerreds*, widows and agricultural workers who paid only 3 or 6 *Akcha*. In general the youth who reached the age of 20 were included in this category. Toward 1455 in Aydın the taxes were 30 Akcha for *Chift*, 15 for half-*Chift* and 12 for *Chiftlü-kara*, 5 for *Jaba-kara* and *kara*. Here we find actually two main groups, namely the peasants with *Chift* and *Kara*. The last category which embraced the poor was divided into three sections as those with a piece of land less than half a *Chift*, those without land and the poorest. Wives, children and the disabled were always exempted from taxation. Certain peasant communities were given a special status because of some services for the state such as guardianship at the mountian passes or specializing in growing rice or in producing butter for the Palace or the army. These peasants usually paid the *Chift-resmi* as half.

Whatever a person's marital situation, bachelor, married or widowed, anyone who possessed a *Chift* had to pay *Chift-resmi* completely. But if the land concerned was less than half a *Chift*, then, marital situation was taken into consideration as well in determining the rate of the tax. Thus it seems that *Chift-resmi* might be considered as a land tax as well as hearth tax. We shall come back to the question of the nature and origin of this tax later on. But here it must be emphasized that the peasantry in the Ottoman empire formed one large class divided into various groups on the basis of the rate of the *Chift-resmi* which was determined in turn by the size of the land possessed and marital status. On the other hand partial tax immunities granted by the state in return for some public services created another large group called *Muâf ve Müsellem*, that is exempted peasants. Putting it another way we can say that the *Chift-resmi* system in the Ottoman empire was an expression of the social stratification among peasantry based on their social and economic conditions. Now before trying to analyze the origin of this system let us review the Byzantine taxation and the status of peasantry as presented in the last studies made by Professor Ostrogorskij. He used in these studies the *praktika*, 20 in number, as his basic source for the subject. The *praktikon* itself is very similar to the Ottoman *Sûret-i Defter*, a document showing land, peasants and taxes assigned to timar-holders and which were actually a certified copy of the official records in the registers. It is interesting to note that Byzantine *praktika* and Ottoman *Sûrets* both recorded widows with land as heads of a household and taxable persons.

Professor Ostrogorskij considers that lands granted as *pronoia* were always regarded as lands under state proprietorship. The same principle was the foundation-stone of the Ottoman timar system. As for the taxation on the Byzantine domanial lands he wrote as follows: "D'une façon générale, les paysans propriétaires des lots les plus importants étaient aussi les plus riches en bétail . . . mais cette règle comporte pas mal d'exceptions . . . Normalement il s'établit un certain rapport stable, un certain équilibre, entre la quantité de terre et la quantité de bétail. De là dérive la classification bien connue des parèques byzantins en zeugarates, détenteurs d'une paire de boeufs, zeugarion, et d'un lot approprié, et de boidates, propriétaires d'un seul boeuf, boidion; et de la moitié d'un lot normal" (Pour l'histoire de la féodalité byzantine, p. 302–3). In Andronic Doukas' domaine (11th century) there were 18 *zeugarate* families, 6 *biodate* and 25 *aktemones*. Each *zeugarate* paid to the seigneur one nomisma as a land and hearth tax. In general boidates paid half a nomisma. It is interesting to note that in some documents half a *zeugarion* is used for *boidate* just as was the case with half a *Chift* in the Ottoman system. Prof. Ostrogorskij seems not quite certain whether *zeugarion* indicates oxen or land. He added: "La notion de *zeugarion* n'est pas absolument liée à un lot de terre et désigne simplement dans le praktikon de Chilandar, comme dans les autres praktika du XIVe siècle, un attelage d'une paire de boeufs" (Ibid. p. 315). When he found that in the praktikon of Chilander 5 families owned jointly one ox he added: "Il est curieux de noter que cet unique boeuf est enregistré comme $^{1}/_{2}$ zeugarion." (p. 318). He also found that the *paroikoi* who did not possess any land but owned oxen still paid the tax of one hyperperon for two oxen and $^{1}/_{2}$ hyperperon for one, and the poorest families usually less than $^{1}/_{2}$ hyperperon.

In view of the parallel system existing in the Ottoman empire we could not think that *zeugarion* always showed the land workable by two oxen and boidion by one. On the other hand Prof. Ostrogorskij himself pointed out that according to some of the *praktika* peasants possessing a plot of about 50 *modioi* were subject to pay one hyperperon. As to the peasants without land other factors such as personal duties were considered in taxation as we shall see later on when we analyze the nature of the *Chift-resmi*. It is further to be noted that one nomisma or hyperperon was worth approximately 22 *Akcha*, the rate of the *Chift-resmi* in 1350 when the Ottomans had established their rule over a quite sizeable part of the Byzantine empire.

As for the *aktemones*, peasants without land, they paid only *kapnikon*, hearth tax at the rate of half nomisma or hyperperon. Special conditions for the varying rates are not quite known. They sometimes paid as low as one sixth of one nomisma. Now *Jaba-bennak* in the Ottoman system who were peasant families without land and paid the tax as $^{1}/_{2}$, $^{3}/_{7}$, $^{2}/_{7}$ of the *Chift-resmi* might be the Ottoman counterpart of *aktemones*.

These indications along with the Ottoman policy about local taxes make us suppose that the Byzantine *zeugaratikion* may be identical with the Ottoman *Chift-resmi*.

At the lowest grade of the social ladder of the Byzantine peasantry came *elevteroi*, the so-called free peasants. As Prof. Ostrogorskij showed their freedom meant simply to have been left out of the registers of the treasury, they were neither the *paroikoi* of the state nor those of *pronoiars* or of monasteries and so possessing no land and being bound to no one they could go around and work as agricultural workers wherever they liked. Originally they were, Prof. Ostrogorskij thinks, mostly run away *paroikoi*.

There is no doubt that this class of Byzantine rural society survived under the Ottoman rule. Actually the Ottoman laws recognized a class of peasants who were not recorded in the *defters*, registers, and called *hârij-re'âyâ*, that is outsiders, or *hârij-ez-defter re'âyâ*, that is peasants not recorded in the state registers, or *haymâne*, nomads. They could go around freely and work on other people's lands as workers while the re'âyâ, peasants recorded in the registers, could not leave their land and timar-holders. The *hârij re'âyâ* had to pay 1 *Akcha* for each 2 or 5 dönüm of land if they cultivated the available land in a timar. This tax was regarded as a fraction of the *Chift-resmi* for small lots. If the *hârij-re'âyâ* stayed on the same land longer than three years they were included among the dependent peasants of the timar-holder to whom they belonged. It will be recalled that we find the same rule with the Byzantine *elevteroi*. The Ottoman *hârij-re'âyâ* originated from run aways as well as from new generations of peasantry who had not been included in the official land and tax registers.

Now we can examine the *Chift-resmi* more closely and try to discover the reasons for differences in its application.

Actually the *Chift-resmi* system in the Ottoman taxation appears to consist originally of some taxes collected in place of certain services which were required differently according to the status of each group of peasants. In the law-book of the Conqueror on the *re'âyâ*, dependent peasants, we find the definition of the *Chift-resmi* as follows: "One *Chift* gives three services or three *Akcha* for services (and there are other services) such as reaping and threashing and wood carrying and yoke-duty. When for these seven services money is required 22 *Akcha* should be collected and *Benlak* pay three services or six or nine *Akcha*." According to the contemporary registers and the law-book of Sultan Suleiman the exact equivalents of these services were as follows: For three days of labour three *Akcha*, for one cart of hay reaped 7 *Akcha*, for half a cart of straw 7 *Akcha*, for one cart of wood 3 *Akcha*, for yoke service 2 *Akcha*, the total sum of these amounted to 22 *Akcha* which is our *Chift resmi*, paid by a peasant in possession of a *Chift*.

Under the Ottoman state the craftsmen in villages had to pay only three *Akcha* for three days of labour and were exempted from all other duties connected with rural occupations. These three days of labour appear to be considered as the basic duty applied to all grown up men in the countryside. Even the peasants without land and the poorest had to pay this minimum head tax. As we have seen, the *Chiftlübennak* (*benlak*), peasant families with small land, had to pay 9 *Akcha* which probably consisted of the yoke-duty which was two akcha and one of the services of hay or straw.

Thus we can conclude that the Ottoman *Chift-resmi* was originally a head tax derived from certain services which can only form a part of a feudal society such as to provide hay, straw and wood and field labour for the seigneur. But a central government with a sufficiently developed money economy tends naturally to convert these services into fixed duties paid in cash.

To come back to the Byzantine *kapnikon* and the similar duties paid by the peasants, I suppose we are justified in considering the origin and nature of these as similar to that of the Ottoman *Chift-resmi*. Perhaps we can explain some seemingly contradictory points in the Byzantine *praktika* by the theory that these Byzantine taxes consisted originally of some seigneurial services which were later on converted into a fixed land and hearth tax and their variations might be connected with this origin as was the case with the Ottoman *Chift-resmi*.

Before concluding we should add that the *Chift-resmi* and its varied forms were applied both to Christian and Muslim peasants in Eastern Thrace and Western Anatolia, where the Ottomans replaced the Byzantine state. But in most of the lands conquered from the Slavs by the Ottomans another *'urfî* head tax called *Ispenje* prevailed. This was paid yearly by all male adults at the rate of 25 *Akcha* and was applied only to the Christians while the *Chift-resmi* continued to be applied to the Muslims there.

As for the other Byzantine taxes included in the *praktika*, one can establish a close relationship between them and the Ottoman *'urfî* taxes on timars. All these should be studied in the framework of a comparative study of the Byzantine *pronoia* and the Ottoman *timar* systems.

III

THE CONQUEST OF EDİRNE (1361)

The question of when and how Edirne (Adrianople) was conquered was most recently discussed by the Bulgarian historian A. Burmov and the Turkish historian İ.H. Uzunçarşılı.[1]

In Burmov's opinion, Edirne must have been taken immediately after the battle of Černomen (Çirmen) (26 September 1371), that is, at the end of September or the beginning of October of that same year.[2] He attempts to establish this date by using information contained in three completely unrelated sources: the Serbian Chronicles, Chalcocondyles and Luccari. He begins by quoting the brief notation in the Serbian Chronicles: "Sultan Otman killed King Vukašin and the Despot Uglješa in Macedonia along the Maritza River ... and took Edirne".

Similarly, Chalcocondyles informs us that the Ottomans took Edirne subsequent to the Černomen battle. Finally Luccari, probably using a Bulgarian chronicle now lost, ties the conquest of Edirne to the Černomen battle. The last two sources mention Süleyman Pasha as the Ottoman commander who took Edirne; according to Burmov, these sources err only on this point.

In reviewing the general situation of that time, Burmov also arrived at the conclusion that the date should be set at 1371. In his opinion, the fact that the Serbian princes suddenly came to Černomen and particularly the fact that Vukašin, who was just then busy in Albania,

[1] A. Burmov, "Türkler Edirne'yi ne vakit aldılar?", Turkish translation by H. Eren, *Belleten* 49 (1949), pp. 97-106; İ. H. Uzunçarşılı, *Osmanlı Tarihi* 1 (Ankara, 1961²), p. 163. Most recently, N. Ormancı, "Edirne'nin fethi tarihine dair", *Türk San'atı Tarihi Araştırma ve İncelemeleri, İstanbul Güzel San'atlar Akademisi, Türk San'atı Tarihi Enstitüsü Yayınları* 1 (1963), pp. 435-438. He ends his writing with the following words: "As of now, we are not able to establish the date of the capture of Edirne".

[2] The most recent article dealing with this battle is G. Skrivanić, "Bitka na Maritsi", *Voynoistorijskog Glasnika* 3 (1963), pp. 71-94. I would like here to express my special thanks to Dr. D. Lukač-Bojanić for her assistance with and translation of the Serbian sources.

rushed to join his brother Uglješa, is to be explained by events of great importance which were taking place in the area. In other words, the battle of Černomen, which took place in 1371, was a campaign undertaken in order to save Edirne from the Turks. When the Serbs were defeated, the city fell to the Turks.

The evidence presented by Burmov is not conclusive to us.[3] First, the Serbian Chronicles often err greatly in information concerning Ottoman advances in the Balkans. There is no reason to prefer the chronology of this source over others.[4] The confusion in the chronology of Chalcocondyles' work, written in the 1480's, is well known.[5] On the other hand, his and Luccari's mention of Süleyman Pasha in connection with this battle is noteworthy since we know that Süleyman Pasha came to Edirne in the autumn of 1352 in order to aid Cantacuzenus, and that he fought with the Serbs.[6] Chalcocondyles seems to have confused the several battles engaged in by the Serbs and Ottomans between 1352-1371.

Finally Burmov holds it significant that the two Byzantine writers contemporary with the events—Cantacuzenus[7] and Demetrius Cydones—never mention the fall of Edirne; had Edirne fallen previous to 1371, that important event would most assuredly be echoed in their writings. But one must not forget that Cantacuzenus was defending himself in his memoirs; perhaps he preferred not to discuss this event which put him and his son Matthew in a difficult position, since he was held responsible for the Ottoman occupation of Thrace. Cydones, in his letters and other writings, striving to show off his literary style, presented a

[3] G. Ostrogorsky rejects Burmov's theory by saying "This suggestion ... is certainly incorrect". *See*, *History of the Byzantine State*, trans. J. Hussey (New Brunswick, N.J., 1969), p. 536, n. 3; M. Tixomirov, *Voprosy istorii* 3 (1948), pp. 691 ff. and F. Babinger, *Revue des études Byzantines* 1 (1950), p. 205 also made objections to Burmov's theory.

[4] The Bulgarian Chronicle, published by I. Bogdan, states that Gallipoli fell after the battle on the Maritsa in 1371 (*see* C. Jireček, *Archiv für slavische Philologie* 18, p. 264).

[5] *See* Ostrogorsky, p. 416.

[6] Ostrogorsky, p. 472. It is in the Ahmedî–Şükrullâh–Ruhî group of the Ottoman sources that we find information about this battle of Süleyman Pasha with the Serbs. The fact that the Düstûrnâme (ed. Yınanç, p. 84) attributes Edirne's conquest to Süleyman Pasha may have something to do with this event. Süleyman Pasha (as the ally of Cantacuzenus) was probably the first Ottoman to enter Edirne. Concerning the Ahmedî–Ruhî narrative *see* my "The Rise of Ottoman Historiography", *The Historians of the Middle East*, B. Lewis – P. M. Holt, Eds. (London, 1962), pp. 159-162.

[7] The memoirs of Cantacuzenus go as far as the year 1364.

general rather than detailed account of the individual events. Let me also add that even the Byzantine *Short Chronicle*,[8] which gives a faithful chronology of important events, contains no mention of the fall of Edirne. In short, we can say that Burmov's thesis about Edirne's fall subsequent to the battle of Černomen is not based on irrefutable evidence.

Previous to Burmov, C. Jireček, rejecting the generally accepted date of 1361 for the conquest of Edirne,[9] took as his basis the death of Orhan in 1362, as given in the Byzantine *Short Chronicle*, and submitted that Edirne must have been conquered only after that date — probably in 1363 — by Murad I who was then *sultan in his father's place*. Later Jireček, basing himself on a notice found in a work of M. Panaretus, written in the fifteenth century,[10] stated that in March of 1362 Edirne was still in the hands of the Byzantines; and he points out that this only strengthens his theory that the city passed to the Turks in 1363.

The Turkish historian Uzunçarşılı, like Jireček, has also attempted to establish the date of the conquest of Edirne through the date of Orhan's death. Today we definitely know that Orhan died in 1362.[11] According to Uzunçarşılı, after Orhan died in 1362 and Murad I ascended the throne, he was faced with the insurrection of his brothers and, in order to subjugate them and bring Ankara under his control, he was forced to undertake a campaign in the east.[12] Taking into consideration that

[8] *See* P. Charanis, "An Important Short Chronicle of the Fourteenth Century", *Byzantion* 13 (1938), pp. 335-362.

[9] *Geschichte der Bulgaren* (Prague 1878), p. 321; also his "Zur Würdigung der neuentdeckten bulgarische Chronik", *Archiv für slavische Philologie* 13 (1891-1892), pp. 255-256.

[10] According to this remark, when the plague broke out John III Comnenus, ruler of Trebizond, who was in Edirne in March 1362, fled from there to Sinop (C. Jireček, *Byzantinische Zeitschrift* 18 (1909), p. 582).

[11] The *Short Chronicle* (*see* Charanis, p. 350) notes that in the year 6870 an epidemic of the plague broke out and in March of the same year (March 1362) Orhan died. Charanis confirms this date with other sources: by comparing with M. Villani's Italian Chronicle from the same period, and with the renovation inscription of the Alâeddin mosque in Ankara. In another unrelated source, the *Calendar* dated 773 A.H. of Zeyn'ül-Müneccim (*Tarihî Takvimler*, ed. Turan (Ankara, 1954), p. 72) the date of Orhan's death is given as 763 A.H. For the inscription on the Alâeddin mosque *see* Mustafa Akdağ, "Ankara Sultan Alâeddin Câmii kapısında bulunan H. 763 t. bir kitabenin tarihi önemi", *Tarih Vesikaları* 18, pp. 366-373, and n. 69 below.

[12] Uzunçarşılı gives in one place 1363 and in another 1362 as the date of this campaign (*Osmanlı Tarihi* I (Ankara, 1961²), p. 164, and p. 165 n. 2). The *Calendar* of Zeyn'ül-Müneccim of Sıvas (ed. Turan, p. 72) gives the date of Eretna-oğlu's march on Ankara as Şevvâl 767 A.H. (the end of July 1364). For Eretna-oğlu's campaign *see* pp. 175-176 below.

these events immediately followed Murad's accession, the author concludes that Murad I could only have undertaken the campaign that culminated in the conquest of Edirne in 1363, or even later in 1364 or 1365.[13]

Both Jireček and Uzunçarşılı accept as a fact that Edirne was conquered only *after the death of Orhan and the ascendance of Murad*, and both arrive at the conclusion that, since Orhan's death has been established at 1362, the conquest naturally took place subsequent to that date. However, the first premise of this syllogism—the supposition that Edirne was conquered after Orhan's death—has not been proved. Both are attempting to prove one unknown by a second unknown. It is these same sources that we have found to be erroneous with regard to dating which states that Edirne was taken by Murad I *after he ascended the Ottoman throne*. No one has yet mentioned the possibility that the sources may have erred on this point too, and that Edirne may have been taken after the death of Süleyman Pasha, but in Orhan's lifetime, by Prince Murad.

In Burmov's opinion, the Ottoman Chronicles, because they give variant dates and contain basically confused and fanciful information, are not to be relied on and should be overlooked on this particular question.[14] Other authors enumerate all the dates offered for the conquest of Edirne by every Ottoman writer from Âşık Paşazâde to Hayrullâh Efendi — *i.e.* 759, 760, 761, 762 or 763 A.H. — and they either select one of them or leave the question completely open. But no one has yet attempted a systematic analysis of these Ottoman narratives.

Without further discussion concerning the dates of the conquest of Edirne, let us, by comparing information contained in Ottoman sources with those of the Byzantine sources, study here the real course of events, and see which of the dates of these events can be clearly established.

[13] Uzunçarşılı, p. 163 n. 2, and pp. 164-165.

[14] The letters given in Ferîdûn Beğ (*Münşeâtü's-Selâtin* I (İstanbul, 1274), pp. 90-96), which, it is claimed, were sent to Karaman-oğlu and Üveys Han (the first one dated 1 Rebîülâhir 767, and Üveys Han's answer of evâil-i Zilkâde 763) concerning the conquest of Edirne are, as the other documents of this collection dating before the time of Beyazid I, not authentic (*cf.* M. H. Yınanç, "Ferîdûn Beğ Münşeâtı", *TOEM*, 11-13, p. 161; 14, pp. 37, 95, and 216). The letter sent to Üveys Han (undoubtedly Şeyh Üveys Bahâdır Han of the Celâyirids, who was sultan between 757 and 776 A.H.) is nothing but the account given in the Ottoman chronicles put into the form of a letter in Persian by an amateur.

Our point of departure will be the death of Süleyman Pasha and the imprisonment of Prince Halil.

Of the old Ottoman narratives, Âşık Paşazâde gives the date 758 A.H. (beginning on 25 December 1356) as the year of Süleyman's death, whereas the *Anonymous Chronicles* and Oruç give 759 A.H. (beginning on 19 December 1357). Pseudo-Ruhî indicates that Süleyman died after waging war in Rumelia for six years; thus, if we keep in mind that he took Cinbi (Tzympe) in 753 A.H. (1352 A.D.), we must accept both for this source and for Pseudo-Ruhî the year 758 A.H. as the year of Süleyman's death. One of the *Calendars*[15] notes that Orhan died five years after Süleyman. Since we know that Orhan died in 763 A.H. (1362 A.D.) this date too confirms Süleyman's death in 758 A.H. The testimony of the contemporary Byzantine historian N. Gregoras corroborates this date (iii, p. 560 = *CSHB* vol. 8). He tells us that Süleyman's death occurred soon after Halil's captivity. We know that Halil was captured in the summer of 1357.[16] Therefore *we can state that Süleyman died either in the summer or the autumn of 1357.*

The detailed information given by Gregoras concerning Halil's release from captivity is important for a better understanding of the situation in which the Ottomans found themselves.

Orhan's eleven year old son Halil was taken captive at sea by pirates and taken to Phocaea (Foça). To save him, Orhan had no other choice but to appeal to the Byzantine Emperor. Emperor John V Palaeologus, who wanted to squeeze the greatest possible advantage from the situation, succeeded in completing an advantageous agreement with Orhan. The conditions of this agreement were that the Ottoman sovereign undertake the establishment of peaceful relations by the cessation of all aggression against Byzantine territory; further, that he assume expenses for the ships which were to be sent against the Phocaeans, cancel the outstanding debts of the Emperor, and promise to support the Emperor by ceasing to aid Matthew Cantacuzenus, who was holding out against the Emperor in Thrace.[17] This last condition was extremely important. The Ottomans

[15] I refer to the Paris *Calendar* which gives the most detailed information concerning the Ottomans (ed. Turan, pp. 16, and 18).

[16] İskender Hoci, who translated this section of Gregoras (iii, p. 560) into Turkish, establishes the summer of 1356 as the date of this event. However, E. de Muralt (*Essai de chronographie byzantine* II (St. Petersburg, 1871), p. 661) gives 1357 as the date of the same event. Gregoras ends his writing with the event of Halil's rescue which took place in 1359 (Ostrogorsky, p. 415). Halil remained prisoner in the hands of the Phocaeans for two years.

[17] John Cantacuzenus (iii, p. 321 = *CSHB* vol. 4) corroborates Gregoras (iii, pp. 504,

had since 1345 been the faithful allies of John Cantacuzenus, who had been struggling against his rivals in Byzantium from his Thracian headquarters in Adrianople and Didymoteichum (Orhan had become his son-in-law when, in 1346, he married Cantacuzenus' daughter Theodora).[18] The Ottomans who through this alliance had first found the opportunity to settle in Rumelia (conquest of Cinbi in 1352) now were able, through their continued support, upon abdication of John Cantacuzenus to his son Matthew, to strengthen their position in Thrace and open up further areas for their activities. In the face of this situation John V Palaeologus in Constantinople had to rely mainly on the cooperation of the Serbs and Bulgars. Now with the agreement with Orhan, John V Palaeologus hoped to stop the advance of the Ottomans, whose activities were the source of great concern in Constantinople, and whose support rendered Matthew a dangerous rival, and to effect, if possible, the evacuation of Thracian cities under Ottoman occupation. According to Byzantine sources, unlike his aged and ailing father, who sought a more conciliatory policy toward Byzantium, Süleyman Pasha was utterly determined in his policy of conquest.[19] Thus he seems to have fully understood the extreme sacrifice involved in the giving up of this bridgehead which was of the greatest importance for the continuation of the *gazâ* and the establishment of the Ottoman state in Europe. An interesting narrative has it that the dying Süleyman's last request was that he be buried in Bolayır, his first conquest on the Gallipoli peninsula, and that his corpse never be left to the enemy.[20] One can understand quite well from the Ottoman and Byzantine accounts the deep and hopeless grief that beset Orhan, the ailing old Ottoman sovereign, at the captivity of Halil by the Phocaean pirates and Süleyman's sudden death.[21]

---

and 561) on this point (*see*, *Histoire de Constantinople* viii, tr. M. Cousin (Paris, 1674), p. 266).

[18] Ostrogorsky, p. 472; P. Lemerle, *L'émirat d'Aydın* (Paris, 1957), pp. 220-221.

[19] In 1354 Orhan was in negotiation with his father-in-law, John Cantacuzenus, concerning the evacuation of the Turks from the places occupied by Süleyman Pasha in Thrace, and it is claimed in Cantacuzenus' memoirs (iii, pp. 276-277; tr. viii, pp. 230-231) that he even agreed to this evacuation in return for financial compensation. From Cantacuzenus' statement it also becomes evident that Süleyman Pasha at that time resisted such a move. Chalcocondyles (i, p. 22, ed. Darkó; tr. pp. 9, and 12) depicts Süleyman as the third Ottoman ruler.

[20] "You will bury me in this province, and should the infidel come you will resist and not flee ... and also you will do your best lest my corpse be left in their hands". (Anonymous, *Tevârîh-i Âl-i Osmân*, ed. Giese (Breslau, 1922), p. ١٧).

[21] Gregoras, iii, pp. 560-561, tr. pp. 241-242; Anonymous, *Tevârîh*, p. 17; especially

Gregoras relates (iii, p. 561) that Orhan's peace agreement with the Byzantine emperor was subsequent to Süleyman's death. This agreement, signed under duress, was a great sacrifice for the Ottomans. It meant the cessation of conquest, the desertion of their ally Matthew, and the abandonment to a bitter fate of Ottomans resident in Rumelia. The indecision and hopelessness that beset these *gazi*s at the loss of their energetic leader Süleyman Pasha is clearly reflected in the *Anonymous Chronicle*. This chronicle relates that, after Süleyman's death, the enemy undertook an all-out attack by land and sea from the direction of Kavak-Tuzlası *i.e.* Saros Bay,[22] but they withdrew when they saw that the Ottomans were determined to fight on regardless of cost.[23] As to Matthew, who had been left to his own resources, he was taken prisoner by the Serbians and turned over to the Byzantine emperor.[24]

Under these new conditions, John V Palaeologus' position on the Byzantine throne was strengthened. In contrast, Orhan's only thought now was to effect the release of his son Halil. He insisted that John V Palaeologus proceed in person with a fleet against the Phocaeans (at that time, Byzantium had three galleys), and the emperor set out in the following spring, *i.e.* the spring of 1358. Orhan had also made an agreement with İlyas Bey, the ruling prince of Saruhan, to attack the Phocaeans by land; together they encircled the city, but without success. The emperor returned to his capital without consulting Orhan. The

---

Düstûrnâme, p. 84. Afterwards Orhan established pious foundations for the convent of dervishes built at his grave in Bolayır. According to Ruhî: "When the heart-breaking news of his death reached Prince Orhan in Bursa, with much crying and sighing he wept and wailed, yet since there was no other way but to accept this grave misfortune, he ordered that an edifice for public welfare (*'imāret*) should be built in Bolayır at the place where the late Süleyman Pasha lay buried". We are preparing for publication an annotated edition of a copy of this important *waḳf* document which was redrawn following an official review during the reign of Mehmed II, and which is at present kept in Istanbul in the Museum of Turkish and Islamic Works.

[22] There is a natural saltpan before the village of Kavak at the Bay of Saros. In Ottoman times it was farmed out.

[23] Anonymous, p. ١٨: In the winter of 1357-1358 the emperor remained with his small fleet in Bozca-ada (Tenedos). We may assume that the Byzantines, in order to profit from the agreement made with Orhan, wanted to put up a show in the hope of taking possession of the places occupied by the Ottomans on the Gallipoli peninsula. However, as can be seen from the Ottoman account, they must have given up their plans when they realized that the *gazi*s there, faithful to Süleyman Pasha's decision, were preparing for a fight.

[24] Ostrogorsky (p. 474) gives 1357 as the date of this event. According to Gregoras (iii, p. 564), this event took place at the time the emperor set out by ship for Phocaea, in the spring of 1358.

Ottoman sovereign then made known to the emperor that, should the latter not return to Phocaea for continued efforts to rescue Orhan's son, he (Orhan) would void the agreement and undertake new assaults against Byzantine territories. The emperor immediately embarked for Priconisum with two ships. He met with Orhan, placated him and within the same year set out for Phocaea. Nevertheless he again returned without a solution. Orhan came to Chalcedon (Kadıköy) in the spring of 1359, and through representatives he conferred with the emperor, who remained offshore on his ship. Orhan accepted the new conditions of the emperor. These conditions stipulated that, as soon as he was rescued, Prince Halil would be engaged to his daughter and there would be a permanent peace between the two states. The Ottoman sovereign also handed over a sum of nearly one hundred thousand gold pieces for Halil's ransom. In the summer of that year the emperor again set out for Phocaea, and the governor of that city surrendered Halil to him. Halil was brought to Istanbul and remained there for a time. He was ceremoniously engaged to the ten-year-old Irene. Subsequently the prince was brought to Nicomedia (İzmit) and returned to his father. The emperor also wanted Halil to be declared heir to the throne, according to Gregoras. Orhan was also so inclined. Since Halil's very person *represented peace between the Ottomans and Byzantium*, the *gazi*s, who wanted the conquest of Rumelia, probably would have preferred Murad to Halil. Halil's return to Ottoman lands can be placed around the end of September 1359. Orhan once again assigned to him his former governorship of İznik.

According to Gregoras (iii, p. 558), the Ottoman threat which had been felt all the way to the gates of Byzantium in the time of Süleyman had receded in the two-year period of Halil's captivity, and a period of true peace and quiet had held sway in Thrace.

The period between 1357 and 1359 was for the Ottomans a period of pause in the conquest of Rumelia. One notices, however, that during this two-year period, the bridgehead established in Rumelia was strengthened by emigrants from Anatolia, and new forces were assembled for an even greater onslaught there.[25] With Süleyman Pasha's conquest

[25] The colonization policy initiated in Süleyman Pasha's time must have been continued also after his death (*cf.* Âşık Paşazâde, ed. Atsız, *Osmanlı Tarihleri* I (İstanbul, 1949), p. 124). We know that of the villages which had been assigned by Orhan as *waḳf*s to the convent of dervishes in Bolayır many carried Turkish names.

of Rumelia was born a new overseas Ottoman governorship, Ottoman Rumelia.[26] Its geographic and military conditions won for this region a status entirely different from that of Anatolia. Of primary importance was the fact that a sea controlled by Christians separated this new realm from the Turkish homeland in Anatolia. Already in 1362, the Crusaders in the West thought that the Turks could be annihilated if the Crusader fleet cut off the Straits and left them helpless in Rumelia.[27] During the administration of Süleyman Pasha, the leader of the *gazis* who formed the backbone of the state at that time, *Ottoman Rumelia assumed the status of a quasi-independent state vis-à-vis Anatolia.*[28] In Gregoras' words (iii, pp. 560-561),[29] Süleyman was "Orhan's designate for the sultanate and entrusted with the general administration of the state". A Serbian source says that "even during his father's lifetime he assumed power and turned toward the west".[30] When Orhan's eldest son Süleyman died, in accordance with Turkic–Mongolian tradition, the oldest brother Murad was sent with his tutor (Lala) Şahin to this most important distant frontier sector of the state in Rumelia.[31] It is more than improbable that in the five year period between Süleyman's

---

Among the villages in Malkara we should mention Bulgurlu, Esendük, Şeyh Halil, Yegen, Pazarlu-Beg, Kara-Ahi, Ulamış and Sasanlar.

26 According to *waḳf* documents, at the time of Süleyman Pasha's death the border line went through the Yayla-Dağ between Keşan and İpsala and the mountainous region that separates Malkara and Hayrabolu. On the shores of the Marmara Sea, Hora and Bakacık-Tepesi to the south of the town Tekfur-Dağı (Rodosto) formed the boundary. The claim that Süleyman captured Tekfur-Dağı, İpsala and Vize (Ruhî) does not seem to be correct. We only know that during his various campaigns he came to these regions and even as far as Edirne.

27 O. Halecki, "Un empereur de Byzance à Rome", *Travaux historiques de la Société des Sciences et des Lettres de Varsovie* 8 (1930), pp. 76, and 117. This plan seems to have been the basis of all Crusade projects in the fourteen-fifteenth centuries. *See* my *Fatih Devri* I (Ankara, 1954), pp. 47-53.

28 As the nucleus of the Rumeli Beylerbeyliği, Paşa Sancağı can be considered as having been established in Süleyman Pasha's time. Most likely the name Paşa Sancağı also originated from that time. In Murad's time and especially after the big campaign under Lala Şahin Pasha's command, Rumelia was to be given to a Beylerbeyi with the title of Pasha.

29 İskender Hacı translation, *TOEM* 1, p. 242.

30 *Lebensbeschreibung des Despoten Stefan Lazarević von Konstantin dem Philosophen*, transl. M. Braun (Wiesbaden, 1956), p. 5. For Süleyman's important position within the state *see* Ahmedî, *İskendernâme*, ed. Atsız, *Osmanlı Tarihleri* I, pp. 12-13.

31 The signature Şahin b. Abdullah that can be seen on the *waḳf* document issued by Orhan in Şaban 761 (June 1360) is most likely that of Lala Şahin himself, and if so he must have been in Anatolia at that time.

death in 1357 and Orhan's death in March of 1362 the Rumelian sector would have been ignored. The *Düstûrnâme* tells us quite clearly that after Süleyman's death, Orhan sent his eldest son Murad to the "holy war" area, and that he made conquests in Rumelia while his father was still alive.[32] At the head of *gazi*s temporarily halted in their drive for conquest, the young prince was to prove himself deserving of the sultanate. The tutor Şahin, a capable commander, and the seasoned march commanders Hacı İlbegi and Evrenuz (Evrenos), after the rescue of Prince Halil in 1359, undertook the conquest with renewed vigor. The peace and amity agreement forced on the aging Orhan by John V Palaeologus for the sake of Halil was signed under abnormal circumstances; a cessation of the advance in Rumelia would have meant for the *gazi*s there certain annihilation. The only way to hold on and survive in this new country was to spread and strengthen themselves, to open up new territories continually for the nomads, *akhi*s and dervishes pouring in every day from Anatolia.[33] On the other hand, as we have seen, John V Palaeologus had driven Matthew, the ally of the *gazi*s, from the Edirne sector and had brought that area under his direct control and rule.[34] Therefore it was only natural that the aim of the new push in Rumelia should be this area long considered by the Ottomans as being under their protection. The Ottomans, even before the conquest, seem to have considered the Edirne region their sphere of influence. The unusual intensity of the renewed assaults by Rumelian *gazi*s in 1359 stirred an echo even in the Western sources. It was then that the systematic occupation of Thrace really began.[35] The Florentine M. Vil-

[32] *Mîr Orhan'ın ulu oğlu Murâd — Ol zaman olubdu kerrâr-i cihâd* (*Düstûrnâme-i Enverî*, ed. Yınanç, text (İstanbul, 1928), p. 84. Further, Chalcocondyles (i, pp. 29-30, tr., p. 17) writes that, as soon as his brother died, Murad hurried to Rumelia. He too, similar to the *Düstûrnâme*, notes that Edirne had been taken by Süleyman Pasha. It is likely that both used the same source of information. P. Luccari (*Copioso Ristretto degli Annali di Rausa*, Libri quattro, Venetia, 1605, p. 64) notes the following regarding Süleyman Pasha: "fu portato sepelire ne' Giardini di Galipoli, lasciando il Regno a Murat suo fratello".

[33] Concerning the first Turkish colonization in Thrace *see* Ö. L. Barkan, "İstilâ devirlerinin kolonizatör Türk dervişleri", *Vakıflar Dergisi* 2 (1942), pp. 279-386; and my "Ottoman Methods of Conquest", *Studia Islamica* 2 (1954).

[34] Concerning the continued support lent to Matthew by the Ottomans *see* Cantacuzenus, iii, pp. 324 ff., tr., p. 437, and Gregoras, iii, p. 564, tr., p. 246.

[35] J. Dräseke, "Der Übergang der Osmanen nach Europa im 14. Jh.", *Jahrbücher für das klassische Altertum* 31 (1913), pp. 476-504.

lani[36] writes that Didymoteichum temporarily fell for the first time to the Turks in 1359 in the course of this assault,[37] and Turkish raiders appeared at the walls of Byzantium in that same year.[38]

Indeed, some Ottoman sources also date to 761 (1359 A.D.) a great attack under Murad's command which resulted in the conquest of Edirne. These sources, however, err in showing this campaign of one and a half years as having taken place in one and the same year. The Ottomans whom Villani mentions as having appeared in front of Istanbul in 1359 must have been the *gazi*s of the Ottoman sources who in 761 (1359) under Murad's command had come to surround a fortress "near Istanbul"[39] as well as the Çorlu stronghold. It is very likely that the panic which developed in Byzantium when Murad marched on Çorlu in the direction of Istanbul aroused such a reaction in Italy. Murad had carried out this attack with the aim of protecting his rear guard from an assault from the direction of Byzantium during his expedition against Edirne. After he took Çorlu, he returned to the West and strove to take the other fortresses on the Byzantium–Adrianople road.

Let us analyze more closely the narratives in the Ottoman chronicles concerning this expedition. These narratives rest basically on two principle narratives, one from Âşık Paşazâde, and another one used by Ahmedî and many after him, the most detailed version of which is found in Pseudo-Ruhî and Neşrî.[40]

Both groups of the Ottoman narratives give 761 A.H. (beginning 23 November 1359) as the date when Murad began his great conquest in Rumelia.[41] Yet those sources generally assume that Murad ascended the throne in the same year. They may have been led into error by the fact that in 1359 Murad, as his brother Süleyman and his father Orhan in Osman Ghazi's time, assumed responsibility for the major affairs

36 F. Babinger, *Beiträge zur Frühgeschichte der Türkenherrschaft in Rumelien (14-15. Jahrhundert)* (Brünn–München–Wien, 1944), p. 46 (M. Villani died in 1363).

37 According to Oruç (p. 20), Dimetoka was conquered in 760 A.H. (December 3, 1358 - October 24, 1359).

38 Ostrogorsky, p. 478 (he mentions Villani).

39 *Cf.* Anonymous, *Tevârîh-i Âl-i Osmân*, ed. Giese, p. 20.

40 Concerning these two groups of narratives *see* my "The Rise of Ottoman Historiography", pp. 152-167.

41 Âşık Paşazâde, ed. Atsız, pp. 126-127; Anonymous *Tevârîh-i Âl-i Osmân*, ed. Giese, p. 21; Oruç, *Tevârîh-i Âl-i Osmân*, ed. Babinger (Hannover, 1925), p. 20; Neşrî, *Ğihānnümā* I, ed. Taeschner (Leipzig, 1951), pp. 52-53.

of state still in his father's lifetime. In the case of the Pseudo-Ruhî account, one may assume that this expedition was confused with the Rumelian campaign undertaken against the Serbs by Murad I after his enthronement.[42] These points will be discussed further below. First we shall look more closely at the two basic accounts.

Âşık Paşazâde's tradition (Chapter 43) reads in short: When Orhan died, Murad "came [straight] to Bursa". He gathered troops from Karesi and from his own governorship. Accompanied by his tutor Şahin, he crossed Gallipoli. He marched straight on the "Banatoz"[43] stronghold and took it without a fight. From there he went on to Çorlu, and seized it after heavy fighting. He levelled the stronghold walls.[44] Then he came before the stronghold of "Misini". The commander (*tekvur*) of this fortress surrendered it.[45] Then the *gazi*s took "Burgus" (Lüle-Burgaz). Its occupants fled. The fortress was burned down.[46]

[42] For the text of Ruhî *see* p. 169.

[43] Âşık Paşazâde has بنطوز (ed. Atsız, pp. 126-28; ed. Giese, pp. 48-51); and Neşrî has بُطنوز (ed. Taeschner I, p. 52; ed. Unat–Köymen, I, p. 192); Oruç has بطّنوز (ed. Babinger, Oxford MS. p. 20, and Manisa MS). We may assume that this fortress was Banatoz (today Barbaros, a district in the Tekirdağ sub-county) on the seashore south of the town of Tekirdağ (Rodosto).

[44] Concerning Çorlu (classical: *Σύραλλον*; Byzantine: *Τξουρουλλός, Τυρολόη*), the Ottoman source is supported by the following observation of B. de La Broquière in 1433: "je vins a une ville que l'on nomme Chourleu qui a esté assés bonne par semblant, car les Turcz l'ont abatue et est repeuplée de Grecz et de Turcz" (*Le Voyage d'Outremer*, ed. Ch. Schefer (Paris, 1892), p. 169). For the pertinent note in Evliyâ Çelebi *see* H. J. Kissling, *Beiträge zur Kenntnis Thrakiens im 17. Jahrhundert* (Wiesbaden, 1956), p. 12.

[45] In Âşık Paşazâde and Neşrî مسنی (Misini); in Oruç and *Anonymi* مسين, مبسين (Misin); in the Byzantine period it was Messene (*Μεσσήνη*) (*see* Babinger, pp. 43-44; Kissling, p. 15, n. 62). Concerning the fortress Misini we find the following note in a Gallipoli statistical register written around 938 A.H. (Prime Ministry Archives, Tapu No. 167): چفتلك در زمين قلعهٔ مسينى ، ذكر اولان مسينى حصار ... Today it is Misinli in Çorlu sub-county. The information given by de La Broquière about this fortress which he called Misterio corroborates that of the Ottoman account; and he says: "de là je alay à une ville que l'on nomme Misterio qui est une petite place fermée et n'y demeurent que Grecz excepté ung Turc à qui Grant Turc l'a donnée" (p. 169). Misinli, which until the exchange of population after World War I was inhabited by Greeks, is today a village of 300 dwellings populated by immigrants from Rumelia. The walls of the fortress are still standing. *See* A. M. Mansel, *Trakya'nın kültür ve tarihi* (İstanbul, 1938), plate XXIII.

[46] Burgaz, later Çatal-Burgaz and Lüle-Burgaz (for the name and historical background of the city *see* Kissling, p. 16). de La Broquière (p. 170) corroborates the

On the other side, Hacı İlbegi had settled in "Burgus"[47] on the banks of the Maritsa River, and was putting pressure on Didymoteichum (Dimetoka). At last he ambushed the fortress's commander (*tekvur*) and took him prisoner; he released him when the fortress was surrendered. Still in the Maritsa valley, Ghazi Evrenuz had seized the Keşan stronghold and was putting pressure on İpsala (Chapter 44).

Murad came to Eski (Baba-Eskisi)[48] from Burgus (Lüle-Burgaz). He found the stronghold empty. The population had fled to seek refuge in Edirne. The fortress was burned (in Neşrî's version). They seized several other strongholds in the environs. Murad sent Lala Şahin with the troops against Edirne. The enemy met them outside Edirne with a large force, and a great battle ensued.[49] The defeated enemy retreated to the stronghold. At this point Hacı İlbegi and Ghazi Evrenuz rejoined Sultan Murad. Then Murad sent them to Edirne as the advance guard of his army. At that time the Maritsa was overflowing. The commander of Edirne[50] boarded a boat and fled by night to Ainos (Enez).[51] When

---

Ottoman narrative and says: "Et de là, je vins à une ville que l'on nomme Pirgasi qui est aussi tous les murs abbatus et n'y demeure que Turcz". de La Broquière mentions the settlements he has seen up to this point, *i.e.* Çorlu, Misterio (Misini) and Pirgasi (Burgaz) in the same sequence as does the Ottoman narrative. Thus it seems clear that the route between İstanbul and Edirne followed the same route in the 1430's also.

[47] Kulelü-Burgaz, to the immediate east of Dimetoka on the Edirne route, is called Phytion today, and may be identical with Eğri Kaleli Burgaz or İlbeği Kalesi mentioned by Evliya Çelebi (V, p. 328; *cf.* also Oruç, pp. 20, and 93). The great tower on the hill dominating the road is still standing today.

[48] Identical with Boulgarophygum of the Byzantines (*see* Babinger, pp. 51-52 and Kissling, pp. 40-41). Also Zambry, the settlement mentioned by de La Broquière after Burgaz, is very likely Baba-Eskisi (Babaeski). He too found the walls of this town destroyed.

[49] İdrîs (*Heşt Behişt*, Topkapı Sarayı Kütüphanesi, Hazine No. 1655, f. 141ʳ) gives Sazlu-Dere as the place of this battle (*cf.*, *Tâcü't-Tevârîh* I, p. 72). In this part, İdrîs follows Neşrî and gives both narratives. Like Neşrî, he too mentions the *Akhi*s of Ankara.

[50] In Oruç (Manisa MS) ادرنوس تكورى (Adranos? Tekvuru); in Hoca Sa'deddin (I, p. 72): "*Edirne Tekvuru* ki اندرنه [Adrine?] demekle meşhur idi".

[51] Enez, today a district of Keşan. It was also written Enoz, Aynoz or Inoz (اينوز). In Byzantine times it was *Αἶνος* and in ancient times *Ἄψυνθος* or *Πολτυοβρία* (*see* Babinger, p. 49). The rent-income of this important harbor, an outlet of the Edirne and Maritsa Valley on the Aegean Sea, and that of the salt-pans there was assigned to the despot Demetrius Palaeologus when Morea was annexed in Mehmed II's time (*see*, *TV* new series 1 i (1955), p. 134). Concerning the conquest of Enez *see* my

news of this was heard the following morning, the inhabitants opened the city gate (Oruç, Manisa version: Kumkale Kapısı) and surrendered. This conquest took place in 761 (45th Chapter).

The *Anonymous Chronicles* and Oruç give a shorter version of this story. Some of the *Anonymi* combined this account with the section in Ahmedî dealing with Murad I, thus giving both versions. The Manisa copy of Oruç, however, gives the date of the conquest of Edirne following the above-mentioned narrative as 761 A.H., and based on the *Calendar*s as 762 A.H.

Âşık Paşazâde's narrative relates the strategic moves for conquest undertaken by Murad after he took command of the frontier forces in Rumelia in place of his brother Süleyman in 761 A.H. (1359); and here the events are set forth in a completely logical order. Thus, while Murad was seizing the vital fortresses along the historic Constantinople–Adrianople road which were, starting from Constantinople: Çorlu, Misini and Burgus (Lüle-Burgaz), commanders of the marches were holding down the fortresses, and especially Didymoteichum which protected Edirne from the south, *i.e.* from the Maritsa valley. In the second and final phase of the expedition, Murad set up his headquarters in Baba-Eskisi, at a distance of fifty-five kilometers from Edirne; from there he sent Lala Şahin against Edirne. The Byzantine forces which gathered in Edirne attempted to scatter the Ottomans by engaging in a battle outside the walls, at Sazlu-dere, but when they were defeated they retreated to the fortress. (The reason why Murad systematically destroyed fortresses abandoned by their population—such as Çorlu and Baba-Eskisi—is easily understood. It was because of the systematic application of this method in the Ottoman conquests that fortresses were prevented from becoming renewed centers of resistance after the Ottomans withdrew.) After his successful attempt at Sazlu-dere, Murad decided to gather all his forces for a last, concentrated attack on Edirne. He summoned the march forces commanded by Hacı İlbegi and Evrenuz (Evrenos) which had been active in the Keşan mountain region and the Maritsa valley. They united with Murad's army and formed the advance guard. Then the entire army moved on Edirne. The tradition that Edirne was taken without a siege seems to conform to the truth. After the defeat at Sazlu-dere, the populace of Edirne had little hope of success against the full complement of Murad's army. It was known of the

---

"Mehmed the Conqueror and his Time", *Speculum* 30 iii (1960), p. 42. Until recent times, communications between Enez and Edirne were accomplished by ship on the Maritsa.

Thracian fortresses (like Banatoz, Misini) which surrendered of their own will, that Murad had protected them from pillage and had allowed the local population to remain; but those fortresses which were subdued after attack were pillaged, destroyed and the local people enslaved.[52] Once Murad had complete control of the Constantinople–Adrianople road there was no hope of aid from Byzantium. According to the narrative, the Byzantine commander fled down the Maritsa to the port of Ainos. Actually, at that time this was the only route of escape from Adrianople to Byzantium. All in all, as we have shown above, the toponymic and topographic data which it contains, and their conformity with the observations of de La Broquière on the situation of the fortresses after the conquest, clearly indicate this account to be a reliable source.

Pseudo-Ruhî, who gives the most complete and detailed version of the second group of accounts,[53] explains events after the ascendance of Murad in this way:

THIRD CHAPTER

ON THE ACTIVITIES OF MURAD, SON OF ORHAN, SON OF OSMAN

When Orhan Bey died the leading men of the state and viziers enthroned his son Murad Han. In the night of the same day Bayezid, the son of Murad was born. People and *bey*s from all over the world congratulated him on his accession to the throne and the birth of his son. Murad I acted in complete justice toward his subjects so that even those rebellious people came to submit to his rule and all subjects enjoyed prosperity and peace. He convened the *'ulemā* in Bursa and at a felicitous moment

[52] It can be said that, in Ottoman times, towns in Thrace which had a large percentage of Greek inhabitants had most likely been taken by peaceful means. For example, according to a statistical register dated 925 A.H. (Prime Ministry Archives, Tapu No. 75, p. 388) in Mürefte there were 107 Christian households compared to four Muslim households. Also from the point of view of taxation, Mürefte and a number of Christian towns like it received special treatment. On the other hand, in places taken *'anvaten*, by force, "the infidels" were taken into captivity and their lands and goods given to Muslims, according to the Islamic holy law. Such places thus rapidly became Muslim towns (*see* above, n. 46, for de La Broquière's interesting observation concerning Burgaz in 1433). Naturally there are also towns which obtained a Muslim or Greek majority later on, prompted by different conditions. But this situation evolved over a long period of time.

[53] Here we use the copy of the Bodleian Library in Oxford (Marsh MS No. 313). For studies on early Ottoman history, it is necessary to establish the original text by comparing this copy, which J. H. Mordtmann attributes to Ruhî (*MOG* 2, pp. 129-136), to other related manuscripts.

laid the foundation of a complex of charitable institutions at Ḳaplūca [in Bursa]. The architects and masons did their best for its completion and so, in a short time, a *medrese* and an *'imāret* were built of an indescribable beauty. To meet the expenses the sultan granted *waḳf*s which were to be given to the *'ulemā*, reciters of the Qur'an, descendants of the Prophet and Muslim poor. Afterwards he intended to pass over to Rumelia in order to make an expedition into Hungary. But before his departure news came to the effect that the *bey*s in various parts of upper Rūm had intentions against Bursa. That is to say, as soon as the sultan crossed the Straits and went to make war against the infidels they would come with their armies over against Bursa to plunder it and make injuries on the Muslims there. Thereupon Sultan Murad asked the leading *'ulemā* of the time whether he should make war against the infidels or repulse the aggressors. Their answer was that the latter was to be done first. So delaying the Holy War and sending orders around, the sultan assembled an army from all over his realm and marched against Rūm. When he reached the border he defeated the enemy who appeared there, and made conquests including Ankara. From there he came to Sultan-Öyüğü and conquered it also. He came to Bursa safely, and, assembling his army again, he crossed over to Rumelia, defeated the Serbian army and conquered Edirne. It occurred in the year 761.

This is how Sultan Murad set out to make Holy War against Serbia. When Sultan Murad had the intention to make Holy War against Serbia he placed his son Bayezid on the throne under the tutorship of Timurtaş Bey, and then he himself assembled a large army and crossed the Strait over to Rumelia in order to march against Serbia...

« المطلب الثالث : فی بیان احوال السلطان مراد بن اورخان بن عثمان.

چون مرحوم اورخان بك بو خراب آباد دنیادن اول بقای سروره رحلت اتدی اکابر و اعیان و وزراء نامدارلر اوغلی سلطان الاسلام و المسلمین سلطان غازی مراد خان تحته کچوردیلر و هم اول کیجه سلطان السلاطین سلطان بایزید بن غازی مراد بن اورخان بن عثمان ظهوره کلدی خلق عالم و اطراف جوانبده اولان بکلر ایلچیلر کوندروب تحت ایچون مبارك باد ایدوب و اوغلیچون تهنیت اتدیلر سلطان مراد خان غازی داخی رعایایه بر وجهله عدل [و] داد اتدی که عدلنوك آوازه‌سی عالمه طولو

اولب صورت عصیان و طغیان ایدن کمسنلر مطیع و منقاد اولوب رعایا داخی مرفه الحال و منتظم الاحوال اولدی کندو داخی دولت و سعادتله بروساده علما و فضلا جمع ایدوب بر مبارك وقتده قبلوجه‌ده بر عمارت بنا اتدردی مهندسلر و بنّالر انوك مصلحتنه و اتمامنه مباشر اولب از زمان ایچنده بر مدرسه وبر عمارت یاپلدی که قابل وصف اولمیا انك مصالحیچون وقفلر قویوب محصولاتن اهل علمه و حافظلره و ساداته و سایر فقرای مسلمینه صرف اولنه دیو امر ایتدی پس اندن صکره قصد اتدیکه روم ایلنه کچوب انکروسه غزا ایده ناکاه بو اثناده خبر کلدیکه یوقرو رومده اولان متفرق بکارك بروسایه قصدلری وار شویلکه خداوندکار دولتله دکزی اوته کچوب غزایه متوجه اولدغی کیب عسکرله کلوب بروسایِ غارت ایدوب مسلمانلره نکبت یتشدوره‌لر. پس اندن سلطان مراد خان اول زمانوك علماسندن و فضلاسندن بو خبر اصلنی استفسار اتدیکه غزا اتمك اوْلی مدر یاخود دشمن دفع اتمك انفعدر پس علمای کرام و فضلای فخام جواب ویردیلر که غزادن ایسه دفع دشمن یِکْرَکْدُرْ دیدوکاری اجلدن غزایِ تأخیر ایدوب اطراف جوانبه نامه‌لر پراکنده ایدوب حوضهٔ تصرفنده اولان مملکتوك عسکرن جمع ایدوب روم طرفنه محاربه و مقاتله اتمکه متوجه اولدی تا روم حدنه یتشوب ظاهر اولان اعدایِ کسر ایدوب ایل ولایت ضبط ایدوب انقرهٔ فتح اتدی اندن سلطان ایوکنه کلوب انی دخی فتح اتدی کیرو صحت وسلامت و عافیت برله محروسهٔ بروسایه کلوب عسکر جمع ایدوب روم ایلنه کچوب سرف لشکرن صیوب ادرنه‌یی فتح ایتدی یدی یوز آلتمش برنجی بیلده. سلطان مراد خان غازی سیرف اقلیمنه غزایه واردغی در :

چون سلطان مراد خان سیرف اقلیمنه غزا نیتن ایدوب اوغل یلدرم بایزید بروساده تحته قویب و تمورطاش بکی یاننده لالا ایدوب کندو عسکر بی نهایه جمع ایدوب دکیزدن روم ایلنه کچوب سرف اقلیمنه متوجه اولدی...»

Neşrî expertly combined the two traditions by transmitting the Ahmedî – Pseudo-Ruhî tradition about events immediately following Murad's accession, then grafting on events from the Âşık Paşazâde narrative of the conquest of Edirne, as if, from a chronological point of view, they had taken place afterwards.[54] However, Neşrî wanted to correct the date of Süleyman Pasha's death to 760, and repeated Âşık Paşazâde's remark saying *Esahh oldur ki oğlu Süleyman Paşa iki ay önden vefat etmiştir*[55] "The truth is that his son Süleyman died two months before him" and transmitted again in the Âşık Paşazâde version the conquest of Edirne. Here, however, he corrected the date to 762. No doubt if Neşrî had given 758 as the date of Süleyman Pasha's death as it is in Âşık Paşazâde, he would have had to accept that Orhan, who he says died two months afterwards, also died in that same year, and that Murad's accession took place in 758. He shows, however, again based on a copy of Âşık Paşazâde, 758 as the year of the conquest of Bolayır. He allowed one year for the following conquests with the remark "all of the aforementioned conquests took place within one year", and set Süleyman's death subsequently for the year 760 A.H. He allowed another year for Murad's enthronement and the Ankara campaign — which he had taken from Pseudo-Ruhî — and set the date of his subsequent return to Rumelia and the conquest of Edirne at 762. We know that Neşrî attempted to resolve such inconsistencies in the sources in other places as well. Thus, although the two ancient traditions — Âşık Paşazâde and Ahmedî–Pseudo-Ruhî — set the conquest of Edirne at 761,[56] Neşrî differed from these traditions by setting the date at 762.[57]

[54] Common with Ruhî (p. 51): *İttifak bir gün ... kavuştu*; and p. 52: *Leşker cem'edip diledi ki ... Sultan-öyüğü'ne gelip etrafını fethedip.* It seems that in the latter Neşrî used a more detailed variant of the same source as Ruhî. The remaining parts are all from Âşık Paşazâde (Neşrî, *Ǧihānnümā* I, ed. Taeschner, pp. 51-53). This important copy from the year 898 was discovered by Th. Menzel; it was not used by F. R. Unat and M. A. Köymen in their critical edition of Neşrî (*Kitāb-ı Cihānnümā*, Ankara, 1949). Here we shall refer always to the Menzel copy.

[55] Âşık Paşazâde, ed. Giese (Leipzig, 1929), p. 46.

[56] The Anonymous *Tevârîh-i Âl-i Osmân* (ed. Giese, p. 31), and Oruç (ed. Babinger, p. 21, and 93) give the date as 761. Kemal Paşazâde, however, who represents a somewhat more recent compilation period, follows Neşrî (*see* MS No. 3078 in the Nuriosmaniye Library) for his report that Süleyman died while on a goose hunt and giving, like Neşrî, the date of his death as 760 A.H. This historian also used the *Anonymi* (the last will of Süleyman Pasha and the narration of the landing of the infidels at Kavak-Tuzlası). For the conquest of Edirne, İdrîs adhered to Neşrî and gave the date as 762, whereas Âlî (*Künhü'l-ahbâr* V, pp. 45-49) and Cennâbî (a good copy of this is in the Selimiye Library of Edirne, No. 1569, f. 700) follow Ruhî.

[57] As we have seen previously, Oruç also gave the date as 762 in the Manisa copy.

After taking notice of this point, let us now attempt to analyze the Ahmedî–Pseudo-Ruhî tradition group. In the Pseudo-Ruhî tradition, the important events are given in the following order:

1. When Orhan died, the influential men of state put his son Murad on the throne.
2. The rebellious elements who caused trouble in the early days of his reign were brought under control and the situation stabilized.
3. Murad had an *'imāret* and *medrese* built at Kapluca.
4. He then wanted to cross to Rumelia and "make Holy War against Hungary" ("*Laz ve Ungurus*" in Şükrullâh's *Behcetü't-Tevârîh*). But it was then that he learned that "the various Begs of Upper Rūm" (in *Behcetü't-Tevârîh*, Mehmed b. Hacı Halil, and Neşrî "the kings of the area") were to attack Bursa during his advance into Rumelia.
5. At this point he went with his army "as far as the border in Rūm, and subduing the enemies who appeared" he made conquests and he took Ankara. From there he passed to Sultan-Öyüğü (Sultan-Önü, Eskişehir), conquered it also and returned to Bursa.
6. Again mobilizing an army he crossed to Rumelia. "Defeating the Serbian army he captured Edirne in the year 761."
7. Subsequently, stationing his son Yıldırım Bayezid in Bursa with his tutor Timurtaş Bey, he again undertook a campaign to Rumelia and "he turned to the Serbian region".

Neşrî transmits this tradition in shorter form but adds to it another account of how the Ankara *Akhi*s received them (Menzel's text, p. 52: "*derler ki . . . kırılışursız*"). Ahmedî, Şükrullâh and Mehmet b. Hacı Halil note that at his ascession, Murad brought in as his vizier Halil-i Çenderî, but Pseudo-Ruhî has no mention of this.[58] On the other hand, the events in Pseudo-Ruhî, cited above in numbers 6 and 7, do not appear in Ahmedî, Şükrullâh and Mehmet b. Hacı Halil. In other words, after the conquest of Ankara and Sultan-Öyüğü, they pass immediately to the Karaman campaign, and do not mention the campaign against the Serbs and the conquest of Edirne. The points in common in all of these sources, including Pseudo-Ruhî, are:

Rather than assuming a direct connection between Neşrî and Oruç, we should consider the *Calendar* as the common source used by both.

[58] Neşrî, adhering to Âşık Paşazâde on this point, states that Hayreddin, the kadi of Bursa, was made kadıasker, whereas Ahmedî and Mehmed b. Hacı Halil maintain that he was elevated to the vizierate. On this contradiction *see* p. 208 below. Mehmed b. Hacı Halil states that in this appointment Mevlâna Şeyh Fahreddin, a disciple of Abdülkâdir Gîlânî, played a role.

1. that Murad at his accession punished those whose loyalty to him had wavered, and
2. that later, moving east to the *serhadd-i Rûm* "border in Rūm", he conquered Ankara and Sultan-Öyüğü. It can be assumed that the common source contained mainly these principal events.

As for those who rose against Murad when he took the throne, Ahmedî expressed it thus:

Oldular yağı ana kardaşları
Kamunun bitti elinde işleri[59]

"His brothers had become enemies
Their fate was sealed by his hand"

According to Uzunçarşılı, the meaning of "*kardaşları*" here is Murad's brothers.[60] He suggests that, at the time of Murad's accession, Prince Halil and İbrahim were alive and had mounted opposition to him in Anatolia. The sources give no date for Halil's death.[61] If he were alive then, at the age of sixteen, he would have to have been in İznik.[62] The Ottomans shared the ancient Turkic belief that God appoints the sovereign.[63] Thus it would only be natural that at Orhan's death (March, 1362) the faction which held Halil felt free to proclaim him sultan in his father's place. Indeed, as we mentioned above, the Byzantine emperor naturally was among those who wanted to see Halil on the Ottoman throne. On the other hand, the then thirty-six year old Murad[64] was in Rumelia in full charge of the main forces of the state. He had won great fame with his conquest of Thrace and, as representative of the war and conquest policy against Byzantium, was doubtlessly supported by the *gazi* groups. On the whole, the conditions in those times may

[59] ed. Atsız, *Osmanlı Tarihleri* I, p. 15.

[60] *Osmanlı Tarihi* I (Ankara, 1960²) p. 160. According to P. Wittek ("Zur Geschichte Angoras im Mittelalter", *Festschrift G. Jacob* (Leipzig, 1932), pp. 352-353) instead of "brothers", the word *kardaş* here is used rather in the sense of "Muslim neighbors".

[61] N. Jorga (*GOR* I, p. 202) writes that Halil died before his father Orhan, but it is not clear how he arrived at this conclusion.

[62] *See* Gregoras (*ibid.*). A *Calendar* written in 773 A.H. (ed. Turan, p. 72) notes that Orhan and someone with the name Halil died in the same year, *i.e.* 763. However, Turan reads خليل آغاء آتا بك as "Atabeg Halil Ağa". We could not check this in the original.

[63] *See* my "Osmanlılarda Saltanat Verâset Usûlü ve Türk Hakimiyet Telâkkisiyle İlgisi", *Siyasal Bilgiler Fakültesi Dergisi* 14 i (1959).

[64] The recently discovered *Calendar*s (*see*, *Tarihî Takvimler*, ed. Turan (Ankara, 1954), pp. 16, and 52) corroborate the year 1326 as the year of his birth.

substantiate the thought that there could have been a struggle among the brothers for the Ottoman throne. However, a struggle between Murad and Halil for the throne can only be guessed at. The only information clearly emanating from the sources is that quarrels broke out in Anatolia in the course of Murad's accession. That the rebels, in a short rhymed version (by Ahmedî) of the tradition, are referred to as brothers is open to interpretation and can not be considered as conclusive evidence.

Orhan's death, on the other hand, must have been considered an opportunity by Eretna-oğlu who counted Ankara within the sphere of his control. We have more definite information concerning the actions of Eretna-oğlu in Sıvas. Ankara was considered under the authority of the Eretna state until the Ottoman occupation; and a certain Melik Nâsireddin Bahtiyâr Beğ was in power there.[65] After Eretna's death (in 1352)[66] a struggle broke out among his sons,[67] and the Ottomans, taking advantage of the situation, undertook a campaign under the command of Süleyman Pasha to Ankara for the first time in 1354[68] and gained control of the city. An inscription[69] placed on the Sultan

65 H. Edhem, *Düvel-i İslâmiye* (İstanbul, 1927), p. 384; H. Hüsameddin, *Amasya Tarihi* III (İstanbul, 1927), pp. 40, 63, and 65.

66 A. Tevhîd, "Beni Ertena", *TOEM* 4, p. 16; Hüsameddin, p. 42.

67 Hüsameddin, p. 44; Tevhîd, p. 18.

68 *See* Wittek, "Zur Geschichte Angoras ...", p. 347. Although it was Nâsireddin Mehmed Bey, the younger son of Eretna, who became sultan in place of his father either toward the end of 754 A.H. or at the beginning of 755 A.H. (1354), his brother Câfer declared himself ruler in Kayseri. Karaman-oğlu Süleyman supported Mehmed Bey (Hüsameddin, pp. 48–49). Concerning the capture of Ankara in Orhan's time we quote here the following official record (Ankara statistical register written in 867 A.H., Prime Ministry Archives, Tapu No. 9): "Ayaş'ta Ahî Bâyezîd çiftliği, kadîmü'l-eyyâmdan vakf olıgelmiş, elinde merhûm Orhan Bey ve Gâzî Hüdâvendigâr ve Sultan Mehemmed bitileri vardır. Elhâletü hâzihi Ahî Bâyezîd oğlu Ahî Elvan vakfiyyet üzere mutasarrıftır".

69 *See* M. Akdağ, "Ankara Sultan Alâeddin Camii kapısında bulunan Hicrî 763 tarihli bir kitabenin tarihî önemi", *TV* NS 1 iii (1961), p. 372, plate II. *Cf.* M. Gâlib, *Ankara* I (İstanbul, 1341), p. 47. The text of this three line inscription is as follows:

عمر هذا لجامع المبارك لولو باشا
دام دولته من جملة المولى المعظم السلطان الاعظم
اورخان خلد الله ملكه فى سنة ثلاث وستين و سبعمائة

There is a record in one of the statistical registers from Mehmed II's time (Prime Ministry Archives, Tapu No. 12, f. 196) that in the village of Eşreflü in Gallipoli Lu'lu' [Lulu] Pasha donated a meadow as a *waḳf* for his caravanseray. T. Gökbilgin

'Alâeddin Mosque in Ankara by Lu'lu' (or Lulu) Pasha in the time of Orhan, and dated 763, clearly shows that previous to March 1362, the date of Orhan's death, Ankara was still subject to the Ottomans, whereas, according to the Ottoman tradition, Murad had to conquer Ankara anew with another campaign. In that case, Ankara was no longer under Ottoman domination after March of 1362. Evidently this too must have been connected with the crisis of indecision which developed in the Ottoman realm after Orhan's death.

The information given by Hüseyin Hüsameddin as pertinent to Central Anatolia and Ankara at this date is rather illuminating.

In 759 A.H.[70] the Karaman-oğlu 'Alâeddin brought Eretna-oğlu Mehmed back to his throne. In this way the Karaman-oğlu and Eretna-oğlu Mehmed once more assumed a superior position in Central Anatolia. It was at this time that the former ruling prince of Ankara, Bahtiyâr Bey, once more got hold of Ankara and began raiding Ottoman territory.[71] Bahtiyâr Bey received encouragement from the Karamanids. Hüseyin Hüsameddin accepts these events as coinciding with the date of Orhan's death and Murad's accession.[72]

The eastern campaign of the new Ottoman sultan, Murad, was conducted, according to Pseudo-Ruhî's version, against *yukaru Rûm'da olan müteferrik beğler* "the various begs of upper Rūm".[73] As is known, the Ottomans had named the area belonging to the Eretna state *Rûm*, and in the fifteenth century the name *Rûm Beylerbeyliği* or *Rûm Vilâyeti* was given to the Beylerbeylik of this region.[74] According to Hüseyin

---

(*Edirne ve Paşa Livası* (İstanbul, 1952), p. 291) shows Lulu Pasha in Murad II's time, which cannot be correct.

[70] Although Hüsameddin gives the date as 762, a contemporary *Calendar* from *Sıvas* (ed. Turan, p. 72) shows the date as 759.

[71] Hüsameddin, pp. 64-65. On this point he uses Müneccimbaşı's *Câmi'ü'd-düvel* and other sources which we could not identify.

[72] But he gives the date of Orhan's death as Receb 761, whereas Orhan's death occurred in March 1362 (*see* above, n. 11).

[73] We know not only of Bahtiyâr Bey in the Ankara region, but many other local beys' names are given in the *awkāf* entries of the fifteenth century Ottoman statistical registers. According to a statistical register from Ankara from the year 867 A.H. (Prime Ministry Archives, Tapu No. 9) even before the Ottomans took over, in the Ankara region there were a number of well known families such as the Yeğen Bey oğulları, Dündar Bey oğulları, Emir Yakub oğulları, Kozan Bey oğulları, Ulu Bey oğulları, Bikâri Bey, Abdullah Bey, Süleyman Bey and Mahmud Bey oğulları.

[74] *See* Neşrî, ed. Taeschner I, pp. 87, and 144. According to Hüsameddin (pp. 142, and 145) Prince Yıldırım Bâyezid was the first vâli in 788 A.H., and Devatdâr Ahmed

Hüsameddin, Sunkur Pasha, one of Murad's commanders, surrounded Ankara; the people of the city, displeased with Bahtiyâr Bey, surrendered the fortress to Sunkur and recognized the sovereignty of the Ottoman sultan. Bahtiyâr Bey fled to Amasya. Neşrî relates how Murad I was greeted by the *akhi*s when he ceremoniously entered the city after the conquest.

On the other hand, a reliable contemporary source has it that Eretna-oğlu Mehmed marched on Ankara the year following Murad's accession, *i.e.* in 765 A.H. (beginning 10 October 1363).[75] (It is noteworthy that this source, written in Sıvas, the capital of Eretna-oğlu, makes special mention of Orhan Ghazi's death.)

Evidently, this Eretna-oğlu campaign must have been made to counter Murad's "border in Rūm" campaign. Its goal was to take Ankara back from the Ottomans.[76]

Essentially, the Ahmedî–Şükrullâh–Mehmet b. Hacı Halil versions explain events subsequent to Murad's actual enthronement, *i.e.* after March 1362. Since Edirne had been conquered previous to that, these sources which transmit the original tradition naturally make no mention of *the conquest of Edirne among the events after Murad's accession.* However, in the Bodleian manuscript attributed to Ruhî (Pseudo-Ruhî), we find the conquest of Edirne simply combined with a campaign against the Serbs. On the other hand, as we have seen above, in the Âşık Paşazâde tradition there are substantial details given concerning the Thracian conquests which culminated in the capture of Edirne. In the Âşık Paşazâde tradition (chapter 47), Murad's giving the Rumelia governorship to Lala Şahin and the Beylik of Marches to Evrenuz must be

---

Pasha became the first beylerbeyi in 789. Fort he naming of the region *Rûm vilâyeti*, *see* P. Wittek, "Le Sultan de Rûm", *Annuaire de l'Institut Oriental* 6 (Brussels, 1938).

75 The Turan edition of the *Calendar* prepared in Sıvas in Muharrem of 773 by Zeynü'l-Müneccim b. Süleyman, p. 72: عزم میر محمد بانکوریة و انهزام بعض لشکر در حوالی آب کرم از مغل در اواخر شوال و جنك بمغل در بوك صاحب وانحطاط دولت میر محمد بیست و پنجم ذی القعده در هفتصد و شصت وپنج اتفاق مغل بامارت بابوق ودخول بقیصریه آخر محرم For the inscription on the tomb of Eretna-oğlu Mehmed (dated 767 A.H.) *see* H. Edhem, *Kayseriyye Şehri* (İstanbul, 1334), p. 113.

76 We know from a note in *Bazm u Razm* (p. 186) that relations between the Eretna-oğulları and the Ottomans were still hostile around 782/1380. When Kadi Burhaneddin got control of the territory of the Eretna house he continued this policy of enmity. From the same source (pp. 390, and 408) we know that, for a while at least, Kadi Burhaneddin pushed his attacks as far as Ankara.

events connected with his accession. The same source states that, with these appointments, Murad secured his hold over Rumelia and, passing through Gallipoli, returned to Bursa where he spent the winter. Also mentioned in the course of these events is the appointment to the "*vezirlik*" of Kara Halil, then the Kadıasker in Bursa. Indeed, the Ahmedî–Şükrullâh account (which is unrelated to Âşık Paşazâde) also tells us that Murad's first act after his accession was the appointment of Kara Halil to the "vizierate". The new sultan had to win over Kara Halil who as kadi was the most important individual administrator in the Bursa capital. There is a strong possibility that the subsequent political influence of Kara Halil and the Çandarlıs may have been a result of the support he rendered Murad in the securing of his throne. It is noteworthy that İznik, which belonged to Prince Halil, later became the center of the Çandarlıs.

After his arrival at Bursa, Murad did not return to Rumelia until 766 A.H. (28 September 1364 to 19 August 1365), this again according to the Âşık Paşazâde tradition. Lala Şahin was compelled to handle all alone the defense actions against the Serbs who were attacking Edirne. It is from the Ahmedî–Pseudo-Ruhî tradition that we learn what sort of difficulties Murad had had to deal with following his accession (the 1362 Ankara campaign; the Eretna-oğlu attack on Ankara in 1363 or 1364).[77]

Thus, after this analysis of the Ottoman accounts as they relate to our subject, we can say that once put into chronological order, the sound historical information contained in these accounts gains its real value. Let us now take up once more the question of the date of the conquest of Edirne.

In the above discussion we attempted to show that the conquest of Edirne does not have to be tied to the 1362 accession of Murad I. The Ottoman tradition gives 761 A.H. (23 November 1359 to 13 October 1360) as the date of the conquest of Edirne. This date, as we pointed out above, marked the beginning of the new mobilization for conquest in Rumelia which was undertaken under *Prince* Murad's direction after the release of Halil in 1359. The goal of this mobilization was, indeed, Edirne,

[77] A third, unrelated narrative occurs in *Düstûrnâme-i Enverî* (p. 84). As we have already mentioned above, this source speaks about the activities undertaken by Prince Murad in Rumelia after Süleyman's death but still in Orhan's lifetime. For the information given in this source concerning the capture of Edirne by Süleyman Pasha *see* n. 6. The *Düstûrnâme* also mentions a defeat of the Serbs at Sazlu-Dere which was brought about after Orhan's death, in 765 A.H.

but the Ottoman source errs when assuming that the fall of Edirne took place within the same year. Indeed, according to another Ottoman tradition, the Manisa copy of Oruç (Muradiye Library, MS 1373, f 41^r), Edirne fell in 762 A.H.; on this we find the following notation: *Kum-kalesi kapısını açıp kaleyi* [Edirne] *verdiler; ol yıl içinde güneş tutulup yıldızlar tamam göründü, Hicretün sene 762 Edirne fetholundu. Hicretün sene 761 vâki' oldu.* ("Opening the gate of Kum-kalesi they surrendered the fortress; in that year the sun eclipsed and the stars were completely visible, in the year 762 A.H. Edirne was taken. It took place in the year 761 A.H.")[78] The essential point here is the notation that Edirne was conquered in the year of the eclipse. Babinger was the first to call attention to this point and calculations have shown that this eclipse had taken place on 5 May 1361.[79] Oruç took this note from the *Calendar*s and added it to the Âşık Paşazâde account, and thus mentions the years 761 and 762 side by side as the date of the conquest of Edirne.[80] The information contained in the Ottoman *Calendar*s [81] about the eclipse is in conformity with the *Calendar* written in 773 A.H. by Zeynü'l-Müneccim:[82]

[78] In the Oxford copy of Oruç (ed. Babinger, p. 23): "in this year the sun had a full eclipse, all the stars were fully seen, Edirne was captured, in the year 761 A.H.". In the Cambridge copy (ed. Babinger, p. 93): "opening the gates of the fortress its populace surrendered the fort, Edirne was captured in 761 A.H. ... Also Evrenos beg captured İpsala in the year of 763 of the Hegira. In that year the sun had a full eclipse and the world became dark".

[79] Babinger first studied this question in *MOG* 2 (1926), pp. 311 etc.; in 1944 he once again reviewed the question in his *Beiträge*, pp. 46-47; lastly he made it clear in the *Revue des Études Byzantines* 1 (1950) p. 205 that the spring of 1361 can be accepted almost certainly as the date of the capture of Edirne.

[80] It seems that his mistake in giving the year of the full eclipse of the sun once as 762 and then as 763 must be attributed to the dating system followed by the *Calendar*s. The *Calendar*s give the date of an event retroactive from the date of their writing (*see* my *Fatih Devri* I, p. 23, and Plate I). Oruç, who seemingly had repeatedly re-written his work (this can be seen especially in studying the Manisa copy) must have made his mistake when trying to coordinate the dating of the *Calendar* with the Hijrî date.

[81] کنش کلی دوتلدن و قرا کو اولب یلدوزلر ظاهر اوللدن و سلطان اولو
ملك ناصر واقعه‌سندن و سلطان ملك اشرف جلوسندن ... برو طقسان بر یلدر
See ed. Turan, p. 44. Actually the Egyptian Mamluk sultan An-Nâsır Nâsırü'd-Dîn Hasan was taken prisoner by Yal-Bogha in March of 1361. The Melik Nâsır incident in the *Calendar* must refer to this event.

[82] ed. Turan, p. 72.

کسوف تمام در شهور هفتصد شصت دو و ظهور ستارهٔ گیسودار در
شرق و وفات اورخان و خلیل آغاء آتابك در سنه هفتصد شصت و سه

The year 762 A.H. given here for the total eclipse falls within 11 November 1360 to 2 October 1361 A.D. Thus the date of 5 May 1361 which Babinger arrived at for this eclipse falls within the year 762 A.H.

On the other hand, Zeynü'l-Müneccim notes that Orhan died in 763, one year after the eclipse; we have already noted above the accuracy of this date.

Our analysis of the Ottoman traditions also confirms the date 762 A.H., *i.e.* 1361 A.D., which Oruç gives for the conquest of Edirne.[83] Further, Halecki[84] notes that, according to Venetian sources, news of the conquest reached Venice on 14 March 1361. Unless this was a false report,[85] shortly before this date, in the year 1361 "at the time the Maritsa was overflowing", Edirne surrendered to Murad.

[83] We attempted to show above that Neşrî must have arrived at the same date of 762 by different means. *Heşt Behişt* also adheres to the view that the capture of Burgus on the Maritsa by Hacı İlbegi, the battle at Sazlu-Dere and the capture of Edirne all took place in 762 A.H.

[84] *Travaux historiques de la Société des Sciences et des Lettres de Varsovie* 8 (1930), p. 75. Halecki (pp. 76-77) points out that in March 1362, upon the fall of Edirne, Venice sent a galley with an ambassador to propose to the emperor an alliance against the Turks. For the joint fleet, Byzantium was to contribute four galleys, and Venice and Genoa two each.

[85] In those times in favorable weather a courier could travel from Istanbul to Venice in thirteen days. We know that from time to time erroneous news concerning the fall of Istanbul reached Italy. According to Matteo Villani (Halecki, p. 75; Babinger, *Beiträge*, p. 46) Dimetoka definitely fell to the Turks in November of 1361. The same source, however, erroneously gives 1361 as the date of Orhan's death.

IV

LAND PROBLEMS IN TURKISH HISTORY

It is a well known fact that the Ottoman empire was based on an agricultural economy. Not only its economic and financial system, but also its military organization were closely dependent on the same base. Landholding and agriculture were carefully organized for the state purposes. Indeed the agrarian policy followed by the Ottoman state contributed most to the rise of the empire. There is no need to say that this system, applied for centuries in many countries under its rule, has resulted in important social and political consequences. Here let it be emphasized also that the system was the result of an historical process.

It may well be asked why all the cultivated lands in the Ottoman dominions were declared state property and why landholding was so closely controlled. The answer lies primarily in the origin of the Ottoman state itself, born as a Gāzī state on the borderland of two rival religions and civilizations, and, in spite of all further developments, it remained essentially a Gāzī state. It was this origin that gave the Empire its conspicuous features and made it a militant state, as well as shaping its culture, based on the composite frontier elements, into a form more tolerant and more capable of receiving new influences than were the old countries of Islam. This needs to be explained a little further.

The Ottomans, like the first Arab conquerors, were making their conquests in new countries, in Dār al-ḥarb, where no previous Islamic occupation left traditions. Thus not being bound by such traditions, they had a free hand to evolve their empire on the new basis they considered most fit for their purposes. Actually the Ottoman state was less successful in remodeling the conditions of land ownership in the Islamic zone of their dominions than in the Balkans. But the first Ottoman Sultans were also realistic enough not to oppose directly the established tradition in the newly conquered lands. In fact, in the Balkan countries the peasantry in general had never been proprietors of the soil which they worked, and this state of things facilitated the Ottoman policy of establishing there a régime of state property. It simply replaced the old native aristocracy and the small Balkan states in the proprietorship of lands. Now a universal state succeeded to the feudal lords and the old practices persisted. It must be pointed out that in this way many instances of *bidᶜa,* that is innovation, slipped into the Ottoman legislation.

But why was the state so anxious to become the real proprietor wherever it made its conquests? State proprietorship was not only a natural consequence of the conditions present at the moment of conquest, but the Ottoman state always sought to take more and more lands under its ownership. It was the militant character of the state that necessitated this policy. For the Ottoman it was necessary to have a standing army ready to march on a moment's notice, because war, for a Gāzī state, was almost a perpetual condition. Considering the scarcity of silver, which was the only currency in those days, the Ottoman state was compelled to collect its principal financial resources that is to say the *ᶜUshr* in goods. Under this necessity it distributed the conquered lands among its numerous soldiers, assigning them these taxes as salary. These cavalrymen were to stay in their *timars*, fiefs, and to collect the *ᶜUshr* themselves. It seems most likely that these practical needs led the state to take the lands under its close control, in other words, under its own proprietorship.

It is not the purpose here to discuss the Islamic literature on land legislation in connection with the Ottoman system. After the critical approach to the sources of Islamic land law by the scholars such as Becker, Poliac and lastly Lökkegaard, we see that the *fiqh* is so rich in principles as to provide foundation for almost any land system. Only after the final formation of their land legislation—that is to say in the 16th century—did the Ottomans try to adapt, or more exactly to interpret, their land legislation to conform to the Sharīᶜah. Prior to this interpretation the land legislation contained *bidᶜa,* innovations. and even violations. We find then the great Ottoman jurists such as Ibn Kamāl and later Abū-l-Suᶜūd who tried to explain the foundation of the Ottoman land system in view of Sharīᶜah. It might be noted that just at that time the Ottoman state developed from a Gāzī state into an Islamic Caliphate ruling over the old capitals of Islam. The greatest of the Ottoman jurists, Shaikh al-Islām Abū-l-Suᶜūd says as follows:

> "In the Islamic countries there are three kinds of land according to the Sharīᶜah. One part is called *ᶜushrī* lands which are recognized as Mulk to the Moslems. These are their real properties. They possess them just like their other properties... They pay only *ᶜUshr.* Examples of this kind of land exist in Ḥijāz and Baṣra... The second part of lands consist of *harâcî* lands which are left in the possession of unbelievers. These also are their real properties. They pay *harâc-i mukâsama* and *harâc-i muwazzafa* which can amount in some cases to as much as the half of the production. If the Moslems took these lands, they also paid the same *harâc* taxes. Now here are the two kinds of land described in the *Sharīᶜah books.* But there is another kind of land that is neither *ᶜusrî* nor *harâcî.* They call it *arz-i memleket.* In principle it is *harâcî,* but the *rakabe,* the real proprietorship is reserved for *bayt al-māl.* According to some *fiqh* books in *Iraq, Sawād* land is of this kind... The lands of the Ottoman dominions are also of this kind. They are not the property of the villagers. They possess it simply in way of *ariyet* lease. They pay *harāc-i mukasama* and *harac-i muvazzafa.* As long as they cultivate the land and pay their taxes, nobody can interfere with them. When they die, their sons inherit it. If they have no son, then some one outside the family can get it by paying a tax called *tapu...* If the land is left uncultivated for three years it is liable to be taken away from the tenant by the decision of the *Qāḍī...* This kind of land cannot be sold, or granted, or given as a *mulk* or *waqf.* Such acts are absolutely against the law."

This land system no doubt existed much earlier than the above description. The real sources for the study of the Ottoman land legislation are the Imperial record-books. They are arranged by special committees, who were sent to the various provinces to inquire and to record all the population and register the lands with their taxes every twenty or thirty years. The Turkish archives possess many thousands of these registers. Recently Prof. Bernard Lewis of London University published an interesting work based on the *daftars* of Palestine. The present writer published the oldest *daftar* of this kind dated 835 A.H. dealing with Albania. It proves that this land system was in force as early as the beginning of the 14th century. Each *daftar* has a *kanunname* in the first page showing the laws and the customs in force in that province. They are used as law books for all land litigations. It might be added that this system existed originally in the Balkans and in Western Anatolia, which were conquered by the Ottomans or by other Gāzī states. In the rest of Anatolia and in other old Islamic countries the system could not be fully applied because of the old *mulks* and *waqfs* established for many centuries according to the Sharīcah.

Nevertheless on several occasions some of the Ottoman Sultans tried to abolish most of these old *waqfs* and *mulks*. Under the weak Sultans the extension of the *waqf* and *mulk* lands became larger and larger. Many influential men obtained grants of land as *mulk* property, and often converted them into *waqfs*. When the energetic and warlike Sultans, such as Bayazīd the Thunderbolt, and Muhammad the Conqueror, attempted the diminution of the *mulks* and *waqfs*, this caused a deep uneasiness in the country. In the Ottoman empire there was always a struggle between the state and the owners of the *mulks* and *waqfs* as in medieval Egypt and Anatolia.

In the first place, the state was supposed to be the real proprietor. It had the *rakabe* that is the real ownership of the land.

In the second place sipahis became the military class par excellence. They were entitled by the charters given by the Sultan to collect certain taxes assigned to themselves on the lands. Also as representatives of the state on this land, they were given some rights of control over its use and its transfer. But the limits of their authority, and the details of their income, were clearly defined in the *daftars* and the *kanunnâmes*. They themselves cannot possess and cultivate the lands of the peasants. Any disagreements were to be settled by the central government. Due to the close control of the central government, these sipahis had no real similarity with the western feudal fief holders with whom they are so often compared. In the third place, came the actual agriculturists who only possessed and cultivated the land. In general the land was divided up in certain units called *Çiftlik,* — a piece of land of approximately 1000 square meters. A peasant family who took a lease of such a *Çiftlik* could not sell or make any change in its original state. And these units were not allowed to be divided up. So they passed, in inheritance only, to the son or sons in common of the deceased. If he left it uncultivated for three years, he lost all his rights on the land.

In the 16th century the inheritance rights were extended a little by recognising priority for the relatives. In this case they were allowed to pay the same *tapu* money as strangers. It is claimed that this land system could be brought under the term of heritable and perpetual lease.

As already pointed out, this system of state property and control was of vital importance for the military organisation. Because only by this system could the sipahi army in the provinces be maintained. On the other hand, this régime resulted in a fairly sound agrarian policy with its maintenance of small farms kept in the possession of the peasants. In this land system the formation of large estates and the division of *Çiftlik* units into too small units was prevented. The land was not left to chance, but it was carefully controlled to serve a definite policy. There are indications showing that the Ottoman government intended not only to guarantee its sipahis income, but also sought a definite control against any régime of landlords. The Ottoman state always fought against the local landed aristocracy. The Ottoman land system was a happy combination of the state's military needs and social security for the peasantry. Indeed this caused too strong a control of the state on land and abolished all liberty of peasant action. For a peasant could not leave his farm without paying a compensation to his sipahi. The land and classes were, so to speak, fossilized in that régime. One must always keep in mind that the state control and the working of the system were possible only by the regular registrations of the land and the provincial population as already described.

This typical régime began to degenerate during the second half of the 16th century when the first signs of decline of the Empire appeared. The principal causes of this breakdown in the agrarian régime can be summarized as follows:

(1) It seems that the American silver was responsible for it to some extent. The increasing production of silver had begun to pour into the Ottoman dominions from 1580, and this sudden increase caused a rise in prices and an economic disorder throughout the empire, which disorganized the old economic system, and also had a serious influence on the land régime.

(2) The weakening of central government and the abandonment of land registration left agriculture to chance.

(3) The Ottoman government neglected its sipahi army in the provinces, because now only the infantry, with fire-arms, could withstand the Christian armies on the European battlefields.

(4) The courtiers and the bodyguard, as well as the officials in the provinces, obtained the sipahi fiefs as personal estates. Through many devious means a large number of former peasant *çiftliks* also passed into the possession of soldiers.

(5) As a result of the disruption of the sipahi régime in the provinces the *mīrī* (state) lands now were subject to a new system of

lease called *Muqāṭaᶜa*. In this way it became possible for the ordinary persons to get together lands in their hands as *Çiftlik* estates.

The *Muqāṭaᶜa* system grew to very large proportions in the subsequent period. The *timar* lands, fallen vacant, were given on lease by the state to ordinary persons, in return for a payment often settled by auction.

Another way of exploitation of *mīrī* lands was to give them to tax-farmers (*multazims*), and this second method began to be used very largely both by the state and the holders of *timar*. Later on the tax-farmers acquired practically the same position as those possessing a *Muqāṭaᶜa*.

As a matter of fact, this rising class of the owners of *Muqāṭaᶜa* and *Multazims*, taking the place of the old sipahis on the land, had only the right of possession. But already in the 18th century, a tendency to consider these lands as *Sharᶜī* properties was observed. Now the state's efforts to hold these *mīrī* lands back were not successful, because it had lost control in the provinces. The resultant situation encouraged all kinds of abuses over land possession.

The fatal results of this new régime were these: (1) The peasantry in dependence on the new land-holders was in a worse situation than ever. In *Muqāṭaᶜa* the peasant had to pay not only the ordinary taxes due to the state, but also he had to give dues which had been established by usage to the land-holder. And when one takes into account the administrative inefficiency of the central government, one can easily guess the oppressive attitude of these new landlords.

(2) In the 17th century the rich and influential people in the provinces had the chance of gathering lands by way of the *Muqāṭaᶜa* system and became so powerful that they assumed some governmental authority. Consequently a landed aristocracy of *aᶜyān*, notables, emerged in the provinces. Moreover some of the *aᶜyān* constituted dynasties and became opponents to the imperial government. They had their own armies and fought each other. In 1808 they forced the Sultan to sign a charter confirming their position. So, with the disruption of the original land régime, the political and social structure of the empire broke down. It may be added that this situation could be seen with its general characteristics in every part of the empire from Egypt to the Danube.

The Ottoman empire passed through a terrible crisis during the period between 1768-1839 which caused a final break down of its political and social organization. It was in this period that an Eastern Question (Question d'Orient) became one of the most arduous questions of international policy. Now an expanding imperialistic Europe was vitally concerned with the Near-East. Apart from the political consequences of European Imperialism, it caused those Near Eastern countries to come under the strong influence of western ideas. Then some of the Ottoman statesmen, who resided for some time in the European capitals as ambassadors, realized that the only chance of survival for the broken down Empire was to reorganize it after Western states. We call this reform movement under Western influence *Tanzimāt,* which was promulgated by a firman in 1839. This firman announced among other things the efficient protection of the peasantry against all kinds of abuses and extortions. It was followed by the promulgation of certain French codes of law translated into Turkish. The land legislation also came under the influence of the new movement. Accordingly in 1840 the Ottoman government promulgated a new law on tithes, according to which they were to be collected literally in a proportion of one tenth in all parts of the Empire. Until then *ᶜushr* varied from one region to another. For instance it used to be taken as one eighth in Rumeli, whereas one fifth in Aleppo.

Another important step was the abolition of the tax-farming system which was the main cause of many social afflictions. The *Multazims* had also some control on the legal changes of a larger part of lands in the Empire.

In 1847 it was announced that a document given by the governmental authorities would be required for all changes of land tenure. In fact a new movement in land legislation was started when the hereditary rights were extended on *mīrī* lands, which, despite all usurpations by individuals, made up the larger part of lands in the home countries. By extending the hereditary rights from the son to other kin, and by recognizing larger and larger rights of use, the state transformed the *mīrī* lands into the real *mulk* properties, in the proper sense as in the West. As a matter of fact, when, in 1858, a new code of land law was promulgated, only father and mother had acquired the rights to inheritance. This important work of codification systematized the Ottoman land legislation with some modification due to the *Tanzimāt.* One of its interesting provisions stated that a whole village was not allowed to be possessed by one person as a *Çiftlik* estate. This is an important indication of the conception of the *Tanzimât* against the large estates. But as usual this remained in the law book. Here it is an interesting subject of inquiry how far the Egyptian land reforms of 1858 are connected with the Ottoman code of law promulgated at the same date.

The evolution in extending the rights of possession on the *mīrī* lands went on. After the Crimean War in 1856 the Western Powers, supporting the Ottoman reforms, supposed that their liberal system would work wonders in Turkey too. They imputed all the misery of the country to the rigidity of land legislation. These views were adopted by the Ottoman intellectuals under Western influence. So, after the promulgation of the land law of 1858, all the subsequent amendments aimed at making the *mīrī* lands real properties for their actual possessors. In 1867 it was announced by a law, that those entitled to inherit *mīrī* land, included also brothers, sisters, grandchildren and husbands or wives. The old *tapu* documents which were originally given only to testify the possession of *mīrī* land, were now accepted as the basis for all kind of rights on land. So in the end this proved a change not in favor of the actual possessors of land, that is to say the peasantry, but for an interposed class who became the main beneficiary of the reform. Because of the *tapu* documents in their hands, the *mīrī* lands became very nearly the real properties of this class who once had obtained these lands from the state as *muqāṭaᶜa*. The peasants remained in these confirmed estates as *ortakci* (metayer) or as simple agricultural workers. The new situation after the reforms was perhaps worse for the peasantry than before. Because now any new social reform on behalf of this large mass of peasants was more difficult, since the lands were confirmed in the hands of their old possessors. Those Ottoman statesmen, unaware of the actual state of things and of the possible consequences of their act, promulgated automatically the reform laws inspired by their liberal advisors, and made everything worse. So, the national states succeeding the Ottoman empire have taken over difficult problems on land. For instance in the second half of the 19th century in Thessaly in Northern Greece 460 villages out of 658 formed estates (*Çiftlik*) owned by the landlords. The peasants had to give half of their produce to the landlord. The Balkan states had to make real land reforms on behalf of the peasants.

The Modern Turkish Republic, one of those national states constituted after the final break down of the Ottoman Empire, also tackled the problem as a major issue. As the first step *ᶜUshr* was abolished.

In 1926 by the adoption of the common law of Switzerland as the Turkish common law, the Western concept of property was now applied without any conditions or stipulations continuing from the former land law. As a result the land law of 1858 with all its amendments has been entirely abolished. It should be also added that the discussion on this fundamental change occupied Turkish jurists for some time. In 1938, Ataturk proclaimed solemnly that the Turkish peasant is, and must be, the real master of the country, and afterwards all the Republican Governments followed this principle in their social reforms. In 1945 a new land law was announced. That was a revolutionary step indeed. In the first paragraph of that law the goal of it was expressed in this way: (a) To provide land and means for the peasants who do not have sufficient to maintain their families (b) to exploit constantly all the arable lands in the country. To reach this goal it was laid down that all landed properties over 500 dönüms (1 dönüm is 0.247 of an acre) would be nationalized for distribution among the peasants who need land. The state would pay for it by shares in 20 years, and the peasants who received these lands would pay their debts to the state, in 20 years without interest. The Government would also furnish these peasants with the required implements, animals and money.

This law, considered a violation of the notion of property in common law and constitutional law, caused a strong opposition. In 1950, after two years of discussion, in the committees in the Grand National Assembly, the law was modified. In the revised new law, the lands liable to nationalization were those over 5000 *dönüms* and if a land of over 2000 *dönüms* was not cultivated by its owner, it might be nationalized too. The state started by distributing first the state domains and mortmains.

From 1947 on, the Turkish government has been distributing the state lands. According to the statistical figures about two million families in Turkey need land. After coming to power, the governments of the new Democratic party have accelerated the distribution of lands. While the total sum of distributed lands was only 50,000 in 1948, the figure has reached 325,000 dönüms by the middle of 1953. It becomes apparent from these figures that there is still a long way ahead. But it must be also pointed out that lands over 500 dönüms in Turkey make up only one eighth of all cultivated areas. Even a nationalization of these lands would not bring a solution to the land problem. So all the arable lands remaining uncultivated at the present, should be changed into cultivated land and distributed by the state to the peasants in need.

University of Ankara.

Addendum:

This paper was written in August, 1953. By the end of 1954 the total area of distributed lands amounted to about 10 million *dönüms* of which 198,730 peasant families had benefited. This figure includes 15,441 immigrant families who obtained 647,512 *dönüms*. In the meantime the rapid mechanization of agriculture has increased the amount of cultivated land considerably. Today it is about 190,000,000 while it was about 145,000,000 *dönüms* in 1950. (These figures show only the area for the cereals). In 1949 there were 1,800 tractors in Turkey. Today this figure has reached 40,000. In accordance with these developments the production in cereals has increased from 23.5 million tons in the three years between 1949-1951 to 36 million tons in 1952-1954. It is also to be noted that the population of Turkey has increased from 21 million in 1950 to 24 million today. (No census has been made since 1950. The last figure is an estimate of the experts.)

V

THE TURKISH IMPACT ON THE DEVELOPMENT OF MODERN EUROPE

Since a Europeo-centric view of history in the West began to be replaced by a true world history concept, the history of the Ottoman Empire, which lasted in a very important part of the world for over five centuries, is gaining a new interest. A number of contributions recently made in Europe and America on the problem of the place of the Ottoman Empire in European history can be considered as a sign of this growing interest. Although some of these new studies were still not free of certain biases, mainly because they did not make use also of the Ottoman evidence, they, however, explored new ideas and had new orientations.

Under the light of these publications we are now able, for instance, to speak of how the Ottoman state became an important factor in the balance of power of European politics. Even during the first stage of the Italian wars from 1494 to 1525 the Ottoman state was an important part in Italian diplomacy. Fr. Babinger and J. Kissling in their studies based on the Italian archival material, and S. Fisher, Pfefferman, Schwoebel, D. Vaughan in their more general treatment of the subject showed how the Italian courts maintained diplomatic relations with the Ottoman Sultan. It is true that the Western archives do not yield much on the subject, for political and military matters were concealed in such negotiations and never put in writing. But sometimes even if an Ottoman military intervention was not really desired the rumor of a secret alliance was used as an intimidation. Hard-pressed Italian states used as a last measure the threat of calling on the Ottomans. In 1525 the French followed actually this Italian policy when their king was made prisoner by the Emperor. The Ottomans welcomed this opportunity to invade Hungary in 1526 and open a sea front against the Emperor in the Mediterranean in 1532 just as in the past they had exploited the situation in Italy against Venice. From 1480 onwards the Ottomans always thought of an invasion of Italy. Two factors made them hesitate for a decisive move, the possibility of resistance of a Europe united under the Pope and Emperor, and their own naval weakness to open an oversea front. In 1537, however, Suleyman thought it was the time for such a move. As early as 1531 the Venetian ambassador was writing to the doge, "Sultan Suleyman says, 'To Rome, to Rome,' and he detests the Emperor for his title of Caesar, he, the Turk, causing himself to be called Caesar." Ottoman attempts to capture from the Venetians strongholds along the Adriatic coast and the isle of Corfu in 1537 and 1538 were in fact a preparation for the invasion of Italy. France was then the ally of the Ottomans. At the siege of Corfu they were reinforced by the French navy. But the King and Emperor saw the great danger for the whole of Christendom in Europe. In July 1538 Francis made peace with Charles V at Aigues-Mortes and what is more he promised to take part in a crusade against the Ottomans. Two months later Barbarossa, Grand Admiral of the Sultan, succeeded in routing at Prevesa a powerful crusading fleet. Then, this victory became useless without French alliance.

What I am trying to emphasize is that the Ottomans became an active part in the second stage of the Italian wars and there was a moment when the Western contenders for Italy saw that the balance of power was lost in favor of the Sultan. It must be added that the Ottomans fully appreciated the value of the French alliance and supported the King financially too. In 1533 the Sultan sent Francis the sum of one hundred thousand gold pieces to enable him to form a coalition with England and German princes against Charles V. Two years later the French King asked the Sultan to send him a subsidy of one million ducats. Later on in 1555 the French King Henri II, pressed for money, floated a loan in France with the interest increased from 12 to 16 percent, and at this time many Turks, pashas among them, found it profitable to invest in this loan. The King borrowed 150,000 scudos from Joseph Nasi, Jewish tax farmer of the Sultan. On his part the French king appreciated well the Ottoman Alliance as the principal power to check the Habsburg supremacy in Europe. In 1532 Francis I admitted to the Venetian ambassador that he saw in the Ottoman Empire the only force guaranteeing the continued existence of the states of Europe against Charles V.

In brief one can say that the Ottoman Empire played an important role in the balance of power in Europe in the sixteenth century and consequently in the rise of the nation-states in the West. This role can be seen to continue in the Ottoman support and encouragement to the English and Dutch in the period after 1580 when these nations proved to be the champions of European resistance to the Habsburg attempts at supremacy.

In the sixteenth and seventeenth centuries support for Protestants and Calvinists was one of the fundamental principles of Ottoman policy in Europe. Already in 1552 Suleyman tried to incite the Protestant princes in Germany against the Pope and Emperor. He said in his letter to them that he himself was about to embark on a campaign and promised on oath that they would not be harmed when he entered Germany. Melanchton was directly in touch with the Patriarch of Istanbul, who was in effect an official of the Sultan. Later on in a letter to Lutheran princes in the Low Countries and in other lands subject to Spain, the Sultan offered military help and saw them as standing close to him, since they did not worship idols, believed in one God and fought against the Pope and Emperor. Under Ottoman rule Calvinism was propagated freely in Hungary and Transylvania, which became a Calvinist and Unitarian stronghold in the seventeenth century. It is convincingly argued that Ottoman pressure on the Habsburgs was an important factor in the extension of Protestantism in Europe.

Also, it should be pointed out that the Ottomans contributed to the rise of Muscovy by supporting, as a great power in the politics of Eastern Europe, the Muscovy-Crimean alliance against the Jagellons and the Golden Horde, which then tried to establish or restore their hegemony in the region. When the Ottomans saw the danger for their Black Sea and Caucasian interests in the Muscovite supremacy and expansion in the middle of the sixteenth century it was too late.

Now I would like to deal in a more detailed way with the economic relations of the Ottoman Empire with Europe.

Speaking of the Ottoman economy one can certainly not ignore the attitude of the Ottoman ruling class towards the productive classes and to the problem of its economic policy in general.

At the outset it must be emphasized that the Ottoman state was *not* a nomadic empire the models of which could be found in the Euroasian steppes. It was a typical Middle East empire with all its age-old administrative principles and institutions. It was concerned primarily with the protection of the settled populations under its rule and promotion of their agricultural and commercial interests. It should be added that this policy was not based on purely economic reasoning but mainly on the financial ends of the state. Even if in the thirteenth century nomadic elements in the Ottoman frontier society played a certain role, the Ottoman state had soon become a typical Islamic sultanate with the basic structure of a Middle East state. Its legislation and actions leave no room for doubt on this point. We know, for instance, that the longest internal struggle the Ottoman state had to make in the fifteenth and sixteenth centuries stemmed from the basic fact that it endeavoured in the interests of the settled population to take under control the semi-nomads of the Uzun-Yayla in Inner Anatolia and of the Taurus range from the Euphrates to Western Anatolia.

The economic system of the Ottoman empire and its basic economic principles derived from a traditional view of state and society which had prevailed since antiquity in the empires of the Middle East. These principles, since they determined the attitude and policy of the administrators, were of considerable practical importance.

In the Muslim state, as in earlier states in the Middle East, all classes of society and all sources of wealth were regarded as obliged to preserve and promote the power of the ruler. Hence all political and social institutions and all types of economic activity were regulated by the state in order to achieve this goal. The populace was regarded as forming two main groups—those who represented the ruler's authority (the administrators, the troops, the men of religion), and the ordinary subjects, *ra'āyā'*. The former were not concerned with production and paid no taxes, while the latter were the producers and tax-payers. A main concern of the state was to ensure that each individual remained in his own class; this was regarded as the basic requisite for politico-social order and harmony.

To increase revenue from taxation the governments of Near East States appreciated the necessity of developing economic activity and promoting the greatest possible increase in production from all classes of the *ra'āyā'*. It was recommended that cultivated land should be increased by the digging of canals and that trade between different regions should be promoted by the construction of roads, bridges and caravansaries, and by ensuring the safety of travelers.

Within the class of the producers, the tillers of the soil and the craftsmen were subject to a code of regulations distinct from that of merchants; the methods of production and the profit margins of the former were under strict state control, since, in this view of society, they were the classes who produced the essential necessities of life and whose labors therefore were most intimately connected with the preservation of social and political order. That a peasant or a craftsman should freely change the methods of production was not countenanced; his activities were permitted only within the limits of the ordinances laid down by the state. In Near East society, it was only the merchants who enjoyed conditions allowing them to become capitalists. "Merchant," *tüjjar*, in this context, means the big businessman who engaged in inter-regional trade or in the sale of goods imported from afar. Craftsmen who in the cities sold goods manufactured by themselves and trades-people who sold these goods at secondhand fell outside the category of "merchant." The merchant class was not subject to the regulations of the *hisba*, that is, rules of the religious law to ensure fair deal in the market.

In an Ottoman Mirror for Princes, Sinan Pasha's *Ma'ārifnāme* written in the second half of the fifteenth century, the ruler is advised :

> Look with favor on the merchants in the land; always care for them; let no one harass them; let no one order them about, for through their trading the land becomes prosperous, and by their wares cheapness abounds in the world; through them the excellent fame of the Sultan is carried to surrounding lands, and by them the wealth within the land is increased.

Going through the state papers issued by the Ottoman Chancery one is struck by the fact that the administration was always most concerned in applying the principles summarized above.

The Ottoman government's concern for promoting the commerce and protecting the interests of the merchants class found its expression in various ways.

It was mainly with the purpose of encouraging trade that the Sultans granted capitulations to the foreigners. It should be emphasized that a capitulation had never been considered as a contractual bilateral document and it maintained its character of a grant of concession by the Sultans until the eighteenth century when they had to give the same privileges to the Habsburgs and Russia. Before this actual change the Sultan retained the authority to decide unilaterally when the pledge of friendship on the opposite side was broken and the capitulation rendered void.

Once its nature as a concession granted by the Sultan is established a capitulation was, however, granted with certain political, financial and economic expectations. The determining factors were usually the opportunities of acquiring a political ally within Christendom, of obtaining scarce goods such as woolen cloth, tin, steel and paper, and especially bullion and increasing customs revenues, the principal source of hard cash for the imperial treasury.

The Ottoman empire was not self-sufficient economically as it is sometimes claimed. It was vitally important for its economy and finances to import western silver. Its import was encouraged by tax exemption and measures were taken to hinder its flow to the Eastern countries where gold was cheaper. The Europeans knew well that the Ottomans were dependent on their commerce in the Levant and when they had to bargain for a special privilege in the capitulations their chief weapon was to use the threat that they were going to boycott the Ottoman ports.

A new period in the economic history of the Ottoman Empire started with the annexation of the Arab countries between 1516 and 1550 which actually gave it the control of the trade routes between the Mediterranean and Indian Ocean. It is now commonplace knowledge that the Near East continued to receive spices directly from India and Southeast Asia throughout the sixteenth century. According to the Ottoman records, in 1562 the customs levied on spices transported from Mecca to Damascus alone amounted to 110 thousand gold ducats. What is interesting to note is that most of the spices imported there went to Bursa and Istanbul to be shipped further north. To give an interesting example, in 1547 we find a Hungarian merchant in Bursa selling kersey and buying a great quantity of spices.

In this period the newly rising nation-states of the West, France, England and the Netherlands, became most anxious to get trade privileges in the Ottoman Empire. The belief was that the Levant was, as in the past, the most promising field for economic growth. It was not solely on religious grounds that the Marrano family of Mendes, then controlling the spice trade in Europe, came to settle in the Ottoman capital in the 1550's.

Against the Venetian dominance in the Levant trade the Ottomans had always favoured the rival nations, first the Genoese, then the Ragusans and Florentines in the fifteenth century.

As to the Western nations, the French made their first progress in Syria and Egypt after Selim's renewal of the Mamluk capitulations in 1517. But they really began to replace the Venetians in the Levant trade only after the Ottoman-Venetian war in 1570-73. Incidentally, the so-called French capitulations of 1536 had never been concluded. The first official Ottoman capitulation to the French is dated 1569. The other Western nations were then to sail and trade under the French flag. At the beginning of the 17th century the volume of the French trade in the Levant rose to thirty million French livres, making up one half of France's total trade at that time. Later on when the English and Dutch proved to be even stronger rivals of the Habsburg power than the French, the Ottomans did not hesitate to favor these nations too by granting them capitulations, to the English in 1580, and the Dutch in 1612. Except during the civil war between 1642 and 1660 the English had the lead in the Levant trade in the seventeenth century. According to a contemporary source the Levant market for the English cloth which was the main article for export, expanded by one-third and was one-fourth of all English manufactures exported to the Levant. As W. Sombart put it, without recognizing the significance of the Levant trade for Western economic expansion it is difficult to comprehend the rise of Western capitalism.

The capitulary privileges were gradually so much extended that Paul Masson and R. Mantran, two French specialists on the Levant trade, could unanimously assert that in the seventeenth century there was no other state in the world practicing a more liberal policy than the Ottoman empire towards the foreign merchants.

The Ottomans had then no idea of the balance of trade, an idea that we find for the first time in a clearly defined form only in the mercantilist England of the sixteenth century. Originated from an age-old tradition in the Middle East, the Ottoman trade policy was that the state had to be concerned above all with the volume of goods in internal market so that the people and craftsmen in the cities in particular would not suffer a shortage of necessities and raw material. Consequently the imports were always welcomed and encouraged and exports discouraged. Hence sometimes we find higher customs rates for exports and even prohibition of the export of such goods as wheat, cotton, hides and beeswax. As for silver and gold no customs dues were levied to encourage their importation and every step was taken to discourage exportation. The Ottomans were definitely bullionists, a stage preceding true mercantilism in the West. The difference with the mercantilist nations of the West was that the Ottomans clung to the guild system as the mainstay of the state and society while Europeans saw in the export of manufactured goods a principal means of getting bullion from outside. In order to achieve a favourable balance of trade they intervened in domestic industries and trade organizations to develop them on capitalistic lines and to export more and more goods and conquer more and more overseas markets. Incidentally, one might speculate that the increasingly unfavourable balance of trade of the West in the fifteenth century pushed them perhaps in this direction and caused a mercantilistic policy to develop, since they had no important commodities other than cloths and minerals to export to the East. The capitulations were complementary to this pattern and it is noteworthy that the mercantilistic nations of the West had been concerned in the first place to found their Levant companies and obtain capitulations. Unwittingly the Ottomans became a part of a European economic system which gave rise to modern capitalism.

VI

THE POLICY OF MEHMED II TOWARD THE GREEK POPULATION OF ISTANBUL AND THE BYZANTINE BUILDINGS OF THE CITY

This paper was prepared for the Symposium entitled "After the Fall of Constantinople," held at Dumbarton Oaks in May 1968. Owing to unforeseen circumstances, Professor Inalcık was unable to be present, and his paper was read by Professor R. J. H. Jenkins.

The Publications Commitee

Note: In transliterating the Turkish, Arabic, and Persian words I have followed the system used in the *Encyclopaedia of Islam*, new edition, with the following exceptions: ج = j, چ = ch, ı = ı, ش = sh, ق = q, خ = kh. The long vowels are rendered with the sign^.

I am greatly indebted to Dr. V. L. Ménage for his translation of this paper from Turkish into English and for his many valuable suggestions.

When in the spring of 1453 the Ottoman Sultan Mehmed II appeared with his immense army before its walls, Constantinople was a half-ruined city whose population might at the most have numbered fifty thousand. As A. M. Schneider has shown,[1] from the time of the Latin occupation in 1204 the city had progressively declined until it was now in effect no more than a collection of villages. Already by the seventh decade of the fourteenth century Constantinople and its immediate neighborhood had formed only a small island surrounded by territories under Ottoman rule, with its communications by sea and its seaborne trade under the control of the Italian maritime states. Economically too the Ottoman capitals of Brusa and Adrianople had begun to overshadow the former imperial center. The old silk route from Persia via Trebizond to Constantinople had, by the end of the fourteenth century, been diverted to Brusa, which had then become the principal trading-center in Oriental products for the Genoese merchants of Galata, and toward which both the silk caravans from Persia and the spice caravans from Syria now converged.[2] In short, Constantinople was the dead center of a dead empire, which George Scholarius described before its fall as "a city of ruins, poor, and largely uninhabited."[3]

Mehmed II did not wish that the city which he envisaged as the future capital of his empire should pass into his hands, after sack, as a mere heap of ruins. In addressing to the Emperor Constantine his three invitations to surrender the city he was, it is true, merely obeying a precept of the Muslim Holy Law; but at the same time he was hoping to win a city which had not been exposed to pillage. To conquer the city by force—the legal term is *ʿanwatan*—would inevitably lead to pillage and destruction; for this is a precept of the Holy Law; and no ruler could rob the fighters for the faith of this right to sack, which was granted to them by Allah. On the other hand, the Sultan was under pressure to bring matters to a swift conclusion. The Venetian fleet was at sea; rumors that the Hungarians would break the state of truce and march into the Balkans were causing uneasiness in the Ottoman camp; and the Grand Vizier Chandarlı Khalîl Pasha was pressing for the abandonment of the whole enterprise.[4] At last, after a council of war had been summoned to make the final decision, the Sultan called for a general assault and proclaimed that the city was given over to sack; a decision dependent, according to the Holy Law, upon the permission of the *imâm*, the leader of the Muslim community.

This proclamation was, of course, welcomed by the Muslim troops, but it is clear that the Sultan had been reluctant to make it. According to Ducas,[5]

[1] "Die Bevölkerung Konstantinopels im XV. Jh.," *Nachrichten der Akad. der Wiss. in Göttingen, Phil.-Hist. Klasse* (1949), No. 9, 234–44.
[2] H. Inalcık, "Bursa and the Commerce of the Levant," *Journal of the Social and Economic History of the Orient*, 3 (1960), 131–47.
[3] Schneider, *op. cit.*, 236.
[4] H. Inalcık, *Fatih devri üzerinde tetkikler ve vesikalar* (Ankara, 1954), 126–32.
[5] Bonn ed., 280; ed. V. Grecu, 349–51.

the ambassador whom he sent into the city before issuing the proclamation had put forward these arguments to induce the Emperor to submit: "Are you willing to abandon the city and depart for wherever you like, together with your nobles and their property, leaving behind the common people unharmed both by us and by you? Or do you wish that through your resistance ... the common people should be enslaved by the Turks and scattered over all the world?" After the conquest the Sultan summoned to his presence the Megadux Lucas Notaras and asked him why he had not persuaded the Emperor to surrender the city, in which case, he added angrily, it would have been saved from all damage and destruction. The Megadux replied that they had indeed been ready to surrender, but that to do so was no longer in the Emperor's power or his own, for the Italians assisting in the defense had flatly refused to consent.[6] Notaras, as is well known, was frequently at odds with the Italian defenders during the siege. An early Ottoman source confirms the report of the Byzantine historian on this point: "When every sector of the walled city was on the point of being destroyed, the Emperor summoned Lucas; they consulted together and took measures for the surrender. But the Frankish infidels were offended and protested; 'We will defend the city; we will not surrender it to the Muslims,' and they persisted in continuing the fight."[7]

The Ottoman Sultan, as a Muslim ruler, was obliged to act in conformity with the Muslim Holy Law, the *sharî'a*. The *sharî'a* decrees that if a community of *ahl al-kitâb* (literally, "people of the Book," in effect, Christians and Jews) rejects the obligatory invitation to surrender and continues to resist, they are to be treated as *mushrik*'s (literally, "those who admit partners [to God]," in effect, polytheists). When they have been subdued "by force"—*'anwatan, qahran*—no rights are conceded to them: their goods are legitimate booty and they and their children are reduced to slavery. In the division of movable property, the Muslim ruler as *imâm*—one might say, the state—is entitled to one fifth.[8] Immovable property—real estate—represents a different category of booty.[9] According to a principle which long before the rise of the Ottomans had been accepted in Islamic land law, the freehold possession over land, whether acquired by force or by peaceful occupation, belonged to the *bayt al-mâl*, the state treasury; in other words, the land belonged to the state. The Ottomans, whose military and administrative organization reposed upon the *tîmâr* (feudal) system, adopted this principle in all its implications; even to propounding that an estate which had been made *vaqf* (i.e., placed in mortmain for the support of a pious object) might, if the pious object ceased to exist, revert to the freehold possession of the state. We shall see later how, in the last decade of his reign, Mehmed II, relying on this theory, "nationalized" a large proportion of *vaqf* estates.

[6] Sphrantzes, Bonn ed., 291 f.; cf. Chalcocondyles, Bonn ed., 390.

[7] Oxford, Bodl. Marsh 313. On this work, see V. L. Ménage, *Neshrî's History of the Ottomans* (London, 1964), 11–14.

[8] For the *jihâd* (Holy War) and its consequences, see the section *Kitâb al-siyar* in Islamic legal textbooks, especially in *al-Durar* by Molla Khusrev, who was *qâḍî'asker* in the reign of Mehmed II; also M. Khadduri, *War and Peace in the Law of Islam* (Baltimore, 1955), 125 ff.

[9] F. Løkkegaard, *Islamic Taxation in the Classic Period* (Copenhagen, 1950), 38–92.

An Ottoman source reports that the Sultan proclaimed the assault and sack in these terms: "The stones and the land of the city and the city's appurtenances belong to me; all other goods and property, prisoners, and foodstuffs are booty for the troops."[10] So Ducas also, who is well-informed in Ottoman affairs, reports[11] that the Sultan reserved the walls and buildings for himself but left all the movable property to the troops.

The Sultan had granted permission for three days of sack, but it is clear that he put an end to the pillage on the evening of the first day.[12] The Ottoman and the Byzantine sources agree in reporting that he felt profound sadness as he toured the looted and enslaved city.[13] Not without significance are the stories told by contemporary sources of the sharp punishments which he decreed for soldiers caught destroying buildings.[14]

According to Tursun Beg,[15] who was in the Sultan's entourage during those days, before leaving the city Mehmed II proclaimed "to his viziers and his commanders and his officers that henceforth his capital was to be Istanbul" and ordered the building of a palace. The word freely translated here as "capital" is *takht*, literally "throne": "My throne is Istanbul." Ever since the time of the steppe empires of Central Asia, a district called "*takht-ili*," the "throne region," had been for the Turks a specific region where the *khaqan*'s (emperors) resided, a sacred territory, the seat of the *khaqan*'s authority; and the most important prerequisite for claiming the title of *khaqan* was *de facto* occupation of this "throne region." This attitude corresponds to the Roman concept of imperial authority. In 1466 George of Trebizond, in a letter to the Sultan, wrote: "No one doubts that you are emperor of the Romans. Whoever holds by right the center of the Empire is emperor, and the center of the Roman Empire is Istanbul."[15a] Mehmed II and his successors regarded themselves, through their possession of the throne of the Caesars, as emperors of Rome and legitimate heirs to all the territories which the emperors had formerly ruled. Thus, to Mehmed II, whose ambition was to establish a worldwide empire, Istanbul provided not merely a strategic center, but also an essential political and legal basis. It is for this reason that throughout his reign one of his main preoccupations and ambitions was to transform the half-deserted and ruined

[10] Tâjî-zâde Ja'fer Chelebi, *Mahrûse-i Istanbul Fethnâmesi*, appendix to *Ta'rîkh-i Osmânî Enjümeni Mejmuası* (hereafter *TOEM*) (A. H. 1331), 19.

[11] Bonn ed., 281. The tale that the entire city, or part of it, surrendered on terms is a fiction invented later to give a legal coloring to the fact that Mehmed II left some churches in the possession of the Greeks; the *muftî* (head of the *ulema*) and, naturally, the Patriarch were willing to give it official sanction. The question is fully discussed by J. H. Mordtmann, "Die Kapitulation von Konstantinopel im Jahre 1453," *Byz. Zeitschrift*, 21 (1912), 129–44; Mordtmann thinks that the peace negotiations before the final assault may have helped to give rise to the story. It is discussed most recently by S. Runciman, *The Fall of Constantinople, 1453* (Cambridge, 1965), 153, 157, 199, 204; Runciman suggests (p. 153) that since the quarters of the city were separated by extensive open spaces, it was possible for the local officials of some quarters to make a last-minute submission.

[12] Runciman, *op. cit.*, 148.

[13] Tursun Beg, *Ta'rîkh-i Abû'l-Fatḥ*, appendix to *TOEM* (1927), 57; Critoboulos, ed. V. Grecu (Bucharest, 1963), 149, English trans. C. T. Riggs (Princeton, 1954), 76f.

[14] Ducas reports (Bonn ed., 298) that the Sultan himself drew his sword on a soldier damaging the pavement of Aya Sofya.

[15] *Op. cit.*, 59.

[15a] F. Babinger, *Mehmed der Eroberer und seine Zeit* (Munich, 1953), 266.

capital of the Caesars, which he had conquered, into a fitting center for this world empire which he sought to create; to rebuild it, to repopulate it, and to raise it to the status of a vital economic and political metropolis. The most faithful account of the Sultan's sustained and vigorous activity in promoting the regeneration of Istanbul is provided by Critoboulos; while in this, as well as in other respects, the most important Ottoman source is Tursun. The details they give, when supplemented by and compared with Ottoman documents relating to *vaqf*'s and Ottoman archive registers, present a clear picture of how the Sultan refounded Istanbul according to the traditions and the institutions of a Turco-Islamic city. Here we shall examine only the treatment which, in order to further this aim, he accorded to the Greeks and the policy which he pursued in dealing with the Byzantine buildings and sites which had come into his possession.

It must be remembered that the Ottomans, in reorganizing a conquered city, followed a series of established principles. According to the *sharî'a*, the inhabitants of a city or town which had responded to the invitation to surrender were left undisturbed in their homes, with the status of *dhimmî*, and their lives, their possessions, and the practice of their religion were fully protected by the Islamic state. By a precept of the *sharî'a*, "if they accept the *jizya* [i.e., the poll tax], that which is due to us [Muslims] is due also to them, and that which is obligatory upon us is obligatory also upon them";[16] in other words, after a Christian population had agreed to pay the supplementary due of the *jizya*, to which Muslims were not liable, they obtained from the *imâm* exactly the same rights and obligations as the Muslims enjoyed.

Bertrandon de La Broquière, who in 1432 travelled through Eastern Thrace along the old imperial road between Constantinople and Adrianople, speaking of the towns then occupied by the Ottomans[17] reports of some of them that their citadels were destroyed and that they were newly populated, either entirely by Turks, or by Turks and Greeks together, whereas others were inhabited entirely by Greeks. When we consult the old Ottoman chronicles, we find that the towns inhabited by Greeks are always those which had responded to the summons to surrender. An early Ottoman chronicler[18] writes:

> [Murâd I] marched against the fortress town of Banatoz [Panados]. The infidels there immediately surrendered the fortress without fighting, and Murâd secured them in their former abodes. Then he went against Chorlu [Tzouroullos]; the infidels fought hard, but finally the lord of the town was struck in the eye by an arrow and they were left helpless. The troops swept into the fortress, there was great looting, and they destroyed the fortifications. Then they came to Misini [Mesene]; and its lord came forth with gifts to meet the Sultan.

[16] *Mevqûfâtî Sherhi* (Istanbul, A. H. 1318), I, 340.
[17] *Le voyage d'outremer*, ed. Ch. Schefer (Paris, 1892), 169–70.
[18] *Ğihānnümā, die altosmanische Chronik des Mevlānā Mehemmed Neschrī*, ed. F. Taeschner, I (Codex Menzel) (Leipzig, 1951), 52–53. Cf. H. Inalcık, "Ottoman Methods of Conquest," *Studia Islamica*, 2 (1954), 112–29.

De La Broquière describes the citadel of Chorlu as being in ruins and the town as being repopulated by Turks and Greeks; Mesene, however, was "une petite place fermée [i.e., walled] et n'y demeurent que Grecz"; on the other hand he says of "Pirgasi" (Pyrgos), which had been taken by force of arms: "tous les murs abattus et n'y demeure que les Turcz."

A second principle which the Ottomans had observed from the earliest days in their reorganization of newly conquered territories was that of compulsory resettlement.[19] Sixteenth-century decrees ordering such resettlement[20] show that it served a variety of social, political, and economic purposes: to restore to prosperity a deserted countryside or a ruined city, to restore to production a potential source of wealth, to move people from an overpopulated to an underpopulated region, to provide a means of livelihood to a landless community, and to remove to a distant territory and break up a rebellious population or a refractory tribe of nomads. When townsfolk were subjected to compulsory resettlement, a certain proportion of the population, e.g., the members of one household in ten, were selected by the *qâḍî* of the town and its prefect (*subashı*), their names and descriptions were recorded in a register, and they were deported to their new home. There the deportees enjoyed a special status; for a specified period they were exempt from taxation but were forbidden to move elsewhere. It was a recurrent cause of complaint that, in the course of such deportations, wealthy and influential individuals who were reluctant to abandon their homes managed to win over the local authorities and procure their own exemption; but the central authorities knew well how essential to the rehabilitation of a city were merchants and craftsmen, and the Sultans made it a principal point of policy to resettle, especially in their capital cities, men of influence, wealthy merchants, and skilled craftsmen of newly conquered territories.

Although Constantinople had been taken *by force*, the Sultan did not hesitate, by using his authority as sovereign, to institute various measures which mitigated the grievous consequences that might otherwise have arisen from this. The preliminary measures which he took before leaving for Adrianople on 21 June concerned the defense of the city and its repopulation. First, says Critoboulos,[21] he presented splendid houses to all his dignitaries and officers, "and to some of them he even gave beautiful churches for their residences." Then he settled the fifth of the enslaved Greeks—his share as ruler—"along the shores of the city harbor," i.e., presumably, mainly in the Phanar region. "He gave them houses and exempted them from taxes for a specified time. . . . He also issued a proclamation to all those who had paid their own ransom, or who promised to pay it to their masters within a limited time, that they might live in the city; to them too he granted freedom from taxes and gave them houses, either their own or those of others." So, too, some of the nobility were granted houses and were resettled. On the question of repopulating the city the

[19] Inalcık, "Ottoman Methods of Conquest," *loc. cit.*
[20] *Ibid.*, 122–29.
[21] Ed. Grecu, 159; trans. Riggs, 83.

Sultan sought the advice of Notaras. He had thought, indeed, of making him prefect of the city and "putting him in charge of its repopulation," but abandoned this idea. (We shall return to the position of Notaras, for it has an important bearing on the Sultan's change of policy toward the Greeks.)

Further measures were taken to promote the repopulation of the city. As Critoboulos reports,[22] "When the Sultan had captured the city of Constantinople, almost his very first care was to have the city repopulated." A number of building projects had to be undertaken without delay: the repair of the walls,[23] the construction of a citadel (Yedikule), and the building of a palace for himself in the Forum Tauri in the center of the city. For this work he used his Greek slaves, paying them a fairly good wage (six aspers or more, corresponding to the daily pay of a Janissary[24]) so that they could ransom themselves with their earnings and settle as free men in the city. He had recourse also to compulsory resettlement, issuing orders that Christians, Muslims, and Jews should be sent to the city from every territory of his domains; Ducas states more explicitly[25] that he commanded that five thousand households be deported to Istanbul by September. Before leaving for Adrianople he appointed Karıshtıran Süleymân Beg as prefect of the city; "He put him in charge of everthing, but particularly of the repopulation of the city, and instructed him to be very zealous about this matter."[26] From a letter of 16 August, published by N. Iorga,[27] we learn that the citadels of Silivri and Galata had been destroyed and their populations deported to Istanbul. In order to encourage people to settle in the city, the Sultan proclaimed that whoever came of his own accord, be he rich or poor, could select whatever abandoned house or mansion he chose, and be granted the freehold of it. Tursun, who reports this,[28] adds that numerous people on hearing this invitation came and occupied houses and mansions; but rich merchants, not being in need, did not leave their homes and ignored the invitation.

The Sultan returned to Istanbul in the autumn of 1453 to survey the progress made in the projects which he had initiated.[29] The chronology of his activities after the conquest has always been confused. During this second stay in Istanbul he appointed (6 January 1454) George Scholarios patriarch.[30] According to Sphrantzes, he did this simply "in order to encourage those Christians who had fled to return and settle in Istanbul." This was no doubt an important factor in the Sultan's decision; but the Ottoman sultans were always careful to represent themselves as protectors of the Orthodox Church against the

22 Ed. Grecu, 171; trans. Riggs, 93.
23 There is an important document in the Archives of Topkapı Sarayı, No. E. 11975, relating to this.
24 *Die Aufzeichnungen des Genuesen Iacopo de Promontorio-de Campis über den Osmanenstaat um 1475*, ed. F. Babinger (Munich, 1957), 36.
25 Bonn ed., 313.
26 Ed. Grecu, 163; trans. Riggs, 85.
27 *Notes et extraits pour servir à l'histoire des croisades au XVe siècle*, IV (Bucharest, 1915), 67.
28 *Op. cit.*, 60.
29 Critoboulos, ed. Grecu, 169–75; trans. Riggs, 89–95.
30 Runciman (*op. cit.*, 155) is somewhat hesitant about this date, but according to the chronology of Critoboulos the Patriarch was appointed in the winter of 1453/4.

Latins. Documents dating from before the fall of Constantinople[31] show that an Orthodox metropolitan or bishop in Ottoman territories was appointed by official patent (*berât*) of the Sultan and might even, like other Ottoman functionaries, be assigned a *tîmâr*. It is thus easily understandable that, in the course of the Ottoman expansion, Orthodox priests frequently cooperated with the Ottomans against the Venetians. This policy of the Ottomans was in no way contrary to the *sharî'a* or to the Muslim tradition of the state.

According to Critoboulos,[32] after appointing the Patriarch, the Sultan went to Brusa where, in the course of a residence of thirty-five days, he dealt with "all that had to do with local disturbances, revolts of leaders and peoples," and dismissed some governors. It is not difficult to see what lay behind these stern measures. We know that wealthy citizens of Brusa resisted deportation; nor should it be forgotten that, during this period in the history of this important commercial and industrial city, the guilds and the merchants engaged in the rich silk trade and industry could feel themselves powerful enough to attempt to resist the Sultan's orders. They failed; for there is documentary evidence[33] that deportations from Brusa were carried out and that the majority of these deportees played the main role in the establishment of the township of Eyüb. The Sultan returned again to Istanbul, and shortly afterward "he set out for Adrianople *in the winter*."[34]

Some years later, in 1459, the Sultan took extraordinary measures to promote the prosperity and repopulation of Istanbul.[35] Chief among them was his summoning of the dignitaries to his presence and commanding each to found, in the quarter of his choice, a building complex consisting of pious foundations —that is, a theological college, a school, a public kitchen, all grouped around a mosque—and of such commercial buildings as a caravansary, a *khan*, and a market. The promotion of commerce and the increase of population were considered to be dependent upon the creation of such facilities. In the following years the Sultan himself, the Grand Vizier Mahmûd Pasha, and other viziers and dignitaries founded such building complexes at various points in the city, each grouped around a mosque; and each such center became the nucleus of a new quarter.[36] At the end of 1459 Mehmed II sent out orders that Greeks who,

[31] See, e. g., *Sûret-i defter-i sancak-i Arvanid*, ed. H. Inalcık (Ankara, 1954), Nos. 148, 162, 186, 200.

[32] Ed. Grecu, 175; trans. Riggs, 95.

[33] In the register (No. A. 3/3) of the *qâḍî* of Bursa.

[34] I.e., early in 1454. For a critique of F. Babinger's interpretation that the Sultan visited Anatolia in the summer of 1453, and that his purpose was to rest, see H. Inalcık's review article, "Mehmed the Conqueror (1432–1481) and His Time," *Speculum*, 35 (1960), 412f.

[35] Critoboulos, ed. Grecu 237–39; trans. Riggs, 140f.

[36] The fundamental sources for these building complexes are the endowment deeds (*vaqfiyye*'s) for the foundations established by the Sultan and his viziers. A list of the *vakfiyye*'s relating to Mehmed II's foundations in Istanbul is given in *Fatih Mehmet II vakfiyeleri* (Ankara, 1938), 6–8. For the subject in general, see Ö. L. Barkan, "Şehirlerin teşekkül ve inkişaf tarihi bakımından Osmanlı imparatorluğunda imâret sitelerinin kuruluş ve işleyişine ait araştırmalar," *Istanbul Universitesi Iktisat Fakültesi Mejmuası*, 23/1–2 (1962–63), 239–96; *idem*, "Fatih Camii ve imâreti tesislerinin 1489–1491 yıllarına ait muhasebe bilânçoları," *ibid.*, 297–341; *idem*, "Ayasofya Camii ve Eyüb türbesinin 1489–1491 yıllarına ait muhasebe bilânçoları," *ibid.*, 342–79. Also, for Mehmed II's endowments, see Maliyeden müdevver deft., No. 2057, the Başvekâlet Archives, Istanbul; for the population of Istanbul, a *Defter-i Hânehâ-i Istanbul, sene 1044*, Belediye Kütüphanesi, Istanbul, Cevdet yazmaları, No. O.

either before or after the conquest, had left Istanbul as slaves or refugees to live in other cities should return. According to Critoboulos,[37] there were then numerous Greek craftsmen who had settled in Adrianople, Philippopolis, Gallipoli, Brusa, and other cities, where they had become rich. All of these were brought to Istanbul, given houses and plots of land, and helped in other ways. That houses were granted not merely to Muslim immigrants but also to Christian deportees was probably one of the reasons for difficult relations between the two communities. Greek immigrants were brought to Istanbul by the Sultan also from his later conquests: from the two Phoceas in 1459; from the Morea after the second campaign of 1460;[38] in the same year a large proportion of the population of Imbros, Lemnos, Thasos, and Samothrace was transferred to the capital;[39] as were some of the inhabitants of Mytilene and the whole population of other towns on the island when Lesbos was occupied in 1462: "On his return to Constantinople the Sultan established the Mytilenians in one quarter of the city. To some *he gave houses*, to others land on which to build houses."[40] When the inhabitants of Argos in the Morea capitulated to Mahmûd Pasha in 1463, "he colonized all of them in Byzantium with their wives and children and all their belongings, safe and unhurt."[41] So, too, Greeks were brought from Euboea in 1470 and from Caffa in 1475, though most of the Christians deported from the latter were wealthy Genoese and Armenians.[42] A population list of 1477 shows these Genoese as numbering 267 families[43] (the figure four hundred given in Italian sources[44] is clearly an exaggeration). These deportees from Caffa founded the pleasant Istanbul quarter of Kefeli.

In the course of the campaigns waged against Karaman in the years 1468–74, numerous deportees—Turkish Muslims and Armenians—were brought to Istanbul from Konya, Larenda, Akseray, and Eregli.[45] Orders were issued that from each city some hundreds of households of craftsmen and wealthy citizens should be selected for transfer. Mahmûd Pasha's overly tolerant treatment of the rich and influential and his substitution of poorer citizens in their stead so angered the Sultan that this conduct was regarded by his contemporaries as one of the main reasons for Mahmûd Pasha's fall.[46] The population list of 1477 notes the immigrants from Karaman as a separate community, composed of 384 families. From the fact that they are noted separately it may be

---

68. A survey register of *vaqf*'s relating to Istanbul in the sixteenth century is being published by the Institute of Istanbul. From these and similar sources it is possible to put together a detailed picture of the development of Istanbul as a Muslim city.

[37] Ed. Grecu, 249; trans. Riggs, 148.

[38] *Idem*, ed. Grecu, 261; trans. Riggs, 157.

[39] *Idem*, ed. Grecu, 265; trans. Riggs, 159.

[40] *Idem*, ed. Grecu, 303; trans. Riggs, 185.

[41] *Idem*, ed. Grecu; 317, trans. Riggs, 197.

[42] M. Małovist, *Caffa, the Genoese Colony in the Crimea*, in Polish (Warsaw, 1947), 338.

[43] This document, drawn up under the supervision of the *qâḍî* Muḥyîeddîn, is in the archives of Topkapı Sarayı, No. D 9524 (see further, p. 247, *infra*).

[44] Małovist, *loc. cit.*

[45] Kemâl Pasha-zâde, *Tevârîh-i Âl-i ʿOsmān*, VII. defter (facsimile), ed. Ş. Turan (Ankara, 1954), 291f. For the Armenians, see Eremya Çelebi Kömürcüyan, *Istanbul Tarihi*, Turkish trans. Hrand Andreasyan (Istanbul, 1952), translator's notes at pp. 93, 175, and (Genoese) 238.

[46] Kemâl Pasha-zâde, *op. cit.*, 291f.; Neshrî, *op. cit.* (see note 18), 203; Tursun Beg, *op. cit.*, 139.

deduced that the other Greeks and Muslims who had, willingly or unwillingly, immigrated earlier, were by this date already so well settled in as to be regarded as the basic population.

In order to ensure the provisioning of the city and palace, the Sultan was concerned also to restore to prosperity the neighboring villages which had been ruined or abandoned before and during the siege. After his later conquests he settled in these villages as slaves large numbers of peasants (30,000 altogether, according to one reckoning), with the status of *khâṣṣ-qul* or *ortaqchı-qul*. They could not leave the village in which they were settled or marry outside it, and half of what they produced belonged to the state.[47] Such settlements of slave peasants were made after the Serbian campaign of 1455 and the two campaigns in the Morea of 1458 and 1460, and after the occupation of the islands of Zante, Cephalonia, and Aya Maura in 1479. (Critoboulos reports[48] that four thousand peasants were deported after the Morea campaign of 1458.) In the course of the sixteenth century these peasants were gradually to acquire the same status as the ordinary *re'âyâ* and to be assimilated in the general population, including that of Istanbul.

It is clear that, in carrying out the repopulation of Istanbul, Mehmed II did not pursue a policy of discrimination against the Greeks, whom he regarded as rightful subjects of the empire. Nevertheless, at various times in his reign, both in this matter and in the larger one of the whole administration, the policy of favoring the Greeks was abandoned for one of hostility toward them. The first sign of this is to be detected in an episode concerning Notaras.

Because of his opposition to the Italians, Notaras had a kind of claim on the favor of the Sultan; and the Ottomans had long since made it their general practice, as a matter of reasonable policy, to take such men into their service.[49] Both Critoboulos[50] and Sphrantzes[51] reveal that at first Notaras, as well as several other members of the Byzantine aristocracy, received unexpectedly good treatment from the Sultan. In considering the reasons for his later unhappy fate, we may detect some matters of policy, more fundamental than was implied by the explanation—given by Ducas and Sphrantzes and adopted and repeated by Western historians[52]—that he refused to sacrifice his son to the Sultan's lust.

In Critoboulos' account the Sultan had at first planned to make Notaras prefect of the city—a step which he must have regarded as necessary toward the promotion of his policy of repopulation. However, this was not without risk. At that time the Venetian fleet was in the Aegean. If, by an act of treachery,

[47] For these slave colonies, see Ö. L. Barkan, "XV ve XVI ıncı asırlarda Osmanlı imparatorluğunda toprak işçiliğinin organizasyon şekilleri," in *Istanbul Üniversitesi Ikt. Fak. Mej.*, 1 (1940), 29ff.; 2 (1941), 198–245.

[48] Ed. Grecu, 229; trans. Riggs, 133.

[49] Inalcık, "Ottoman Methods of Conquest," 112–22.

[50] Ed. Grecu, 159–63; trans. Riggs, 82–85.

[51] Bonn ed., 292f.

[52] Most recently S. Runciman, *op. cit.*, 157. For J. Moschos' work on the life of Notaras, see A. E. Bakalopulos, "Die Frage der Glaubwürdigkeit der Leichenrede auf L. Notaras von Johannes Moschos," *Byz. Zeitschrift*, 3 (1959), 13–21.

the city, conquered with such difficulty, were to fall to the Latins, a second and harder siege would be required. According to Critoboulos[53] (who had high respect for Notaras), some influential members of the Sultan's entourage opposed this measure, saying that they (i.e., Notaras and the nine members of the Byzantine nobility who were his followers) "would do all they could against the city, or would desert to the enemy, even while remaining here"; it was this argument that made the Sultan change his mind and execute Notaras and his associates. Sphrantzes, who is hostile to Notaras,[54] maintains that he endeavored to win the Sultan's favor, wishing to preserve his former high position; but that the viziers persuaded the Sultan to execute Notaras. Now, it is well known that Mehmed II, again following practice, took into the Palace several sons of the Byzantine nobility to be brought up within the established system of training slaves for administrative posts—a system which, before the end of the century, was to produce two Greek-born Grand Viziers, Rûm Mehmed Pasha and Mesîh Pasha. The former Megadux, realizing that he would not be able to recover his previous position, must have decided not to hand over his son and son-in-law[55] to serve as Palace pages—in effect, hostages.

Immediately following his account of the execution of Notaras, Critoboulos notes that the "influential men" who had advised it were *shortly afterward* dismissed by the Sultan for this treachery and were severely punished. We know who they were: the elderly Shihâbeddîn Pasha and Zaganuz Pasha, who had played most important roles in the conquest of Constantinople. It was they, too, who had been mainly responsible for the execution of Chandarlı Khalîl Pasha and who had made every effort to secure for themselves all the reins of power.[56] It is not impossible to trace the reasons for Mehmed II's sudden coldness toward these two men, his former tutors who had paved the way to his success. The execution of Khalîl Pasha had been regarded by the Janissaries, the intellectuals (*ulema*), and the people in general as having been prompted by spite,[57] and had caused much sorrow. After the execution of the Megadux, the Sultan, realizing that the recovery of the city was not progressing and now regretting the execution of Notaras, blamed the two Pashas. Thus, in 1456 both Zaganuz (the Grand Vizier) and Shihâbeddîn (the second vizier) were dismissed.[58] Shihâbeddîn Pasha had urged that houses vacated in the city should be granted to Muslim immigrants as freehold, and that the city should be quickly turkicized. As related above, Mehmed had returned to Greeks their former homes and distributed uninhabited houses among them; further, he had granted empty houses and mansions as freehold to immigrants who came voluntarily. ʿÂshıqpashazâde reports that houses were granted also to deportees. The passage runs:

[53] Ed. Grecu, 161; trans. Riggs, 84.
[54] See Bakalopulos, *op. cit.*, 19.
[55] His younger son was taken into the Palace (Bakalopulos, *ibid.*).
[56] See Inalcık, *Fatih devri üzerinde tetkikler ve vesikalar*, 55–136.
[57] Sphrantzes, Bonn ed., 294.
[58] Inalcık in *Speculum*, 35, p. 413f.; *idem*, *Fatih devri üzerinde tetkikler ve vesikalar*, 135.

> And he sent officers to all his lands to announce that whoever wished should come and take possession in Istanbul, as freehold, of houses and orchards and gardens, and to whoever came these were given. Despite this measure, the city was not repopulated; so then the Sultan commanded that from every land families, poor and rich alike, should be brought in by force. And they sent officers with firmans to the cadis and the prefects of every land. And they, in accordance with the firman, deported and brought in numerous families, and to these newcomers, too, houses were given; and now the city began to become populous.[59]

The procedure was that each immigrant, after choosing the house he wanted, went to the city prefect and received from him a note of recommendation; he took this note to the Porte—we recall here that real estate belonged legally to the Sultan and was therefore within his gift—and applied there for a freehold deed, a *mülknâme.*[60] Some of these documents have come to light in the archives of Topkapı Sarayı. The *mülknâme's* are of various dates, the oldest I have found being of Ramaḍân 861, that is to say, July 1457. They grant full freehold tenure of real estate, according to the principles of the *sharî'a*, so that they read: "It is to be in his possession; he may, as he wishes, sell it, or give it away, or make it *vaqf*; in short, he may enjoy it as freehold however he wishes." (There is a distinction here between this and real estate which remained *mîrî*, i.e., state property: the freehold of the latter belonged to the state, and the holder who enjoyed it could *not* sell it, give it away, or make it *vaqf*.)

When, however, as a result of these various measures, the population had increased and the houses had been occupied, the Sultan gave orders that these houses should be subjected to survey and enregistered, and that *muqâta'a* should be collected in respect of them. In Ottoman state finances the term *muqâta'a* means in general the leasing or farming out to an individual—after agreement on the sum which the individual will pay—of a source of state revenue. In the context under consideration the term is to be understood as "rent," and in what follows the word "rent" will be used. The grounds for the Sultan's new decision were that the freehold had been granted only in respect of the building, not of the land which it occupied; and land could not be held without payment of rent.[61]

The task of making the survey was entrusted to Jübbe 'Alî Beg, city prefect of Brusa, who took with him as his clerk his nephew Tursun Beg, the historian, later an important official in the financial administration. Tursun himself tells[62]

59 'Âshıqpashazâde, ed. Çiftçioğlu N. Atsız, in *Osmanlı Tarihleri*, I (Istanbul, 1949), 193 (= § 124; cf. German trans. R. F. Kreutel, *Vom Hirtenzelt zur Hohen Pforte* [Graz, 1959], 200); cf. Neshrî, *op. cit.*, 181.

60 Tâjî-zâde Ja'fer Chelebi, *op. cit.* (see note 10), 24.

61 Tursun Beg, *op. cit.*, 60.

62 *Ibid.*, 61f. According to the register of 1490 for the inspection of the *vaqf*'s of Aya Sofya (see note 67), some houses which had been made over to the church before the conquest were confirmed as *vaqf* by Mehmed II. A typical Arabic note recording this reads: *al-manâzil...kulluhâ yutaṣarrafu bi'l-muqâṭa'a al-mawdû'a qadîman fî zamân al-kufr wa'l-jâhiliyya al-muqarrara ba'd al-fatḥ 'alâ mâ kân 'alayhi fî zamân al-fatḥ wa-huwa al-marḥûm Sulṭân Muḥammad Khân al-mufattaḥ lahu abwâb al-raḥma va'l-ghufrân wa'l-riḍwân* (fol. 50b; other such notes at fols. 43a, 45a).

how every house was visited, how every house, great or small, every orchard, and every garden was listed in a register, and how rent was imposed on each according to its value. In the course of the survey many houses changed hands because holders, finding themselves too poor to pay the rent demanded, moved to houses better suited to their circumstances. When the operation was completed, it was found that these rents would bring to the treasury an annual income of a hundred million aspers (*aqche*), that is to say, over two million Venetian ducats. For the period, this is an enormous sum: the total revenue of the Ottoman Empire around 1432 had been estimated at only two and a half million ducats.

Shortly after this survey, we find the Sultan issuing new orders, by which he abolished this rent "for his officers and his subjects" and again granted *mülknâme*'s. According to Tursun Beg,[63] who was closely concerned in the survey, the Sultan explained to one of his intimates why after so short a time he had taken this second decision which contradicted the first: the first measure had been prompted by the fact that many people had obtained freehold of houses beyond their means and status; they could not sell them, for there was no one to buy; but if these large houses and mansions remained in their possession they would inevitably fall into disrepair and ruin. Rent had been imposed, therefore, to induce everyone to take a house that suited his means; the primary intention had not been to raise revenue for the treasury.

The real reasons which prompted the Sultan to abandon this rich source of revenue are revealed by another historian, ʿÂshıqpashazâde, who, unlike Tursun, was writing for the general public:

> They imposed rent on the houses which they had given to these people [the deportees]. When this happened, the people found it more onerous and said: 'You forced us to leave our old homes, which we owned. Did you bring us here that we should pay rent for these houses of the infidels?' And some of them abandoned their wives and children and fled. The Sultan had an officer named Kavala (Kephalia) Shahin [that is, Shihâbeddîn Pasha] who had served under the Sultan's father and grandfather and who had been vizier. He said to the Sultan: 'Come now, Your Majesty! Your father and your grandfather conquered numerous territories, but in not one of them did they impose rent; nor is it fitting that you should impose it.' The Sultan accepted what he said and abolished the rent and issued new orders: 'Whatever house you give, give it as freehold.' Then they gave a document in respect of every house that was given, stating that the house should be the freehold of the possessor. When things were arranged thus, the city began to be more prosperous; people began to build mosques, some built dervish convents and some built freehold properties, and this city returned to its former good state.[64]

This passage shows clearly that the attempt to raise such a large revenue from the inhabitants of the city had given rise to strong opposition, and the

[63] *Op. cit.*, 61f.
[64] See *supra*, note 59.

outspoken language of ʿÂshıqpashazâde doubtless reflects popular sentiment. To induce the Sultan to retract this measure had required the intervention of Shihâbeddîn Pasha—the old and influential vizier who had been the Sultan's tutor and his greatest support. This change of policy must have occurred before 1457, for in that year we find that Shihâbeddîn Pasha had already been dismissed.[65] The Topkapı Sarayı archives contain *mülknâme*'s belonging to the years immediately following, that is, 1457 to 1459.[66]

In A. H. 861 (29 November 1456–20 October 1457) many of the houses surviving from the Byzantine period were, we find, made over by the Sultan to the *vaqf* of the mosque of Aya Sofya, the income arising therefrom as rent accruing to the *vaqf*. At various times further properties were made over as *vaqf* to the mosque; and these *vaqf* properties were inspected and checked twice during the reign of Mehmed II (once by the *qâḍîʿasker* Kebelü-zâde Muhyîeddîn Mehmed, and then by the *qâḍîʿasker* Fenârî-zâde ʿAlâeddîn ʿAlî). In an inspection and survey made in 1490, during the next reign,[67] it is noted that some of the houses had been given to the *vaqf* in 861 (1456/7). According to this survey, in 1490 the real estate in Istanbul, Galata, and Üsküdar that belonged to the *vaqf* of the mosque consisted of 2,350 shops bringing in an annual rent of 458, 578 aspers; four caravansaries, various "rooms" (*ḥujarât, odalar*),[68] two baths, thirty shops selling millet beer (*boza*), twenty-two sheep-head shops bringing in a rent of 174,175 aspers; and 987 houses let at a total rent of 85, 668 aspers. (We note in passing that at the then current rate of forty-nine aspers to the ducat these rents represented an annual income of some 14,500 ducats.) Most of the 987 houses must have survived from the Byzantine period. As to 111 of them, there is the following note: "After the conquest, before they were made *vaqf*, these houses were granted as freehold and their holders were given *mülknâme*'s; subsequently an annual rent of 9,655 aspers was imposed upon them; . . . and 178 houses, bringing in a rent of 11,509 aspers, were held by servants (*qul*) of the Sultan; thus, in 887 [1482] some of these holders were given *mülknâme*'s and others were given certificates cancelling the rent." Besides these houses belonging to the Sultan's servants whose freehold tenure was

[65] Inalcık, *Fatih devri üzerinde tetkikler ve vesikalar*, 134–36.

[66] Nos. E. 7222, E. 7232, E 3056/2. The city prefects (*subashı*) named as recommending the grant of *mülknâme*'s are Chakır Beg/Agha (1457), Murâd Beg (1462), Chakır Agha (again, 1466), Ilyâs Beg (1468). The register of the *vaqf*'s of Aya Sofya refers to houses in respect of which *mülknâme*'s had been granted in Rejeb 860 (= June 1456). It records also that in 861 (29 Nov. 1456–20 Oct. 1457), when there was a general inspection, many old houses and shops were made *vaqf*, the *mülknâme*'s being cancelled (same register, fol. 56a), these changes may be connected with the survey carried out by Jübbe ʿAlî Beg.

[67] This register is No. 19 in the series "Maliye'den müdevver" in the Başvekâlet Arşivi in Istanbul. Composed by Kestelli Yusuf b. Khalîl, its preface states that the inspection was made on the basis of registers drawn up by Kebelü-zâde and Fenârî-zâde. It contains a detailed listing of the *vaqf*-properties of Aya Sofya situated in Istanbul, Galata, and Üsküdar. Another survey register of the Aya Sofya properties, made in 926 (= 1520), is in the Belediye Kütüphanesi, M. Cevdet yazmaları, No. 64. The annual accounts for the years 893, 894, and 895 have been published by Ö. L. Barkan (see note 36: "Ayasofya Camii . . . .").

[68] In such contexts *ḥujra* or *oda* usually means a fairly large room used as a separate workshop or lodging, as appears from the entries in the Aya Sofya register. At the same time, complete houses were sometimes apparently called *ḥujra* or *oda*. Such "rooms" were built in markets and bazaars as workshops and lodgings (T. Gökbilgin, *Edirne ve Paşa Livası* [Istanbul, 1952], 503).

recognized or whose rent was cancelled in 1482, there is reference to other houses for which the rent had been cancelled earlier, in Fenârî-zâde's previous survey, because they were held by servants of the Sultan. It may be said in general that houses surviving from the Byzantine period which had been granted to such servants were always given special treatment and made rent free.

As to the houses granted in freehold to private individuals, they became the subject of controversy once again in the years 1471 and 1472. When Rûm Mehmed Pasha was appointed Grand Vizier in 1471,[69] he embarked on a series of extraordinary financial measures. These were mainly prompted by the sudden increase in expenditure brought about by the stubborn resistance of Karaman, and by the sack of Tokat and the invasion of Karaman by Uzun Hasan's forces in the following year.[70] Once more we find in 'Âshıqpashazâde —who was violently hostile to Rûm Mehmed Pasha—the pronounced reaction to the change made at this date. He says:[71]

> There came to the Sultan a certain vizier who was the son of an infidel and had won high favor with the Sultan. The former infidel inhabitants of this city of Istanbul had been friends of this vizier's father. They came to him and said: 'What do you think you are doing? These Turks have restored the city. Have you no spirit? They have taken your father's home and our homes and occupy them before our very eyes. Come now! You are the favorite of the Sultan. Exert yourself so that these people may cease the restoration of this city, and it may be left, as it was before, in our possession.' The vizier said: 'Let us reimpose on them that rent which was imposed earlier on, so that they may refrain from building freehold houses; thus the city will again fall into ruin and finally be left in the possession of our people.' One day this vizier found an occasion for suggesting this idea to the Sultan and got the rents reimposed. They sent out one of these deceitful infidels, accompanied by a nominally Muslim servant of the Sultan, who did whatever this deceitful infidel told him to do, and they wrote it all down.
>
> Question: Who is this vizier?
>
> Answer: It is Rûm Mehmed Pasha, whom the Sultan caused to be strangled like a dog.
>
> . . . and because of this rent the people began to refrain from restoring Istanbul.
>
> If the Sultan is capricious in the decrees he makes
> Then his territory always suffers harm.
> And if his vizier should be an infidel,
> He always seeks to cause damage to the true faith.
>
> And the blame for the reimposition of this rent which we now have to pay rests with this Rûm Mehmed.

[69] For the date, see Inalcık, in *Speculum*, 35 (see *supra*, note 34), 414.

[70] See Inalcık, *s.v.* "Mehmed II," in *Islâm Ansiklopedisi*, VII, p. 525; Babinger, *Mehmed der Eroberer und seine Zeit*, 326f.

[71] *Op. cit.*, § 124 (see *supra*, note 59).

Although this bitter passage of ʿÂshıqpashazâde has been quoted by historians,[72] its true historical significance and the reasons prompting it have not been considered. It should be recalled that, in other contexts too, ʿÂshıqpashazâde gives vent to his hostility to Rûm Mehmed Pasha and thereby reflects also the feelings of a specific group in Ottoman society. Behind his hostility lie the facts that among the various financial measures taken by Rûm Mehmed Pasha there was, besides his reimposition of the previously cancelled rent, his abolition (doubtless for reasons of economy) of the gifts and bounties customarily distributed by the Palace to dervishes and sheykhs,[73] the class to which ʿÂshıqpashazâde himself belonged. These measures evidently caused a violent reaction among the Muslim populace, especially in religious circles. It may be true that the Pasha's descent inclined him to favor the Greeks and that at this period Greeks exercised some influence in the Palace and in state affairs;[74] but ʿÂshıqpashazâde's assessment of Rûm Mehmed Pasha's motives must be viewed with some reserve, for the measures the Pasha had instituted remained in force, even after his dismissal and execution,[75] during the rest of Mehmed II's reign. Under his successor, however, these questions were reconsidered.

In 887 (1482), shortly after Bâyezîd II's accession, when many of his predecessor's financial measures were abolished, the Sultan considered also the matter of the rents and cancelled them, particularly in respect of houses held by what the documents call *qul*'s. This word, translated here as "officer" or "servant," is applied to state officials of whatever rank; it embraces, and sometimes specifically means, the Janissaries, the group which in 1481 had helped Bâyezîd to the throne.[76] A firman dated Rebîʿ I, 889 (April 1484) reads:[77]

[72] Cf. Babinger, *Mehmed der Eroberer und seine Zeit*, 487.

[73] ʿÂshıqpashazâde, ed. Atsız (see *supra*, note 59), 243–44. For specimen entries in a register recording such donations made by the Palace, see Gökbilgin, *op. cit.*, 470–85.

[74] After the conquest of Constantinople, Mehmed II caused young members of the Byzantine nobility to be brought into his service in the Palace—i.e., to be trained for state service in the various "chambers" of the Palace School (see Critoboulos, ed. Grecu, 163–65; trans. Riggs, 85f.); after the occupation of Aenos and of Trebizond too he took into the palace groups of children of the nobility (Critoboulos, ed. Grecu, 197, 287; trans. Riggs, 110, 175). The Palaeologue Khâṣṣ Murâd (for whom see F. Babinger, "Eine Verfügung des Paläologen Chaṣṣ Murad-Paša...," in *Documenta Islamica inedita* [Berlin, 1952], 197–210) was appointed beylerbey of Rumeli in 1471, i.e., during the Grand Vizierate of Rûm Mehmed Pasha (*Die frühosmanischen Jahrbücher des Urudsch*, ed. F. Babinger [Hanover, 1925], 126). It may be significant that in his history, written for presentation to the Sultan, Critoboulos did not hesitate to express his sorrow over the executions of the members of the Byzantine aristocracy.

[75] He was executed in 1474; see Inalcık, in *Speculum*, 35, p. 415.

[76] According to the Aya Sofya register, the *qul*'s whose houses were exempted from rent were described as *yenicheri, sekbân, sipâhî, jebeji, topju, arabajı, yayabashı*; the Palace servants as *helvajı, qapıjı, sarrâj*, also *kâtib* and *münejjim*. There are notes of several Janissaries engaged in commerce and industry in the markets and holding shops at a rent. The register shows also that high-ranking members of the military class—*beg*'s and *ulema*—held several houses by virtue of *mülknâme*'s; thus the governor of Istanbul, Chakır Agha, had houses in various quarters of the city; a big house in the Germiyan quarter was granted by *mülknâme* to the *khatîb* of Galata, Mevlânâ ʿAlî, and another to the children of Zaʿîm ʿAlî. Non-Muslims also possessed houses: in Shawwâl 863, houses were granted by *mülknâme* to "Manul Komnen," "Nikefor," and the sons of "Yorgi"; the house belonging to "Angelina," in the same quarter, was given to the bootmaker Davud, and a house belonging to a Greek woman, "Zabya," to Re'îs ʿAlî. "Pandeliyo Moris," who had lost his *mülknâme*, was given a new one in A. H. 889 (his house was a big one, assessed at a rent of 250 *aqche*'s).

[77] The register "Maliye'den müdevver," No. 19 (see note 67), fol. 52.

> I have abolished rent in respect of all my servants who receive a stipend from me and are actually living now in houses and on sites liable to rent in Istanbul[78] and Galata which belong to the *vaqf*'s of the Aya Sofya Mosque; from such as these, rent is not to be demanded. But, as for those who are my servants and do not receive a stipend, as they are brothers or relatives of my servants, from them rent is to be demanded for the houses and the sites they occupy which are liable to rent and belong to the *vaqf*. For the future, whoever takes over a house or a site liable to rent, whether he be a servant of mine receiving a stipend or not, from him the rent for the house and site where he lives is to be collected, not cancelled.

Bâyezîd thus cancelled the rents only for those who at that date were actually in his service.

When he issued this firman, in April 1484, he was making preparations for his first major campaign, in Moldavia, the success of which was to strengthen his own prestige as Sultan. Now it was at this very time that ʿÂshıqpashazâde was writing his history,[79] and he was evidently prompted to devote a separate chapter to the question of rents because their partial cancellation then had once more made them a subject of discussion in Istanbul. From his account it is clear that public opinion objected to the rents on the grounds that they were contrary to the *sharîʿa*, that they favored the Greeks, and that Mehmed II, having first granted the properties as freehold, then, "led astray" by Greeks, had gone back on his word. It should be remembered also that, upon Bâyezîd's accession, the appointment of Khalîl Pasha's son Ibrâhîm as *qâḍîʿasker* reflected a reaction against the too frequent recourse, during Mehmed's reign, to the doctrine of the Sultan's executive authority (*ʿörf*)[80] to justify measures which many felt to be contrary to the *sharîʿa*. When, in these years, such measures were abolished, it was always the *sharîʿa* which was adduced to require their abolition. All the Ottoman historians writing in Bâyezîd's reign—ʿÂshıqpashazâde, Neshrî, Tursun, Idrîs, Kemâlpasha-zâde—praise him for reviving the authority of the *sharîʿa* and for promoting "justice."

From the record of the inspection made in 1490 of the imperial *vaqf*'s of the Aya Sofya mosque, which included many house properties liable to rent, it is possible to identify other principles which had been laid down in applying the new policy.

First, as we have seen, rent has been cancelled for houses owned and occupied by *qul*'s who are in the immediate service of the Porte; it remains in force, however, for houses owned by *qul*'s who have been granted a *tîmâr* and thus have left the immediate service of the Porte, and for houses which have passed by sale or inheritance into the possession of others. Second, "in accordance with the precept of the *sharîʿa*," rent has, in principle, been cancelled

[78] The register used the name Islambol (a folk etymology meaning "full of Muslims") rather than Istanbul; elsewhere the register speaks of "Qostantaniyye."

[79] See the Introduction to Giese's edition.

[80] On this subject, see H. Inalcık, in *Islâm Ansiklopedisi*, *s.v.* "ʿÖrf."

for houses which had been granted in freehold by *mülknâme* to private individuals before the endowment was made, but upon which rent had later been imposed; thus we find that rent has been cancelled for some houses by an "imperial document of cancellation" (*ref'nâme-i hümâyûn*), but for the great majority it has been confirmed. In the register of the *vaqf*'s each property has a separate note affirming its position.

A third case is that of houses subject to rents which have been made over to the *vaqf*. These represent houses which had fallen into ruin and upon whose sites new houses or shops had been built: in this event, they were subject to rent only in respect of the land on which they stood, in accordance with the principle "rent due on land does not lapse with the deterioration of the building upon it."

The Byzantine houses which came into the hands of the Ottomans thus presented the Ottoman authorities with an awkward problem of policy, a problem which not only affected the Ottoman financial departments but also had repercussions upon the questions of the settlement of Muslims in Istanbul and of Ottoman policy toward the Greeks; it became more and more complex in relation to the further factors that some were occupied by *qul*'s and some had been made over as *vaqf*.

Generally speaking, and admittedly with the intention of restoring the city to prosperity, Mehmed II gave favorable treatment to the Greeks. The census of the city made under the supervision of the *qâḍî* Muhyîeddîn in 1477 shows the following population figures, by households, for Muslims and Greeks:

	Istanbul	*Galata*
Muslims	8,951	535
Orthodox Greeks	3,151	592

All the other communities collectively—Armenians, Latins and Gypsies—amount only to 3,095 households.[81] As we have seen, a large proportion of the Greeks had been brought to Istanbul by compulsory resettlement from the Morea and elsewhere.

It is a prominent characteristic of Mehmed II's policy that he sought to give prime emphasis in state affairs to the principle of *'örf* (in Arabic, *'urf*), the executive competence of the ruler, and thus win absolute and unlimited authority for his own decisions. His contemporaries thought that he had pushed the principle too far. At his death, as we have seen, many of the measures which he had taken—although responsibility for them was imputed not to him but to his viziers—were declared to be contrary to the *sharî'a*. In a letter of advice addressed to his successor,[82] the writer maintained that Mehmed, "by the counsel of mischiefmakers and hypocrites," had "infringed the Law of the Prophet and impaired the good order of the land," and advised the new Sultan to follow in the steps not of his father but of his grandfather

[81] For this document, see *supra*, p. 238 and note 43. It may be noted that it records 3,667 shops in Istanbul and 260 in Galata.

[82] The letter is found in a MS of the *Menâhiju'l-inshâ*, in Izzet Koyunoğlu's library at Konya.

Murâd II. Certainly, Mehmed II was a man of a different stamp from his son Bâyezîd II; also from his great-grandson Süleymân, upon whose orders the *muftî* Abû's-Su'ûd tried to bring the executive regulations of the Empire into conformity with the *sharî'a*. In settling Greeks in Istanbul and leaving churches in Christian hands, which Mehmed II undertook in order to promote the city's prosperity, he invoked the principle of *'örf* rather than the authority of the *sharî'a*, as being in the best interests of the state. It is true that the religious scholars of his day—chiefly the *qâḍî'asker* Molla Khusrev, who had been closely connected with him since his childhood—did not regard these measures as contrary to the *sharî'a*, precisely because they served the best interests of the Muslim community.[83] But when Mehmed's protection of the Greeks enabled them to form a substantial proportion of the population of the city, and when they began to gain wealth and influence in trade, in the guilds,[84] and through the farming of rich customs and mineral concessions,[85] then, not unnaturally, a certain hostility between them and the Muslim Turkish population developed; or, rather, the hostility, already apparent immediately after the conquest in the incident of Lucas Notaras, was exacerbated. Thus, from time to time in the reigns of Mehmed's successors the question was raised whether it was not contrary to the *sharî'a* that Greeks should be living in a city taken by force of arms and that some of its churches should be left in Christian hands. In 1538, when for various special reasons[86] this question was raised again, it was necessary to obtain a *fetvâ* (i.e., a written opinion of the *muftî*) in order to protect the Greek population. The *fetvâ* justified the situation on the fictitious grounds that during the siege the Jews and the Christians had made a secret compact with Mehmed II and had refrained from assisting the Byzantine

[83] For this question, see *Islâm Ansiklopedisi*, *s.v.* "'Örf."

[84] According to the Aya Sofya register of 1490, among the leading merchants of the Bedestan there were only two Armenians, five Jews, and three Greeks, all the remaining 122 businesses belonging to Muslims. In the market guilds, too, the Muslims were greatly in the majority (the names of non-Muslims appearing, without distinction, in the lists of Muslim names): thus, in the market around the Bedestan, of forty-one carpenters' shops only one belonged to an Armenian; of forty workshops making pots and pans sixteen belonged to Greeks (from Mitylene, the Morea, and Galata); of thirty-four grocers only four were Greeks; and all the 142 shops in the saddlers' quarter belonged to Muslims. But the Greeks were particularly active in big tax-farming operations and in the trade by sea (see note 85).

[85] Under Mehmed II the Greeks were enabled to engage in commerce under more favorable conditions than had existed before. Since they were *dhimmî* subjects of the Sultan, the whole Empire was open to them as a field for their commercial activities and they enjoyed protection, especially against the Italians, who were subjected to a higher customs tariff than the Greeks. Thus, they gradually supplanted the Italians, particularly in the Black Sea trade and in trade with the countries of Northern Europe. The customs registers for the ports of Kilia (on the estuary of the Danube), Akkerman (at the mouth of the Dniester), and Caffa show that toward the end of the fifteenth century Greek ship captains and merchants were numerous: of twenty-five ships calling at Akkerman in 1490, fifteen belonged to Greeks (of the rest, six belonged to Muslims, three to Italians, and one to an Armenian). I am preparing a study on this trade; for the present see my article, "Bursa and the Commerce of the Levant" (*supra*, note 2). For the customs system and for Greek farmers of taxes, dues, and concessions, see my "Notes on N. Beldiceanu's translation...," *Der Islam*, 43 (1967), 152–56.

[86] The fall of Coron in the Morea to the Emperor Charles V's fleet in 1532 caused consternation in Istanbul, and was attributed to treachery on the part of the Greeks; a Venetian report of 1535 (*Calendar of State Papers, Spain* [London, 1838], V/I, doc. 197) said: "Albania and the surrounding provinces, chiefly inhabited by Christians, are only waiting for news of the Emperor or his fleet going to Constantinople to rise in rebellion."

Emperor: it was allegedly for this reason that the Sultan had not enslaved them but left them in their homes.[87] Similarly, too, in the course of the sixteenth century it was felt to be scandalous that Christians should hold *tîmâr*'s and serve the Sultan as *sipâhî*'s (cavalry), whereas in the reign of Mehmed II, and before, it had been regarded as completely normal that Christians, Greek Orthodox among them, should serve as *sipâhî*'s.[88] Furthermore, shortly after 1500 the historian Idrîs had commented that in leaving these Christians undisturbed the Sultans had had in view the prosperity of the world and of the Muslim religion.

Postscript: After this article had gone to press Professor B. S. Baykal, of the University of Ankara, brought to my attention a photocopy of a survey-book of Galata produced toward the end of 1455. How this new original source will affect the points dealt with in this paper can be discussed only when Prof. Baykal's publication of the survey-book makes it available for study.

[87] See note 11, *supra*.

[88] For Christian *sipâhî*'s, see Inalcık, *Fatih devri üzerinde tetkikler ve vesikalar*, 137–84.

[illegible] for this reason that the sultan had not [illegible] their houses.[illegible] Similarly, too, in the course of the sixteenth century it was felt to be scandalous that Christians should hold fiefs and serve the Sultan as sipahis (cavalry), whereas in the reign of Mehmed II and before, it had been regarded as completely normal that Christians [illegible] among them, should serve as sipahis. Furthermore, [illegible] after [illegible] historian [illegible] had commended the sultan for giving these Christians a [illegible] he had tried to revive the prosperity of the world [illegible]

Postscript: after this article had gone to press Professor [illegible] of the University of [illegible] brought to my attention a photocopy of a survey book [illegible] prepared toward the end of 1455. How this new document would [illegible] on the points dealt with in this paper can be discussed only when [illegible] publication of the survey book makes it available for study.

[illegible]

[illegible]

VII

SULEIMAN THE LAWGIVER AND OTTOMAN LAW*

Suleiman I, "the Magnificent" (1520—1566), reputed to have published a fundamental code of laws and to have shown a keen interest in establishing the authority of the law in his dominions, was first idealized as a legislator during the period of disorder and decline after 1580, when a nostalgic Ottoman Empire looked back to his age as one of order and prosperity. An official expression of this viewpoint can be found in a passage of the rescript of justice *(ʿadālet-nāme)* decreed by Mehmed III (1595—1603) upon his accession to the throne. It reads: "In the time of my great ancestor Sultan Suleiman, a law-code *(Ḳānūn-nāme)* was composed and distributed to the law courts of the cadis in the provincial cities and towns, and thereafter decisions were given in accordance with its provisions; then no one suffered any injustice or exaction and all the affairs of the empire followed an ideal course, and the subjects, placed by God in the custody of the Sultan, were prosperous. But now this law-code guaranteeing a just administration is discarded and forgotten, and all kinds of unjust innovations introduced in the administration. . . ".[1] These sentences reflect a contemporary view of Suleiman's age and the then generally held theory of the decline of the Ottoman Empire. Selānīkī Muṣṭafā and ʿĀlī, historians of the late sixteenth century, blamed the various disor-

* This paper was originally written for the Conference commemorating the four hundredth anniversary of the death of Suleiman the Lawgiver which was held in Istanbul in 1966. I want to thank Professor Jean Aubin who read this article and made valuable suggestions. The system of transliteration we used in this article is that of *Encyclopaedia of Islam*, second edition, with these differences: ج = c, چ = ç, خ = ḫ, ش = ş, غ = ġ, ı̣ = ı.

[1] M. Ç. Uluçay, *Saruhan'da eşkiyalık ve halk hareketleri* (İstanbul, 1944), p. 164; H. İnalcık, "Adâletnâmeler", *Belgeler* II (1965), p. 105.

ders of their own day on the neglect of Suleiman's laws and regulations. Around 1610, the author of the *Kitāb-i mustaṭāb*, one of the sources for Koçi Beg's treatise on the Ottoman decline, followed the same line of reasoning in explaining the decadence of the Empire. The common argument was that the unparalleled greatness and prosperity enjoyed under Suleiman were due primarily to the strict application of traditional laws and regulations. Thus if the old legal system were restored and rigorously enforced the Empire could be expected to recover from its decline. Seen in this light, Suleiman and his laws grew ever more significant in Ottoman statecraft. Later generations came to know him as *ḳānūnī*, an epithet which can be translated as 'lawgiver' and as 'law-abiding'. A popular *gesta et vita (Menāḳibnāme-i Maḥmūd Paşa)* copied in the sixteenth century, called him *ṣāḥib-i ḳānūn Sulṭān Süleymān Hān* 'Suleiman Khan, Law-giving Sultan'.

In his own day he was already renowned in the Christian West for "son humanité, justice et fidélité".[2] His keen interest in law and justice was stressed in various contemporary sources. In his famous work *Estat de la court du Grant Turc* published in 1542, Antoine Geuffroy wrote: "Il est estimé doulx et humain, gardan sa foy et parolle quoy qu'il promette et qui facilement pardonne à ceux qui l'on offencé. Son passe temps de lire ès livre de philosophie et de sa loy en laquelle il est tellement instruit . . ."[3] Apparently it was Suleiman himself who permitted the author of the inscription on the gate of his great mosque in Istanbul (completed in 1557) to call him "the propagator of the sultanic laws" *(nāṣir al-ḳawānīn al-sulṭāniyya)*.

But what were the real accomplishments of Sultan Suleiman's legislation and his efforts to establish the rule of law in his dominions?

[2] G. Postel, *De la République des Turcs*, la tierce partie (Poitiers, 1560), p. 87; "Egli (Suleiman) ha fama di essere molto giusto" (B. Navagero [1553], in *Relazioni*, ed. E. Alberi, III, p. 73); "molto giusto ma sopra modo crudele contro quelli che tentano o che a giudicio suo tentar possono alcuna cosa o contra il suo imperio o contro la sua persone" (Andrea Dandolo [1562], *ibid.*, IX, p. 164).

[3] *Estat de la court du Grant Turc* (Paris—Antwerp, 1542), p. 30. For Geuffroy, *see* C. D. Rouillard, *The Turk in French History: Thought and Literature (1520—1660)* (Paris, 1943), pp. 185—89.

1. THE IDEA OF LAW AND ITS EXPRESSION IN THE TURKISH STATE

The Ottoman concept of State and Law was for the most part a continuation of the tradition of earlier Turkic-Muslim rulers, combining in the person of the sultan the Turkic and Persian ideals of the sovereign. According to the Persian conception, the ruler was omnipotent. For him justice and law were mere creatures of an act of grace.[4] The Turkic ideal of the ruler, by contrast, considered justice to be the result of the impartial enforcement of the *törü* or *yasa (yasak)*, the traditional law of the steppes, sanctioned by great Kagans.[5] The Persian tradition of sovereignty became virtually predominant under the Abbasid Califate and was further strengthened under the newly rising sultanates in Iran. As in Sassanian times, the most important public function of the Muslim ruler was believed to be the holding of the meeting of the Divan or *Dār al-ʿadl,* in which he heard the complaints of his subjects against abuses of authority and gave summary decisions regardless of formalities and regulations.[6] Presumably this displayed his limitless power and justice. Not infrequently, and for the same purpose, the ruler personally received the complaints of his subjects while out hunting or when otherwise engaged in some public functions, such as going to the mosque. Such scenes were sometimes staged to show the country the fairness and mercy of the ruler. Poets, story-tellers and miniaturists took such scenes as their subject matter, and as indispensable instruments of the royal prestige and propaganda, received generous gifts from the sovereign in return. In Middle Eastern states, from antiquity on, the public life of the ruler was always depicted in terms of such acts, and the *naṣīḥat-nāmes*, the 'Mirrors for Princes' of medieval Islam, abounded with stories about them.

Ḳutaḍġu bilig, a Turkic *naṣīḥat-nāme* written in 462/1069 under the Karakhanids, rulers of the first important Turkic Muslim state

[4] R. N. Frye, "The Charisma of Kingship in Ancient Iran", *Iranica Antiqua* IV, pp. 36—54; A. K. S. Lambton, "Medieval Persian Theory of Kingship", *Studia Islamica* XVII (1962), pp. 91—119.

[5] *See* H. İnalcık, "Kutadgu bilig'de Türk ve İran devlet ve siyaset nazariye ve gelenekleri", *Reşit Rahmeti Arat İçin* (Ankara, 1967), pp. 259—271.

[6] *See* E. Tyan, *Histoire de l'organisation judiciaire en pays d'Islam* (Leiden, 1960), pp. 433—526.

(840—1212), shows us how strongly the Turkic concept of State was influenced by the Persian tradition.[7] Yet in this same source these Muslim Turks are shown following the example of their pagan ancestors in the Kök-Türk empire (552—745), considering *törü* 'law' as the most important foundation of the state. The *törü* was inseparable from sovereignty. *Ḳutadġu bilig* says: "The sovereignty of a ruler stands by the law"; "Sovereignty is a good thing but better still is the law *(törü)* and it must be enforced with justice".[8] It was clear from the inscriptions of the Kök-Türks that the Kagans who founded or saved the Turkic empire had always promulgated their own *törü* and thus established and legitimized their sovereignty through its enforcement. Temüçin apparently followed the same tradition in 1206 when he declared himself Genghis-Khan, universal emperor, and allegedly at the same time issued his *yasa*. In the old Ottoman tradition Osman Ġazi, the founder of the Ottoman dynasty, was supposed to have declared his 'laws' *(ḳānūn)* immediately after gaining his independence. In *Ḳutadġu bilig* the main duty of a ruler is his impartial application of the *törü*. The predominance of the *törü* in the original Turkic concept of State might be explained by the fact that it originally included sacred rules of tribal life.[9]

According to Islam there could be no law but the *şarīʿa*, the religious law of Islam. However some authorities on Islamic law accepted the principle of *ʿurf*, that is, the power of a ruler to decree independently from the *şarīʿa* those regulations which seemed necessary for the welfare of the Islamic community. These regulations were generally called *ḳānūn* (plural *ḳawānīn)*, or rather, with reference to their origin, *ḳawānīn al-sulṭāniyya* or *ḳawānīn al-ʿurfiyya*. The Turkic Islamic states maintained such laws and regulations, especially in the spheres of administration and public welfare.[10] But it must be recalled that the *ʿulemā*', who did not

[7] *Cf.*, İnalcık "Kutadgu bilig'de...", pp. 261—67.

[8] Yūsuf Hāṣṣ Hācib, *Ḳutadġu bilig* (text ed. R.R. Arat) (İstanbul, 1947), couplet no. 5285.

[9] V. A. Ryazanovskiy, *Obichnoye pravo mongolskih* (Harbin, 1924); G. Vernadsky, "Çengiz Han Yasası", *Türk Hukuk Tarihi Dergisi* I, p. 109; *cf.*, A. Temir, *Moğolların Gizli Tarihi* (Ankara, 1955), pp. 58—215; K. Alinge, *Mongolische Gesetze* (Leipzig, 1934), chapter III.

[10] H. İnalcık, "Osmanlı hukukuna giriş", *Siyasal Bilgiler Fakültesi Dergisi* XIII (1958), pp. 102—126; R. Levy, *The Social Structure of Islam* (Cambridge, 1957), chapter VI.

accept the principle of *ʿurf*, fought against this dual system in the Islamic state.[11] In the states founded by the Oghuz Turkic tribes following the collapse of the Ilkhanid empire in the fourteenth and fifteenth centuries, the word *yasa* meant all the *ʿurfī* laws and regulations issued by the ruler *(lex principis)*. Around 1485 Tursun Beg,[12] Ottoman statesman and historian, defined *ʿurf* as the *yasaġ (yasa)* of the monarch *(pādişāh)* issued to secure public peace and order.

In order to strengthen his centralistic government, Mehmed II, conqueror of Constantinople and the real founder of the Ottoman empire, became the first historically known Ottoman sultan to proclaim *ḳānūn-nāme*s (law-codes) and many *ʿurfī* laws, under the names of *ḳānūn* and *yasaḳ-nāme*.[13] His first *ḳānūn-nāme*, issued about the time of the conquest of Constantinople, contained penal laws as well as laws concerning *ʿurfī* taxes to be paid by the *reʿāyā'*, the Christian and Muslim subjects. His second law-code, issued towards the end of his reign, contained statutes and regulations concerning the court and the government.[14] Both of these law-codes were issued as imperial decrees and never refer to the *şarīʿa*. The reign of his successor, Bayezid II (1481—1512), was a reaction against the Conqueror's radicalism in the sphere of *ʿurfī* legislation as in other fields. Bayezid's reign was greeted as the restoration of justice and the *şarīʿa*. Tursun Beg wrote that among the most important things to be recorded about a sultan were his efforts to restore the religious sciences.[15] During this period *ʿurf* and *şarīʿa* entered into open conflict. But it must be added that the *şarīʿa*-minded policy of Bayezid II was dictated by certain political and social circumstances prevailing at the time of his accession: on the one hand, his brother Cem Sultan's struggle for the throne and, on the other, the deep discontent of the *şayḫ*s and the ancient landholding aristocracy, who had been deprived of their lands either

[11] For instance Ulugh Beg, Tamerlane's grandson, was denounced by the ulema as a follower of the *yasa* (*see* Z. V. Togan, *Umumi Türk tarihine giriş* [İstanbul, 1946], p. 376.)

[12] *Tā'rīḫ-i Abu'l-Fatḥ* (ed. in *Tarih-i Osmani Encümeni Mecmuası)*, (İstanbul, 1330 H.), p. 13.

[13] *Ḳānūnnāme-i Sulṭānī ber mūceb-i ʿörf-i ʿOsmānī* (ed. R. Anhegger—H. İnalcık), (Ankara, 1956), pp. XV—XVII.

[14] H. İnalcık, "Osmanlılarda raiyyet rüsûmu", *Belleten* XXIII (1959), p. 576

[15] *Tā'rīḫ-i Abu'l-Fatḥ*, p. 28.

wholly or in part under certain *ʿurfī* laws promulgated by Mehmed II. Under Bayezid II, the principle of the independence of the *ʿurfī* laws and executive power was, however, maintained. Moreover, some of the decrees of Mehmed II were later restored, especially when Bayezid II felt securely established on the throne. We shall see that this sultan was responsible for putting together the law-code attributed to Suleiman I. The successor of Bayezid II, Selim I (1512—1520), proved to be an autocratic ruler, jealous of his independence of action. He took some harsh steps which were apparently felt by public opinion to be violations of certain fundamental principles of the *ṣarīʿa.*

Suleiman's first acts after his accession to the throne in 1520 were undoubtedly intended to present him to the world as a just and law-abiding ruler. He declared that a group of fifteen hundred exiles, mostly artists, scholars and merchants, who had been taken by Selim from Tabriz and Cairo to Istanbul, were to be allowed to return to their homes if they so desired. Selim I, during the war of 1514—1516, had also prohibited the importation and sale of Iranian silk in his dominions; in 1515 the silks and cloths of the Persians at Bursa were confiscated, and the merchants themselves were banished from Bursa and Istanbul and sent to Rumelia.[16] Once on the throne, Suleiman I released the merchants and either returned their goods or compensated them. Suleiman also ordered an investigation of Caʿfer, *sancaḳ-beg* of Gallipoli, an influential but cruel officer of Selim I who was found guilty and sentenced to death. Performed immediately after Suleiman's accession to power, this execution — a warning to the governors who were inclined to misuse their authority — was quite obviously designed to show that during his reign the public would enjoy an age of justice. Suleiman continued to give similar proofs of his dedication to equity. For example in 1528, when informed of the outrageous behaviour of the *sancaḳ-beg* of Scutari, in Albania, Suleiman immediately sent two *çavuş* of his Porte to execute the *sancaḳ-beg* and eight of his men on the spot. Such severe acts of justice were celebrated in the magnificent miniatures of the *Hünernāme.*[17]

[16] *See* art. "Ḥarīr", *EI*² III, p. 213.

[17] *See* Öz, "Hünernâme ve minyatürleri," *Güzel Sanatlar Mecmuası* I (1939), pp. 3—17

Summary punishments, considered as manifestation of the authority and power of the potentate, were grouped under the term of *siyāset (siyāsa* in Arabic), a word which also meant the political and executive power of the ruler as against his religious functions, defined by the *şarīʿa* as *imām*.[18] The main function of a ruler, according to Middle Eastern theories of the state, was to establish public order in his dominion through *siyāset*. Men in society, it was argued, could not survive without *siyāset*, personified by one absolute monarch. In brief, *siyāset* was the essence of what we call the Middle Eastern State. In all his initial deeds Sultan Suleiman attempted to present himself as a perfect example of this type of ruler. ʿĀlī wrote: "Emulating Nūshīnrevān the Just, (Sultan Suleiman) rendered service to the creatures of Allāh with justice and moderation for all forty-eight years of his reign."[19]

Suleiman was appreciated even more for establishing justice in his dominions through the strict rule of law than for the use of his limitless power against abuses. It seems that in taking action against his own sons Muṣṭafā and Bāyezīd, he himself considered the idea of law and order to be more important than anything else in his empire. In his opinion, they were guilty because they acted against the laws of the empire. Tired of such accusations, his son Bāyezīd wrote in protest that whatever he did was considered to be against the law.[20] In his famous letter in rhyme to his son, Suleiman, while expressing his tender paternal feelings, accused Bāyezīd of being a rebel who caused bloodshed among innocent people. Suleiman went so far as to say that it was his duty as protector of his subjects to eliminate him if necessary. He concluded by saying: "O my dear son Bāyezīd, if you return to the right path I will certainly forgive you. In any case, do not say that you are not guilty, but do say, my dear son, that you repent for what you have done."

2. SULEIMAN'S LEGISLATIVE ACTIVITY

Suleiman distinguished himself by publishing a number of *ʿurfī* laws, following the tradition of his great predecessors in Turkic history. These can be classified in three categories: (1) the *ḳānūn-*

[18] *See* Tursun Beg, *op. cit.*, p. 13; Tyan, *op. cit.*

[19] *Kunh al-aḫbār*, Ms. in the Library of Dil ve Tarih-Coğrafya Fakültesi, no. 1783.

[20] Ş. Turan, *Şehzade Bayezit vakʾası* (Ankara, 1961), p. 209.

nāmes for each *sancaḳ*; (2) the *ḥukms* (decrees) containing specific laws; and (3) a *ḳānūn-nāme* of general character.

1. For each *sancaḳ* in the Ottoman Empire an official survey of land and population *(mufaṣṣal defter)*[21] was prepared and this was introduced by a *ḳānūn-nāme*. The *ḳānūn-nāme* of a *sancaḳ* was generally intended to detail: (a) tax rates and the way taxes were to be collected by the timar-holders; (b) rules concerning land-possession, transference and inheritance under the timar-system; (c) exemptions and immunities; and (d) rules concerning the statutes of the military. The *ḳānūn-nāme* of a *sancaḳ* was primarily intended to be used by government or courts to settle differences between the *tīmār*-holders and the *reʿāyā*ʾ or between them and other officials, or between tax farmers and *waḳf* agents. These *ḳānūn-nāmes* were an integral part of the *defters* 'registers', which, when ratified with the sultan's seal *(tuġra)*, became *official* laws of the empire. Typical *sancaḳ ḳānūn-nāmes* are found only after the reign of Mehmed the Conqueror (1451—1481).[22] It seems that the Conqueror's first *ḳānūn-nāme* for *reʿāyā*ʾ and his penal law were used without distinction in every *sancaḳ* until the reign of Bayezid II.[23] In the *defters* of the *sancaḳs* of the time of the Conqueror there were indeed laws and regulations on specific matters and statutes for certain groups, recorded in full or in summary form, and derived from original imperial decrees. But typical *sancaḳ ḳānūn-nāmes* as described above appeared first in the *defters* of the reign of Bayezid II. Under Suleiman's reign we find one *ḳānūn-nāme* for almost every *sancaḳ*, arranged systematically[24] and similar to the Conqueror's general *ḳānūn-nāme* for the *reʿāyā*ʾ.

2. The *ḳānūn-ḥukms* contained laws and regulations on a particular subject, and bore all the formal characteristics of an imperial

[21] For *defters*, *cf.*, H. İnalcık, *Suret-i defter-i sancak-i Arvanid* (Ankara, 1954), pp. XVIII—XXII.

[22] *See* Ö. L. Barkan, *XV ve XVI-ıncı asırlarda Osmanlı Imparatorluğunda zirai ekonominin hukuki ve malî esasları I, Kanunlar*, (İstanbul, 1943).

[23] The first typical *ḳānūn-nāme* of a *sancaḳ* which came down to us is a *ḳānūn-nāme* of the *sancaḳ* of Ḫudāvendigār (Bursa) dated 892/1487 (edited in Barkan, *op. cit.*, pp. 1—6). In the *defters* of Mehmed the Conqueror's time we find only laws and regulations concerning special groups (*see* H. İnalcık, *Fatih devri üzerinde tetkikler ve vesikalar* [Ankara, 1954], pp. 137—165).

[24] *See* Barkan, *op. cit.*

decree. They were either in the form of a *berāt* (diploma) or of a *firman* (order) addressed directly to a person or group.[25] Such *ḥukm*s were the original source of most of the provisions in the *ḳānūn-nāme*s of *sancaḳ*s and the *ḳānūn-nāme*s of a general character. Some of the *ḥukm*s containing detailed regulations and laws can hardly be distinguished from the general *ḳānūn-nāme*s. We have examples of *ḥukm*s in full text which were later converted into the provisions of the *ḳānūn-nāme*s. The original legislative activity of the Ottoman sultans was to be found primarily in the *ḳānūn-ḥukm*s, and a systematic study of Ottoman law will be possible only when a complete record of those *ḳānūn-ḥukm*s still in the State Archives has been established.[26] It should be pointed out that many of the *ḳānūn-ḥukm*s issued during Suleiman's reign were actually no more than reproductions of the previous *ḥukm*s with only the necessary modification of some details.[27] But we can never know exactly whether an act of Suleiman depended in part or in the whole on a prototype since we do not have for comparison a complete collection of the *ḳānūn-ḥukm*s issued in the previous reigns. There are, of course, certain *ḳānūn-ḥukm*s of Suleiman I with the clear statement of the modifications which they brought to the existing situation. A systematic study of these changes under Suleiman I will be taken up in another article.

*Ḳānūn-ḥukm*s were usually written out by the bureaucrats *(kātib)* in the departments under the *vezīr-i aʿẓam*, *defterdār* or *nişāncı*. The *nişāncı* and his assistants, the *reʾīs ül-küttāb* and the *beglikci*,[28] were responsible for their final formulation. In wording them they generally followed earlier examples, often verbatim. The sultan usually ratified them by the formula "*mūcibince ʿamel oluna*", 'let (them) proceed in accordance with its provisions'. The origin of such *ḳānūn-ḥukm*s was usually a situation or problem

[25] For *ḥukm*, *see* L. Fekete, *Einführung in die osmanisch-türkische Diplomatik der türkischen Botmässigkeit in Ungarn* (Budapest, 1926), pp. XXX—XLVII. For *berāt*, *see* Anhegger — İnalcık, *op. cit.* pp. XIV—XV.

[26] Some *ḳānūn-ḥukm*s which we collected from the cadi records of Bursa of the time of the Conqueror are published in *Belleten* XII, pp. 693—708; *see* also Anhegger — İnalcık, *op. cit.*

[27] This becomes apparent even from a rapid comparison of the *ḳānūn-ḥukm*s of the Conqueror (in Anhegger — İnalcık, *op. cit.*, pp. 56—59, 61—65, 82—84) with those of Suleiman (Ms. Revan no. 1936).

[28] *See* art. "Reîs-ül-küttâb", *İA* IX, pp. 671—676.

which called for the formulation of a general rule in one of the three administrative departments. It was not uncommon for a petition submitted by the people to result in the issuing of a *ḳānūn-nāme*. Also cases *(ḳaḍiyye)* submitted by commissioners of surveys often found their response in special *ḳānūn-ḥukm*s.

Only seldom did a sultan directly formulate a *ḳānūn-ḥukm*. Mention must be made here of an example from the reign of Suleiman. Our source reads: "*Ḳānūn* on the retinue of vezirs, *mīrmīrān*s and *mīrān*s. When Ferhad, *sancaḳ-beg* of Semendere,[29] was ordered to convene the army and, at the end of the inspection, reported to the Sultan that many the *sipāhī*s holding *tīmār*s called *ḳılıc* were not present because they were included in the retinue of high-ranked persons, on this occasion the late Sultan Suleiman wrote this *ḳānūn* with his own hand: From among the *tīmār*-holders each vezir may keep twelve persons in his service, each *beglerbegi* eight, each *sancaḳ-begi* seven, and they shall not have more than these specified numbers."[30]

Imperial orders prescribed that such *ḳānūn-ḥukm*s be copied by the cadis into their record books and be referred to when necessary by the commissioners in the registers of surveys, or by other authorities. The numerous *ḳānūn-ḥukm*s that were issued under Suleiman are to be found scattered in the survey *defter*s, the official records *(sicillāt-i ṣarʿiyya)* of the cadis, and in books kept by the central government, the most important of which are the *mühimme*, and *muḳāṭaʿāt*. Several collections of documents which were arranged originally under Suleiman by the scribes at the imperial Divan or by other officials for their own use,[31] contain a number of important *ḳānūn-ḥukm*s of Suleiman's time. Among these are:

(a) A collection of documents preserved in Âtif Efendi Library, Istanbul, Ms. no. 1734. Arranged towards the end of Suleiman's time, it contains about thirty of his *ḳānūn-ḥukm*s on various subjects.

(b) Several closely associated collections: two in the Topkapı Sarayı Museum Library, Ms. Revan no. 1935 and no. 1936; one in

[29] Ferhad was governor of Semendere (Smederovo) in 1523—1524.

[30] Ms. in Süleymaniye Kütüphanesi, Reisülküttab no. 1004, 32r.

[31] At the Ottoman chancery, directly under the *vezīr-i aʿẓam*, we find a scribe whose function was to see whether the outgoing documents were in conformity with the laws *(ḳānūn)* in force, *cf.*, art. "Reîs-ül-küttâb", *İA*, *loc. cit.*

the Üniversite Kütüphanesi, Istanbul, no. T 2753; one in the British Museum, Or. no. 9503; two in the Bibliothèque Nationale, Paris, fonds turc ancien no. 35 et no. 85. These collections were apparently arranged during Suleiman's time, and the *ḳānūn-ḥukm*s issued after him were added in the later copies of these collections, but most of the documents come from his reign.

(c) A manuscript of the Orientalni Institut, Sarajevo, Turcica no. 3 (previously no. 1076), copied in 969/1561, contains many *ḳānūn-ḥukm*s of Suleiman's time together with the so-called "*Ḳānūn-nāme* of Suleiman".

(d) The manuscript Velîyüddin no. 1970, Bayezid Umumî Kütüphanesi, Istanbul; arranged in the last years of the sixteenth century, this compilation contains many *ḳānūn-ḥukm*s of Suleiman's time.

(e) The manuscript Reisülküttab no. 1058, Süleymaniye Library, Istanbul, embodies a collection of legal decisions by the famous Celāl-zāde Muṣṭafā, *nişāncı* of Suleiman's reign (*cf.* fol. 1 and 29r) and some *ḳānūn-ḥukm*s of Suleiman (compiled towards the beginning of the seventeenth century).

3. The next general *ḳanūn-nāme* subsequent to that of the Conqueror was that ascribed to Suleiman. The origin and nature of this *ḳānūn-nāme* will be the main subject of the following part of this article.

It has been asserted that this *ḳānūn-nāme* "was not at all an official law-book, made to replace the genuinely official *ḳānūn*s (*i.e.*, the *ḳānūn-nāme*s of *sancaḳ* and *ḳānūn-ḥukms*) in the departments of the government . . . but rather a collection designed to give the Sultan and his administrators a general idea of the organization and institutions of the Empire. In fact it was never used as an official law-book in practice . . . and to date, no one has found an official text of such a *ḳānūn-nāme* confirmed by the Sultan."[32] However, we know that the general *ḳānūn-nāme*s of the Conqueror and Suleiman were officially declared and used in the courts and government departments. In the introduction to the general *ḳānūn-nāme* of the Conqueror, it is made clear that it was composed "because it was deemed necessary to make a *ḳānūn-nāme* to be observed for ever in the imperial Divan".[33] Originally arranged by the *nişāncı*, the highest authority in the matter of *'urfī* laws, it

[32] Barkan, *op. cit.*, p. XXII.

[33] Ed. F. Kraelitz in *MOG* I (1921—1922), p. 13.

was modified by the Sultan and ratified by his personal handwritten order *(ḫaṭṭ-i şerīf)*. It reads: "This *ḳānūn-nāme* is the law of my ancestors and now it is my law too. My exalted descendants, generation after generation, must observe its provisions." As to the so-called "*Ḳānūn-nāme* of Suleiman"[34] it states in its introduction: "Because an imperial order was given to compose a *ḳānūn-nāme*, the rules for government and *ʿurfī* laws, which are the foundation of the world's welfare and the support of the affairs of all the people, were collected and divided into three chapters and each chapter into seven subdivisions." In the *ʿadālet-nāme* (rescript of justice) of 1595, "the *ḳānūn-nāme* of Suleiman" is said to have been officially imposed in courts throughout the empire.[35] Such references as these may also be found in *sancaḳ ḳānūn-nāme*s "They [fines and other occasional fees] were to be levied according to the provisions of the imperial law",[36] meaning the penal laws in the *ḳānūn-nāme*s of the Conqueror and "Suleiman".

This clearly indicates that there was an official *ḳānūn-nāme* of a general character besides those pertaining to the *sancaḳ*s. On the other hand, the cadis were to give decisions both in criminal cases and in disputes between *tīmār*-holders and *reʿāyā*', as well as certify title deeds, transferences, etc. They needed *ḳānūn-nāme*s such as those of the Conqueror and "Suleiman" since the *defter* containing the *sancaḳ ḳānūn-nāme* was written in only two copies per *sancaḳ:* one for the *defterhāne*, a department attached to the central government in Istanbul, the other for the use of the *beglerbegi* in the *sancaḳ*. The cadis used to make a copy of it in their own books. In giving decisions on the *ʿurfī* cases they were not obliged to use the officially ratified copies of the *ḳānūn-nāme*s, just as they were free to use their own personal copies of the *şarʿī* law-books on the *şarʿī* cases. It seems that Suleiman was the first to have the idea of officially distributing copies of the general Ottoman *ḳānūn-nāme* to the courts of law.

The general *ḳānūn-nāme*s were subject to change at any moment as a result of the issuance of new *ḳānūn-ḥukm*s, — a fact which explains numerous marginal notes and additions found in the

[34] Edited on the basis of five manuscripts by M. Ârif as a supplement to *TOEM* (İstanbul, 1329 H.). A new critical edition is needed. For manuscripts, *see* also note 73.

[35] *See* above note 1.

[36] Barkan, *op. cit.*, pp. 268, 311, 317, 362.

copies of the general *ḳānūn-nāmes*. The *ḳānūn-nāme* of the *sancaḳ* of Silistre, which dates from Suleiman's reign, provided that if a proper provision were not found on a particular *ʿurfī* case, the cadi was to inquire about it at the Sultan's Porte and give his decision according to the imperial order he would receive. He would then make a record of the decision in his record book *(sicill)* and this was to constitute a legal precedent for future decisions.[37] This is one of the reasons why the Sultan forbade dismissed cadis to take away the *sicill*s of their period in office.[38] Cadis were generally ordered to give their decisions according to the official records in the *defter*s, the *şarīʿa* and *ḳānūn-nāmes*.

New *ḳānūn-ḥukm*s were either appended at the end of copies of the general *ḳānūn-nāmes*, or given — at least their main provisions — in the margins of the text. They were often interpolated in the text of the *ḳānūn-nāme* by later copyists.[39] Thus, for the history of Ottoman law, every copy, especially the annotated ones at the courts, had the merit of an original.

3. THE SO-CALLED KĀNŪN-NĀME OF SULEIMAN

A comparison with the ḳānūn-nāme of the Conqueror

In the earliest copies, one of them anterior to Suleiman's time,[40]

[37] Barkan, *op. cit.*, p. 276, art. 20; *cf.*, Tyan, *op. cit.*, p. 344.

[38] *Ḳānūn-nāme-i Āl-i ʿOsmān* [Suleiman's *Ḳānūn-nāme*], suppl. *TOEM*, p. 42.

[39] From this point of view the following copies of the so-called Suleiman's *ḳānūn-nāme* are of particular interest: Mss. Velīyüddin no. 1969, Esad Efendi no. 2362, Revan no. 1936 (*see, infra* note 73).

The following explanation of how the *ḳānūn-nāme* of slave-duty *(pencik)* was drawn up in 1520 is of particular interest for the study of the preparation of a *ḳānūn-nāme*. It runs: "Formerly when there was need of a specific *ḳānūn-nāme* on slave-duty at the port of İnebolu, the responsible people there demanded from the Porte such a *ḳānūn-nāme*. In a memorandum we asked for a copy of the *ḳānūn-nāme* of slave-duty at the port of Istanbul which was in the possession of the late Mustafa, a scribe at the office of slave-duty collection. He sent us a copy following which a *ḳānūn-nāme* of slave-duty was written for the port of İnebolu, and its copy was recorded in the register of copies of issued firmans. Now as this *ḳānūn-nāme* was originally copied from the *ḳānūn-nāme* of slave-duty of Istanbul, it was found at the register of copies of Anadolu, and it was copied from there and sent. Thus the text of the ancient *ḳānūn-nāme* on slave-duty is that . . ."

[40] The Ms. Koyunoğlu is dated 907/1501 (*see* below); Library of the Turkish Historical Society Y. no. 75; Velīyüddin no. 1969; Revan nos. 1935 and 1936.

the so-called "*ḳānūn-nāme* of Suleiman" is simply entitled *Ḳānūn-nāme-i ʿOsmānī* 'The book of the Ottoman Law'. It is divided into three parts *(bāb)*, the first part having four chapters and the second and third parts seven chapters each.

The first three chapters of the Conqueror's code, concerning offences and fines, are generally identical with the first three chapters of the "*ḳānūn-nāme* of Suleiman" edited by M. Ârif. The latter has only one additional provision at the end, to the effect that half the fines were to be paid if the author of the offence was a non-Muslim. The additional fourth chapter in "Suleiman's *ḳānūn-nāme*" under the heading *Mücerred siyāseti* is obviously a posterior version of an imperial *ḥukm* called *siyāset-nāme*. Two early copies of this have come down to us, one published in the reign of Bayezid II, probably between 889—894 H. (1484—1489),[41] and the second under Selim I.[42] The first is addressed to Hüseyn, *sancaḳ-beg* of Aydın, and the second to crown prince Suleiman, then governor of Saruhan. This was to be applied to criminal cases whenever evidence could not be established through the *ṣarīʿa*, hence its name *siyāset-nāme* 'the book of corporal punishment', laid down directly by the ruler. In its second version we already find additions and important modifications in the text.[43] It was Selim's *siyāset-nāme* which was reproduced almost verbatim as that of Suleiman. We have a later copy of the *siyāset-nāme* which was issued in the middle of May 1556, and addressed to Pertev Pasha, *beglerbegi* of Rumeli.[44] It is identical to the one found in the so-called "*Ḳānūn-nāme* of Suleiman". In the seventeenth century copies of the "*Ḳānūn-nāme* of Suleiman" we find further additions and modifications made apparently according to the new *ḳānūn-ḥukm*s and *siyāset-nāme*s.

The second and third parts of the "*Ḳānūn-nāme* of Suleiman" are much more detailed than the Conqueror's corresponding part, which constitutes the fourth and last chapter *(faṣl)* of it. Many articles are reproduced in the "*Ḳānūn-nāme* of Suleiman", sometimes with differences in style and arrangement and with changes in

[41] Ms. Wien, Nationalbibliothek, Orient. Handschr. AF no. 554.

[42] Edited by E. Z. Karal, in *Belleten* VI (1942), pp. 37—44.

[43] For example, in Bayezid's *siyāset-nāme* a pimp was to have his nose cut off, whereas in Selim's *siyāset-nāme* and Suleiman's *ḳānun-nāme* he is branded on the forehead.

[44] A copy of the *siyāset-nāme* adressed to Pertev Pasha can be found in the Ms. Âtıf Efendi no. 1734, pp. 33—36.

the rates of the taxes and other more essential points. Such articles concern the tax on building plots;[45] tithes on cotton, flax, madder and saffron;[46] privileges of timariots in selling the revenue of wine in kind;[47] the tithes on hives;[48] marriage dues;[49] hog tax.[50] Also the articles about *reʿāyā'* being unable to cultivate the land[51] and *reʿāyā'* having abandoned their cultivated lands[51] are the same in both *ḳānūn-nāmes*. Though somewhat different in its wording, the famous article on forced labour is also the same.[52] The articles on market dues in the Conqueror's *ḳānūn-nāme* were reproduced in Suleiman's. Thus, for the most part, the Conqueror's *ḳānūn-nāme* was embodied in that of "Suleiman".[53] The missing parts of some articles in one or other *ḳānūn-nāme* were left out, I think, mostly by accident by the copyists.[54] The changes in style and expressions must have been made largely by later generations of scribes *(kātib)* at the Ottoman chancery.

Fundamental differences in the articles are few. The "*Ḳānūn-nāme* of Suleiman" left out the article on *çift-resmi* and *ispence*,[55] which reflected the earlier conception of these taxes, and which were probably considered as unnecessary. The rate of the tax on sheep was one *akça* for three sheep for Muslims and non-Muslims in the Conqueror's *ḳānūn-nāme;* it is one *akça* for two sheep in the "*Ḳānūn-nāme* of Suleiman", except in the frontier *sancaḳ* of Vidin, where the previous rate was maintained.[56]

The basic differences between the *ḳānūn-nāme* of the Conqueror and that of "Suleiman" consist in subsequent additions concerning

[45] The Conqueror, chapter III; Suleiman, p. 17.

[46] The Conqueror, chapter IV, art. 12—13, 21; Suleiman, p. 32.

[47] The Conqueror, *ḳānūn-i cebelūyān*, art. 4; Suleiman, p. 34.

[48] The Conqueror, chapter IV, art. 23; *cebelūyān*, 3; Suleiman, p. 37.

[49] The Conqueror, chapter III, art. 18; Suleiman, pp. 36, 39.

[50] The Conqueror, *cebelūyān*; Suleiman, p. 57.

[51] The Conqueror, chapter IV, art. 7; Suleiman p. 16, and The Conqueror, chapter III, art. 14; Suleiman, pp. 51, 53 respectively.

[52] The Conqueror, *cebelūyān*, art. 1, 2; Suleiman, pp. 57, 58.

[53] The Conqueror, chapter IV, art. 30, 32; *cebelūyān*, art. 9—28; Suleiman, pp. 21—23.

[54] For example, in the Conqueror's *ḳānūn-nāme*, art. 4: *Eger zinā eden ḳız olursa . . .* ; art. 3: *Eger ḳoyun veya ḳovan oğurlasa . . .* ; art. 5: *Eger sığır oğurlasa . . .* ; in Suleiman's *ḳānūn-nāme*, p. 2: *Eger zinā eden dul olsa . . .* ; p. 6: *İnek girse dört çomaḳ . . .*

[55] The Conqueror, chapter IV, art. 1—4, 14.

[56] The Conqueror, chapter III, art. 13; *cebelūyān*, art. 5; Suleiman, p. 30.

subjects which previously were treated slightly or not at all. Some of these additions come from the later *ḳānūns* issued by the Conqueror himself. For example the statutes on the Eflaḳ (Vlachs) of Braniçevo and Vidin and Semendere (Smederevo) were obviously copied from survey books arranged about 1477.[57] It is to be noted that the taxes paid in kind by Vlachs in 1468 were converted into cash by 1477.

Hersek-zāde Ahmed Pasha's amendments

An undated copy of a document tells us that Ahmed Pasha, *beglerbegi* of Anatolia, had sent a *ḳānūn-nāme* to the *niṣāncı* at the Porte, who corrected it according to the "*ḳānūns* newly issued by the Sultan" and returned it to the Pasha.[58] The text of this *ḳānūn-nāme* is not given in the manuscript, which says that it was about "*reʿāyā' ve berāyā', beg ve paşa, ewḳāf ve emlāk, yaya ve müsellem.*" This could only be found in a *ḳānūn-nāme* of a general character. Another document in the same manuscript informs us[59] that Hersek-zāde Ahmed Pasha was asked by Selim I to amend a *Ḳānūn-nāme-i ʿOs̱mānī*, and names the subjects changed. The headings of the chapters referred to in these amendments are the same as those in the so-called "*Ḳānūn-nāme* of Suleiman". The first six amendments are found interpolated in the text of the "*Ḳānūn-nāme* of Suleiman" and the last two were added to it as an appendix in a copy of Suleiman's time.[60] This appendix gives us the further information that the amendments were made by *vezīr-i aʿzam* Ahmed Pasha, son of Hersek (Hersek-oğlu or Hersek-zāde) on the 15th of ramaḍān 906 (5 April 1501). Now Hersek-zāde Ahmed Pasha was *beglerbegi* of Anatolia several times under Bayezid II (1483—1486, 1487—1488, 1490—1492), but he was not Grand Vizier in April 1501. He became Grand Vizier first in 1497—1498, and then for a second time in 1502, shortly before December. He stayed in this post until 7 September 1506. We find him Grand Vizier again in

[57] N. Beldiceanu et I. Beldiceanu-Steinherr, "Quatre Actes de Mehmed II. concernant les Valaques des Balkans slaves", *Südost-Forschungen* XXIV (1965), p. 105; İnalcık, "Adâletnâmeler", pp. 63—67.

[58] In Revan no. 1936; Revan no. 1935 does not contain it.

[59] Also Revan no. 1935 and Westdeutsche Staatsbibliothek, Marburg, Orient. no. 2730 (*see*, N. Beldiceanu, *Les actes des premiers sultans* II (Paris, 1964), p. 41, note 1) contain it without the first document concerning Ahmed Pasha.

[60] Velîyüddin no. 1969.

1511, and again between 1512—1514 and 1515—1516 under Selim I. He died on 21 July 1517.[61] In April 1501 Mesih Pasha was Grand Vizier and Hersek-zāde Ahmed Pasha second vizier. Most probably he made the above-mentioned amendments when he held this post.

It is interesting to see how these amendments were interpolated into the text of our *ḳānūn-nāme*. For comparison we shall use certain copies made in the time of Suleiman I.[62]

1. The first amendment regards the minimum age for participation in the campaigns by the sons of *sipāhīs* holding a *tīmār*. Some late copies lack this section. In the copy of Velîyüddin it is interpolated in the text. But in the margin of the copy of 975/1567 we find the following note: "Now the *ḳānūn* applied in this matter holds that when he is still a child and if he has not been granted a *tīmār* by the Sultan's order on condition of sending an *eşkinci*,[63] he can not possess a *tīmār* at all; and as to his participating personally in the expeditions, only his ability to fight is considered."

2. The second amendment concerns the *aḳıncı*, raiders, who were exempted from the emergency taxes and services (*ʿawāriḍ)* only in the years when they actually joined the army for an expedition.

3. The third amendment deals with the exemption from the taxes of *çift-resmi* and emergency taxes and services of every *şeyḫ* running a *zāviye*, a religious hostel serving passers-by, and of every *sipāhī-zāde*, members of the pre-conquest military class in the province of Karaman. We found the same exemption recorded in an official *defter* of Karaman dated 906/1501.[64] In the copy of Velîyüddin, however, we find this marginal remark: "This too is abolished because if the lands originally belonging to the *reʿāyā*' are somehow in the possession of *sipāhīs*, these lands cannot be considered as theirs. They too have to pay all the taxes." And the marginal note in the copy of Revan no. 1935 reads: "If the *şeyḫs* running a *zāviye* are actually serving the travellers, and if the *sipāhī-zādes* actually take part in the expeditions in the service of the *beglerbegis* with the hope

[61] *See* H. Šabanović, "Hersek-zāde, Aḫmed Pasha", *EI*[2] III, pp. 351–352); H. Edhem, *Hersek-oğlu Ahmed Paşa'nın esâretine dair Kahire'de bir kitâbe*, in *TOEM* V, pp. 202—222, 272—295.

[62] *See* note 73.

[63] For that term, *see* H. İnalcık, "Eshkindji" in *EI*[2] II, pp. 714—715.

[64] *Tapu defterleri*, no. 40.

of obtaining a *tīmār*, then they are exempted from those taxes, but all others are to pay them."

These marginal notes, made apparently in the time of Suleiman, meant restriction of the exemptions formerly accorded to the *şeyḫ*s and *sipāhī-zāde*s in the province of Karaman at a time when the critical situation there necessitated a lenient policy.[65] The later changes implied the strict application of the Ottoman principles of taxation, according to which those who came into possession of lands originally belonging to the *reʿāyā'* paid all the taxes as *reʿāyā'*. On the other hand, the Ottoman law recognized exemption from emergency taxes and services only while some service was being performed for the State. Under Suleiman it was a general policy to abolish as far as possible special privileges and exemptions everywhere in the empire. The amendment was expressed in the *ḳānūn-nāme* of the *sancaḳ* of Karaman dated 935/1528, as follows: "Those people who are recorded as *sipāhī-zāde, zāviyedār (şeyḫ*s) or the like, are exempted from *ʿawāriḍ*, extraordinary taxes and services. Those among them who were exempted for generations from *çift-resmi* and the like are likewise not to pay these taxes, but those who were subjected to *çift-resmi* are to pay them except for the *ʿawāriḍ*, unless recorded otherwise in the *defter*."[66] Thus the *defter* was an authority to decide on each particular case since the commissioner of the survey saw and recorded the actual application of the principle.

4. The fourth amendment is of particular interest for us. It abolished tax exemptions in the province of Rūm (Amasya—Sivas) and compelled the families who enjoyed such exemptions to be registered as simple *reʿāyā'* in the *ḫāṣṣ* lands of the sultan. Nevertheless the *müsellemiyye*, members of the native military class and *şeyḫ*s of *zāviye*s in the province of Rūm[67] who enjoyed tax exemp-

[65] From 1468 down to 1514 the submission of the Karaman territory became the most complicated question for the Ottomans. It was not only an internal question, but also a matter which determined the Ottoman relations with the Mamluks in Egypt and Akkoyunlus and later on Safavids in Iran. The actual leaders of the terrible insurrection of Şāh-ḳulu in 1511 were the *sipāhī*s of Karaman (*see* the documents published in Ç. Uluçay, "Yavuz Sultan Selim nasıl padişah oldu?" *Tarih Dergisi* VI, pp. 53—90, 117—142; H. Sohrweide, "Der Sieg der Safaviden in Persien und seine Rückwirkungen auf die Schiiten Anatoliens in 16. Jahrhundert", *Der Islam* 41 (1965), pp. 95—223).

[66] Barkan, *op. cit.*, p. 47, art. 21.

[67] *Müsellemiyye* were maintained on their pre-conquest lands, mostly pasture-lands (BVA, *Tapu defteri*, no. 13).

tions under this name were maintained in their status of *müsellemiyye*. Here too we find a lenient measure evidently introduced by Hersek-zāde. The argument was that the *müsellemiyye* did not possess lands belonging to *reʿāyā'* and furthermore they were doing military service in the Ottoman army. But the marginal note in the manuscript Revan no. 1936 reads: "They are maintained in this status (of *reʿāyā'*). The *müsellems* in the province of Rūm are definitely registered as *reʿāyā'* and become *reʿāyā'*." This again showed a return to the original Ottoman policy, as in the case of Karaman.

The other four amendments of Hersek-zāde were concerned with the important tax called *tapu-resmi*, which was to be paid to *sipāhīs* by *reʿāyā'* upon the possession and transference of land. Introduced in the *ḳānūn-nāme*, the first two of these amendments were later modified and completely changed under Suleiman.

The Koyunoğlu manuscript of the ḳānūn-nāme

A recently discovered manuscript of this *ḳānūn-nāme*, belonging to the private library of Mr. İzzet Koyunoğlu in Konya,[68] and dated 907/1501, confirms that we are not justified in attributing "Suleiman's *ḳānūn-nāme*" to Suleiman. This manuscript (hereafter Koyunoğlu Ms.), entitled *Kitāb-i Ḳawānīn-i ʿUrfiyye-i ʿOs̱māniyye* 'Book of Ottoman *ʿurfī* laws', begins with the introduction common to all other copies of the so-called "*Ḳānūn-nāme* of Suleiman", and includes all the chapters with the same headings which were found in the later copies, concluding with these words: "This book has been written and completed with the help of God, all bountiful, by Muṣṭafā b. Ramaḍān,[69] who is poor and wretched and in need of His mercy, may God forgive his sins and those of his parents, and accord His favors upon them, in the middle of rabīʿ I, in the year of 907" (the last days of September and first days of October 1501).

[68] Dr. V. L. Ménage informed me about this manuscript after his visit to Konya in 1962, and Mr. Koyunoğlu was kind enough to let me have a microfilm of it. For the description of the Ms. *see* Beldiceanu and Beldiceanu-Steinherr, *op. cit.*, p. 104. I think their interpretation of the sentence in 59r: *ilk yaz* ... is not altogether convincing *(ibid.*, p. 108). I read it as *ilk yaz Hızır Ilyas günü dillerinde fuluri diyen zamanda bir kuzılu koyun.*

[69] The famous Mehmed Çelebī Ramaḍān-zāde (*see* ʿĀlī, *Kunh al-aḫbār*; M. Tahir, *Osmanlı müellifleri* III, p. 53; M. Süreyya, *Sicill-i ʿOs̱mānī* IV, p. 120) might be a relative of our Muṣṭafā b. Ramaḍān.

In the margin we find records of some important events with dates. The earliest of these concern an insurrection on 1 muharrem 934/27 September 1527, and the battle between Prince Selim and Prince Bayezid on 1 ṣaʿbān 966/9 May 1559. The text itself contains nothing to make us doubt the date of the manuscript. For example, no mention is made of the provinces which were annexed to the Ottoman empire under Selim I or Suleiman I.

A comparison of this *ḳānūn-nāme* with a *ḳānūn-nāme* of the *sancaḳ* of Ḫudāvendigār (Bursa) dated 892/1487[70] shows that the latter was one of its main sources. This is quite comprehensible if we remember that the *ḳānūn-nāme* of Ḫudāvendigār, the birthplace of the Ottoman State, embodied the classic Ottoman laws on taxation and land possession. For example, the Koyunoğlu Ms. and the *ḳānūn-nāme* of Ḫudāvendigār give an identical provision on runaway animals and slaves, but a copy of our *ḳānūn-nāme* dated 936 H./1529[71] and later copies contain an additional note with this introductory phrase: "Afterwards an imperial firman arrived to the effect that . . .". The Koyunoğlu version contains the amendments introduced by "*vezīr-i aʿzam*" Hersek-zāde Ahmed Pasha which were declared on 5 April 1501. On the other hand, Suleiman Pasha, who is mentioned in the Koyunoğlu manuscript with a reference to his previous governorship in Semendere (Smederovo), was a *sancaḳ-begi* there between 1489—1492.[72] In conclusion we can say that the so-called "*Ḳānūn-nāme* of Suleiman" must have been composed originally between 1492 and 1501.

In comparison with the Koyunoğlu Ms., the copies made under Suleiman I, contain only a few modifications and additions.[73] Each copy of this general *ḳānūn-nāme*, with modifications in the text or with marginal notes summarising the *ḥukm*s, actually represents an independent document in itself, exhibiting a certain stage in the evolution of Ottoman law. The *ḳānūn-nāme*

[70] Barkan, *op. cit.*, p. 2.

[71] Ms. Library of the Turkish Historical Society, Y. no. 75.

[72] *See* H. Šabanović, *Beogradski pašaluk*, in *Encyk. Yugoslavija* I.

[73] The important copies made under Suleiman are: (1) The above mentioned Ms. Library of the Turkish Historical Society, Y. no. 75, copied on 11th muharram 936/15 September 1529; (2) Ms. Bayezid Umumî Kütüphanesi, Velîyüddin Kitapları, no. 1969, (3) Ms. Orientalni Institut, Sarajevo, Man. Turcica, no. 3, copied in 969/1561; and (4) Ms. Âtıf Efendi Kütüphanesi no. 1734.

received further modifications after Suleiman's death, and we find a seventeenth century copy with a new arrangement of the chapters, some of which were substantially extended or completely omitted.[74] I think it is no exaggeration to assert that *one Ottoman law-book existed which evolved throughout Ottoman history*. The new *ḳānūn-ḥukm*s, issued according to new conditions and needs, were incorporated later on into the body of this *ḳānūn-nāme*.

In even the earliest available copy of the general *ḳānūn-nāme*, *i.e.*, the Koyunoğlu Ms., dated 907/1501, we find that the bulk of its provisions come mainly from the *ḳānūn-nāme*s of the provinces of *Anadolu* (Anatolia, *i. e.*, Western Asia Minor), *Karaman* (Central Southern Asia Minor), and *Semendere* (Smederovo, in upper Serbia). The *ḳānūn-nāme*s of *Rūm* (Central Northern Asia Minor) and of *Vidin* (on the Danube) were less frequently referred to. It appears that the author of the general *ḳānūn-nāme* went through the *defter*s (survey registers) at his disposal and gathered information not only from the *ḳānūn-nāme*s which introduced the *defter*s, but also from the legal statements on specific matters in them. Supporting this view are such phrases as: "No tax on linseed oil presses was found in the *defter*s other than that of Karaman".[75] "The *ḳānūn-nāme*s of the Anatolian *sancaḳ*s, especially that of Ḫudāvendigār of which we have a copy dated 1487,[76] thus became the source for most of the general provisions in our general *ḳānūn-nāme*. The different provisions which were found in the *ḳānūn-nāme*s of other provinces were usually introduced in the general *ḳānūn-nāme* with the phrase: "But in the province of Karaman (or Semendere) the matter is . . . ".[77] The laws on the Vlachs were collected from the *defter*s of Braniçeva (Braniçevo), Vidin and Semendere.[78] The law on the market duties and custom duties of Semendere found in our *ḳānūn-nāme*[79] is taken verbatim from a *ḳānūn-nāme* found in an official *defter* of

[74] Ms. Üniversite Kütüphanesi, Hâlis Efendi, T. no. 2730.

[75] M. Ârif edition, p. 43.

[76] Barkan, *op. cit.*, pp. 1—6.

[77] For the provisions from the *Ḳānūn-nāme* of Karaman in the M. Ârif edition, *see* pp. 18, 21, 33, 34, 42, 53, 62—63, 67—68, and for those from that of Semendere, pp. 23—27, 32, 35, 46, 52, 56, 64, 68.

[78] For the laws on the Vlachs in the survey books of the time of Mehmed II, *see* İnalcık, *Fatih devri . . .*, pp. 152—158; *cf.* Beldiceanu and Beldiceanu-Steinherr, *op. cit.*, pp. 103—105.

[79] M. Ârif edition, pp. 23—27.

this *sancaḳ* dated awāi'l-i ṣafar 922/6—15 March 1516;[80] the other provisions of the said *ḳānūn-nāme* concerning the *re'āyā'* are scattered in the pertinent sections of our *ḳānūn-nāme*. But a copy of this official *defter* dated earlier than 922/1516 must have been used.[81] The provisions on *çift-resmi* in our *ḳānūn-nāme*[82] were gathered from the *defter*s of *sancaḳ*s of Anadolu. The first part of the law on *müsellem*s and *yaya*s,[83] the law on the people who come from outside to cultivate lands in *tīmār*s,[84] the law on the property of foreigners who died in the Ottoman territories,[85] and laws on the conscription of the *'azab*s,[86] the abolition of unlawful practices in Konya[87] and the wood supply for the imperial court,[88] were apparently reproduced from the original *ḳānūn-ḥukm*s or their copies in the *defter*s. Future investigations in the archives may produce the original *ḥukm*s. In conclusion we can say that the laws which were used in our *ḳānūn-nāme* must have been issued either under Mehmed the Conqueror, or during Bayezid II's reign before 1501. It is possible that a general survey made in 892/1487 may have been the occasion for this legislative activity under Bayezid II.

4. AN OUTLINE OF THE EVOLUTION OF OTTOMAN LEGISLATION IN THE SIXTEENTH CENTURY

Thus about 1500 A.D. an Ottoman law-book came into being with clearly defined rules and principles covering a wide range of matters concerning the *re'āyā'* and their relations with the military. The principles that gave Ottoman law its particular quality and its internal unity were of course in force long before Bayezid II, as we

[80] BVA, *Tapu defterleri*, no. 1007. I am indebted to Dr. D. Bojanić-Lukać for the information on this *defter*.

[81] The correct form of the phrase *yer ıssına* 'to the possessor of the land' is found in our *kānūn-nāme* whereas it was rendered mistakenly as *yer üstüne* 'to the surface of the land' in the *defter*.

[82] M. Ârif edition, pp. 27—30.

[83] *Ibid.*, p. 43.

[84] *Ibid.*, pp. 55—56.

[85] *Ibid.*, p. 58.

[86] *Ibid.*, pp. 59—61.

[87] *Ibid.*, pp. 65—69

[88] *Ibid.*, pp. 69—70.

have seen from the Conqueror's law-book. Yet under Bayezid II Ottoman law found its definite broad expression in his *ḳānūn-nāme*, which seems to have become the main source for the typical Ottoman laws that were to be applied in the newly conquered lands under Selim I and Suleiman I.

Faithful to an old Ottoman tradition, Selim I generally maintained pre-Ottoman taxation in the lands he conquered from the Safavids in Eastern Asia Minor and from the Mamluks in Syria and Egypt. Suleiman I at first did the same in Iraq and to some extent in Hungary. Even so, both of them abolished certain practices which were believed to be flagrantly contrary to the *ḳānūn-i ʿOs̱mānī*. For example, in 1518 when the taxation laws of Uzun Hasan, the Akkoyunlu ruler, were maintained in Eastern Asia Minor (Diyārbekr and Erzurum provinces), extra levies on crops taken after the collection of tithes were immediately abolished as contrary to the *şarīʿa* and Ottoman law.[89] In Hungary, pre-conquest royal taxation was maintained only after adapting it to basic Ottoman laws.[90] The florin tax, which required that one Hungarian gold piece be paid to the royal treasury by each family during the time of the Hungarian kings, was accepted under the Ottomans as the *resm-i filuri*, a tax corresponding to *cizye*, the Islamic poll-tax.[91] Actually it ended up being called *cizye* by the end of the sixteenth century. Also *ispence*, an Ottoman *ʿurfī* tax, was collected under the name of *ḳapu-resmi*, 'gate tax' which was in force under the Hungarian kings.[92]

Since the foundation their State, the Ottomans had followed this conciliatory policy of allowing the older taxes, obviously because it was easy for the *reʿāyā'* as well as for Ottoman administration in its early stage.[93] But in 1540 almost everywhere in Eastern Asia

[89] Barkan, *op. cit.*, p. 156, art. 16; W. Hinz, "Das Steuerwesen Ostanatoliens", in *ZDMG* CX/CXI, pp. 181—185.

[90] Barkan, *op. cit.*, p. 323, art. 10; Gy. Káldy-Nagy, "Bevölkerungsstatistischer Quellenwert der Ğizye-Defter und der Tahrīr-Defter", *Acta Orientalia Hungarica* XI (1960), pp. 259—260.

[91] Barkan, *op. cit.*, p. 30, art. 1—2; p. 303, art. 1; p. 306, art. 1; p. 316, art. 1; p. 318, art. 1; p. 319, art. 1; p. 322, art. 1; and H. İnalcık, "D̲jizya (Ottoman Empire)", *EI*² III, pp. 562—566.

[92] Barkan, *op. cit.*, p. 301, art. 3; p. 316, art. 2; p. 320, art. 4; p. 322, art. 2. For *ispence*, *see* İnalcık, "Osmanlılarda raiyyet rüsûmu", pp. 602—608.

[93] *Cf.*, H. İnalcık, "Ottoman Methods of Conquest", *Studia Islamica* II (1954), pp. 103—129.

Minor standard Ottoman taxation law replaced that of Uzun Hasan because "the *reʿāyā*ʾ wanted the Ottoman law to be put in force in their province too".[94] In the preamble to the *ḳānūn-nāme* of Erzurum in 947/1540, it was made clear that "as the tribal communities, as well as merchants and other communities [in the province of Erzurum] could not bear the heavy load resulting from the so-called laws of Hasan Pādişāh [Uzun Hasan], they wanted the Rūm [Ottoman] law to be put into force [in their own province]. Their request was submitted to the Sultan's Porte and, as a result of his feelings of compassion and justice in their favor, he issued the order that the *ḳānūn-nāme* of Rūm should be applied to them too."[95] In Syria too, Ottoman law was imposed after a period of transition which seems in some places to have lasted longer than in Eastern Asia Minor. For example, in the *sancaḳ* of Maʿarra the pre-Ottoman taxes of *dawra* and *ḥimāya* were maintained as corresponding to the Ottoman *çift-resmi* until as late as 959/1552, whereas the *çift-resmi* system was by then applied in the province of Aleppo in Northern Syria. In Iraq the so-called laws of both Hasan Pādişāh (Uzun Hasan) and of the Safavids were left in force in 1537. Then by a firman dated the 14th of February 1537, the practices which were ascribed to the Safavids *(Ḳızılbaş)* were abolished as totally unjust innovations.[96]

It can safely be said that the basic rules of the *ḳānūn-i ʿOsmānī*, traditional Ottoman law concerning the *reʿāyā*ʾ, took definite form as a result of fusion of Ottoman laws with pre-conquest practices and antedating the Conqueror's law-book which we know was proclaimed around 1453. The Conqueror's long and dynamic reign witnessed the issuance of a number of laws and statutes on specific matters,[97] some of which seem to have been codified into the law-

[94] Barkan, *op. cit.*, pp. 117, 63.

[95] Barkan, *op. cit.*, p. 63.

[96] Velîyüddin no. 1970.

[97] A collection containing some of these *ḳānūn-ḥukm*s was published in 1956 by R. Anhegger and H. İnalcık, quoted above note 13, the publication of which had been announced in my *Sûret-i defter-i sancak-i Arvanid* (Ankara, 1954), p. XIX, note 85. In 1956 there appeared a facsimile edition by F. Babinger, *Sultanische Urkunden für Geschichte der osmanischen Wirtschaft und Staatsverwaltung am Ausgang der Herrschaft Mehmed II. des Eroberers* (Munich, 1956). For the French translation of it by N. Beldiceanu, *Les actes des premiers sultans* I (Paris—La Haye, 1960) *see* my remarks in *Der Islam XLIII* (1967), pp. 139—157.

book of Bayezid II as found in the Koyunoğlu Ms. Under Suleiman I Ottoman culture reached its classic period with an absolute faith in the perfection of Ottoman institutions and laws. The Ottomans rejected, as *bidʿat*, innovations and unjust practices, all the pre-conquest customs and laws which were incompatible with their own legal system.

We shall try to demonstrate what the main features of the *ḳānūn-i ʿOsmānī* were in the form which it took until the middle of the sixteenth century.

First of all, it was asserted as a fundamental principle that "*reʿāyā*ʾ and land belong to the sultan". This meant primarily that no one had any right to exercise authority over land and *reʿāyā*ʾ without a specific mandate from the sultan. Thus the absolute sovereignty of the sultan within the empire was secured and all sorts of local lordships in the provinces were sooner or later eliminated. Also under the same principle the sultan was able to apply the *tīmār* system within his empire, the *tīmār* system being the basic institution used to organize conquered lands. The same principle gave the sultan the right to interfere with *waḳf*s (religious foundations) and private estates and to place certain obligations on them. The theory was that there too the land and *reʿāyā*ʾ belonged fundamentally to the sultan.[98] In brief, this principle became the very foundation-stone of Ottoman absolutism and the centralized empire.

On the other hand, appointees to whom the sultan had assigned *tīmār*s and authority in the provinces were not to dispose of anything beyond what was stated in their diploma of investiture *(berāt)*, imperial survey registers and *ḳānūn-nāme*s. A *beg* or *sipāhī*, as *tīmār*-holder, was given the authority to collect certain taxes directly from the *reʿāyā*ʾ living on his *tīmār*, and could force them to comply with the rules applying to the cultivation and possession of the land. It is easy to surmise that, if not properly controlled, such authority might have given rise to all sorts of abuses to the detriment of the *reʿāyā*ʾ. The sultan always had to be vigilant, and we know that he reacted strongly against such abuses of authority in order to uphold the principle that no one was allowed to establish personal authority over *reʿāyā*ʾ and land beyond his own. Many feudal practices from pre-Ottoman times, that had given uncheck-

[98] *See* the *ḳānūn-nāme* of Diyārbekr in Barkan, *op. cit.*, p. 135, art. 23.

ed control to local military classes over land and population, were abolished by the Ottomans. One of the central points in the *ḳānūn-i ʿOs̱mānī* was that "*(tīmār*-holders) were not to take anything more from the peasants once they had obtained that which was defined in the *ḳānūn-nāme*s and registers". Also, there was the article prohibiting forced labour which appeared in the *ḳānūn-nāme*s, including the Conqueror's, and which ran as follows: "[*Tīmār*-holders] are not to take and use forcibly horses and carts of the *reʿāyāʾ* or make them work in their own service".[99]

In spite of this principle, in the Ottoman *tīmār*-system as in European feudalism there always existed services for which the *reʿāyāʾ*'s cooperation was deemed necessary. The main ones were to provide fuel for the *tīmār*-holder and hay for his horses in wintertime, to carry and store the tithes taken from products of the soil and till the *tīmār*-holder's *ḫāṣṣa*, his own personal land and orchard. As a matter of fact, the *ḳānūn-i ʿOs̱mānī* tried to abolish these or at least limit their scope. Even in the period prior to the *ḳānūn-nāme* of the Conqueror several services, such as providing wood and hay for the *tīmār*-holder and working for three days for him, were abolished in most parts of the Balkans and Anatolia in return for a fixed cash tax of 22 *akça* to be paid to the *tīmār*-holder as a compensation.[100] Called *çift-resmi*, this tax was to be paid by a peasant possessing a piece of land of one *çift*, varying in size from about sixty to hundred fifty *dönüm* (one *dönüm* = 939.3 sq.m.). Those possessing half of it, or less than half, paid lower rates. The *ispence* was a tax parallel to *çift-resmi* that applied to non-Muslims. *Çift-resmi* and *ispence* taxation were established as the most typical Ottoman laws in the *ḳānūn-i ʿOs̱mānī*. They were also called "taxation of *raʿiyyat*" (singular of *reʿāyāʾ*), representing personal obligations of *reʿāyāʾ* to the military. Thus the *ḳānūn-i ʿOs̱mānī* in general brought to the *reʿāyāʾ*, a simpler and easier system of taxation than the previous complicated system of feudal services, which had been much more open to malpractice. It must be added that in many places the military found ways to continue the old practices, and what is more, certain *sancaḳ ḳānūn-nāme*s included these as recognized customs even after the collection of the *çift-resmi* and *ispence*.

[99] Barkan, *op. cit.*, p. 305, art. 9.

[100] *See* İnalcık, "Raiyyet rüsûmu" in *Belleten* XXIII, pp. 575—600, and "Čift-resmi" in *EI*².

The Ottoman law-maker endeavoured to limit the scope of certain services recognized by custom. *Reʿāyā'* were to mow and heap grass on the *ḫāṣṣa* (reserved) land of the *tīmār*-holder, but not to carry it as far as the barn, to transport tithes to the nearest market-place, but never farther than one day's distance, and to build a barn, but not a house, for the *tīmār*-holder. In the middle of the sixteenth century, by which time the origin of *çift-resmi* had been long forgotten, the three days forced labour for the *tīmār*-holder in the newly conquered areas of Eastern Asia Minor (Diyārbekr) was converted into an extra tax of two *akça* per familiy,[101] and in Hungary fifteen *penez* (1 Hungarian ducat = 100 *penez)* for one cart-load of wood and twenty five *penez* (Hungarian *pénz)* for one cart-load of hay were to be paid per family.[102]

The *ḳānūn-i ʿOsmānī* allowed *beg*s and *sipāhī*s to levy provisions for themselves and especially for their horses only under special conditions (for example in the province of Trabzon where a shortage of wheat and barley was chronic).[103] For all kinds of emergency levies of provisions and demands of services *(ʿawāriḍ, salma, salġun)*, the principle was that there must be a real need for the provisions and services for the good of the country and a special order of the sultan to impose such levies was required.[104] Otherwise, provisions were to be bought at market prices from *reʿāyā'*. This was the law. Repeated orders sent to the provinces for its strict application and public declarations to prevent abuses[105] leave no room for doubt that the *ḳānūn-i ʿOsmānī* itself distinguished between a recognized innovation and custom *(bidʿat-i maʿrūfe)* and a rejected innovation and custom *(bidʿat-i merdūde)*. For more onerous innovations the terms "injustice" *(ḥayf)*, "oppression" *(ẓulm)* or "foulness" *(ṣenāʿat)* were used.

As for tithes, which made up the second most important group of taxes, the *ḳānūn-i ʿOsmānī* adopted a simple system, as with *raʿiyyet* taxation. For grain it was one tenth, usually with an additional tax of one fortieth called *salarlıḳ* or *sālāriyye*, which made one

[101] Barkan, *op. cit.*, p. 132, art. 8. For straw and wood taxes to be paid to *sipāhī* guards at the fortresses in Ḫudāvendigār in 1487, *cf.*, Barkan, *op. cit.*, p. 2.

[102] Barkan, *op. cit.*, p. 323, art. 6.

[103] Barkan, *op. cit.*, p. 61, art. 14.

[104] Barkan, *op. cit.*, p. 270, art. 21—22.

[105] *See* İnalcık, "Adâletnâmeler", pp. 49—145.

eighth altogether. The latter was interpreted as corresponding to fodder taken for the horses of *tīmār*-holders.[106] Once *salarlıḳ* was taken, no other extra imposition on grain in the guise of *salma* (levy) or otherwise was allowed. In Hungary the proportion of one tenth was adopted for tithes, but in the *sancaḳ* of Lipova (Lippa) it was one ninth without *salarlıḳ*, as in the time of the Hungarian kings. In the Eastern provinces of the empire, those annexed in the sixteenth century, namely Eastern Asia Minor, Syria and Iraq, where the *ḳānūn-i ʿOs̱mānī* was extended fully only under Suleiman I, the proportion of one fifth, that is, the proportion adopted by the *şarīʿa* on the so-called *ḫarāc* lands,[107] was applied without *salarlıḳ*. The proportion of one fifth for tithes on grain was applied also in some of the Balkan provinces (in Albania in 1570), and in the newly conquered lands, such as Cyprus and Georgia, in 1570.[108] This change can be ascribed to the influence of Abu's-Suʿūd, the famous *şeyḫü'l-islām* of Suleiman I, who zealously embarked upon the adaptation of Ottoman *ʿurfī* laws to the *şarīʿa*.[109] His interpretation of state owned *(mīrī)* lands as *ḫarācī* lands according to the *şarīʿa* was followed faithfully in the new *ḳānūn-nāmes*.

At any rate, the Ottomans abolished all sorts of local grain taxation practices wherever they brought in their *ḳānūn-i ʿOs̱mānī* with its typical tithe system. In Eastern Asia Minor the old practices of taking a certain amount of grain per heap on harvest floor or per farm (4 *kile* per farm in the province of Diyārbekr, 5 *kile* per farm in Ruhā, 1 *kile* per farm in Çermik, etc.) or collection of straw in

[106] *Sālāriyye* means 'due for lord' (also *ağalıḳ*). It is a supplementary tax to tithes, and taken for straw (*ḳānūn-nāme*, Ms. DTC Fakültesi Kütüphanesi, Ankara, İsmail Saip no. 5036). It is taken only from wheat, barley, millet, rye, oats. The proportion is one fortieth in general. But in Sirem it was one thirtieth. On the island of Eğriboz (Euboea) it was one load *(denk)* of wheat. (*Cf.*, Barkan, *op. cit.*, p. 341, art. 4.)

[107] *See* Abu's-Suʿūd's commentary on land in Barkan, *op. cit.*, pp. 297—299. It is also found in the form of a *fetwā*. It exercised a sweeping influence on the Ottoman land law later on.

[108] Barkan, *op. cit.*, p. 291, art. 3; p. 349, art. 2; p. 197, art 2.

[109] In the introduction to his famous *Maʿrūḍāt* (in *Millî Tetebbuʿlar Mecmūʿası* I, pp. 336—337), he said that Sultan Suleiman asked him to give an opinion on the basis of religious authority on certain questions which he thought should conform to religious law before he gave his orders on them. Abu's-Suʿūd's activities in strengthening the influence of religious law on the administration went much deeper than our present knowledge indicates.

addition to tithes, were abolished when the *ḳānūn-i ʿOs̱mānī* was extended to this part of the Empire in 1540. Under the name of *harman-resmi* (harvest-tax) a similar tax was found in territories which once were part of the Byzantine empire in the Balkans, as in the case of the Aegean islands. It consisted of a certain amount of wheat and barley (usually two *kile* of both but half a *luḳna* of wheat and half a *luḳna* of barley in the *sancaḳ* of Semendere)[110] collected by the *tīmār*-holder from every family at harvest time in addition to the tithes. The Ottomans identified it with their *salarlıḳ*. It survived indeed in some parts of the empire as an ancient custom. During his campaign against Belgrade in 1521, Suleiman abolished it upon the *reʿāyā*'s complaint in the province of Vidin. But later on *sipāhī*s protested, saying that it caused a substantial diminution of their *tīmār* revenues. The Sultan ordered inquiries which showed that it was an ancient tax surviving from pre-Ottoman times.[111]

The third category of taxes in the *ḳānūn-i ʿOs̱mānī* was the so-called *bād-i havā*, occasional dues such as the bride-tax, tax on title-deeds, and especially fines (*cerāʾim*). In order to prevent abuses, the *ḳānūn-i ʿOs̱mānī* included in its first chapters quite a detailed law on fines, and laid down the rule that no fine was to be taken unless the local cadi had given a decision.[112]

It becomes clear that one of the main purposes of the *ḳānūn-i ʿOs̱mānī* was to protect the *reʿāyāʾ* from the abuses of the local military class. The principle *bidʿat*s, innovations, contrary to the Ottoman law in Hungary, as expressed in the *ḳānūn-nāme* of this region in the middle of the sixteenth century,[113] were as follows:

1. Forced labour imposed upon *reʿāyāʾ* by *tīmār*-holders who were trying to use them and their carts in their own service.

[110] For *kile, cf.*, W. Hinz, *Islamische Mässe und Gewichte* (Leiden, 1955), pp. 41—42.

[111] *See* İnalcık, *Fatih devri* . . . , p. 178. It has been historically established that as early as the reign of Czar Samuel of Bulgaria (976—1014 A.D.) the Bulgarian peasant gave as a tax on grain one measure of wheat and one measure of barley (C. Jireček, *Geschichte der Bulgaren* [Prag, 1876], p. 410).

[112] See İnalcık, "Adâletnâmeler", p. 78. The rates of dues to be taken by cadis on legal matters and documents were also carefully tabulated in the *ḳānūns*. *Cf.*, an order of Mehmed II dated 884/1479 in *Belleten* XLIV (1947), p. 700, doc. 10.

[113] Barkan, *op. cit.*, p. 305, art. 9.

2. Attempts to extract extra dues, such as *resīd-aḳçası*, and *icāzet-aḳçası*, after collection of the sheep and hog tax, and demands for a cartload of hay.

3. Refusal to accept tithes in kind, while demanding instead the value in cash.

4. Forcing the *reʿāyā'* to provide food and fodder upon their visits to the villages.

Such *bidʿat*s were repeatedly prohibited in most parts of the empire, demonstrating that they were actually widespread and well rooted malpractices throughout the Ottoman dominions.

The immediate preoccupation of the Ottoman law-maker was to protect the *reʿāyā'* and increase the revenue sources for the State treasury. According to the traditional Middle Eastern concept of State, the more prosperous the *reʿāyā'* the more powerful the State, and the prosperity of the *reʿāyā'* depended on a just and merciful government. Supreme authority and law existed primarily to prevent those having authority and power from oppressing the *reʿāyā'*.[114] These ideas were leading principles of the Ottoman law-maker, and for this reason the *ḳānūn-i ʿOs̱mānī* was principally concerned with arranging the relations of the military with the *reʿāyā'*. Local cadis were responsible for administering the *ḳānūn-i ʿOs̱mānī* as well as the *şarīʿa*, and for seeing to it that the local authority acted in accordance with them. Most of the *ḳānūn-ḥukm*s and firmans ended with a sentence such as: "If the *reʿāyā'* bring to your attention their complaints against *beg*s or other military persons or tax-farmers, you have to stop them from committing injustices; if you think you are not able to do so you should immediately notify this to my Porte. If you fail, you will be punished yourself. My supreme desire is to maintain the *reʿāyā'* in peace and comfort and the country in prosperity."[115]

The words of the introduction to an order to the *beglerbegi* of Bagdad for the application of a new *ḳānūn-nāme* in 1537 are particularly significant: "As upon my order the provinces of Bagdad were surveyed and a survey book was composed, and at the same time all the *ḳānūn*s and rules which were maintained under the just sultans as well as the unjust practices and innovations which

[114] *See* İnalcık, "Kutadgu biligde...", p. 264, and "Adâletnâmeler", pp. 49—52.

[115] İnalcık, "Adâletnâmeler", pp. 67—84.

were introduced under the *Ḳızılbaş* (*i.e.*, Iranian domination) were submitted in a report to my attention . . . I confirm the practices already in force during the late Hasan *Pādişāh* (Akkoyunlu) and abolish all the unjust practices and innovations introduced in the time of the *Ḳızılbaş*, and I declare that from now on nobody will do anything contrary to the *şarīʿa* and *ḳānūn* towards the people living in the towns and villages of the province of Bagdad, and I order that as soon as you (the governor general and cadi of Bagdad) receive this firman of mine you will have it announced and read in public from beginning to end in all the cities, towns and meeting places, and afterwards you are to take care to forbid all innovations and make known the *ḳānūn*s and rules which I order, so that they shall know their own obligations, for which they are incumbent, and pay them accordingly, and thus nobody will have any idle excuse to exact them . . ."[116] In the introduction of a seventeenth century copy of "Suleiman's *ḳānūn-nāme*" we read: "Seeing that they [people with authority] oppress the *reʿāyā*ʾ beyond all limits and reduce them to a wretched situation, my late ancestors laid down the Ottoman *ḳānūn* [*ḳanūn-i ʿOsmānī*]".[117] Thus, in the minds of the Ottomans the proclamation of a *ḳānūn-nāme* was identified with justice. In the *ʿadālet-nāme* of 1595, quoted above, Mehmed III complained publicly of the neglect of the *Ḳānūn-nāme* of Suleiman by part of the members of the ruling class, and then banned under threats of unusually severe punishment a series of abuses and exactions introduced by its members into the administration of the provinces.

An *ʿadālet-nāme* is a document drafted to clarify and sanction the provisions of general *ḳānūn-nāme*s, and to prohibit abuses in connection with them.[118] This document was to be recorded in the *sicill*s of the cadis and a certified copy of it from the *sicill* could be obtained without charge. Thus the concept of justice in the *ḳānūn-nāme*s as protection of the *reʿāyā*ʾ against abuses of authority and illicit exactions comes out clearly in the *ʿadālet-nāme*s. Sultan Suleiman himself announced several *ʿadālet-nāme*s abolishing certain malpractices and deviations from the Ottoman law in the provinces.[119] This institution of making public declarations to protect

[116] Ms. Velîyüddin no. 1970.

[117] Ms. Fatih Millet Kütüphanesi, Ali Emîrî no. 74, fol. 1v.

[118] İnalcık, "Adâletnâmeler".

[119] *Idem*; especially the one declared in muharrem 947/May 1540.

the subjects from the malpractices of local authorities was not an Ottoman invention. One can see in the Mamluk and Ilkhanid inscriptions which abolish exorbitant taxes and duties particularly susceptible to exactions,[120] a prototype of the Ottoman *ʿadālet-nāmes*. Placed upon the walls of the mosques or the main gate of the cities, the Ilkhanid or Mamluk tax inscriptions were intended to reach the attention of everybody. These inscriptions, like the *ʿadālet-nāmes*, were obviously a joint product of the ancient Persian idea of the justice of rulers and the Turco-Mongol tradition of *törü (türe, tüzük)* and *yasak*. The Ottoman sultans after Suleiman I published *ʿadālet-nāmes* instead of *ḳānūn-nāmes* and their content became more and more elaborate. Even the proclamation of the *Ḫaṭṭ-i Şerīf* of 1839, which open the Tanzimat period of reform, can be linked with this tradition.

If the Ottoman sultans ceased to publish new *ḳānūn-nāmes* and preferred to issue *ʿadālet-nāmes*, this must have been due principally to the fact that the *şarīʿa* began to be considered as the source of legislation even in matters that hitherto had been the subject of legislative activity on the part of the political power. From the first decades of the seventeenth century on, the *ḳānūn-nāme-i ʿOs̱mānī*, general Ottoman law, became increasingly overloaded with *fetwās*, the legal opinions of the *şeyḫ ül-islām*, based on religious authorities.[121]

POSTSCRIPT

When I completed this paper I discovered that some new publications of Dr. N. Beldiceanu were closely related to the problems with which I have dealt above. In his article on the Vlachs ("Sur les Valaques des Balkans slaves à l'époque ottomane", *Revue des Études Islamiques* XXXIV [1966], p. 88) he wrote: "Ahmed Pacha est l'auteur d'un recueil d'actes juridiques ottomans". The text which led him to formulate this idea is the same one which we used above (*see* note 58). The text is not just one document, as Dr. Beldiceanu

120 W. Hinz, "Steuerinschriften aus dem mittelalterlichen Vorderen Orient", *Belleten* XIII (1949), pp. 745—769. For the Mamluks *see* J. Sauvaget, "Décrets Mamluks de Syrie", *Bulletin d'Études Orientales* II (1932), pp. 2—52; III (1933), pp. 1—29; XII (1947—1948), pp. 1—56.

121 *See* for example the *ḳānūn-nāme* published in *Millî Tetebbuʿlar Mecmūʿası* I, (1331 H.), pp. 49—112, 305—348.

thought, but is made up of two different documents. In the first document the *ḳānūn-nāme* in question is one of the Sultan's, not one of Hersek-zāde Ahmed Pasha's, as Dr. Beldiceanu supposed. In order to settle cases cencerning the *tīmār*-holders and *reʿāyā*ʾ under his jurisdiction Ahmed Pasha, then *beglerbegi* of Anadolu, must have had in his possession a general law-code of the Sultan. The document informs us that he wanted to check it with the *ḳānūn-nāme* in the hands of the *nişāncı*, who was the responsible authority for the compilation and correction of the *ʿurfī* laws of the empire.

As for the second document concerning Hersek-zāde Ahmed Pasha, it speaks of the revision of a *ḳānūn-nāme* when he was a vezir under Selim I. A detailed analysis of it is to be found above. At any rate, there can be no *ḳānūn-nāme* of Hersek-zāde Ahmed Pasha.

Dr. Beldiceanu also published in facsimile the Koyunoğlu Ms. dated 907 A. H. *(Code de lois coutumières de Mehmed II* [Wiesbaden, 1967]). In his introduction he tried to prove that this codification was originally made between 1477 and 1481. Dr. V. L. Ménage in his recent review of Dr. Beldiceanu's edition (*BSOAS* XXXII i [1969], pp. 165—67) examined his arguments on these dates and expressed doubts whether the *terminus ante quem* for it was actually 1481. The Koyunoğlu Ms. contains in the text the date of 19 dhu'l-ḳaʿde 900 (August 11, 1485). Dr. Beldiceanu himself admitted that there may be additional entries in the text made after 1481. I tried to explain in the article above that the *Ḳānūn-nāme* was composed some time between 1492 and 1501 and contained, of course, various *ḳānūns* which were issued under Mehmed II and Bayezid II.

In her book *Kniga zakonov Sultan Selima I* [The Code of Law of Sultan Selim I] (Moscow, 1969) A. S. Tveritinova discusses two Ottoman codes of law. These two codes, both of which carry the title "Kanunname-i Sultan Selim Han" [The Code of Law of Sultan Selim] and are listed under the numbers B1882 and A250, are among the Turkic manuscripts of the Asian Museum of Leningrad. In the book in question, Professor Tveritinova has published the facsimile of the code listed under B1882 together with the Russian translation of the text; in addition, in the notes to her book she gives the variants found in the code listed under A250.

The opinions which she offers concerning the origin and nature of the Ottoman codes of law and concerning the development of the "Ottoman feudal system" clearly show that, in her work, Professor Tveritinova has completely disregarded the literature of the last thirty years on this question. Further, it is more than disconcerting to find twelve errors in the Latin transcription of a thirteen line Turkish text from the code's introduction.

As to the question of whether or not these documents really belong to Selim I, the answer can be seen quite clearly from the headings. One should not forget however that later copies can be misleading; they can contain additions and changes. The copy-date of the manuscript numbered B1882 is 1564 (it is not *1 receb* 971, as Professor Tveritinova reads it, but *evāḫir-i receb* 971). Since throughout the manuscript the changes are indicated as marginal notes, the main text can be accepted as dating from Selim I's reign. Although no date is given on the A250 manuscript, valuable information is gained from a remark at the end. Here the copyist states that the original of the manuscript was given to Nişāncı Celāl-zāde, who indicated changes in articles at the margins of the pages, and he himself wrote them similarly on the margins of the pages. The fact that the copyist refers to Celāl-zāde as *hazretleri* clearly shows that at the time the copy was being made Celâl-zāde was still alive. And since we know that Celāl-zāde first became nişāncı in Suleyman's time, the date of this copy [A250] has to be sought between 1534 and 1567. Professor Tveritinova is indeed mistaken when she mentions Celāl-zāde as the author of the code.

We had the opportunity to compare the B1882 code with the Koyunoğlu manuscript which dates back to the time of Beyazid II and found that the two copies differ greatly; B1882 manuscript lacks certain sections (*e.g.*, sections relevant to the *reʿāyā'*, the *müsellem*s and the *yaya*s), while these sections are to be found in all copies from Suleyman's time. Some sections also appear out of order.

In the article above we tried to show that various codes of law from the reigns of Mehmed II, Beyazid II and Suleyman I are known to us and that all of them are versions of the same original, enlarged and modified with the times. At the same time, one must keep in mind that, among the Ottomans, laws and legal dispositions had to be validated by the new Sultan in order to become effective. Thus it was only natural that there should be a legal code dating from the time of Selim I, and Tveritinova's publication shows that such a legal code exists.

VIII

OTTOMAN POLICY AND ADMINISTRATION IN CYPRUS AFTER THE CONQUEST

In Cyprus, as in their earlier conquests, the Ottomans followed different policies towards the ruling class and the native population. They proclaimed that the war had been declared against the "Franks", but that the Ottomans did not look upon the Orthodox native population as their enemies. As early as in February 1570, the Sultan, in a firman directed to the Sanjak bey of İç-ili who reported currently to İstanbul about the situation in the island, ordered him "to do his utmost to win the hearts of the masses", pledged word that, in case the island is captured, the population shall in no way be molested, that any property they have owned for a long time, and their families shall suffer no attack, and demanded that the people should be informed about this solemn promise of his[1]. Ever since the dawn of Ottoman history, this policy of **istimâlet,** i. e. leniency aimed at winning the hearts of the peasants played a prominent part in the Ottoman expension.

The Ottoman command took care never to depart from this policy while the conquest was proceeding. One of the first regions to submit was the fortress of Kyrenia (Girne) and the surrounding villages[2]. The serdâr (commander-in-chief of the army) Lâlâ Mustafa Pasha gave strict orders that no harm be done to the people. There a captain having transgressed this order he had him severely punished, thus demonstrating that no tolerance would be shown in this respect[3].

---

(1) The document was published by Safvet in *Tarih-i Osmanî Encümeni Mecmuası* (hereafter TOEM), IV, 1181-82.

(2) Army Diary *(ruznâmche)*, Başvekâlet Archives, İstanbul, *Mühimme* collection, No. 8, in Safvet, p. 1191.

(3) The record concerning this incident (Army Diary, 5 Safer 978) is as follows: "Though the reaya around the fortress of Kyrenia (Girne, Kirine) had made obeisance and had been entirely subjected, and though orders to the effect that the reaya be left unmolested had been repeatedly issued, the above mentioned zaîm came on his vessel with the *Levends* (corsairs) and plundered a great number of villages under the authority of the fortrees of Kyrenia, and captured their population, in retaliation for the offense his zeâmet was taken from him and granted... to Mehmed, son of Bayezıd Bey."

Owing partly to the subjection of the Orthodox Church[4] to the Latins, partly to the severe conditions under which the serfs **(paroikoi, parici)** lived (see below), there prevailed among the peasants of the island a widespread discontent with the ruling class, a situation about which the Ottomans had been informed through their intelligence channels. Didaskalos who in 1562 made an attempt to stir up the islanders against the rule of Venice[5] kept secretly in touch with Iskender Pasha, the the Beylerbey of Anatolia[6]. According to a contemporary witness[7] "it was supposed that there were some fifty thousand serfs who would be ready to join the Turks".

When the Turkish army set foot on the island, the Venetians began to worry earnestly about the probability of an uprising of the Greeks. A movement against the Venetians was observed at Lefkara. In order to prevent it from spreading to the rest of the Island, the Venetians suddenly made a surprise attack and put some 400 men to the sword[8]. Let it be stated here that, when the Ottomans subsequently arrived, they meted out an especially favourable treatment to the people of this village and freed them from taxes for a certain period.

It is an established fact that the peasants were reluctant to fight on the side of their former masters against the Ottomans. The following statement by G. Diedo[9] reflects the Venetian disappointment: "The inhabitants, through inconsistency of temperament, or because the yoke of slavery imposed upon them by the Chypriot nobles made them flatter themselves that they might find better luck under a new master, even offered them provisions and gave them the fullest information as to the position of affairs and the condition of the island".

In spite of all, a number of villagers of the plain within the area of the military operations, had taken refuge in the mountainous region. Even before Nicosia was captured, the **Serdâr** sent letters about through his men, in order to inspire the **reaya** with confidence and practised **istimâlet.** These letters caused a great many persons from the reaya to come and make their obeisance[10]. Similarly, we are informed

(4) G. Hill, *A History of Cyprus,* III (London), p. 839-41.

(5) İbid., p. 840.

(6) İbid., p. 840.

(7) İbid., p. 842, note 2.

(8) İbid., p. 961-62.

(9) C. D. Cobham, *Excerpta Cypria,* Cambridge 1908, p. 92.

(10) The record in the Army Diary reads *verbatim* as follows: "The same having reached their destination with the letters aiming at *istimâlet* on the reaya in the Island of Cyprus (Kıbrus), Mustafa was granted three thousand akcha of promotion and Yusuf and Memo three thousand *akcha timar* each, as a reward for inducing large numbers of the *reaya* to come to make their obeisance."

that the Orthodox priests were sent for the same purpose[11]. When in 1572 a census of the population and revenues of the island was completed it was seen that, in the Masarea and Mazoto region, 76 villages did not harbour any reaya.

After the capture of Nikosia (8 Rebiülahir 978/9 September 1570) we see that the native people everywhere made their submission **en masse,** and that the Ottoman rule was normally organized in the Island[12].

It was a tradition with the Ottomans to appoint first of all a **Bey** and **Kadi** (Judge) for the territories which they intended to annex to the Empire. The Bey represented there the political and executive authority of the Sultan, the **Kadı** the Religious Law and the imperial regulations. In addition to these, a **Defterdâr** (imperial accountant) was appointed in the great centres to handle the revenues belonging to the Central Treasury of the Empire. Those three officials were the Ottoman government authorities in that place. As to the Beylerbey who exercised a general supervision over them he symbolized the unity of the administration.

The Ottoman government was especially eager to win the hearts of the islanders. We find it reflected in the firman of may 6, 1572 adressed to the Beylerbey, Kadı and Defterdar of Cyprus in the following terms[13]: "The Island of Cyprus has been captured by force; therefore the situation of the reaya somewhat deteriorated. So no violence should be done to them; they should be treated with justice. It is important both in the enforcement of the decisions of the Shari'a (Religious Law) and in the levying of state taxes, to regard and protect them, so that the country may thus revert to its former prosperous state. Thus I order that you must be careful in giving the reaya who are a trust from god to us, as much protection and mercy as you can, abstaining from such actions as may lead to their dispersion. It is my desire to ensure that everybody may attend to his daily work and concerns with a mind free from discomfort and anxiety, and that the Island may be restored to its former flourishing condition. Those responsible for scattering the reaya through oppressing them and imposing too heavy taxes on them, shall be chastized".

---

(11) Hill, III, 961-62.

(12) The fortress of Kyrenia made obeisance on the 18th of Cemâziyülâhir 978. A man by the name of Gaspro had acted as a go-between in this surrender. The Serdâr bestowed on him a pension of 10 akça per day (Army Diary). But the fortress commanders of Kyrenia actually submitted on the 5th of Safer 978. Piero, son of Jamarta, who has induced them to do so was rewarded with an exemption from the *Avâriz,* extraordinary levies (ibid).

(13) A. Refik, in *Edebiyat Fakültesi Mec.* V (1926), p. 71, document 47.

In the above lines we find expressed the century old principles of Ottoman rule: The sources of income of the State depend upon the prosperity of the country, and this, in turn, is made possible through the tax-paying population being ruled within the bounds of justice and law, and through the taxes being levied by the local authorities in conformity with the provisions of the law[14].

Until the time when he left the Island, its conquest having been completed, Mustafa Pasha, in his quality of vizir and **serdâr,** was entitled to take all kinds of measures, give orders and appoint officials in the Sultan's name. His decisions had been recorded in an official army diary. According to this diary which has been preserved in the Ottoman Archives[15], Mustafa Paşa, on the very day that Nikosia was captured, appointed immediately a Beylerbeyi (Muzaffer Pasha, the former Bey of the Sanjak of Avlonya) and a Kadı (Ekmel Efendi). About the same time, ten communal Kadis were also nominated. The Serdâr, wishing to complete the staff of the **Beylerbeylik** administration, instituted a **Defter Eminliği** and a **Timar Tezkereciliği** to deal with the timar affairs of the Beylerbeylik and appointed a **defterdâr** for the financial affairs.

He installed troops in Nikosia to ensure its protection. He farmed out the revenues of the Island in the name of the Ottoman treasury, but he freed the reaya from that year's jizye, capitation.

When Famagusta fell on the 1st of August 1571, the conquest of the Island was complete. The **Serdâr** Mustafa Pasha having made over the administration to the Beylerbey, left Cyprus, on the 24th of September, 1571[16].

The organization of a territory and the actual establishment there of the Ottoman rule was deemed complete only after the so-called **tahrîr,** i.e. the survey of population and sources of revenue was performed. In the **mufassal defter** (detailed register) based upon the **tahrîr,** all the taxable inhabitants in cities and villages were entered with their liabilities to taxes, and, if any, their immunities; similarly, during the execution of the survey, laws related to taxation and possession of land as well as the methods of levying taxes in the sanjak concerned were determined and inscribed in the beginning of the register. When once approved by

(14) For the sources of these principles of government *vide,* H. İnalcık, "Kutadgu Bilig'de Türk ve İran Siyaset Nazariye ve gelenekleri", in *Reşit Rahmeti Arat için,* Ankara 1966, pp. 259-271.

(15) Başvekâlet, Mühimme defterleri, No. 8. The book contains the orders issued by the Serdâr from the 10th of Zilhicce 977 to the 19th of Rebîülevvel 978.

(16) Hill, (III, 1035) prefers the sources giving the 20th of September as the date.

the Sultan, this register was resorted to in all controversial cases, assumed the character of a **statute** on which judgments of the Bey and the Kadi would be based.

On the 9th of October 1571 (19th of Jumada II, 979 AH.), shortly after the capture of Famagusta, a firman was sent to Sinan Pasha, the newly appointed Beylerbey of Cyprus, ordering a tahrîr of the Island[17].

What details Kyprianos reported about this tahrîr on the basis of Italian sources seems to be true[18]: "Mustafa now (after the conquest of Famagusta)" he says "returned to Nikosia, and ordered that a census should at once be made of the inhabitants remaining in Cyprus. In making this census of the villages and their inhabitants, he not only used the books and accounts of the Latin sovereigns, to discover how much revenue the Island yielded to the royal treasury... The **parici** and **perpiriarii,** who were slaves of the chiefs and upper classes, who could not own land, and whose veryselves and children were their master's property, never ceased to help the Turks, for they hoped under their yoke to find freedom and rest. They made known to the commission of enquiry and to the Pasha the revenues, estates, villages, and even in detail the families in each village and their houses."

In fact the Ottoman **tahrîr**[19] used to be carried out as follows: A commissoner **(emîn)** and a scribe **(kâtib)** were appointed, they proceeded to investigate the old records, to travel about the country and, assembling the notabilities, carry out some researches. They thus collected information about the heads of families, the extent of lands they possessed, the number of bachelors and widows. They found out how much of the different crops had been raised in the past three years and calculated the average annual income. They also ascertained the annual yield of such sources of revenue as customs, fisheries **(dalyan)**, salt-pans and the like.

Mehmed, who had been appointed **defterdâr** to the Island, was selected to be at the head of the commission charged with the **tahrîr,** and the **tezkere emîni** Halil was added to the commission as scribe. To ensure a satisfactory progress of the operation and to avoid any departures from strict justice, the Beylerbey was appointed as **nâzir**

---

(17) This firman was first published by A. Refik: "Official Documents, relating to the Cyprus and Tunis Campaigns", *Edebiyat Fakültesi Mecmuası,* V, 1-2 (1926), document 32. Sinan Pasha's nomination took place in September 1571 (vide H. Sahillioğlu, "Osmanlı İdaresinde Kıbrıs'ın ilk bütçesi" (First Cyprus Budget under Ottoman Rule), Belgeler IV. (1967), pp. 7).

(18) In *Excerpta Cypria,* p. 345.

(19) On the tahrîr vide H. İnalcık, "Ottoman Methods of Conquest", *Studia Islamica* II (1954), pp. 103-130.

(inspector) to the commission[20]. They completed their job on the 18th of October 1572 and submitted the **mufassal defter** (detailed register) to the Sultan for approval[21].

In the order on the **tahrîr** the sultan enjoined the Beylerbey to find out whether the population wished to remain under the pre-conquest statutes or prefers the Ottoman laws in force in the neighbouring Arab provinces or in some other parts of the Ottoman empire. The people of Cyprus, in order to free themselves from the feudal charges of the Frankish period, accepted readily the Ottoman law.

Thus the Ottomans applied a typical ottoman régime to Cyprus. The status of the reaya, their rights respecting landownership, the taxes imposed on them were all based on the same principles that were applied to the sanjaks in Rumelia and Anatolia in the 16th century[22].

Cyprus being a country that had been conquered by the use of force, the Islamic principles for such a land were applied to the land: All agricultural land in the villages passed under the state's proprietorship as mîrî (public) land. Actually, before the conquest, the land was owned partly by the State and partly by the Frank nobility. In 1562, there were 246 villages belonging to the State and styled **Real;** those belonging to the nobility and the Church numbered 567[23]. The peasants had no title to the land. The Ottoman Law, as in other reigons so also in Cyprus, allowed the peasant to possess the land he tilled, and to leave it to his male offspring as a heritage without any indemnity. The only due paid by the peasant to the State in this connexion was a lump sum payable at the beginning called **hakk-i karâr** or **tapu-resmi.** This sum, generally amounted to the yearly income derived from the land. In fact this was a régime of perpetual lease securing for the peasant the perpetual usufruct of the land. This change was so important that even the authors hostile to the Ottomans could not help pointing to the advantageous situation which the new régime brought for the peasant[24]. It must

(20) A. Refik, *ibid.,* document 28. There we find stated the following justification for this appointment: "For it is very important that the revenue belonging to the treasury be increased and that the situation of the reaya be determined in full justice."

(21) This register is now preserved in Ankara at the Directorate General of the Cadastral and Land survey, Section of Old Records, N. 506/64; *Defter-i Mufassal-i Kıbrus.*

(22) In the Cyprus Register *(Defter)* no detailed *kanunnâme* is added as in the registers of the other sanjaks. We find there verbatim, only the firman that we shall summarize. The provisions about market dues figure singly at the beginning of the register. On the typical Ottoman kanunnâme and its basic principles see "Adâletnâmeler", in *Belgeler,* II (1965), pp. 53-58.

(23) B. Sagredo in Mas Latrie, *Hist. de l'île de Chypre,* III, Paris 1855, 541.

(24) See Kyprianos, in Excerpta Cypria, p. 345.

be added that immediately after the conquest the land possession became subject of speculation in Cyprus as the abandoned lands were sold through the tax-farmers to anyone who paid the **hakk-i karâr**. Some military men and speculators bought such **mîrî** lands and demanded much higher prices for them when later on the reaya wanted to buy them. By a specific order the Sultan prohibited such a speculation and asked the Beylerbey and defterdar to interfere in such transactions and make the reaya to pay only the original purchase price for the land. He emphasized the point that "the prosperity of the country depended on the fact that the reaya settled and tilled the land. The authorities should act accordingly and not estrange the reaya on the Island[25]".

There were good reasons to believe in the sincerity of the Ottoman government in bettering the conditions on the Island and contenting the reaya. The measures adopted were, in the first place, considered as one of the conditions for the maintenance of the Ottoman rule in Cyprus, and secondly, they were necessary to ensure the prosperity of the Island and the development of its sources of income, so that it should cease to be a burden on the Ottoman treasury. There were some further reasons, specific to Cyprus, for such a policy: Before the invasion the peasant population in the central plain of the Island, had taken refuge in the mountainous region, so that the fields remained unsown and that scarcity and even famine broke out before the harvest of 1572[26]. The allied crusaders had destroyed the Ottoman fleet in 1571. It was feared that the crusaders might attack Cyprus in 1572. According to the information supplied by Calepio, who was then on the Island[27] a panic had broken out among the Turks in February 1572. Obviously, the policy pursued during the **tahrîr** and in the following year should be viewed also in the light of this situation.

Let us now proceed to a comparative study of the taxes imposed on the peasant under the Ottoman rule, and in the Frankish and Venetian periods.

The reforms to be carried out under the Ottoman law are stated in the firman[28] of October 1572 addressed to the **tahrîr emîni** (commissi-

(25) See the document in A. Refik, İbid., p. 75. The date is 1573. A revenue of 283,780 akcha was obtained by the sale of such houses, gardens and lands (see Sahillioğlu, 22).

(26) Kyprianos p. 345, 347. For the measures of the Ottoman government to remedy this situation see A. Refik, İbid., p. 56, 61, 63 and 67 document 40.

(27) In *Excerpta Cypria,* p. 162.

(28) This important firman has been set at the beginning of the detailed register (Directorate general of the Ankara Cadastral and Land survey, n. 506/64: Vide Ö. L. Barkan, in İktisat Fakültesi Mecmuası II-1 (1941), 46-47; Hill (IV 27-28) made use of it.

onar of the survey) Defterdar Mehmed. This document informs us that, before the Ottoman conquest, the peasant in Cyprus had to surrender one sixth of his crops in one region, one fifth, one fourth or even one third in another. The peasant group called **parikoz (parici)** before the conquest, used to perform two days a week forced labour for the feudal lord on whom they depended, and to surrender to him one third of their produce. Again before the conquest, each peasent used to pay a given annual amount as poll-tax. This might amount to 60, 80 or 90 akça[29] according to the personal situation of the taxpayer. In addition the peasant had to pay for himself, his sons and daughters a tax styled salt-tax amounting to five akcha, as well as several dues for his new born animals. Besides, he paid one akcha for every one of his sheep. The peasant of the region of Limason (Limasol) and Avdim had to surrender one third of the produce of his vinyard and, pay for every **dönüm**[30] of plot a due amounting to 1½ akcha.

Table I.

Synoptic Table of the Taxes abrogated or changed under the firman dated 980 Cemâziyülâhir/October 1572[31]

Taxes	Before the conquest (Akcha)	After the Conquest (Akcha)	
Poll-tax	60, 80, 90	60, 80, 100	only non-Muslim adults
Ispenje	—	30	only non-Muslim adults
Tithes	From 1/6 to 1/3	Maximum 1/5	Parikoz pay maximum in pre-Ottoman regime
Sheep-tax	1 Akcha for each sheep	1 akcha for each 2 sheep	
From new-born animals	for mules 60 akcha " colts 25 " " calves 5 " " lambs 1 "		abrogated by the Ottomans
Salt due	5 akcha		abrogated by the Ottomans
Vineyard due	Tithes and 1½ akcha for each **dönüm**	Tithes or 2 akcha for each **dönüm**	

(29) About these times one gold ducat or Ottoman piece of gold was worth 60 *akcha*. Ottoman silver coin.

(30) One *dönüm* is approximately 1000 sq.m.

(31) See above note 28.

The Cyprus peasant appears to have been subjected to three kinds of poll-taxes bearing different names prior to the Ottoman conquest.

A poll-tax paid by the majority of the population in Cyprus in the opening years of the Frankish period is mentioned. This tax amounted to 2, 6 or 16 Hyperper (**besant,** Byzantine gold) per head. As Peter I (1358-69) was in need of money **in consequence of war expenses,** he freed from this tax those who paid a lump sum of 2000 **hyperper.** Another poll-tax made its appearance in the time of James I. When in 1388, he had to pay a ransom exacted by the Genoese for his son, he imposed on rich and poor a temporary tax. The owners of property or income had to pay out 4 % of their fortune. As to the peasants, every one of them above the age of 15 had to pay a piece of gold **(hyperper)**[34]. This tax, which had been imposed owing to an extraordinary situation, though it had been introduced in the beginning as temporary, was subsequently repeated and, in the end, assumed a permanent character[35]. It is obvious that this tax too was imposed on the peasant as a poll-tax.

There was still another kind of poll-tax which the Cyprus population had to pay prior to the Ottoman conquest: It was styled **Stratiata.** As it was exacted per household, it should rather be called a hearth-tax. While the island of Cyprus was under Byzantine rule, a kind of guardian troops called **stratiotes** were sent to the island to protect its shores from Arab raids, and to maintain these soldiers, each peasant household was required to pay three gold hyperper, and each urban family one gold hyperper. This Byzantine tax which went by the name of **Stratiata,** lasted until the Ottoman period[36].

Jizye, although a capitation, was collected in Cyprus, as in certain regions of the Ottoman Empire, as a kind of hearth-tax[37]. Women, children those unable to work, i.e. the old and the cripped were exempted from it. The amount of Jizye has been determined for Cyprus as 100 from the wealthy, 80 from the medium status and 60 from the poor. However, as the jizye collected in the 1571-72 budget from 23000 heads of family totalled

(34) L. Makhairas, *Chronicle,* ed. Dawkins, Cambridge 1908, I, p. 141. Cf. *Chronique de Strambaldi* ed. Mas Latrie, Paris 1893, 161, F. Bustron (Mas Latrie, *Mélanges Historiques,* V, Paris 1886, p. 353) writes: "Ogni huomo et ogni femina per tutta l'isola dovesse pagar un bisante all'anno, e che togliela qual imposition montova ogni anno bisanti ottanta mila".

(35) The Ottomans, owing to extraordinary situations, used to exact from all their subjects, as a temporary measure, this kind of tax or service. It was styled *avâriz-i divâniye.* With the Ottomans also, in their period of decay, this tax assumed the character of a permanent tax in cash collected each year.

(36) See Dawkins' note in Makhairas, II, p. 9.

(37) See "Djizya", in *Encyl.* of *Islam,* new edition.

23220 gold pieces (1 393 213 akcha), it seems obvious that one piece of gold was due from each head of family[38].

As to ispenje[39] this tax which was introduced into the Ottoman tax system as early as the 14th century, seems to be a relic of the Byzantine tax system. In newly conquered regions, generally, ispenje used to be collected along with jizye. Ispenje is like jizye a capitation collected from peasants and town dwellers, from bachelors and married men, in short, from all adult males. It amounted in general to 25 akcha, but in Cyprus it had been fixed at 30 akcha (half a gold piece). Another tax connected with ispenje was **bîve** resmi, a due which was imposed on widows owning an independent income and was fixed at 6 akcha.

The most important tax imposed on the peasants is without doubt **a'shâr** (tithes). This is an Islamic tax collected in kind in a given ratio from every kind of crop[40]. By order of the Sultan it was fixed in Cyprus at one fifth for all the reaya alike. In the 1572 **tahrîr** register it is pointed out with each village that it amounted to one fifth **(khums)**[41]. But under the typical Ottoman Law the tithe, together with an additional tax called **salarlık** or **sâlâriyye** was fixed at one eighth in the Empire in general. We see that, towards 1570 the ratio one fifth was preferred[42]. Then to find the total volume of each crop, we have only to multiply by five the fraction surrendered[43].

(38) According to Sagredo (Mas Latrie, İbid, 562), jizye *(harâj)* was levied in this way: "le carach, qui était d'un sequin ou ducat par tête payé par tous les habitants de l'île, de l'âge de quinze ans jusqu'à soixante ans".

(39) On *ispenje* see H. İnalcık, "Osmanlılarda Raiyyet rüsûmu", Belleten No. 92, 602-608.

(40) See my "Adâletnâmeler", p. 72-75.

(41) However, Kyprianos (in *Excerpta Cypria,* p. 345), states that the tithe ratio varied from place to place and was one seventh here and one eighth there.

(42) Under the 1570 Georgia (Gürcistan) law the Christians must surrender one fifth. In 1570, when in Albania the *sanjak* of İskenderiye (Işkodra) was the subject of a new survey, it was ordered that "kharâj-i mukâseme" should be levied. The Sheyhülislâm Ebûssuûd efendi, in the famous *fetvâ* he made concerning the Ottoman land law, ruled that land belonging to Christians was to be regarded as subject to "kharâj" which involved the payment of one fifth. This fetvâ became the basis of subsequent Ottoman legislation on land. Evidently Cyprus was one of the first provinces where it was applied.

(43) In the register the quantities in *kîl* for cereals, in *qantâr* for cotton, in bunch for flax as well as the values in akcha are given. The prices were as follows.

Wheat	1 kîl (25.656 Kgr.)	12 akcha
Barley	1 " "	6 "
Vetch	1 " "	6 "
Olive	1 " "	11 "
Lentil	1 " "	13 "
Cotton	1 qantâr (56.443 Kgr.)	300 "
Flax	1 demed (bunch)	2 "

Prior to the Ottoman conquest, the serfs called parici **(paroikoi)** used to surrender one third of their crops to the feudal lord or to the King. On the other hand, the class of peasants called **lefteri** (eleutheroi) or **francomati** used to surrender one fifth, one seventh, one eighth or one tenth. The relative size of these two types of peasants at different times were as follows:

	Parici	Francomati	Total of the peasant population
The end of the 15th century (*Relatione*, Mas Latrie, III, 493)	47,185	77,066	124,251
1540 (F. Attar, M.L. III, 534)	70,050	95,000	165,050
1562 (B. Sagredo, M.L. III, 541)	83,653	47,503	131,156

This list shows that, towards the end of the Venetian period, the group surrendering one third was the overwhelming majority. In establishing the rule for all peasants indiscriminately to surrender one fifth of their crops, the Ottoman régime effected a considerable decrease in the total yield of the tithes.

As to the **tuz-hakkı** (salt-tax)[44] which was completely abolished by the Ottomans, it occurs in the Frankish period under the name of **mète du sel.** It caused a lot of abuses and the peasants bitterly complained of it, so much so that numerous peasants used to run away from the island because of it.

B. Sagredo notes that the salt-tax brought in anually 300 thousand gold pieces to the Venetian treasury[45]. He points out that this revenue, under Ottoman rule, fell to 8000 gold ducats. The 1571-72 Ottoman budget gives a revenue of only 1183 gold pieces from the salt works[46].

There have always been attempts to account for this sharp decrease in the salt revenue by a corresponding decrease in the production[47]. All

(44) Cyprus salt has been famous ever since antiquity, the white salt obtained from the salt-lake near Larnaka being in keen demand. Another centre of production was the salt-lake near Limassol. In the Frankish and Venetian periods the production and sale of salt was a state monopoly. The Ottomans maintained this position. The salt revenue constituting a special *mukataa* (lease), was managed by an *emîn* (commissioner) or *mültezim* (tax-farmer).

(45) Also estimated at 800 thousand or at 100 thousand (Hill, III, p. 814).

(46) Sahillioğlu, p. 21. About 1792 the British consul H. de Vezin reports that the Larnaka salt-works yielded 10.000 araba (1 *araba* = 1000 okka) and those of Limassol 15000 araba of salt. The Larnaka salt cost on the spot five and half *kurush* (piastre) an araba (in *Excerpta Cypria,* 271).

(47) The latest being Hill, III, 814.

travellers, relying on the information obtained from the local Greeks, insisted on the decrease in production due to Turkish neglect[48]. However the decrease of the revenue is in reality the result of the abolition of the **mète du sel** which was actually a complicated heavy tax.

The salt-tax called **mète du sel** was introduced by James I (1382-1398), who, having to pay the Genoese a ransom for his son, exacted from all the serfs and **the francomati,** as a kind of taille, one **besant** per head, forcing them in addition to purchase one measure of salt[49]. In this way he secured for himself an annual income of 80000 gold pieces. Besides, the forced labour connected with the extraction of salt and its transport to the stores went on[50]. It was possible to free oneself from the forced labour by paying a given tax. The Ottomans found the salt-tax to amount to 5 akcha per head (one twelfth of a gold ducat). There is no doubt about the fact that this was not one hyperper tax per head. The tax due must be tax paid to be freed from forced labour at the salt works. In 1490, just after the Venetian rule was being established over the Island, the peasants complained much about the **mète du sel,** clamouring for its abolition. They reported that, this tax being axacted even from girls and boys below the age of 15, a lot of peasants had run away from the Island. The Venetians could not renounce this huge source of revenue. They limited themselves to taking steps in view of checking abuses[51]. Thus the high amount given by Sagredo must be considered as the total, with the profit accruing from the salt monopoly and sales, of all the other dues[52].

It was a good policy on the part of the Ottoman government to abolish this odious tax.

Furthermore, the salt-tax, constituting a kind of extraordinary levy was felt to be incompatible with the Ottoman Law. In addition to that, the Ottomans collecting already **Jizye** and **ispenje,** must have considered the enforcement of another tax of one gold piece per head as an abuse.

Together with the abolition of the salt-tax went that of forced labour consisting in the obligation for the peasant to work for two or three

(48) For instance Cotovicus (in *Exc. Cypria,* 189); Della Valle (ibid., p. 212).

(49) Makhairas, ed. Dawkins, I, 609-615.

(50) Stocker, in 1519, saw 700 people at work in the salt-works (Hill, III, 814).

(51) Hill, III, 815.

(52) In 1482, I. van Ghistele (Hill, 814, note 72) points out that the salt extracted brought an income of 20000 ducats. In 1940, the two large salt lakes under state monopoly yielded annually a quantity of salt valued at 32000 pounds sterling. While still under Turkish rule and a short time before it was taken over by England, the yearly revenue amounted to 25000 pounds. Anyhow it is difficult to admit that, in the Venetian period, salt sales alone yielded 300000 pieces of gold.

days per week on the land of the feudal lord. This constituted another factor of the considerable decrease in the state revenue experienced in the Ottoman period.

There was probably no considerable difference between the Frankish feudal regime over the peasant class and the situation in the former Byzantine period. Under Byzantine rule the peasantry fell into two main categories: the **paroikoi** being attached to the land under the control of state or seigneur and the **eleutheroi** who were not attached to the land of anyone. This division was maintained under Frank rule[53] the former being styled **parici,** the latter **elevtere, eleftri** or, in Italian, **francomati.** The **parici** in Cyprus like the serf in Czar Stefan Dushan's Law, had to do forced labour for three days a week on the land of the owner, state or seigneur. As for the **eleutheroi** or **francomati** they were peasants free to move, and as a result, not subject to forced labour. There seems to have been little difference between the two categories. It seems that any **francomati** who settled on the land of a lord passed automatically into the parici category. We have seen above that towards the close of the Venetian period, the number of **parici** increased very considerably. In the Frankish period the **parici** were under the obligation to render a variety of corvées whether they lived on the king's lands, or on the fiefs of the Frankish nobility[54]. These obligations were defined in the documents concerning the emancipation of serfs as in this example: "(Nous) avons franchi et délivré Vasilis Thodoru tou Therianou, nostre serf dou tous liens de servage, **chevage, anguaires** dimois, apaut et de tout autre manière de drotures que serfs paient ou sont uzés ou accoustumés de faire ou paier"[55]. **Chevage** was a kind of

---

(53) The situation of the peasantry in the Byzantine Empire and its successor States in the Balkans, as investigated in particular by G. Ostrogorsky, must be kept in mind when studying the situation in Cyprus. Professor Ostrogorsky's researches on the *eleutheroi (Quelques Problèmes d'Histoire de la Paysannerie Byzantine,* Bruxelles 1956, sheds light on the real situation of the *paroikoi* and *eleutheroi.* In the Ottoman period, the reaya non-registered in relation to the state-owned *(mîrî)* lands were styled hâric-ez-defter (not on the register), and were nothing but the *eleutheroi* of the former period. The *hâric-ez-defter* members of the reaya, when they settled in one place, became attached to the land like the *yazılı* (registered) members of the reaya and were no longer allowed to leave the land and its owner unless they paid an indemnity.

(54) The fact that Guy de Lusignan, in distributing fiefs in Cyprus, adopted certain changes (Mas Latrie, I, pp. 43-44), is interesting. The problem of the influences in this respect of local institutions and customs going back to the Moslem or the Byzantine period has not been investigated.

(55) Mas Latrie, III, p. 269 (the document is dated 1468).

capitation which serfs had to pay[56]. **Anguaires** were various kinds of forced labour and especially services to be rendered to the lord on week days in connection with transportation on horse back or in carriages. **Apaut** or **apat** were some contributions arranged by mutual promise[57]. But the most important type of forced labour imposed on the **parikoz** was the obligation to work three days a week for the lord. A serf could free himself from these obligations by paying to the lord or to the king a rather considerable lump sum in money (e.g. in the above case 50 gold ducats), whereupon he would become an **elevtère**. The **francomati** payed reduced tithes as one seventh, one eighth or one tenth of their crops. If they worked for the lord they received wages[58]. The **parici,** owing to their difficult conditions, used to run away from their lands, and fled from the Island. The majority of the royal acts dated 1468-1469 that have come to us, deal with the flight, the recapture and the emancipating of serfs[59]. When Venice took over the Island, she did not effect any change in the social status of the **parici.** Signory became the owner both of the **real** lands, that had belonged to the king, and of the **parici.** During this change hopes were aroused among the **parici** and they showed some agitation. It is interesting to note that, by the same date, the Ottomans had achieved complete control of the Anatolian shores north of the Island, and that the first Ottoman landings and raids on the Karpas area had started.

In 1488 Nicolas le Huen reported this:"No man can leave it without permission, therefore at times, many of the dwellers in the land go to give themselves up to the Turks, so as to escape from the place and its government"[60].

Under the circumstances the Venetian government gave to the **captain** sent to the Island in 1489 the instruction that "every care was to be taken to prevent serfs being removed from the Island[61]."

---

(56) See Godefroy, *Dictionnaire de l'ancienne langue Française.*

(57) *Dimois* might be the same as the *dimos* or *deymus,* found in Syria. *Dimos* denotes in Syria a lump sum agreed upon beforehand, in the case of taxes payable in cash or kind (See R. Mantran et J. Sauvaget, *Réglements fiscaux Ottomans,* Paris 1951, p. 5)).

(58) F. Attar (about 1540) describes them as follows: "Di poi, in diversi tempi, essendo venuti altri habitatori per i casali, furono, a differentia de parici chiamati leufteri, cioè liberi, altri li chiamano francomati, alli quali non furono imposte salvo picciole angarie, nel numero di quali si connumerano quelli parici che per diverse vie sono stati liberati" (Mas Latrie, III, 520).

(59) These important documents were published by Mas Latrie (III, 89-307).

(60) Cobham, *Excerpta Cypria,* pp. 51-52.

(61) Hill, III, pp. 864-75, article 12.

The Ottoman pressure on Cyprus, which started in 1488 naturally encouraged the parici. It was known that the Ottomans abolished forced labour in the places they had conquered[62]. At last, the Venetian government felt the necessity to take decisive steps to give them satisfaction. Forced labour was reduced to two days, and, in some regions a small wage started being paid on the days that labour was done for the lord. Later on projects were prepared for the granting of their freedom to the parici in return for an indemnity. Bernardo Sagredo, who was sent to the Island in the capacity of **proveditor** in 1562, reported in warning that the land owners forced the peasants to labour for them gratis, that, in addition, they also kept them for long stretches of time in their estates in return for a small pay, and that the **parici** suffered **greatly from it**[63].

When the Ottomans declared war in **1570**, it is true that Venice decided to grant all **parici** their freedom in return for an indemnity, but it was too late[64].

It seems that, immediately after the capture of Nicosia, when the administration was being first organized, forced labour must have been declared **bid'at** (an unlawful innovation), for when, as early as in the year **1570**, the sources of revenue in the Island were officially listed, it was not admitted that, in return for "the forced labour **(ücretsiz hizmet)** performed by the reaya at the time of the Infidels" any compensation whatsoever should be collected: The tax-farmers, stating that they had farmed out all the revenues of the Island "on the basis established at the time of the Infidels", calculated for each individual of the reaya a payment of three akcha a day of forced labour and asked each to pay **200-300 akcha**[65].

---

(62) See H. İnalcık, "Adâletnâmeler", in *Belgeler,* vol. II, 53-55, 65.

(63) "Et il mio precessore gli obligo che debbano servire alli patroni delli loro casali giornate 36 l'anno, con pagamento de soldi 12, un paro de bovi senza spese, dalche è entrato un grandissimo odio, et quel che è peggio, sono alcuni di loro patroni che non li pagano, ma ben in loco di pagamento li mettono in ceppi et gli danno delle bastonate; et li giusdicenti non hanno autorità contra li feudatarii et gentilhuomini" (in Mas Latrie, III, 541). Under the Frankish feudal laws the serf who raised his hand against his lord, had his hand cut off (Makhairas, I, p. 25).

(64) Hill, III, 798-800.

(65) This method of indemnification was in force at the time of the Franks. The calculation of the Ottoman tax-farmers shows that the days for forced labour amounted to 67-100 days a year. Cf. note 63.

The conflict was put before Mustafa Paşa, who said that "the tax-farmers were not entitled to collect such taxes[66]".

As there were about 80,000 parikoz on the Island in 1562, the revenue thus sacrificed amounted to a minimum of 260,000 gold pieces[67].

In a firman dated October 1572 (Cemâziyülâhir 980 A.H.)[68] the Sultan declared forced labour abolished in the following terms: "The class known by the name of parikoz are reported to have formerly served their lords and knights on two days a week... Now I have shown great mercy to the reaya on the aforesaid Island and decided that the above mentioned class shall do one day service for me in the sugar mills, the fallow fields and other appropriate places, and the fifth part of their crops shall be collected in kind from them, as is done in the case of other members of the reaya".

This firman orders that forced labour be reduced to one day only and that it be resorted to only for the tasks connected with the Sultan i.e. the central treasury. But we learn that even this one day forced labour was never enforced, as no record occurs in the official documents mentioning it. Similarly the Christian travellers who visited the Island after the conquest fail to mention any such thing. On the other hand some of them emphasize the fact that the serfs were actually liberated from servitude when the Turks came[69]. Kyprianos reported as follows about the situation of the peasants after the conquest[70]: "Leave then was given to those people at a very small ransom to hold land, and cultivate it as their own, and without further charge to hand it down to their children, being bound only to pay so-called third of produce"[71].

So much for the consequences of the introduction of the Ottoman tax system. Now in order to see the actual situation we present in the following table as examples some typical villages as found in the register of 1572.

---

(66) See Sahillioğlu, p. 8.

(67) This important document has been published by Sahillioğlu (İbid., pp. 29-31).

(68) See above note 28.

(69) See S. Gerlach, *Tage-Buch,* Frankfurt-am-Main, 1764, p. 123 (quoted by Hill, p. 798, note 3).

(70) Excerpta Cypria, p. 345.

(71) Cf. Makhairas, I, 89-91.

Table II.

The names of the villages	Population: Household	Population: Bachelor	Population: Widow	Ispenje: Adult male	Ispenje: Total of the tax	Tithes: Wheat	Tithes: Barley	Tithes: Vetch	Tithes: Flax	Tithes: Cotton	Tithes: Fruits	Tithes: Olives	Dues: Bee hives	Dues: Cocoons	Dues: Garden produce	Dues: Sheep-tax	Dues: Pig-tax	Dues: Fines and other occasional dues	Dues: From properties without heirs etc.	Dues: Rural guardianship	Dues: Mills	Dues: Tavern	Total
Lurikina (Louroujina)	24	3	—	27	810	900	1050	—	—	—	975	55	10	—	—	20	40	95	75				4084
Damadya (Aay. Dhometios?)	3	—	—	3	90	360	162	—	20				12		10	10	5	12	9				696
Potamya (Potamia)	16	2	—	18	540	384	174	72	20	600	1100			15		55	30	43	37	18			3124
Sha	16	4	—	20	600	1800	450	18	—	—	175	495	—	—	—			63	47				3688
Aya Varvara	14	—	5	14	420+30	900	600	120	70	Lentil 91	—	550	—	—	—	15	25	45	25	25			2949
Ayo Sozomano (Aiyos Sozomenos)	16	—	—	16	480	1380	696	—			255	440	10	30		20	30	57	43				3513
Lakatamya	90	9	3	99	2970+18	5964	12900	30	750	3000	2750	8250		50		800	175	175	50	75	240	200	38598
Nisu	42	2	—	44	1320	4110	4500	270	60	600		715	78	Lentil 75	rent 2500	350	85	75	54	46	350	rent from garden 2680	17956
Pera	60	16	—	76	2280	3900	3490	105	20			1045			rent 1320	250	130	43	35	42	120	150	13082
Anaya	33	1	3	34	1020+18	1380	1500	330		450					rent 2350	55	57	52	35	46	350	rent 2000	9436

Table III.

(All figures are in akcha)

	Jizye	Total of all taxes	Percentage of the taxes in kind	Average tax burden per adult male	
Lurikina	1620	5704	54	210	
Damadya	180	876	65	287	
Potamya	1080	4204	55	236	
Şa	1200	4888	60	250	
Aya Varvara	840	3789	57	286	
Ayo Sozomano	960	4473	61	274	
Lakatamya	7920	46518	67	500	
Nisu	2640	20596	51	465	rents: 5180
Pera	4560	17642	45	220	rents: 1320
Anaya	2040	11476	36	374	rents: 4350

In general the taxes collected from villages under the Ottoman laws consist in 1. Capitation, 2. tithes, 3. dues for animals, beehives, orchards, mills, garden produce ect. 4. fines and occasional dues grouped under the names **bâdihavâ** or **niyâbet.** Naturally certain taxes such as mill and tavern dues or rent for public properties were levied from certain villages only. The special urban taxes, i.e. in the first place the market-dues and the rents obtained from sectors monopolized or controlled by the state do not exist in villages.

As will be seen from the comparison of the tables II. and III. the percentage of the taxes collected in kind was between 45 and 67. We find the same ratio in the most parts of the Ottoman Empire in the same period. Taxation in kind was preferred by the peasantry in the Ottoman Empire mainly because it relieved them from the obligation to convert their crops into cash which was difficult and disadvantageous especially for the villages too far away from big centers. In need of cash to pay their obligations of jizye and ispenje the peasants had often to borrow money from usurers.

That the percentage of the taxes to be paid in cash was higher than those in kind in the villages of Anaya and Pera is evidently due to the fact that the annual rents paid for the public domains by the villagers made up an important part of the revenue there (in Nisu 25, in Anaya 40 percent of the total revenue). Lakatamya could not be put in the same category because it produced in great quantities such valuable crops as cotton, olive and fruits subject to tithes. It is also to be observed that the tithes in grain made up the greater part of the revenues from tithes in the villages in general.

The second largest part of the tax revenue in the villages was capitation which consisted in jizye and ispenje. It made up one third of the total sum of the tax revenue. As to the tax burden per adult male in the villages the average was 250 akcha (around four gold ducats). It was twice as much in Lakatamya and Nisu because of the extra sources of revenue.

IX

LEPANTO IN THE OTTOMAN DOCUMENTS

THE following account of the Ottoman policy leading up to the battle of Lepanto and of its immediate effect on the Ottomans is based exclusively on documents from the Turkish archives.[1]

In Febraury, 1571 the Porte had intelligence from the Begs of Kilis (in Bosnia) and Delvina that the Venetians were assembling their forces near Korfu, and waiting for the Spanish fleet.[2] Further reports coming from various sources confirmed the news. The Beg of Morea reported that the Venetian fleet in Crete thirty vessels strong was badly in need of provisions and was planning to capture the merchant ships carrying provisions from Egypt and Syria to Istanbul.[3] The news about the Christian fleet caused great concern and excitement in Istanbul and the imperial Divan took drastic measures to meet the imminent danger. The Porte was primarily concerned with Christian attempts to break the Ottoman siege of Famagusta. The strategy to prevent such an intervention consisted of first sending reinforcements to the Ottoman commander-in-chief in Cyprus to

---

[1] The main collection of documents which I used for this paper is the *Mühimme defteri* (see for this series of documents, URIEL HEYD, *Ottoman Documents on Palestine, 1552-1615*, Oxford, 1960, XV-XVI) « Başvekâlet Arşivi », Istanbul, No. XVI. An important court chronicle in Persian, *Selîmnâme* by Lokman, (Topkapı Sarayı Library, R. 1537) is perhaps the most important narrative source of the event. Some documents from the *Mühimme* series are published by AHMED REFIK (*Kıbrıs Seferine ait Vesikalar; Tunus seferine ait Vesikalar*, in « Darülfünûn Edebiyat Fakültesi Mecmuası », Istanbul, 5 (1927), pp. 29-76); SAFVET, *Sıngın Donanma*, in « Tarih-i Osmanî Encümeni Mecmuası », II, p. 558 and by I. H. UZUNÇARŞILI, *Kıbrıs Fethi ile Lepanto (Inebahti) Muharebesi...*, « Türkiyat Mecmuası », 3 (1935).

[2] REFIK, *ibid.*, doc. 9.

[3] *Ibid.*, doc. 13.

complete the conquest of the Island, and then assembling all the Ottoman naval forces under one command to prevent the Christian fleet from coming to the aid of the besieged in Famagusta and of destroying the allied fleet. The Porte's decision to attack the Christian fleet was a fateful one which would determine the course of events henceforth.

For this purpose the following steps were taken: the Beg of Rhodes who was on the watch over the Venetian ships at Crete was immediately reinforced by twenty ships sent from Istanbul under Kaya Beg of Koca-ili in the middle of February. Şuluk Mehmed, Beg of Alexandria was appointed commander of all the forces to be assembled at Rhodes [4] with instructions to attack any Venetian ship attempting to infiltrate in the waters of Cyprus,[5] and to transport troops from Tripoli (in Syria) to Cyprus. Also a decision was taken to accelerate work at the imperial arsenal in Istanbul to complete the ships under construction. (Later on, after the defeat at Lepanto, it was said that the failure at this was one of the reasons for the defeat). Müezzin-zâde Ali Pasha, admiral of the Ottoman fleet, left for Istanbul with thirty galleys on March 21, and reached Cyprus the end of March. He was ordered to assemble all the forces in the Aegean and proceed to Cyprus. He brought to Cyprus soldiers (18 thousand according to Paruta), ammunition from Tripoli, and took part in the siege of Famagusta. In the meantime the Porte assigned the second vizir Pertev Pasha commander-in-chief of of all the naval forces sailing from Istanbul with the remaining ships, 124 in number, on May 4, 1571. He was to assemble all the forces under his command, and attack the allied fleet wherever he found it. The inspection showed that the total number of the oared ships – *çektiri* – was 227, of which 35 had slaves as oarsmen and the rest Muslim *kürekci*, oarsmen conscripted from the Ottoman provinces. Twenty ships were to be left in Cyprus to serve as guard and transportation. The Kapudan Pasha Müezzin-zâde was informed that the decision to attack the Christian fleet was final and strongly supported by all Muslims. In the words of the document: « When the news about the Infidels' intention to attack became known by everybody here the *ulema* and all the Muslim community found

---

4 *Ibid.*

5 Uzunçarşili, *ibid.*, doc. 25, by the end of January 22 galley entered the port of Famagusta.

it most proper and necessary to find and immediately attack the Infidels' fleet in order to save the honor of our religion and state, and to protect the Land of the Caliphate, and when the Muslims submitted their petition to the feet of my throne I found it good and incontestable. I remain unshakable in my decision ». This passage vividly reflects the fact that the Ottomans fully realized the gravity of the moment. The war for Cyprus thus entered a new phase with an intense holy war spirit on both sides. Now the Ottomans tried to mobilize all their resources for the fateful struggle. The Sultan appointed the third vizir Ahmed Pasha commander-in-chief of the land army which included 1500 Janissaries and about 1500 cavalry of the Porte with the provincial cavalry (timariote sipahis) under Hüseyin Pasha, beglerbegi of Rumelia. Ahmed left Istanbul on April 29, and soon reached Üsküp (Skoplje) to concentrate the troops.

Müezzin-zâde left Cyprus to join Pertev Pasha on May 9.[6] Hearing the news that the Venetian fleet at Crete was in a bad position because of the loss of its crew as a result of an epidemic and the unwillingness of the local population to serve, the Porte sent an order to Pertev Pasha, commander-in-chief of the naval forces, to attack the enemy in Crete, raid in the islands and fortresses in the area and assault the Venetian ships which had assembled at Corfu. If this proved successful, he was to attack the Venetian coastal fortresses and destroy the fortress of Parga. The land forces under the Begs of Joannina and Delvina were to cooperate with him in the last enterprise.[7]

In the Ottoman chronicles of Selânikî, Âlî, Lokman and Zeyrek the account of the naval operations is very brief. Zeyrek[8] tells us that the Ottoman forces made devastating raids in Crete, Cerigo (Çuha Adası), Zante (Zaklise), Cephalonia and Corfu, and took and destroyed the fortresses of Sopot (in Albania), Dulcigno (Ülkün), Antivari (Bar) and Budua. Uluč Ali, beglerbegi of Algeria had joined the fleet with his twenty galleys near Crete. We find further details in the contemporary court chronicle *Selîmnâme* by Lokman (Topkapı Sarayı Library, R. 1537) which was illustrated with fine miniatures. He describes how Ahmed Pasha arrived in Shkodër (Işkodra) and stormed Dulcigno in

---

[6] UZUNÇARŞILI, *ibid.*, doc. 31.
[7] REFIK, doc. 38.
[8] *Tarih-i Feth-i Kıbrıs*, Ms. Nationalbibliothek, Vienna.

cooperation with the naval forces under Pertev Pasha. The news of the capture of Dulcigno was received with great joy in the Ottoman capital, and Ahmed Pasha was rewarded for it by the Sultan. It is interesting to note however that during this operation many of the Ottoman combatants who had landed to fight deserted and never returned to their ships. Selânikî adds that many ships were thus left without soldiers.

When Ahmed and Pertev were about to move against Kotor they learned that the allied fleet had finally appeared in the Adriatic Sea but decided to retreat. Thereupon the Porte speculated that the enemy's intention was to strike Ottoman possessions on the Adriatic coasts; energetic measures were taken to prevent this. In July the information came form Avlona (Vlorë) that the Venetian fleet moved to Messina. In August several orders were sent out to the begs and cadis in Rumelia with a warning to be prepared against an enemy attack. The Beg of Küstendil was to guard the coast from Alessio (Lesh) down to Durazzo (Durrës) in Albania, and the cadis of Rumelia were ordered to supply provisions and materials whenever requested by the captain of the fleet from his winter quarters.The following order is of particular interest in showing the situation on the Ottoman side in September. It reads: « Order to Ali Pasha, admiral of the imperial fleet. In your letter of September 9,1571 you reported that my previous firman about your wintering together with the Beglerbegi of Algeria at the port of Kotor reached you at Lepanto (Inebahti), you indicated that in a letter Ali, one of the captains of Algeria who was sent to Messina to capture prisoners for intelligence wrote to you that the fleet of the infidels had entered the port of Taranda (Otranto), and captured a small vessel from their fleet. The captives informed him that Spain and Venice had fitted out all their ships including those at Crete and had decided to come to Corfu under the command of Don Juan, brother of the King of Spain in order to attack either the imperial fleet or a place on the coasts of our dominions. You add that the whole situation would be discussed at the war council and the best will be done for the things concerning our religion and state. All that you have reported was known to us. Moreover Mustafa, one of my Chavushes, brought the news which he heard from Bayezid, Beg of Delvina, that the fleet of the Infidels had already reached Corfu. Pertev Pasha, my commander-in-chief also reported to me the things which you wanted to submit to my knowledge. Now I order that after getting reliable news about the enemy, you attack the fleet of the Infidels fully trusting in God and his Prophet. As soon as my order arrives you are to go to Pertev Pasha and hold a council together with the Beglerbegi of Algeria, other beys, *zuamā* and sea captains acting all in perfect agreement and unity in accordance with what is found most suitable . . . If you think my imperial fleet should winter by God's will in those waters as I had considered in my previous order, you may make up your mind about staying in the port of Kotor or in another port after consulting with Pertev Pasha, and submit to me the measures you will take in order to be able to act in accordance with whatever my imperial command will be ».

We learn from an order to the Kapudan Pasha dated September 17, that when the Ottoman fleet set out for Avlona a squadron of five enemy galleys came to the strait of Kotor, but Kasim, Beg of Hersek (Herzegovina) repulsed them and took prisoners. He learned from them that the Christian fleet composed of 130 Spanish and 130 Venetian vessels was to lay siege to Nova (Castelnuovo). Thereupon an order dated September 25, was sent to the effect that the Kapudan Pasha together with the Beglerbegi of Algeria were to winter at Kotor with the imperial fleet of 230 vessels. The provisions for six months were to be provided for the navy and fortress of Nova. In addition Ahmed Pasha, commander of the land forces was ordered that the sipahis of Rumelia under Beglerbegi Hüseyin were to move quickly to wherever an enemy attack was expected. In order to guard Nova the Beg of Küstendil was sent. The Begs of Herzegovina and of Shkodër were to communicate with the commanders, and go into action in cooperation with them. On September 27 chavush Mustafa wrote from Delvina of the arrival of the Christian fleet near Corfu.

In September Ahmed Pasha arrived in Albania with the Beglerbegi of Rumelia to quell the Albanian rebels in Ohrida, and to reinforce the garrisons in the fortresses of Preveza, Patras, Delvina, Avlona and Durazzo with timariot sipahis. He assigned the Begs of Küstendil and Vidin to guard the Albanian coast, and inspected all the dangerous points in this region. Ozkur oglu Mahmud, apparently a member of the old Albanian family of Sguras, offered his services to guard the coasts with two thousand volunteers. Later on, Ahmed Pasha wrote to the Porte that the troops were in a bad situation as a result of rain and a dearth of provisions in Albania, and they insisted on returning home. Also the Begs guarding the coasts sent complaints about the scarcity of provisions claiming that it was impossible for them to stay in Albania through the winter. In an order dated October 10, that is to say three days after the battle of Lepanto, the Porte informed Ahmed Pasha that the Christian fleet was at Corfu and no Ottoman troops were to leave for their home provinces (the timariot sipahis as a rule served only during the campaign season, that is from Spring to Autumn), and that the exhausted troops in the ships were to be replaced by fresh ones from the land forces. He was to give the contingents urgently required by the navy, inspect the garrisons in the fortresses, and then go with all the forces under his command to a point near where the enemy attack was expected.

In early October the Porte received news that the Christian fleet under Don Juan included 130 galleys, 70 *fregate*, 28 *barche* and six *maone*. On October 19 still uninformed of the defeat at Lepanto, the Porte thought that the campaign season was over and sent permission for the land forces to return home with the warning that they should be ready for the expedition next Spring. All these facts support the view that the Porte did not seriously expect an enemy attack at that time, and that the battle came rather as a surprise. Âlî, a contemporary Ottoman chronicler, said: « The fleet cruised for a long time on the sea. No one appeared. The Ottomans believed that the Christians lacked the courage to meet them. The winter approached. The corsairs and Begs of the coastal provinces asked the Porte for permission to return home. Thus the army there disintegrated ». When it was learned that the enemy was on the way to attack the Ottoman fleet the Ottoman commanders hastily recruited crews for the ships from among the garrisons in the coastal fortresses and even from the local population.

There is no detailed Ottoman report available on the battle of Incirli Liman in the Bay of Lepanto. The report of Pertev Pasha, mentioned in a firman, has not yet been discovered in the Turkish archives. Chronicles give only a very brief account of it. The Sultan, then in Edirne (Adrianople), received news of the event by a special emissary of Uluč Ali Pasha on October 23 (according to Selânikî, a few days earlier). In a firman dated October 28 sent to Pertev Pasha only this was said about the event: « Now a battle can be won or lost. It was destined to happen this way according to God's will ». Actually overconfident after the fall of Famagusta (Magosa) (August 1, 1571) which thus completed the conquest of Cyprus and the capture of the Venetian fortresses of Dulcigno and Antivari in Albania during the summer, the Ottomans were shocked at the news. The Ottoman historian Âlî noted that since the creation of the world and Noah's construction of the first ship no such disaster had been recorded. Discussing the causes of the defeat the Ottoman chroniclers emphasize the unusually early departure of the fleet from Istanbul in the spring, the exhaustion of the crews as a result of a long period of operations on the sea, the desertion of the timariot sipahis from the ships, the unexpected attack of the Christian fleet at a time when the Ottomans believed the campaign had ended, the initial definite order from the Porte to meet the Christian navy and the Kapudan Pasha's insistence on complying with this directive, his disregard of Uluč Ali's tactics for battle, his rush into enemy lines while 40 or 50 of his ships were driven ashore and the desertion of many of his troops. But all the chroniclers end by saying that it was God's scheme to warn the Muslim believers of their sins.

The meeting of the Imperial Divan on the day following the arrival of the emissary demonstrate high spirit and confidence in restoring matters to a better course. The register of the Divan's[9] decisions contained a number of energetic measures after this meeting: an order to Kılıç (Uluč) Ali Pasha, beglerbegi of Algeria and now Kapudan Pasha, who had saved his 20 ships at Lepanto, to assemble all the scattered ships of the fleet and stay on guard in a line between Greece and Scio, another order to Ahmed Pasha, beglerbegi of Rumelia, to recruit and place soldiers in the fortresses on the coasts, to watch and repulse the enemy if they came ashore, to inspect the area of Preveza and then move to the Morea with all the forces assembled to meet any enemy attack there. The Morea was thought to be in great danger since the navy before the battle had taken aboard a great number of the soldiers from the fortresses and the Mainots were in rebellion.

The Sultan reproached the soldiers who had left their positions before the battle in these terms: « There has been no similar situation before. There is no excuse for saying that the terrain was rough while in spite of the winter the enemy was on

---

[9] *Mühimme*, No. XVI, p. 70 ff.

its way to destroy our country and their evils were mounting each day. That you give such excuses simply shows a lack of religious zeal and public spirit on your part ».

On October 24 new orders were sent to all the cadis on the coasts of the Mediterranean to place watchmen at dangerous points, to take the local populations up to heights difficult to reach, to complete or increase the garrisons in the fortresses. Special orders were dispatched to the wardens of the castles at the Straits, Rhodes and Modon to be armed and on the alert. All this showed that the Porte was seriously considering the possibility of an attack on the coasts and even on Istanbul itself. The newly conquered Cyprus was believed to be particularly vulnerable especially when the news about 42 Venetian ships moving towards Crete arrived. The Beblerbegi of Karaman and Begs of the four Anatolian provinces namely Içel, Tarsus, Alâiye and Teke, now all incorporated into the province of Kıbrıs (Cyprus), with all the forces under their command were ordered to pass immediately over to the Island. The captains of Paphos and Kyrenia were also ordered to return to Cyprus with their ships.

After receiving Ahmed Pasha, conqueror of Dulcigno, and Lala Mustafa, conqueror of Cyprus, with great ceremony into his presence the Sultan returned from Edirne to Istanbul on October 28. He had, Âlî says, a kind of melancholy after the news of « the defeated fleet » (*Sınghın Donanma*) reached him.

In the middle of November, the Kapudan Pasha informed the Sultan of his coming to Istanbul with the fleet. We know that Don Juan was already back at Messina on November 1. According to Selânikî, an eyewitness, Kılıç Ali arrived in Istanbul on December 19 with 32 ships, some of which were apparently those scattered after the defeat. As soon as he reached the capital he went to the imperial arsenal to oversee the building of the new fleet.

ECONOMY

X

The Ottoman Economic Mind and Aspects of the Ottoman Economy

I. THE RISE OF THE OTTOMAN COMMERCIAL CENTRES

It was a deliberate policy of the Ottoman government that was primarily responsible for the development of Bursa, Edirne (Adrianople) and Istanbul, successive Ottoman capitals between 1326 and 1402, 1402 and 1453 and from 1453 onwards, into major commercial and industrial centres. The measures which the Ottomans took to this end varied.

Following a very old tradition of Middle Eastern states, the Ottoman government must have believed that merchants and artisans were indispensable in creating and developing a new metropolis. It used every means to attract and settle them in the new capitals. By granting tax exemptions and immunities the imperial government encouraged them to come and settle or in a summary fashion forcibly exiled them to the capital.

After the conquest of Constantinople Mehmed II made every effort to convert the ruined city into a real metropolis, the seat of a universal empire, and in his policy of settlement he gave central importance to bringing into the city merchants and artisans. He was furious when in the fall of 1453 he learned that well-to-do people in Bursa did not comply with his order to come and settle in Istanbul. In 1475 after the conquest of Caffa a group of rich merchants were exiled and settled in Istanbul in a district where they numbered 267 families in 1477. With the same end in view he encouraged the Jews in Europe to migrate to his new capital and their number reached 1,647 families in 1477. When later under Bayezid II the Ottomans welcomed an exodus of Jews from Spain, Italy and Portugal who were settled in the main ports of the empire the idea was always that their commercial activities would bring prosperity to these ports. Jews made up an important part of the population of Istanbul in the sixteenth century (by 1535, 8,070 families) and turned Salonica into one of the most developed commercial and industrial centres of the empire. In 1554 the house of Nasi, the Ottoman Fuggers, came and settled in Istanbul under the special protection of Suleiman I. The method of forcible settlement was used by Selim I who drove to Istanbul about 1,500 merchants, artisans from Cairo and Tabriz.

In rebuilding the Ottoman cities and regenerating commerce and the economy, the construction of *ʿimarets*, each a complex of religious and commercial institutions, played a decisive part. Always established as a pious foundation, an *ʿimaret* consisted of religious and charitable institutions such as mosque, *medrese*, *mekteb*, hospice and hospital on the one hand and mercantile establishments such as *bedestan* (*bezzazistan*), caravanserail, *han*, covered bazaars, market places on the other. The latter group was designed to provide for the expenses of the former. As in classical Islamic cities, the bazaars and industries of an Ottoman city developed around the *bedestan*, which was a building serving as a stronghold in the centre of the city to store and guard the precious merchandise as well as the fortunes of the ordinary citizens. It was also employed as the city hall for important transactions and exchange. Many Ottoman towns owed their development into commercial centres to their having a *bedestan*. In the seventeenth century Evliya Çelebi divided the Ottoman cities into those with a *bedestan* and those without it. Similar complexes were also built on the important trade routes and later on gave rise to thriving cities.

Caravanserails, *hans* and *zaviyes* in the cities or on the routes completed the system, which was designed to facilitate the caravan trade and make the trade routes converge on the capital city. The interesting point was that the state took a keen interest in promoting it. In 1459 Mehmed the Conqueror convoked the high dignitaries to his presence and required them to build *ʿimaret*-cities wherever they liked in Istanbul. Thus the main districts of Turkish Istanbul came into being with their monumental religious institutions as well as bazaars and *hans*. On the other hand the *bedestan* and *ʿimaret* which Minnet-oğlu Mehmed Beğ built at the beginning of the fifteenth century at Tatar-Pazarcığı became the nucleus of the thriving city with the same name in Bulgaria. The *uc-beğis* like Minnet-oğlu were responsible for the building of several provincial towns. The state encouraged such foundations, especially by granting property rights on the lands which were to be made *waqf* for them. It should be noted that in most cases such land was *mawāt*, waste or abandoned land, and the founder of the *ʿimaret* undertook to bring it under cultivation. The usual procedure was as follows: the founder came to the Porte with a project, saying that if such and such lands with property rights were granted, he would revive them by settling there people who were sometimes the founder's slaves and by building dams and digging canals; and the revenues of the land were to be assigned as *waqf* for the upkeep of the *ʿimaret*. Thus such projects gave rise to commercial centres and to the creation of new farm lands and villages in the countryside. Incidentally, the letters of Rashīd al-Dīn give examples of such projects in Iran under the Ilkhānids. The idea goes back apparently to ancient Iran as reflected in *Siyāsatnāmes* and Ṭabarī's account of the Sassanian kings. The state's main concern was to extend the sources of revenue for the treasury.

Zaviyes of dervishes, with the obligation of sheltering travellers in the cities and on the routes, were established on the same principles and must be considered as part of the same system. In early Ottoman history they played a pioneering role in Turkish settlement in the newly-conquered lands, and many Turkish villages in western Anatolia and the Balkans came into being around *zaviyes*. On the original *waqf* lands granted by the Sultan, the dervishes themselves or their slaves provided labour to bring them into cultivation.

When in the late fifteenth and sixteenth centuries most of the *waqfs* of *zaviyes* lost their original function, they were returned to the state's ownership. These reforms caused widespread social and political reactions in the empire. But it is interesting to add that when Suleiman I wanted to bring back prosperity to the major trade route from Iran to Erzurum, it was found necessary to restore the *zaviyes* on this route.

To come back to the rise of commercial centres in the Ottoman empire, it can safely be said that the Ottomans tried to bring about a route system around their capital cities, and that many of their conquests were motivated by the desire to take control of certain trade routes.

II. THE OTTOMANS AND THE TRADE ROUTES

With the fall of the Mongol Ilkhānid empire in Iran in the early fourteenth century, and the rise of the Ottomans in western Anatolia, the political, and subsequently, the commercial centre of gravity gradually shifted to western Anatolia. Concomitantly there was a change in the pattern of commercial routes. Bursa, which until the end of the fourteenth century was both the political and commercial centre of the Ottoman domains that stretched from the Euphrates to the Danube, became the most important trading city of Anatolia. It was the hub of the Anatolian commercial network. The former emporia of western Anatolia, such as Palatia, Altoluogo (Ephesus) and Smyrna, had already fallen under Ottoman control in 1391, and were now linked to Bursa. Caravans arriving from Iran now reached these seaports by way of Bursa. Moreover, by extending his domains eastwards as far as Erzincan, through Amasya and Tokat, Bayezid I (1389–1403) took control of this caravan route. Iranian silk caravans began to penetrate overland as far as Bursa. In the fifteenth century the cities of Amasya and Tokat, located on this route, became the most important political, economic, and cultural centres in Anatolia after Bursa.

The Ottomans did not neglect the trade routes in the southerly direction. In 1391 Bayezid I incorporated into his domains Antalya and Alanya, the principal ports of entry in southern Anatolia for Indian and Arabian goods. The main overland route followed by this trade was the ancient Aleppo-Adana–Konya–Istanbul road that cut diagonally across Anatolia. Complete Ottoman hegemony over this route that connected Bursa with the southern countries was established in 1468 when the Ottomans put an end to the Karamanids.

Muslim traders could now come to Bursa from Iran and Arabia in complete security. In addition, European traders from Venice, Genoa and Florence operating from Istanbul and Galata, which had been the most important centres of the Levant trade, now found Bursa the closest market in which they could purchase eastern goods and sell European woollens. This situation must have been apparent quite early, for Ibn Baṭṭūṭa mentioned, around 1330, that Orhan was considered the richest of the Turcoman sultans in Anatolia, and as early as 1352 the Genoese had concluded a commercial agreement with the Ottomans. At the end of the fourteenth century Schildtberger compared Bursa's silk industry and trade to that of Damascus and Caffa. He noted that Iranian silk was sent from Bursa to Venice, and to Lucca, which was then the centre of the European silk industry.

Bursa's development stemmed primarily from the Iranian silk trade. The silk industry in Europe experienced a great expansion in the fifteenth century, and Bursa became the international market place for the raw material upon which that industry depended, the esteemed silk of Astarābād ('Strava' in Italian) and Gīlān in northern Iran. J. Maringhi, the representative in Bursa of the Medicis and other Florentine houses, noted in 1501 that every year numerous silk caravans arrived in Bursa from Iran. In his letters is reflected the anxiety with which the merchants awaited the arrival of those caravans, and the eagerness with which the goods were bought in sharp competition. The rewards were handsome, for in Italy each *fardello* (about 150 kgr.) fetched seventy to eighty ducats profit. About a thousand silk looms in Bursa consumed five *fardelli* of silk a day. The price of silk rose constantly, fifty *akça* in 1467, seventy in 1488, and eighty-two in 1494. An average caravan brought about two hundred *fardelli* of silk. The table below gives the value of customs receipts from silk in Bursa for various years:

Year	Gold Ducats
1487	120,000
1508	100,000
1512	130,000
1521	40,000
1523	50,000
1557	70,000

The sudden decline after 1512 is a result of the wars with Iran. Although an upward trend is discernible after the peace of 1555, the level is far below that of the fifteenth century.

Even after Istanbul became the capital of the empire, Bursa continued to flourish as a principal trade centre of the empire for another century. Her rival in the silk trade, Aleppo, had been of importance for a long time. The silk caravans from Iran would arrive at Aleppo by way of Erzurum, following the Euphrates valley, or more often along the Tabriz–Van–Bitlis–Diyarbekir–Birecik route. In 1516–17 the Ottomans assumed control of these routes and of the Aleppo market as well. As a result, all outlets for Iranian silk open to Europeans were now in Ottoman hands. Not content with control of the outlets, the Ottomans attempted in the sixteenth century to place the north Iranian centres of silk production, such as Shīrvān and Gīlān, directly under their own domination.

Iranian silk, however, was not the only item traded in Bursa. Musk, rhubarb and Chinese porcelain assumed an important place among the merchandise coming to Bursa from China and Central Asia. Iranian merchants sought to take back with them mainly European woollens, precious brocades and velvets, and especially gold and silver specie, since it was scarcer and had a higher value in Iran.

A description of the diagonal land route from Damascus to Bursa in 1432 has been left to us by the noted traveller Bertrandon de la Broquière. He had joined in Damascus a three thousand camel caravan of pilgrims and merchants returning from Mecca. The Turkish group in the caravan included many notable men and was placed by appointment of the sultan under a merchant of Bursa. De la Broquière reached Bursa after a journey of some fifty days. There he found Florentine as well as Genoese merchants from Pera who were interested in buying spices.

Goods in transit on this caravan route tended most often to be merchandise light in weight and expensive in price, such as spices, dyestuffs (indigo and gum lac), drugs, and textiles. This caravan trade was totally in the hands of Muslim merchants. Among them was Abū Bakr, a substantial merchant of Aleppo, who in 1500 had brought to Bursa a shipment of spices worth 4,000 gold ducats, and Mahmud Gavan of India who in the 1470's annually sent his commercial agents to Bursa with Indian merchandise. In 1481 some of his agents even passed over the Balkans to trade textiles and other goods.

About 1470 Benedetto Dei, a Florentine, was able to claim that his fellow citizens could provide in Bursa not only cotton and wax, but also spices. From the reports of Maringhi we know that spices were exported to Italy from Bursa, however small the quantity. In 1501 he wrote to his associate in Florence that he had consigned three sacks of pepper to him, and if he wanted, he could send more. As it turned out, however, the difference in price between Bursa and Florence was not large enough compared to the profits obtainable in the silk trade. Maringhi wrote in 1503 that the price of pepper might go up to twenty-seven gold ducats a *kantar* (about 56 kilos) in Pera if new supplies did not arrive. The official price in Edirne in 1501 was only eighteen gold ducats a *kantar*. Connected with this crisis, of course, was the fact that at this time the Portuguese had already circumnavigated Africa and had begun to transport spices by sea. Antwerp received its first shipment of spices over this new route in 1501.

Selman Reis' famous report of 1525 demonstrated how the Ottomans reacted to the threat. In his report he tried to emphasize how easy it was for the Ottomans to wipe out the small Portuguese garrisons from their fortified posts on the Indian Ocean in order to re-establish the traffic between India and the Red Sea and thus to restore the state's revenues accruing from the spice trade in Egypt. He suggested the necessity for the Ottoman government to extend its rule over the Yemen and Aden, which would give it complete control of Indian trade. He further added that these conquests would bring to the Ottoman treasury hundreds of thousands of gold pieces and jewels every year as tax revenue. The port of Aden, he said, was visited by fifty or sixty ships every year and the tax revenue of this trade amounted to 200,000 gold ducats a year. He further argued that Sawākin, the rival of Aden, and Jidda would yield a huge amount of revenue for the Ottoman treasury if the Ottomans established their control there. Interestingly enough all his arguments to persuade the Ottoman government to take action against the Portuguese related to profits for the treasury. This is not the place to discuss the Ottoman struggle against the Portuguese in the Indian Ocean. It is now an established fact that the spice trade through the Middle East continued to be as important as before all through the sixteenth century.

Contemporary Venetian observation on Suleiman's policy of making Istanbul the centre of the world spice trade needs comment. It was a fact that half of the spices reaching Cairo and Damascus were conveyed to the Turkish markets, especially to Bursa and Istanbul, and from these cities it was re-exported to the Balkans and to the northern frontiers via Akkerman, Kilia and Caffa. On the other hand when in 1562 the English negotiated with the Shah of Iran to establish a direct trade route through the Caucasus and Russia, the Ottoman diplomatic mission then in Qazvīn insinuated that the Ottoman government would consider it a sign of hostility. But none of these attitudes was actually translated into a well-defined policy on foreign trade or the economy of the empire which could be compared to what we find in the same period in the West. The benefits of the state treasury and the needs of the internal market seem to be the only concern of the Ottoman government. In the late sixteenth and early seventeenth centuries the deterioration of Ottoman finances and increase of various duties and exactions at the ports of arrival were among other causes of the rising prices of Indian goods and Persian silk in the Ottoman markets which made the

English and Dutch intensify their efforts to establish direct relations with India and Persia.

The wars with Persia in the sixteenth century seriously affected the silk trade and had profound repercussions on the economies and finances of the two countries. The first stage began with Selim I's imposition, as a weapon of war, of a commercial blockade. He intended to prevent the Persians from acquiring war materials, silver and iron, and, by forbidding the trade in silk, to reduce the Shah's income from dues, one of his main sources of revenue. But the blockade had no effect, since most merchants began using the routes through Aleppo and Iskenderun. Thereupon Selim I resorted to more violent measures. Arab, Persian and Turkish merchants with stocks of Persian goods had their goods confiscated. The silks and cloths of all Persians at Bursa were confiscated and listed, and the merchants themselves were transported to Rumeli and Istanbul in 1515. The import and sale of Persian silk was forbidden. Anyone proved to have sold silk was fined its value. When Suleiman I came to the throne he released the merchants and restored their goods or paid them compensation. Nevertheless the ban on the import of and trade in silk by Persian merchants was maintained for a time. This blockade had important effects: it increased state control of the sale and distribution of silk; the scarcity and high price of silk obliged many merchants and weavers to go out of business; instead of Persian and Turkish merchants, Armenians began to gain control of the trade; and finally the government encouraged the production of silk within the Ottoman empire. When the silk routes were reopened under Suleiman, the industry again became dependent on Persian silk, and there was a new expansion in the trade and manufacture of silk. Yet in this reign too, during the wars with Persia, the Ottoman government imposed restrictions on the movement of gold and silver currency into Persia: the consequent shortage of silk harmed the Bursa industry and led to a fall in the revenue derived from it. In the ensuing period of peace the silk trade flourished again, but in the long period of war from 1578 to 1639 silk became an important political weapon for each side. As early as 1579 the Ottoman revenue from the trade had been halved, and the Ottomans again imposed a strict control on the export of gold and silver. In 1586 the shortage of silk had left three-quarters of the looms of Bursa idle, and the quality of the fabrics produced had begun to decline. The peace of 1590 extended Ottoman sovereignty over the silk-producing regions of Ganja and Shīrvān north of the river Kura. In the following year the ruler of Gīlān, Aḥmad, attempted to exchange Persian for Ottoman protection. The restrictions on the export of gold and silver caused an acute shortage of currency in Persia. Before Shah ʿAbbās launched his counter-attack in 1603, he sought means (no doubt at the suggestion of the Sherley brothers) to export Persian silk direct to Europe, via the Indian Ocean, whereby the English would escape the need to pay customs in the

Ottoman empire and the Shah would deprive his enemy of a rich source of revenue. In 1610 he sent an embassy to Lisbon and exported 200 loads of silk by sea, hoping to prove that this route was cheaper. When the attempt to make an agreement with Spain failed, the Shah turned to England, and in 1617 Sir Thomas Roe opened negotiations with the Shah. Of the 3–4 million gold pieces which Persian silk cost annually, England undertook to pay two-thirds in goods and one-third in coin. In order to maintain control of it, the Shah made the silk trade a state monopoly and forbade the export of silk to Turkey. The Ottomans and Venice—the two states most affected—watched these developments with anxiety. In 1619 and 1622 consignments of silk were indeed sent to England by sea. After the Ottoman-Persian peace of 1618, Persian silk was again exported to Aleppo, Bursa and Foça. Shah ʿAbbās's policy was not followed by his successor, who abolished the state monopoly of silk, and the use of the Indian Ocean route did not develop as was expected mainly because England was reluctant to provide the gold and silver currency required for it. Nevertheless in 1633 the Venetians were concerned at learning that English merchants were buying large quantities of silk at Bandar ʿAbbās. In 1664 the French too were attempting to divert the Persian silk-trade through the Persian Gulf and Surat.

The Ottoman government often used the trade privileges which it granted as a political asset. The grain of western Anatolia, Thrace, Macedonia and Thessaly was vitally important for feeding Venice and the cities of Northern Italy. In his excellent study M. Silberschmidt demonstrated how Bayezid I (1389–1403) in his relations with Venice could influence Venetian diplomacy by regulating grain export. Showing himself generous by letting Venice export grain from his dominions, Mehmed II (1451–81) kept Venice unsuspecting about his intentions before the siege of Constantinople.

It can be said that the capitulations were often granted on political considerations rather than economic. It was true that the Ottomans could not do without European cloths, an indispensable luxury for the higher classes, English tin and steel, and especially bullion on which the finances of the empire relied. So I think there is some exaggeration in saying that the Ottoman empire was economically self-sufficient. But it was equally true that from the outset, when the Ottomans favoured the Genoese against the Venetians by granting the capitulations of 1352, down to those granted to England in 1581 and to Holland in 1612, the Ottomans believed that they were favouring and supporting the friendly nations against the hostile ones by giving them trade privileges. I think one should first consider changes in Ottoman political attitudes to understand the fluctuations in the trade of a particular western nation in the Levant. Also it must be added that the extension of the capitulations to the western nations was very beneficial for the Ottoman economy in the sixteenth century, for such a policy kept the Levant markets alive and enabled the Ottoman Empire to compete successfully with other routes for the trade in spices and silk. In the early seventeenth century it was argued in England that the Levant Company was more important than the East India Company. The English capitulations were granted just at the time when England renewed its attempts to set up a trade route through Russia, the Caucasus and Iran to Hormuz. The fact that the Ottoman market consumed a large amount of cloth made a great difference for the English who were trying to pay for oriental goods with as little bullion as possible. It was along the same line that Naʿīmā, the Ottoman chronicler of the early eighteenth century, wrote: 'People in this country must abstain from the use of luxury goods of the countries hostile to the Ottoman empire and thus keep currency and goods from flowing out. They must use as much as possible the products of native industries . . . One may argue that such a policy might result in a decrease in the customs revenues, but one must not forget that if foreign merchants spend the money they earn by selling their goods here to buy what they need of Ottoman products, the money remains within the country. Moreover duties are paid more than once on these transactions. The European merchants import woollen cloths and buy for export wool, mohair, alum, gallnuts, potash and other goods, and pay for them at Smyrna, Payas, Ṣaydā and Alexandria with shiploads of silver and gold. This money is spread over the country, especially in Ankara, Ṣaydā, Tripoli and the Lebanon. But the Muscovites sell us expensive furs but purchase nothing in the Ottoman dominions and keep the money for themselves. Also we spend so much for Indian goods but Indians purchase nothing here. As a matter of fact they have nothing to buy here. Consequently incalculable fortunes are amassed in India. The same can be said about the Yemen from which we import coffee.' It is interesting to note that Naʿīmā avoided mentioning among the goods exported to Europe wheat, cotton, textiles and hides the export of which in the traditional thinking of the Ottomans was not desirable as they were necessities for the internal market.

In peace as in war the Ottoman government forbade the export of certain goods. In the list were usually included cotton, wax, leather, hides, grain. The idea was to protect the domestic market and prevent scarcity and higher prices.

III. THE OTTOMAN GOVERNMENT AND THE GUILDS

The attitude of the Ottoman government towards the guilds and domestic commerce is of particular interest in understanding the Ottoman economic mind.

The Ottoman guild system (called *esnaf*, *hirfet* or *lonca*) was actually a continuation of the *akhī* organization with this difference that the independent and powerful position of the guilds in the thirteenth and fourteenth centuries weakened under the centralist system of government of the Ottomans.

Let us first have a glance at the internal organization of an Ottoman *hirfet:* the number of *ustas* (from *ustādh*, master-craftsman) was limited. They elected from among themselves a council of control known as 'the Six', *Altilar*, who were, in descending order, the *shaykh*, spiritual head, the *kâhya* (from *katkhudā*), the *yiğit-başı*, *işçi-başı* and two *ehl-i hibre*, experts. The local kadi would confirm the election and register the result in his official *sicil.* The Sultan's diploma was to be obtained for the *kâhya*, actual leader and representative of the *hirfet* as was the *akhī* in earlier times. The principal duties of this council were to ensure that regulations concerning the quality and prices of manufactured goods were enforced, to carry out the examinations for promotion from apprentice (*şagird*) to journeyman (*kalfa*, from *khalīfa*) and from journeyman to master, to issue licences (*icaze*), to investigate and settle disputes and malpractices in the guild, to represent the guild in dealings with the government, and most important of all to prevent competition and underhand practices in the employment of workmen and in the buying of stocks. In carrying out these duties the *kâhya*, usually acting as the principal officer, the *yiğit-başı*, and his assistant the *işçi-başı*, would investigate complaints and make a report to the *ehl-i hibre*, on the basis of which they made the final decision. The guild co-operated closely with the government, and if there was any resistance to the decision of 'the Six', the latter could call upon the local state officers to enforce it. The regulations of the guild were confirmed by the Sultan, so becoming an *ihtisab* law, and as such, their application became the responsibility of the kadi. The work-people were divided into three main groups: *kuls* (slaves), *şagirds* (apprentices) and *ecirs* (wage-earners). The masters sold their products at specified shops in the market and were not permitted to sell their goods elsewhere. When one branch of a *hirfet* expanded, its members could easily form themselves into a new *hirfet* but the Sultan's diploma for recognition was required.

The government's control of a guild was carried on through various agents such as the local kadi, the *muhtesib* and various *emins*, agents of the Sultan. In Istanbul in certain professions the *kâhyas* had first to obtain a high official's certificate to get the Sultan's diploma. For example, the chief architect at the Porte was authorized to give such certificates to *kâhyas* elected by the guild of architects. The government usually respected the decision of the guild. There are indeed many instances in which the guilds imposed their own choice instead of a *kâhya* favoured by the local authority.

The disputes in a guild or between guilds or malpractices and deviations from the rules often made the government interfere in the affairs of the guilds. Almost without exception the Ottoman government adopted the views of the guilds about new trends against the rules. In the thriving cities of Bursa and Istanbul masters working outside the guilds and cheaper production to meet growing demand for goods at popular prices appeared to be the two principal threats against the guild system. Usually the guild denounced them at the Porte as working without licence and producing defective goods in violation of the regulations. The government interfered in favour of the guild and tried to restore the old regulations apparently without great success. A firman reduced the number of looms weaving brocade from 318 to 100 in 1564 but a new inspection in 1577 found 268 looms still working. Measures were taken to prevent hoarding of raw material. A special market or hall was assigned for each major item such as wheat, butter, honey, cloth, silk, leather and it was brought, weighed, taxed and then distributed to the representatives of the *hirfets* there. For the necessities such as wheat and meat for the Istanbul market the government established a close supervision from the producer in the provinces down to the retailers in Istanbul in order to provide a regular and sufficient supply of these goods and eliminate speculators. For purchase on a large scale in the provinces the government appointed rich persons, sometimes without their consent. The strict regulation and close control of domestic trade and industry was dictated, as seen above, by the government's major concern to meet the needs of the population at normal prices. Under the Islamic *ḥisba* rules the community was to be protected from unjust practices in the market. Especially in a city like Istanbul where a shortage or abnormally high prices of basic goods might rouse the military and the common people against the government all this was of vital importance with far-reaching political implications. We have also seen above how concern over scarcity and high prices made the government forbid the export of certain goods and thus affected foreign trade. In general the export of goods was not something desirable. When not forbidden, goods for export were subject to customs duties as high as those for import.

Conclusion

The Ottoman economic mind was closely related to the basic concept of state and society in the Middle East. It professed that the ultimate goal of a state was consolidation and extension of the ruler's power and the only way to reach it was to get rich sources of revenues. This in turn depended on the conditions making the productive classes prosperous. So the essential function of the state was to keep in force these conditions.

The society is, in this philosophy of state, divided into the ruling class who are not engaged in production and consequently pay no taxes and the subjects who are engaged in production and pay taxes. The latter is subdivided into city-dwellers engaged in commerce and industry and peasants engaged in agriculture. In the Middle Eastern state the belief prevailed that the peace and prosperity of the state depended on keeping the members of each class in their own place. It was such a concept of state and society that was prevalent in the minds of the *kuttāb*, actual administrators in a Middle Eastern state formulating all the measures to be taken. It called for an economy and economic organization the ultimate aim of which was to increase the state revenues as much as possible without impairing the prosperity of the subjects and to keep the traditional organization of the society from alteration.

By developing commercial centres and routes, encouraging people to extend the area of cultivated land in the country and international trade through its dominions, the state performed basic economic functions in the empire. But in all this the financial and political interests of the state were always prevalent and the Ottoman administrator could never have realized within the political and social system in which he lived the principles of a capitalistic economy of the Modern Age; while Europe, equipped with the knowledge and organization of such a system, came to challenge the Middle Eastern empire of the Ottomans.

XI

BURSA AND THE COMMERCE OF THE LEVANT

I. Turkey's trade with Arabia and India, 1480-1500.

It is not an exaggeration to say that European historians of the Levant trade viewed it essentially from Venice or Genoa. They drew their evidence mainly from documents preserved in the archives of these cities. This evidence was bound to be often misleading, for the Venetians and Genoese showed little interest in internal developments in the Levant and viewed the measures taken by the Ottoman rulers only in terms of their effect upon the Levant trade. Thus it is not astonishing to find even in such a great scholar as W. Heyd the general judgements of decline and destruction of the Levant trade as a result of the Ottoman expansion [1]). Just as the assertions of decline for a whole period and region in European economy in later middle-ages have been subjected to revision and often modified [2]) under the light of the recent investigations, which have indicated that there were actually shifts of activities from one section to another rather than a general decline, so our own inquiries in the native sources concerning the commerce of the Levant are tending now to alter some of the widely held views since W. Heyd wrote his authoritative work.

There are indeed local sources for the history of the Levant trade. The Turkish archives contain some important collections concerning the conditions of the Levant trade for the last decades of the 15th

1) *Histoire du commerce du Levant au Moyen-âge*, transl. F. Raynaud, IIe réimpression, 2 vols. Leipzig 1936, pp. 258, 317, 349, 507.

2) See *Relazioni*, X. International Congress of Historical Sciences, vol. vi, Rome 1955, pp. 803-957.

century when world trade and economy was going through momentous changes [1]).

In this first article we shall deal with how Bursa, early capital of the Ottoman state, became a center of the trade between the Ottoman dominions and Syria and Egypt, and what effects this new situation had on the commerce of the Levant [2]).

Let us start by examining the table below which is based upon the material from the records of the *Qâḍîs* of Bursa.

1) The principal collections which we are going to use in this study are: I. The customs day-books called *müfredât* or *rûznâmče*. The day-books which were kept at the principal ports recorded day by day ships coming and going with the name and origin of the captain, the port of origin, merchants or agents aboard with their name and origin, the wares they brought specifying each item and its quantity and value and the duties levied. Precise tables and diagrams can be drawn up on the basis of this material to show at a given port and date the imports and exports, prices and the volume of trade. Unfortunately, of these books only a few are available now in the archives for the 15th and the early 16th centuries. The most important ones for our subject are the *rûznâmče* for the ports of Akkerman and Kilia covering the period between 1495 and 1515, in Başvekâlet Archives, Istanbul, Maliye, no. 6; the *rûznâmče* for the port of Kaffa for the years between 1484 and 1489, in the same archives, Kâmil Kepeci tasnifi, No. 5280; another *rûznâmče* for the Danubian ports from Tulča to Smederevo (Semendere) in which the books of Tulča and Yergögü (Giurgiu) of the years 1506 and 1514-1522 and of Smederovo of the year 1514 are noteworthy. The oldest available *rûznâmče* for the port of Antalya (Satalia, Adalia) in the Archives is dated 1560, Maliye no. 102. II. The *muqâṭa'ât* registers containing the accounts of the revenues which were farmed out make up a second category. They contain the customs duties revenues of various zones, customs regulations and other taxation. The most important single register of this type is a *defter-i muqâṭa'ât* covering almost the entire reign of Mehemmed II (1451-1481), in the Başvekâlet Archives, Maliye No. 7387 and 6222 and 176. III. The third important category of sources is composed of the books kept by the Qâḍîs who in their capacity as judge, notary public and supervisor of the state finances in their zone have left us a large collection of court decisions on commercial matters, contracts, certificates, notarial deeds, and deeds of the properties of the deceased. We are fortunate to have a rich collection of these books kept by the Kâḍî of Bursa of the last decades of the 15th century. They are now preserved at the Museum of Bursa, see for details *Belleten*, No. 44, p. 693, and, *İktisat Fakültesi Mecmuası*, vol. 15, No. 1-4, pp. 51-73. Some of the documents from these books are published in *Belleten*, No. 44, pp. 693-708, and, No. 93, pp. 45-96. This collection will be our main source in this study.

2) In the subsequent articles we shall deal with the trade with Persia especially the silk trade which made Bursa an international market for this stuff between Persia and Europe, the European cloth trade in Turkey and customs duties and prices will be also dealt with.

Merchants in Bursa from the Arab countries

Name and origin	goods	value (in akča)	sold to	bought from	date
Khodja Surûr, Aleppo	pepper, cloth of Yaman	33242	Dâvûd, Adrianople	—	1479
Khodja Zayn al-Dîn, Aleppo	pepper and clove	1070	Yaʿqûb, Jew in Bursa	—	1480
ʿAbd al-Wahhâb	pepper, clove and indigo	3900	Radjab b. Ismaʿîl, Aleppo	—	1480
Mohammed, Damaskus	raw silk	2100	—	Al-Ḥâdjdj Kemâl	1479
Khodja ʿAlî b. Fâḍil	gum lac and other goods from Yaman	16700	Yaʿqûb, Jew from Balat, Istanbul	—	1479 1479
ʿUmar b. Shayʾ Allâh	lynx furs, damask (*kemkhâ*)	12400	Khayr al-Dîn and Shams al-Dîn	—	1480
ʿAlî, from Bursa settled in Aleppo	damask (*kemkhâ*)	1000	—	Ḥadjdjî Mohammed, *kemkhâ* manufacturer	1480
ʿAlî, Damaskus, settled in Pera	saffron	2500	—	Ḥadjdjî Khalîl	1480
Khodja Moḥammed, Hamâ	mohair of Angora, satin	250 Ashrafî gold	—	Ḥadjdjî ʿAbdî, silk manufacturer in Bursa	1480
Ḥadjdjî Hasan	woollen cloth and cotton	3200	ʿAbd ʾAllâh, Mossul	—	1480
Khodja Ḥusayn	sable furs	?	—	Khodja Muḥyî al-Dîn.	1481
Khodja Muṣliḥ al-Dîn	pepper	17925	Mûsâ, Jew in Istanbul	—	1480
Khodja Shahâb al-Dîn, Damaskus	*aladja* [1]) cloth	2500	ʿAdjam Moḥammed, Bursa,	—	1481
Khodja Ibrâhîm b. Karam Allâh	pepper	527 Ashrafî gold	Dâvûd, Jew	—	1484

1) *Aladja* was any kind of cloth with stripes of different colours. In the 15th century documents we find *aladja* of Bursa, a kind of silk cloth, cotton textiles called *aladja* and *aladja* of India. For the import of Indian textiles see below p. 141.

Name and origin	goods	value (in akča)	sold to	bought from	date
Khodja Ḥusayn, Damaskus	sable furs	?	—	Khodja Muḥyî al-Dîn	1481
Ya'qûb, Aleppo	raw silk	3330	Ilyâs, velvet manufacturer in Bursa	—	1481
Ḥusayn, Andalusia	mohair	350	Meḥemmed	—	1501
Zayn al-Dîn, Aleppo	woollen cloth	1600	—	Khodja musliḥ al-Dîn	1500
Al-Hâdjdj Yûsuf, Aleppo	indigo, gum lac	9500	Mustafa, attar in Seferihisar	—	1501
Ḥadjdjî Abu Bakr, Aleppo	pepper (50 cantar), ginger (15 cantar) and other spices	200000	?	—	1500
Dja'far, Aleppo	pepper	22000	Ahmad, Aleppo	—	1500
Khodja Sandemur	corals	25000	—	Karagöz, Bursa	1500

Among the Arab merchants in Bursa in this period the example of Khodja Ṣadr al-Dîn b. 'Abd al-Raḥîm al-Shâmî is of a particular interest for us because of his wide-range activities. Here is a list showing the business he carried on in the years 1479-1480.

goods	price (in akča)	sold to	bought from	date
pepper, gum benzoine etc.	15000	Hamza b. 'Abd Allâh	—	May 1479
silk	1000	—	Mustafa	May 1479
damasks (*qemkhâ*), brocades (*kadîfa mudhahhab*, *munaqqasha*) of Bursa	3005	—	Mehemmed, Beglerbeg of Anatolia	Aug. 1479
Woollen cloth and mohair (*ṣûf*)	30000	—	Mehemmed, Beglerbeg of Anotolia	Aug. 1479
Damask of Bursa	4000	'Umar, Damaskus	—	Sept. 1479

goods	price (in akča)	sold to	bought from	date
Indigo, pepper, clove, and other spices	12900	Khodja Moḥammed, Aleppo	—	Sept. 1479
pepper, clove, indigo, gum benzoine etc.	52040	Dâvûd b. Ilyâs, Jew of Istanbul	—	Sept. 1479
gum lac	4500	Yûsuf b. ʿAbd Allâh, silk manufacturer in Bursa	—	April 1480
silk	960	Mehemmed	—	March 1480
mastic of Chios (133 cantar), European woollen cloths	11600	—	Ḥüsâm al-Dîn Čelebī	Oct. 1480

The most active of the Arab merchants in this period, Khodja Ṣadr al-Dîn of Damaskus, traded, as appears from our list, in spices and dyes imported from his native town as well as in Bursa silk cloths, European woollen cloths and Angora camelots (mohair). It is interesting to note that Bursa was then a market of gum mastic of Chios[1]) for the Arab merchants from Syria too. He sold spices in large quantities to the merchants of Bursa and Istanbul. Apparently he had settled in Bursa and engaged himself in the import as well as export trade. Among his customers we find Arab merchants such as ʿUmar of Damaskus who bought from him Bursa cloths which he himself had apparently bought

---

[1]) Chios, closely dependent on the Bursa market for its trade with the East and North in this period, exported a considerable part of its mastic to Bursa, a fact that is confirmed by the large scale sales of it there. The Island greatly benefited from its transit trade which enabled the merchants of the Western nations without commercial priviledges to trade with the Ottoman dominions. By 1450 there is a reference to English kersey cloths in Chios. The merchandise that the English got in exchange were silk, jewels, cotton, wines, mastic, Turkish carpets, camelots, rhubarb, pepper and other kinds of spices (see Ph. Argenti, *The Occupation of Chios*, Cambridge 1958, pp. 500-501). Cotton and camelots (mohair) were imported from Turkey. The great transit center of the Angora camelots in this period was Bursa. In his general tendency to show the Island as the main producer of its exports, and to minimize the exports of Turkish products, Argenti assumed that the trade of camelots depended on the production in Chios itself (p. 509). We have no indication of a Chian industry large enough to provide of the large scale export of camelots from the Island.

in Bursa. He must have been doing business with the Italians there too, since a Qâḍî deed showed that he had a credit of a large sum of 86000 akča on Alessio, son of Piero, a Florentine merchant, who died in Bursa in February 1479 [1]).

Most of the Arab merchants doing business in Bursa were from Damaskus and Aleppo. In our table 10 out of 28 Arab merchants were from Aleppo, 6 from Damaskus, one from Hamâ, one from Damiette and one from Andalusia. K͟hod͟ja Muṣliḥ al-Dîn of Bursa, mentioned in our table as selling a great quantity of pepper to a Jew named Mûsâ of Istanbul, is an example of the many other Ottoman merchants who were buying spices from the Arab merchants or importing it themselves from Mecca, Damaskus or Aleppo. Also it is not a coincidence that the merchants in our table buying spices and dyes in Bursa were in majority Jews of Istanbul. These were found in great numbers in the trade of spices, European cloths and silk, not only in Istanbul, but also in the ports of Akkerman, Kaffa, Giurgiu and Kilia as the customs registers show.

Our table contains only a small part of the Arab merchants mentioned in the records of the Qâḍî of Bursa in those years. We have listed the merchants considered most typical. The table indicates that the principle imports by them were spices, dyes (indigo, gum lac) and textiles (cloths of Yaman, *Alad͟ja*). It is a question whether the mohair sold by an Andalusian merchant was a product of Andalusia or of Turkey, for Turkey itself was producing and exporting mohair in great quantity. Trade in raw silk between Turkey and Arab countries must also have been limited since Turkey was getting it in great quantity directly from Iran. Syria was then producing a fine quality of cotton [2]), but Turkey was at the same period a great producer of cotton and met domestic needs sufficiently. As for the spices and dyes they appear to be regular imports in great quantity from Syria and Egypt. Under the Ottomans Bursa appears to have become a transit center of spices for Constantin-

---

1) See *Belleten*, No. 93, p. 72, document 8.

2) F. C. Lane, *Andrea Barbarigo*, 1418-1449, Baltimore 1944, p. 60-65, 101-113; B. Lewis, *Notes and documents from the Turkish Archives*, Jerusalem 1952, pp. 16-17.

ople (Istanbul), the Balkans and the Northern countries (Moldavia, Poland, Russia).

In 1432 Bertrandon de La Broquière, who came to Bursa in a caravan from Damaskus, tells us that part of the spices brought by the caravan was bought by the Genoese merchants from Pera [1]). About 1470 a Florentine, Benedetto Dei, was able to claim that his fellow citizens in Bursa could provide not only cotton, wax etc. but also spices, and that they would be in a more favourable position there than the Venetians in Alexandria, for while the latter had to pay cash for spices in Alexandria the former could barter their cloths for the oriental goods in Bursa [2]). A more precise indication of the importance of the spice trade in Bursa was that the revenue of the duties from the imported saffron, gum lac and pepper in Bursa amounted to 100.000 akča (over 2000 Venetian gold ducats) in 1487 [3]). This had been even higher (135.000 akča) before, and the decrease can be ascribed to the conflict between the Ottomans and the Mameluks after the accession of Bâyezîd II (1481-1512). As 2 akča per cantar [4]) was the usual duty on such goods the annual import of these three items together can be estimated as about 2500 tons (saffron was a product of Asia Minor and must have constituted the larger part of this total amount). It can also be noted that in 1500 Abû Bakr of Aleppo sold in Bursa at one time spices worth 200.000, that is over 4000 gold ducats.

From the reports of Maringhi, a Florentine agent in Pera, we know that even in 1501 spices were exported, however little, from Pera to Florence. In May 1501 he wrote to his associate in Florence (Ser Nicolo Michelozzi) that he had consigned three sacks of pepper to him

1) *Le Voyage d'Outremer de Bertrandon de La Broquière, premier tranchant et conseiller de Philippe Le Bon, Duc de Bourgogne*, publié et annoté par Ch. Schefer, Paris 1892, pp. 135, 137.

2) Heyd, II, pp. 349-50, 354.

3) H. Inalcīk, *Bursa, Belleten* No. 93, p. 56. The three items were listed together in the *defter*.

4) Cantar, kantar or *qintâr* is shown as equal to 40 *okka* (one *okka*-1,282 kgr.) in the customs registers of this period. In a *qanûnnâme* of 972 of H. one cantar was 44 *okka* (see *Belleten*, No. 60, p. 677, cf. W. Hinz, *Islamische Masse und Gewichte*, Leiden 1955, p. 27).

and if wanted he could send more. It turned out, however, that the differences in prices between Bursa and Florence were then not large enough to make as good a profit as in the silk trade. Maringhi thought that if sold at 24 ducats a cantar, their pepper would make a good profit[1].) We learn from his letters that other companies too were importing spices from Bursa[2]). Galilei and Co. had imported at 24 ducats (The official price of one cantar of pepper in Adrianople was 18 ducats at this date[3])). Maringhi asked Michelozzi to send back the unsold part of the pepper that he had consigned, and added: "In any case there is no bargain to be expected from the spices"[4]). Soon he learned that all the pepper he had sent was sold out, and he asked if any more was wanted. In 1503 he wrote[5]) that the price of pepper might go up to 27 ducats in Pera if new supplies did not arrive.

There is no doubt that for the sole reason of the transportation difficulties on the long overland route from Mecca to Bursa, the spice trade of Bursa with the West was never to be a flourishing one, and later on the decrease in prices in the European markets after the Portuguese discovery of the sea-route to India was, as it appears from Maringhi's letters, an additional factor to discourage this trade in Bursa and Pera. But, the Ottoman unifying policy and expansion in the Balkans and Anatolia followed by the replacement of the Italians by Ottoman subjects (Muslim or non-Muslim) in the spice trade with the Northern countries, kept the Bursa and Istanbul-Pera spice market alive. This

---

1) G. R. B. Richards, *Florentine Merchants in the age of Medicis*, Cambridge Mass., 1932, p. 108.

2) Idem, p. 108.

3) *Kanûnnâme-i Ihtisâb-i Edirne*, ed. Ö. L. Barkan, *Tarih Vesikaları Dergisi*, No. IX, p. 173. Here is a list of pepper prices in Turkey in this period according to the customs registers:

Adrianople	950	akča per cantar around 1502
Akkerman	1440-1800	akča per cantar around 1504
Kilia	2000-2400	akča per cantar around 1504
Tulča	1700	akča per cantar around 1506
Akkerman	1800	akča per cantar around 1515
Yergögü (Giurgiu)	1800	akča per cantar around 1525

4) Richards, *op. cit.* p. 117.

5) Ibid. p. 272.

market continued to be supplied with spices in the 16th century by the Syria-Bursa caravan route and the Bursa-Antalya-Alexandria sea-route on the one hand, and the Alexandria-Chios-Istanbul route on the other [1]).

The customs registers of Akkerman, Kaffa, Kilia (Kili) and Yergögü (Giurgiu) attest to an active trade with the northern countries in this period. From the reign of Mehemmed II (1451-1481) onwards not only were all kinds of manufactured goods and natural products of the Ottoman lands [2]) brought to these ports by the Ottoman merchants, Muslim, Jew, Greek, Armenian, but imported spices, dyes, sugar and European cloths were also brought by them [3]). Yergögü received about 30 cantar (1501 kgr.) pepper in eight months in 1506 and 43 cantar (2112 kgr.) in six months in 1515. It is also interesting to note that in Lwow (Lemberg), the center of the Levant trade in Poland, the Italians were replaced by Armenians, Greeks, and Jews coming from the Ottoman empire [3]), and Sučeava, in Moldavia on the trade-route from Kaffa and Akkerman to Lwow, seems to have expanded its Levantine trade during this period. When in 1455 Petru III

---

1) The view that the India-Arabia trade route was not completely cut off and Indian goods continued to arrive in Mecca and Cairo in the 16th century (Lybyer, Lane, Braudel) finds a strong confirmation in the Turkish sources (see *Belleten*, No. 60, pp. 661-676). Even in 1671 a report submitted to the Levant Company in France reads: „De sept à huit caravanes des Indes qui y (Aleppo) abordaient tous les ans et qui vont à Smyrne il n'y en vient à présent qu'une." (P. Masson, *Hist. du commerce français au Levant au 16e siècle*, I, p. 374).

2) The customs registers of these ports included such goods as silks of Bursa, damasks, brocades, satin, tafetta, raw silk, cotton goods from Adrianople and Salonica, woollen blankets, copper hardware, mohair of Angora and natural products such as dried raisins, nuts, rice, opium, soap, wines, alum. Among the shipowners are found such names as Yani of Trebizond, Dimitri, Ali Reîs, Bernardo of Chios, Yorgi of Trebizond, Nikefor of Crete, Kemal Reîs, Sava, Angelos, Manul, Uways of Istanbul, Toma b. Zano, and among the merchants Marko, Yusuf of Adrianople, Andrea of Pera, Avram of Istanbul, Musa the Jew, Hamza, Kirkor, Mahmud, Lefteri, ʿAbd Allâh of Bursa, Mihitar, Kosta, Trândafilos, Hadjdjî ʿAbdʾ Allâh, Timur, Mustafa of Karahisar, Shaʿbân the Jew, Yaʿqûb the Jew, Hamza of Bursa, Emre of Istanbul, Süleyman of Adrianople, Yehuda of Moldavia.

3) See L. Charewiczowa, *Handel Lwowa z Moldawja i Multanami w wiekach srednich*, in *Historyczny*, I, (1924), pp. 36-67.

Aaron recognised Mehemmed II as his suzerain by paying a yearly tribute of 2000 gold ducats, his subjects were granted freedom of trade in the Ottoman dominions, especially in Adrianople, Bursa, and Istanbul [1]). By becoming *kharâdj-guzârs*, people paying tribute, they also enjoyed a reduction in customs rates which seemed to offset the burden of the *kharâdj* paid [2]).

By the end of the 15th century Russian merchants appeared not only in Kaffa, Akkerman, Kilia and other Black Sea ports but also in Anatolia and Bursa. An order of the Sultan to the Qâdîs of Anatolia makes it clear that three Russian merchants, named Alexi, Gavril and Stepan, should be exempted from paying any *kharâdj* while they visited Anatolia on commercial purposes. At the Porte they declared: "Previously we had done business importing goods from Russia and had travelled freely in this country, but this time when coming from Bursa to Usküdar (Scutari)" the tax collector tried to subject them to taxation claiming that they were run away slaves [3]). The goods imported from Russia were enumerated in the customs registers as well as in the orders to the collectors of the customs duties [4]). These goods were furs, especially Russian foxes, sables, martens, fine leather (called *Bulgârî*), harnesses, woollen cloths (called *Trski* and *Chkmet*?), Russian linens, knives and other arms. It can be assumed that the Russian-Ottoman trade was quite extensive in this period and the first diplomatic relations between the two countries, established through the Khan of Crimea in 1492, had commercial as well as political (conflict with the Jagellons) motives [5]).

As for Ragusa (Dubrovnik) we can not emphasize here too much how

---

1) The text of this berât in F. Kraelitz, *Osmanische Urkunden in türkischer Sprache*, Wien 1922, p. 44.

2) J. Nistor, *Die auswärtigen Handelbeziehungen der Moldau*, Gotha 1911; see the important collection of documents: *Documente privind istoria Romîniei*, ed. M. Roller.

3) *The Qâdî deeds of Bursa*, The Bursa Museum, Şer'iye sicilleri, No. 18/17, v. 358 a.

4) For the registers see above p. 132 note 1.

5) B. Spuler, *Europäische Diplomaten in Constantinopel*, *Jahrbücher für Geschichte Osteuropas*, vol. I, No. 3, p. 425; H. Inalcık, *Yeni vesikalara göre Kırım Hanlığının Osmanlı tâbiliğine girmesi ve ahidnâme meselesi*, *Belleten* No. 30, pp. 185-229, F. Koneczny, *Sprawy z Mengli-Girejem*, Vilno 1928.

greatly the Ragusans expanded their trade in the Levant at the expense of the Italians by becoming a *kharâdj*-paying city to the Ottomans [1]).

Even at the present stage of research it is safe to say that with the conquest of Constantinople (Istanbul) and the unification of the Eastern empire by Mehemmed II, the commerce of the Levant achieved a significant internal development in favor of the native elements, and, in particular, the international trade route of Arabia-Bursa-Istanbul and the Black Sea ports experienced a renewed prosperity.

In this period not only the Ottoman and Arab merchants were active in this trade but also merchants were coming to Bursa and the Balkans directly from India to do business.

Maḥmûd Gâwân or Gîlânî, powerful vizier of the Bahmanî kingdom in India [2]), organised regular trade relations with Turkey by 1480. According to the records of the Qâḍîs of Bursa [3]) he sent three commercial agents to Bursa with cloths and other commodities (not specified in the document) in April 1479. In February 1481, a larger group of six agents who were his salaried men (*wakîls*) sent by him reached Bursa. From their usual headquarters in Bursa some of them passed over to Rumelia (the Balkans) to trade their goods, textiles and Indian goods. A statement in one of these documents makes it clear that they came via Arabia [4]). From a document dated 1548 [5]), apparently comprising the previous Mameluk practices, we learn that spices and cloths of India were arriving in Syria from Mecca or from Egypt by caravans similar to the one which B. de La Broquière joined in 1432. At Kisve near Damaskus, a customs duty of seven gold pieces and half a gold of *Mubâshiriyya* were collected per load of camel. If these goods were sold at the Damaskus market to the Western merchants the seller paid

---

1) Now see I. Božic, *Dubrovnik i Turska u XIV i XV veku*, Beograd 1952.
2) See Journal of the Asiatic Soc. of Bengal, I-2, 1935.
3) See the documents published in *Belleten*, No. 93, pp. 69, 75, 95.
4) Idem, p. 75.
5) Ö. L. Barkan, *Kanunlar*, I, Istanbul 1943, p. 221; its translation into French in R. Mantran-J. Sauvaget, *Règlements fiscaux ottomans, les provinces syriennes*, Paris 1951, pp. 8-9. For the practices under the Mameluks see, *Diplomatarium Veneto-Levantinum*, II, Venice 1899, pp. 325, 338.

a duty at the rate of 10 per cent and the buyer 9 per cent *ad valorem*. If this was between Muslims only a small duty of broker (*dellâliyye*) (1 per cent *ad valorem* on spices and dyes) was to have been paid. The Westerners paid other duties, a 2 per cent *ad valorem* and a duty of 7 1/3 per camel before they took their purchases to Beyrouth to ship. Thus, Muslims could take the Indian goods further to Bursa without being subject to the taxation that the Europeans had to pay in Damaskus.

The land-route from Aleppo to Bursa followed roughly the ancient diagonal route across Anatolia [1]). B. de La Broquière has left us a description of this route in 1432. As we have seen, in Damaskus he joined a caravan of pilgrims and merchants coming from Mecca with three thousand camels. The Turkish group in it included many notable men and was placed by appointment of the Sultan under a merchant of Bursa [2]). De La Broquière arrived in Bursa after a journey of about fifty days via Aleppo, Adana, Konya, Akshehir, Kara-hisar (Afyon) and Kütahya. At Akshehir he came across twenty five Arabs in a caravanserail, and in Bursa he found Florentine and Genoese merchants [3]). This land-route passed through Karamanid territory and was at the mercy of the Karamanid princes, irreconcilable rivals of the Ottomans. Certain passage duties were levied at the three mountain passes in the Taurus range. These duties were six Aleppo *akča* (at this time about 120 of this silver coin were worth one Venetian ducat) for a camel load, four for a horse and two for a donkey load [4]). The Ottomans first secured control of the Bursa-Antalya-Alexandria sea-route in 1390 and only after a long struggle between 1464-1474 did they eventually occupy the whole territory of the Karamanids [5]). They then abolished all the passage duties (Kosunlu-*badj* and Kara-isalu *badj*,

---

1) See Fr. Taeschner, *Das anatolische Wegennetz nach osmanischer Quelle*, 2 vols. Leipzig 1924-26.

2) "*Hoyarbara, quy estoit chief de la caravane et des plus grands de la cité de Brousse*" (B. de La Broquière, p. 59).

3) The activity of the Italian merchants in Bursa according to the records of the Qâḍîs of Bursa will be dealt in a separate article.

4) Barkan, *Kanunlar*, p. 201.

5) See H. Inalcık, *Mehmed II.*, *Islâm Ansiklopedisi*, cüz 75 (1956), pp. 506-535.

obviously named for the two Türkmen tribes) except for one at the famous Gülek pass [1]).

The sea-route we have mentioned, it appears, was not less important for the Bursa-Arabia trade than the land-route, especially before the Ottoman conquest of the Karamanid territory.

Already under the Seldjukids in the 13th century, Antalya (Satalia, Adalia) was a very important transit center for the export of the products of Anatolia and the import of merchandise from Egypt and Syria, as well as from Europe [2]). From an incident we learn that in 1289 an Anconian ship was carrying sugar, linen and pepper from Alexandria to Alâiye (Alanya-Candelore), a port near Antalya [3]). Ibn Batûta, who came from Lâdhikiya (Lazkiye), a Syrian port, to Alâiye and thence passed to Antalya, described it as "one of the best cities of the world" [4]) and Malipiero toward 1470 wrote that it was the greatest spice market for Asia Minor [5]). Antalya, and the area where the main routes leading to Bursa lay, belonged to the Hamîd dynasty until the Ottomans invaded this region in the years 1381 and 1390. The century-long struggle between the Ottomans and the Karamanids for the control of this area seems to have been determined by its economic importance. The Ottomans did everything to ensure this direct route from Bursa to Egypt and Syria which were under the Mameluks with whom commercial and political relations were considered very important by the Ottomans [6]). This direct sea route was also much shorter than the land

---

1) According to the Kânûnnâme of Sis dated 1519 (Barkan, *Kanunlar*, p. 201).

2) See W. Heyd, I, p. 548; S. Lloyd and D. Storm Rice, *Alanya* (*Ala'iyye*), London 1958. I. H. Konyali, *Alanya*, Istanbul 1946.

3) W. Heyd, I, 547.

4) *Voyages d'Ibn Batutah*, ed. C. Defrémery and B. R. Sanguinetti, II (Paris 1877), p. 258.

5) *Annali Veneti*, I, p. 74 (mentioned by Heyd, II, 356).

6) Facing the constant Karamanid threat at their rear the Ottomans, nevertheless, insisted upon getting control of Akshehir, Begshehri, Seydishehri, Isparta region, and Bâyezîd I (1389-1402) as well as Mehemmed II endeavoured persistently to fix a border line at the Čarshanba river which was to ensure, on its west, the Bursa-Antalya route (see my *Fatih Devri*, I, Ankara 1954, pp. 36-37; and *Mehmed* II, *Isl. Ansiklopedisi*, pp. 523-527).

route for it took only one week or so from Alexandria to Antalya [1]), and while light precious stuff could be taken by the land-route it was necessary to use the sea-route for the bulky freight such as lumber, pitch and iron exported from Anatolia. But there too there were some obstacles. Rhodes and Cyprus were in Christian hands and the piratical activities of the Catalans and others who often found shelter in these islands, constituted a real danger to the sea communications of the Muslims in the East Mediterranean [2]). Along with other causes (the threat of the Timurids and, then, Uzun Hasan) this situation accounts for the long friendly relations between the Ottomans and the Mameluks until their interests came to an acute clash in Central and Southern Anatolia by 1464 [3]). When the Mameluks attempted at the conquest of Cyprus in 1426 and the Ottomans pressured the Knights of Rhodes in 1454, relations were strengthened between Cairo and the Porte. By 1430 when the Ottomans were at war against the Venetians the Mameluk-Venetian relations came to the breaking point [4]). Venice, the Karamanids and the kingdom of Cyprus were then preparing an alliance [5]). A similar alignment was to be seen later in the years 1471-1473 when Venice and Uzun Hasan, the powerful ruler of Iran and Eastern Anatolia, made an alliance against the Ottomans and Uzun Hasan sent letters to the king of Cyprus and the Knights of Rhodes exhorting them to cooperate with the army he was to send under the Karamanid princes [6]). Upon the sack and burning down of the outer parts of Antalya by a strong Christian fleet under the Venetians in 1472, the

1) See *Fatih Devri*, I, p. 65. Shams al-Dîn Djazarî used the sea-route fleeing from Egypt to the Ottoman territory in the time of Bâyezîd I. His voyage from Alexandria to Antalya took only three and a half days.The Egyptian ambassadors to the Ottoman court in the same period usually took the same route (see Al-ʿAynî, *ʿIkd al-Djumân*, the events of 799 of H.)

2) For the Catalans now see N. Coll y Julia, *El corso catalan en relacion con el commercio en el Proximo Oriente, en Flandes y el Mediterraneo*, Estudios de His. Moderna, Barcelona 1955.

3) See *Mehmed II*, *Isl. Ansikl.*, cüz 75, p. 524-525.

4) N. Iorga, *Notes et Extraits*, vol. II, p. 519-521.

5) Idem, pp. 501-503.

6) Original copies of these letters were captured and preserved in the Ottoman archives (Tokapı Sarayı Müzesi Arşivi, No. 3127/2, 8334, 9662).

besieged threatened to make reprisals on the Venetian merchants settled in Syria, that is, in the Mameluk territory. It is also interesting to note that the quantities of spices found then at Antalya made a great impression on its pillagers [1]). It was apparently to protect the Ottoman merchants against the Christian pirates that the state-owned ships were hired to the Muslim merchants there [2]). Mehemmed II made a major effort in 1480 to conquer Rhodes from the Knights "to put an end to their attacks on the Muslim ships and coasts" [3]). The Ottomans succeded in taking the Island only in 1522, five years after the conquest of Syria and Egypt. Thus the Ottomans secured complete control of the direct line between Alexandria and Istanbul which seems, in the long run, to have adversely affected the activity of the old Antalya-Bursa route.

Turkish merchants, especially from Bursa, were actively engaged in the import and export trade with the Arab countries using the land as well as sea routes. One of these merchants, Khayr al-Dîn had his will recorded in the book of the Qâḍî of Bursa which contains interesting details for our subject. It reads: "He said: between Hadjdjî Koçi, a slave freed by Khodja Mehemmed [4]) and myself there was an association with a capital at the amount of 545.500 akča the half of which belonged to me and the other half to aforesaid Khodja Mehemmed. From the aforesaid amount lumber, wood, and pitch worth 105.000 akča has been taken by my son Yûsuf and the aforesaid Khodja Mehemmed's son Ibrâhîm from Antalya to Alexandria, also Yûsuf and Hasan, slaves of the aforesaid Mehemmed, have gone overland to Egypt taking 123.000 akča worth of Bursa cloths and saffron, also 112500 akča worth of iron, wood and lumber were sent (to Egypt) with the Sultan's ships; these were sent by my son Yûsuf; also 12000 akča worth of leather were sent by me to my sons in Egypt via the

1) See W. Heyd, II, p. 355; Zinkeisen, GOR, II, p. 404 note 2.
2) *Belleten*, No. 44, p. 701, document 12.
3) Sa'd al-Dîn, *Tâdj al-Tawârîkh*, I, 572.
4) For the important place of slaves and freed slaves in the industrial and commercial life in Bursa see, H. Inalcık, 15. *asır Türkiye iktisadî ve içtimaî tarihi kaynakları*, *Iktisat Fakültesi Mecmuası*, Istanbul, vol. 15, No. 1-4, pp. 58-59.

Antalya port with a man named Seydî Alî, and a slave of the aforesaid Khodja Mehemmed named Süleyman took sables, lynx furs and Bursa cloths worth 125000 akčas, and also they (Khayr al-Dîn and Khodja Mehemmed) declared that 75 Ashrafî flori were due to them by a person in Egypt named Wazzânî Shahâb al-Dîn . . ." [1])

The capital invested in this enterprise, about 11000 gold ducats, was a sizeable one for the period [2]). The goods exported to Egypt were mostly products of Turkey: lumber, pitch, Bursa cloths, sables and lynx furs. But among the goods in their joint possession mention is also made of 11.400 Wallachian knives imported from Wallachia, soap and ginger (*Zancabîl Hirbânî*) imported from Arabia. Khayr al-Dîn stated in the same document that he had sold 22.000 akča worth of soap to several people in Antalya. A regulation of the customs duties of Antalya dated 1477 [3]) shows that cloths, raw silk, camelots (mohair), iron spades and the like, wood and lumber were the most important items of export and that spices, sugar, indigo and other dyes were the leading imports. In a detailed day-book of the Antalya customs dated 1560 [4]) we find imports and exports specified in more detail. They included lumber, iron, carpets, rugs, leather and hides, opium, slaves (white), Wallachian knives, dried fruits, pitch, a kind of light cotton textile called *bugasi*, lynx furs, London cloths (*čûka-i Londra*) as principal exports, and black slaves, rice, pepper, linen, sugar, dyes, and a cloth called *aladja* as imports. From Tripoli of Syria soap, cotton and olive oil were shipped to Antalya. Again, in this document slaves, rice, linen, and sugar come first in importance as imports and wood, leather, carpets, opium, slaves, iron, and woollen cloths as exports. Export of lumber to Egypt from Asia Minor had always been important [5]), and under the

1) For the full text see *Belleten*, No. 93, pp. 91-93.

2) For a comparison see A. Barbaro's capital (about 15000 ducats) in F. Lane, *op. cit.* p. 32.

3) Başvekâlet Archives, Maliye, No. 7387.

4) Başvekâlet Archives, Maliye, No. 102.

5) References to the import of wood from Asia Minor to Egypt in the Arabic sources (Ibn Tagribirdi, Ibn Iyâs) are abundant. I am indebted to Dr. Ayalon who drew my attention to them. One of the earliest references to it is quoted by P. Wittek, *Das Fürstentum Mentesche*, *Istanbuler Mitteilungen*, 2, Istanbul 1934 p. 2.

Ottomans it continued on a large scale. According to the official records the customs duties levied on wood, lumber, and pitch exported from Antalya in 1477 amounted to 150.000 akča (about 3000 gold ducats) and to 50.000 akča at Alâiye [1]). The export trade of lumber was put under state monopoly and farmed out to private individuals [2]). A regulation of 1477 [3]) provided that the undertaker of this monoply was to buy a piece of lumber from the workers for three akča and to sell it for seven, a cantar (51, 280 kgr.) of pitch was to be bought for 60 akča and sold for 120 [4]). (These workers were customarily only Türkmen nomads living on the Taurus mountains who, because of their occupation, were called *Tahtadjı*, that is lumbermen and until recently a large group of nomads there bore this appellation). Heavy goods such as wood, lumber, pitch, iron, and leather were transported by ships from Antalya to Alexandria and as we have pointed out the Sultan's ships were hired [5]) for this purpose.

As another positive proof of the expanding Ottoman-Mameluk trade in this period we can mention the fact that the Egyptian gold coin called *Ashrafî* was then widely used [6]) in the Ottoman dominions, especially in Bursa. Its official rate varied between 42.5 and 43 akča a piece while the Venetian ducat (*Efrendjî*, *Afrandjî*) and the Ottoman gold coin varied between 45.5 and 46. [7])

1) Başvekâlet Archives, No. 6222.
2) Some regulations of state monopolies in the second half of the 15th century in the Ottoman empire are found in *Kānūnnāme-i Sultānī ber muceb-i ʿörf-i Osmānī*, ed. R. Anhegger-H. Inalcık (Ankara 1956).
3) Başvekâlet Archives, Maliye, No. 7387.
4) Pitch was extracted at a village called *Hisardjık*.
5) See above p. 145.
6) *Belleten*, No. 93 (1960), documents No. 9, 26, 28, 34.
7) *Idem*. Both the florin and the Venetian ducat were called *efrendjî* or *florî* since both of them contained about 3.5 grams of gold.

XII

Capital Formation in the Ottoman Empire

THE economic system of the Ottoman Empire and its basic economic principles derived from a traditional view of state and society which had prevailed since antiquity in the empires of the Near East. This theory, since it determined the attitude and policy of the administrators, was of considerable practical importance.

In the Muslim state, as in earlier states, all classes of society and all sources of wealth were regarded as obliged to preserve and promote the power of the ruler.[1] Hence all political and social institutions and all types of economic activity were regulated by the state in order to achieve this goal. The populace was regarded as forming two main groups—those who represented the ruler's authority (the administrators, the troops, the men of religion), and the ordinary subjects (*raʿāyā*); the former were not concerned with production and paid no taxes, while the latter were the producers and the taxpayers. This latter group comprised, in a strictly regulated hierarchy of classes, the tillers of the soil, the merchants, and the craftsmen. A main concern of the state was to ensure that each individual remained in his own class; this was regarded as the basic requisite for politico-social order and harmony.[2]

For the transcription of the Turkish, Arabic, and Persian words, we have in general followed the transcription lists of the *Encyclopaedia of Islam* (new ed.) as far as available type permitted. Some words—*cadi*, vizier, etc.—are kept in the forms used in current English.

[1] The legitimacy of the exercise of unbounded power by a single ruler was based in the Islamic state upon the assumption that it was the sole means of ensuring the application of the *Sharīʿa*, the holy law of Islam. For the traditional view of the state in the Near East, see A. Christensen, *L'Iran sous les Sassanides* (Copenhagen, 1944); A. Mez, *Die Renaissance des Islams* (Heidelberg, 1922); D. Sourdel, *Le Vizirat Abbaside de 749 a 936* (2 vols.; Damascus, 1959-60); S. D. Goitein, *Studies in Islamic History and Institutions* (Leiden, 1966), pp. 149-213; and H. Inalcik, "Kutadgu Bilig'de Türk ve Iran Siyaset Nazariye ve Gelenekleri," in *Reşit Rahmeti Için* (Ankara, 1966), pp. 259-71. The original source of the traditional view of the state is to be found in the Mirror for Princes (*Nasīhatnāme*) literature: N. Ch. Bandyopadhyaya, *Kautiliya: Or an Exposition of His Social and Political Theory* (Calcutta, 1927); *Tarjuma-i Kalīla wa Dimnah*, ed. M. Mīnovî (Tehran, 1343 H.); *The Nasīhatnāma known as Kābūsnāma of Kai Kāʾus b. Iskender*, ed. R. Levy (London, 1951); Nizām al-Mulk, *Siyāset-nāma*, ed. H. Darke (Tehran, 1962); M. Minovi and V. Minorsky, "Nasīr al-Dīn Tūsī on Finance", in *Bulletin of the School of Oriental and African Studies*, cited hereafter as *BSOAS*, X (1940-41), p. 755. The chapters on politics and economics in the classic works on ethics, namely *Akhlāk-i Nāsiri*, by Nasīr al-Dīn Tūsī, *Akhlāk-i Muhsinī*, by Husayn Wāʿiz, *Akhlāk-i Jalālī*, by Jalal al-Dīn Dawwānī, and *Akhlāk-i ʾAlāi*, by Kinalizāde ʾAlī, were written under the strong influence of this literature.

[2] It should be noted that the governments of Near East states appreciated the

Within the class of the producers, the tillers of the soil and the craftsmen were subject to a code of regulations distinct from that of the merchants; the methods of production and the profit margins of the former were under strict state control, since, in this view of society, they were the classes who produced the essential necessities of life and whose labors therefore were most intimately connected with the preservation of social and political order.[3] That a peasant or a craftsman should freely change the methods of production was not countenanced; his activities were permitted only within the limits of the ordinances laid down by the state. In Near East society, it was only the merchants who enjoyed conditions allowing them to become capitalists. "Merchant" (*tüjjār*) in this context, means the big businessman who engaged in international and interregional trade or in the sale of goods imported from afar.[4] Craftsmen who in the cities sold goods manufactured by themselves or tradespeople who sold these goods at secondhand fell outside the category of "merchant." Although merchants were organized into trade guilds according to the type of merchandise in which they dealt, yet they were not subject to the regulations of the *hisba* (to be discussed later). This is the most important feature distinguishing them from the craft guilds. Whereas the craftsmen were strictly controlled in their buying of raw materials and in the production and sale of their wares, the merchant remained free to accumulate, by any means in his power, as much capital as he could, and to seek

---

necessity of developing economic activity and of promoting the greatest possible increase in production from all classes of the *re'āyā*. In the *Nasīhatnāmas* it was recommended that cultivated land should be increased by the digging of canals and that trade between different regions should be promoted by the construction of roads, bridges, and caravansaries, and by ensuring the safety of travelers. But the object of all such activity was to increase revenue from taxation and hence fill the ruler's treasury.

[3] In *Akhlāk-i 'Alā'ī* (ed. Bulak, 1274 H.), p. 9, a work on ethics written in 1565, Kinalizāde emphasized that in production certain kinds of activities were necessary for "the good order of the society" while some others were not.

[4] This type of merchant is usually referred to in Ottoman sources as *bāzirgān*. More respectful titles for the big merchants were *khwāje* (in colloquial Turkish, *hoja*) and *khwājegī* (the exact equivalent of "maestro"). The *khwājes* were usually the richest merchants operating from a city. Another common Ottoman term is *matrabāz*. My colleague, Hasan Eren, thinks that it comes from the Greek word, ματαπράτης, grocer. It is used especially of wholesale dealers in foodstuffs. Possessors of large cash fortunes, *māl*, were called *māldār* or *mutamawwil*. In the official language, *asl al-māl* or *ra's al-māl* were used as the equivalent of capital. The Persian words, *sermāye* and *sermāyedār*, were used to denote capital and capitalist in their modern meanings only in the nineteenth century under Western influence.

always to increase this capital; and the types of activity in which he could engage were neither prescribed nor limited.

In discussing the ways of making "capital," *māl*, the Muslim jurists agreed on the three principal ones, namely, commerce, handicrafts, and agriculture. Some added to them political power. But commerce was always regarded as the best way of making a "capital." If some jurists of a later period considered agriculture preferable it was because, Kinalizāde argued,[5] they in their own time found too many malpractices in commercial transactions.

Muslim sources emphasize that the basic wealth of the merchant consists of money-coin, which for them is the only real "wealth."[6] All the same it was recommended that as a precaution the merchants' wealth might be held in various forms, by being laid out for the purchase of pearls, precious stones, rich stuffs, slaves, land, or animals; and the Ottoman "registers of effects" (*tereke defterleri*) reveal beyond all doubt that the rich indeed followed this recommendation. They did not entirely abandon the method of burying their wealth in the ground; but the hints provided by these sources that money should always be "set to work" and not left idle are the expression of a real general tendency. In all classes of Ottoman society there was apparent a great desire to put cash into making profit; and the most profitable field for investment of cash wealth was commerce.

In the *Kitāb al-Ishāra*,[7] of the eleventh to twelfth centuries, merchants are divided into three categories: (1) *Holders of stocks:* these buy at times when supply exceeds demand, i.e., when prices are low, and sell when the converse situation maintains and prices rise; in other words, they profit from the change in price brought about by *the lapse of time*. From the examples quoted, it is clear that these merchants dealt particularly in products dependent on the season, especially cereals. They were obliged to put their goods on the market gradually, to watch closely the rise and fall of prices, and to keep an eye on the political situation in the country where they were operating. (2) *Traveling merchants:* these merchants, who carried goods from one region to another, profited from

[5] *Akhlāk-i 'Alā'ī*, pp. 7-8.

[6] See M. Rodinson, *Islam et Capitalisme* (Paris, 1966), pp. 49-50, citing Ibn Khaldūn. This was a general opinion expressed in the works on ethics. For example, see Kinalizāde, pp. 6-7.

[7] H. Ritter, "Ein arabisches Handbuch der Handelswissenschaft," in *Der Islam*, VII (1917), pp. 15-17.

the variations in prices in *different regions;* it was therefore important for them to watch carefully the differences in price, taking into consideration the costs of transport and customs duties. (3) *Organizing merchants:* these appointed a reliable agent in the place to which the goods were to be sent, the goods being sent to him in the care of trustworthy men; the agent would sell the goods, and buy other goods with the proceeds; the agent was free to make his own decisions and had a share in the profits.

Although the *Kitāb al-Ishāra* is based upon the work by the Neo-Pythagorean Bryson, the types of merchant portrayed there are close to the real situation in Muslim society. Muslim jurists, from the earliest times, had distinguished two types of commerce, *hādira,* that engaged in on the spot, and *ghā'iba,* that carried out over long distances. Accordingly Ottoman documents relating to commerce distinguish two types of merchant, the traveling *tājir-i seffār,* who engaged in trade by overland caravan or by sea, and the *tājir-i mutamakkin,* who ran his affairs from a center in which he resided.

All these types are concerned with commerce between different regions, the distinctions being derived from the legal basis of the enterprise rather than the type of trade. The commercial principles dealt with in textbooks of Muslim law—the section on *shirka,* dealing with various types of partnerships; the section on *buyū*ᶜ, dealing with commercial transactions, including *murābaha* and *ribā',* i.e., money-transactions and types of credit; the section on *muḍāraba,* dealing with *commenda*—had been codified over the centuries in order to meet the needs of Muslim society;[8] and the register books of *cadis* (Muslim judges) and other documents of the Ottoman period show that these principles were in fact applied. Here we need mention briefly only a few of these principles which are of immediate relevance to our subject.

The forms of partnership lay down clear and sound principles for the formation of capital and for investment. Partnerships on credit (*shirkat al-wujūh*) and *commenda* (*muḍāraba*) were important means of bringing together capital and specialist skill and so ensuring profit from the union of enterprise and capital;[9] ex-

[8] A. Udovitch, "Credit as a Means of Investment in Medieval Islamic Trade," in *Journal of African and Oriental Studies,* LXXXVII (1967), pp. 260-64; S. D. Goitein, *Studies in Islamic History,* p. 219.

[9] Udovitch, "Credit," p. 262; Udovitch, "Labor Partnership in Early Islamic Law," in *Journal of the Economic and Social History of the Orient,* cited hereafter as *JESHO,* X-1 (1967), pp. 64-80. On these problems we refer to Mewkūfāti's com-

amples of how this worked in Ottoman society are given below. The parties in a *shirkat al-wujūh* traded on credit, and at the end of a stipulated term returned the capital to its owner, the profit being divided among the parties on a 50-50 basis, or however else had been agreed. *Muḍāraba* is a partnership in which one party provides the labor and the other the capital, and both share in the profit. The example given in the law books is as follows: A gives money to B, and B travels and trades with this money; they divide the profit. B, while traveling, has complete use of the goods, but cannot use them for a loan or a pledge. A condition laid down beforehand with regard to the profit may invalidate the *muḍāraba* contract. If the goods are lost, B is not obliged to recompense A. B has a share of the profit, but cannot claim it all. If the contract of *muḍāraba* becomes void, B can demand wages, whether or not a profit was gained. *Muḍāraba* applies only when the capital is applied to goods obtainable in partnership. If the capital is used not for trade but for the manufacture of goods, this creates an entirely different type of partnership (*shirkat al-sanā'iᶜ wa 'l-takabbul*); in this case one party supplies only capital and the other only labor and skill, or else both parties obtain capital from outside and undertake jointly a manufacturing enterprise, sharing the profit. It will be seen that these legal principles permit the use of capital in investment, the invested capital naturally receiving its share of the profit.[10] Hence, by various means, the taking of interest (*fā'iḍ, ribā'*) is rendered legal. In Islamic society the use of money at interest and other forms of credit are both very old and widespread.[11] As shown below, among the Ottomans, not merely non-Muslims but Muslims, men of religion included, indulged freely in putting out money at interest. According to some jurists, the principal goods on which interest may legitimately be taken (*māl ribāwī*) are gold and silver.

There is much truth in the suggestion that Islamic law and the Islamic ideal of society shaped themselves from the very first in accordance with the ideas and aims of a rising merchant class; but this tendency should be linked not specifically with the religion of Islam but rather with the traditional concept of state and society

---

mentary on *Multakā' al-Abhur* by Ibrahīm Halabī (d. 1549), which became the standard law book at the Ottoman courts: Vol. I (Istanbul, 1318 H.), pp. 360-65, vol. II, pp. 124-30.

10 Mewkūfātī, II, pp. 28-33.

11 Rodinson, pp. 52-62.

that had prevailed in the Near East in pre-Islamic times. *Shaybānī*, one of the founders of the Hanafite School of Law, "had to prove that the vigorous striving of the new Muslim trading people for a decent living was not only not opposed by Islam, but actually regarded by it as a religious duty;" he did not regard luxury as contrary to religion; indeed he considered it praiseworthy.[12]

In the *nasīhatnāmes* and similar traditional sources reflecting the bias of the administrative class, the merchant is portrayed favorably. In its advice to the ruler, the eleventh-century *Kutadgu Bilig* says[13] that the merchant, "who is always in search of profit and travels the whole world," brings to the ruler and his people from distant regions of the world valuable and rare goods, silk-stuffs, furs and pearls; the ruler should remember that merchants are very sensitive in matters of profit and loss. The work points out that they render him valuable service by bringing news from afar and by publishing his fame abroad, and that they should therefore always be given good treatment. Also many traditions attributed to the Prophet on the merchant are favorable: "the merchant enjoys the felicity both of this world and the next"; "He who makes money pleases the God",[14] etc. In an Ottoman *nasīhatnāme*[15] written in the second half of the fifteenth century, the ruler is advised: "Look with favour on the merchants in the land; always care for them; let no one harass them; let no one order them about; for through their trading the land becomes prosperous, and by their wares cheapness abounds in the world; through them, the excellent fame of the sultan is carried to surrounding lands, and by them the wealth within the land is increased."

In brief, since the merchant class of Near East society, through the various functions it fulfilled, formed an indispensable element in the state, the state and the law accorded it a privileged position. Of these functions, the most important were that the merchants could be of service to the state in various ways thanks to their accumulated fortunes of ready money; they made loans to the state, they acted as intermediaries between the state and the mass of the

12 Goitein, *Studies*, pp. 219-29.

13 *Kutadgu Bilig*, tr. R. R. Arat (Ankara, 1959), p. 320, verses 4419-38.

14 For further examples, see Ahmed Nazmi, *Nazar-i Islâm'da Zenginligin mevkii* (Istanbul, 1340-42 H.). According to the law school of Abu Khanīfa, which prevailed in the Ottoman Empire, there was nothing wrong in accumulating wealth (cf. Kinalizāde, p. 11).

15 Sinān Pasha, *Ma'ārifnāme*, ed. I. H. Ertaylan (Istanbul, 1961), p. 271.

population in matters of taxation, they ensured a steady revenue from customs charges, they supplied the administrative class with goods produced far afield, and they acted as agents and ambassadors. This close cooperation with the state enabled the merchants to put their wealth to profitable use and increase it greatly.[16]

Yet it would be incorrect to explain the privileged position of the merchants only by their common interests and their cooperation with the administration; we must also remember their exceptional economic function in an economic system which had taken shape as a result of particular conditions. International trade not only supplied luxury goods, but also provided the large cities with their essential food and raw materials. In particular it imported the raw materials for the weaving industries of the cities (silk, wool, cotton, dyes, alum) and distributed the products to distant markets;[17] if this trade slowed down or stopped, the results for the city could be disastrous. Again, since communications were very difficult and dangerous, and since the merchant's was a profession demanding a large capital, specialized knowledge and skills, an enterprising spirit, and considerable personal courage, the exchange of goods between distant regions attracted only a limited number of people. Thus the movement of goods from an area of plenty to an area of scarcity was carried out only to a small degree and in a small range of commodities. Merchants were attracted only when discrepancies of price were large enough to promise adequate profits. It is for these reasons that interregional trade in the Near East assumed an exceptionally capitalistic and speculative character and thus constituted that form of economic activity which chiefly led to capital formation.

On the other hand it is quite clear that in the large centers of population of the Near East there was a strong current of popular hostility to the class of merchants, *bāzirgān* and *tüjjār*, (these terms always refer to merchants engaged in trade between distant regions), to the class of the bankers and money changers (*ṣarrāf*), to luxury, and to the capitalist mentality—that is, to the tendency

[16] For the situation in Syria under the Mamluks, see I. M. Lapidus, *Muslim Cities in the Later Middle Ages* (Cambridge, Mass., 1967), pp. 116-42.

[17] For the traditions showing that the cloth trade was regarded as the most important, see Ritter, p. 29; Goitein, *Studies*, p. 222, n. 3. It was not a coincidence that the business center in the Muslim cities was called *bezzāzistān*, the hall of *bezzāz*, dealers in textiles. We will see that in the Ottoman Empire too the *bezzāz* were among the wealthiest in the cities.

to accumulate money fortunes and to increase them by investment. This hostility found expression in the religious confraternities (in earlier days in the *Karmatiyya,* under the Ottomans particularly in the *Malāmitiyya,* the *Bayrāmiyya* and in the order of Sheykh Badr al-Dīn), which reflected popular interests and sentiments.[18] So too, orthodox Islam, especially one strand of thought represented by *al-Ghazali,* was hostile to the capitalist mentality. This doctrine held that a man's profit should be expended only for religious purposes and for the maintenance of his family; and that profit must not be an end in itself. A man engaged in trade should leave the market-place when he had made a sufficient profit; he should work not to win the good things of this world but with the next world in view; to pursue unbounded profit was a religious and a moral failing.[19] This scheme of ethics recommended as an ideal a middle course between a complete asceticism on the one hand and the capitalist mentality on the other.[20] *Al-Ghazali* condemns as evil acts a trader's switching from market to market or from commodity to commodity, or his embarking overseas in quest of greater profit—a point of some interest as indicating what class he was addressing.

The unfavorable view of the merchant–capitalist held not merely by some *ulema* and in the circles of the religious confraternities but also by most of the population of the great cities is apparently to be connected not so much with strictly religious attitudes as with the basic social and economic structure of Near East society. In the Near Eastern city, production and distribution depended ultimately on the guild system. If we leave aside the few great cities producing for distant markets, we find that the rest depended on a method of production geared to supplying only the immediate neighboring region, that is, a clearly defined and limited market; and these cities, in view of the difficulties of communication, depended for the raw

18 C. Cahen, "Mouvements populaires et autonomisme urbaine dans l'Asie musulmane du Moyen Age," in *Arabica,* V, pp. 225-50, VI, pp. 25-58, 233-65; B. Lewis, "Islamic Guilds," in *Economic History Review,* VIII (1937), pp. 20-37. For the *malāmatī* movement in the Ottoman Empire, see A. Gölpinarli, *Melāmilik* ve Melāmiler (Istanbul, 1931); V. A. Gordlevski, *Gosudarstvo Seldjukidov Maloy Azii* (Moscow, 1941).

19 Ritter, "Ein arabisches Handbuch," pp. 41-45.

20 Sabri Ülgener, *Iktisadi Inhitat Tarihimizin Ahlâk ve Zihniyet Meseleleri* (Istanbul, 1951), pp. 67-68. Criticizing the attitude of the mystics (*sūfī*) who preached the giving away in alms of everything that was not needed for subsistence, Kinalizāde (p. 11) said that it was necessary to accumulate wealth in order to maintain good order in this world.

materials of their industries on a similarly defined and limited area. Thus the guild system, which completely did away with competition, was for them an ideal organization ensuring the harmony and subsistence of the society it served. The competitive spirit and the profit motive were regarded as crimes threatening to overthrow this system and the existing social order. The *futuwwa* ideal,[21] which prevailed among the artisans and the shopkeepers linked together in the guild system, represented the very principles which *al-Ghazālī* had formulated; to strive after profit, to seek to make more money than one needed to live on, was regarded as the source of the most serious moral defects. If a guildsman became too rich, his fellows would expel him from the guild and treat him as a "merchant." The merchant's profits were regarded as a sort of profiteering, the result of speculation, an illegitimate gain; whereas what had been produced by the work of the hand and the sweat of the brow—this only was legitimate. In order to prevent competition and to stop one of their number from overproducing and making too much profit, the guildsmen, through the agency of their representative, bought the raw materials of their guild in bulk; this raw material was distributed among the members openly; and the goods produced were sold, in the name of the guild, in one specific place. To change the quality or the style of the goods produced was not permitted, and production was supervised. The object in all this was to prevent any one of their number from upsetting the market by increasing his business—for where the purchasers were limited, if one man increased his share another must be left in want. This social class, therefore, became increasingly hostile to the principle of unlimited profit. Moreover, the merchant trading with other regions might, in order to profit from a price discrepancy, seek to buy up all the raw materials in one place and take them off, and by offering a higher price he could force up the price of raw materials and even provoke a shortage. The guildsman therefore regarded him as an enemy, a social menace (Ottoman documents reveal that the guilds frequently complained to the authorities on this account). So this economic rivalry between guildsmen and merchants led to flat hostility between them. That neutral terms like *bāzirgān* and *matrabāz,* which are used for merchants in official documents, gained in popular speech such pejorative implications as "profiteer" and "trickster" as

[21] See Fr. Taeschner, *Futuwwa,* in *Encyclopaedia of Islam,* new ed., II (1965), pp. 961-69.

the expression of this social hostility. Nevertheless, as will be shown, capitalist tendencies leading to some disruption of the guild system did manifest themselves in Near Eastern society, particularly in the big cities and in branches of industry supplying external markets.

The state was always being called upon by the guildsmen to resist these new tendencies, and the state did in fact always seek to support the guilds, obliged as it was to fulfill the duty of *hisba.* In the Islamic states of the Near East certain ancient and traditional rules, intended to protect the interests of the populace by preventing profiteering, fraud, and speculation, had been taken over by the religious law under the name of *hisba,* so that their application had become one of the principal obligations of the Muslim state. Hence the *imām,* the leader of the Muslim community, was obliged to fix the "just price" and to see it observed, and it was with this particularly that *hisba* was concerned, punishing as crimes all types of speculation. In the supervision of the quality and weight of commodities and their price, the state and the guilds worked hand in hand: Together they laid down the principles to be observed; then, during the process of manufacture, supervision was entrusted to the guild, and when the goods were exposed for sale, to the *muhtesib,* the official appointed by the state. The recognized profit (after all expenses had been met) was 10 percent, though for some commodities it might, exceptionally, be 15 or even more.[22] It must be emphasized that merchants were not subject to the *hisba.* The rules of *hisba* were fitted to, and upheld, the guild system, and as such conformed to the classical Near Eastern ideal of the state, which sought to protect the traditional class structure as being the mainstay of social harmony. Indeed it may be said that, from the economico-social point of view, the principal characteristic of the Near Eastern state is that it reposed basically on the guild organization.

Although in general the *hisba* rules were not applied to trade between regions, yet strict state control had been imposed on trade in various essential commodities. The Near East state had comprehended the necessity of preventing profiteering and speculation in commodities essential for the provisioning of large populations, a shortage of which might provoke serious popular disturbances. It was presumably as a result of this experience that the religious law forbade *ribā'* (that is, speculative profit-making) in certain com-

22 H. Sahillioglu, "Osmanlilarda Narh Müessesesi," in *Belgelerle Türk Tarihi Dergisi,* No. 1 (1967), p. 40.

modities, notably cereals. Yet we find that trade in cereals was in fact one of the principal methods of large-scale speculation and hence of the accumulation of large fortunes.

Another basic reason for popular hostility to those who accumulated cash fortunes was the shortage of precious metals, especially silver. Not only the taxpayers but also the guildsmen complained bitterly of the lack of coin in circulation. As early as the eighth century, the people of Bokhara had asked the government to take measures preventing the movement of silver money outside their own region.[23] In accordance with the explicit command in the Koran (IX,34-35) al-Bīrūnī (eleventh century) wrote that to hoard gold and silver and remove them from circulation was a crime against society.[24] The issue of paper money in Persia in the Mongol period was connected primarily with the acute shortage of silver.[25] That imperial governments should heap up treasuries of gold and silver to meet the needs of their palaces and armies and to finance their campaigns had been condemned in popular sentiment from Sasanian times, and governments so acting were regarded as failing in "justice." According to the *Kutadgu Bilig*,[26] a good government is one which distributes the contents of its treasury. Merchants who were known to have accumulated large stocks of cash were therefore looked on with as much hostility as those that profiteered in wheat. Furthermore, it was known that merchants and money changers cooperated with the state by farming taxes. Occasionally the state, appearing to share the popular sentiment against those made wealthy by speculation, would confiscate such fortunes; but in general the state refrained from confiscating the fortunes of ordinary merchants. Confiscation was employed particularly against the tax farmers and officials who had made their money through their connections with the Finance Department. It must be added that the shortage of coin had important consequences, particularly in dealings among merchants; barter was widespread, as were various forms of sale with delayed payment. Since the latter entailed a credit transaction, the price of the commodity was increased by a not inconsiderable element of interest.

These then are, in outline, the basic conditions governing capital

[23] W. Barthold, *Turkestan Down to the Mongol Invasion* (London, 1928), p. 204.

[24] Z. V. Togan, *Tarihte Metod* (Istanbul, 1950), p. 161; H. Inalcik, "Türkiye'nin Iktisadî Vaziyeti," in *Belleten*, No. 60 (1951), p. 652.

[25] H. Inalcik, *ibid.*

[26] Tr. R. R. Arart, verses 5479-90. *Cf.* n. 20.

formation in the traditional empires of the Near East, of which the Ottoman Empire was one.

BURSA

There is no doubt that the most important group of sources upon which studies on capital and the capitalist in the Ottoman Empire may be based is the records kept by the *cadis.* These records consist of the *sijill*-registers, in which all kinds of commercial transactions were recorded, and the *tereke*-registers,[27] in which (in view of the *cadi's* duty to supervise the division of estates) the possessions of the deceased, together with their values, were listed. In what follows we shall, on the basis of the fifteenth-century *sijill*- and *tereke*-registers of Bursa and of the sixteenth- and seventeenth-century *tereke*-registers of Edirne, consider those persons who may be called "capitalists," the sources of their wealth, and the fields in which they invested capital.

In the fifteenth and sixteenth centuries, Bursa rose to be one of the most important commercial and industrial centers of the Near East.[28] Commodities coming from the East, from Central Asia and Persia, and from Arabia and India were there distributed to the countries of the Balkans and northern Europe. At the same time Bursa was an important center of the silk industry, exporting light and heavy silk stuffs of various types to supply both the internal and the external market. About 1502, there were over 1000 silk looms in Bursa (while in Istanbul, in the middle of the sixteenth century, there were only about 300). It is at Bursa therefore that we can look for individuals who may be called "commercial and industrial capitalists."

First we classify the personal fortunes, according to the *tereke*-registers of the fifteenth century[29]:

Of 319 estates for the years 1467-8:

Those under 10,000 *akches*[30] constituted 84.1 percent
Those between 10,000 and 50,000 constituted 12.6 percent

[27] For *sijill*-registers, see *Belleten,* No. 44, pp. 693-96. For the *tereke*-registers, see H. Inalcik, "15.asir Türkiye Iktisadî ve Ictimaî Tarihi Kaynaklari," in *Iktisat Fakültesi Mecmuasi,* III, pp. 57-76, and Ö. L. Barkan, "Edirne Askerî Kassâmina ait Tereke Defterleri," in *Belgeler,* III (1966), pp. 1-9.

[28] H. Inalcik, "Bursa," in *Belleten,* XXIV (1960), pp. 45-96, and in *Encyclopaedia of Islam,* new ed., s.v.

[29] See H. Inalcik, "15.asir," pp. 5-17.

[30] On Ottoman silver coin, see *Encyclopaedia of Islam,* new ed., I: "akče."

Those over 50,000 constituted 3.3 percent
(in these years the Venetian ducat = 44-45 *akches*)

Of 402 estates for the years 1487-8:

Those under 10,000 *akches* constituted 89.8 percent
Those between 10,000 and 50,000 constituted 8.2 percent
Those over 50,000 constituted 3.0 percent

It is worth noting that the largest fortunes rarely exceed 200,000 *akches* (4500 ducats); these belong, in descending order, to money changers/goldsmiths, to merchants (particularly those dealing in silk stuffs and silk thread), and to silk weavers. The fortunes of those leaving more than 50,000 *akches* consist primarily of coin; then follow in descending order real estate, male and female slaves, rich stuffs, and silk (it was natural that in Bursa, the center for international trade in silk and for silk manufacture, these last two should be such an important vehicle for capital). Yet the greatest fortunes were those of the money changers (*ṣarrāf*), who dealt in money and made loans at interest; ʿAbd al-Rahman, for example, evidently a moneylender, left an estate of 199,035 *akches,* of which 127,500 consisted of money out on loan. It is noteworthy too that the rich generally owned several male and female slaves, who were employed mostly as weavers or as commercial agents.

By contrast, the fortune of 67,420 *akches* left by Ḥajji ʿIvaz Pasha-oghly Mahmūd Chelebi, a member of a famous family of government servants, is very differently constituted, consisting mainly of cereals and domestic animals on his farm and of income from his father's *wakf.* (We shall find the same pattern with members of the military and administrative class in sixteenth-century Edirne.)

It is a point of considerable interest from the sociological point of view that many of the wealthy individuals are the sons of "*khojas,*" that is, of rich merchants, manumitted slaves, and "*chelebīs,*" that is, sons of the higher-ranking members of the administrative class. There are also some members of the *ulema* engaged in trade and in silk manufacture. The manumitted slaves had gained experience in business by serving their masters as weavers or as commercial agents and then, after winning their freedom, had set up in business independently; such former slaves, vigorously carving out new careers for themselves, came to form an energetic and enterprising element in Ottoman society.

We now consider first the merchant class in Bursa and its activities. Many merchants traveled to Bursa from Syria—from Damascus and especially Aleppo—bringing large consignments of pepper and other spices and expensive dyes such as indigo and gum lac.[31] These commodities came by caravan along the diagonal route from Aleppo via Konya and Kutahya, and represented consignments of great value: In 1479 khoja Surur of Aleppo sold to Dāvūd of Edirne, in one lot, pepper worth 730 ducats; in 1484 khoja Ibrahim sold to the Jew Dāvūd pepper worth 527 ducats; and in 1500 Abū Bakr of Aleppo sold pepper worth 4000 ducats.[32] The *sijill*-registers reveal that Turkish merchants of Bursa also engaged in important transactions, usually by sending agents to Aleppo and Damascus.[33]

This trade was not confined to luxury goods: Turkish merchants exported by sea to Arabia such bulky commodities as timber, iron, pitch, and hides. One of these merchants, Khayr al-Dīn, had his will recorded in the book of the *cadi* of Bursa, which contains interesting details.[34] It reads: "He said: between Hadjdji Koçi, a slave freed by Khoja Mehemmed, and myself there was an association (*shirka*) with a capital to the amount of 545,000 akches (about 11,000 gold ducats), the half of which belonged to me and the other half to the aforesaid Khoja Mehemmed. From the aforesaid amount, lumber, wood and pitch worth 105,000 akches has been taken by my son Yūsuf and the aforesaid Khoja Mehemmed's son Ibrāhīm from Antalya to Alexandria, also Yūsuf and Hasan, slaves of the aforesaid Mehemmed, have gone overland to Egypt taking 123,000 akches worth of Bursa cloths and saffron; also 112,500 akches worth of iron, wood, lumber were sent (to Egypt) with the Sultan's ships; these were sent by my son Yūsuf, also 12,000 akches worth of leather were sent by me to my sons in Egypt via Antalya with a man named Seyyid 'Alī; and a slave of the aforesaid Khoja Mehemmed named Süleyman took sables, lynx furs and Bursa cloths worth 125,000 *akches,* and also they (Khayr al-Dīn and Khoja Mehemmed) declared that 75 flori were due to them from a person in Egypt named Wazzāni Shihāb al-Dīn." It is clear that Khayr al-Dīn and his partner used Bursa and the port of Antalya as their centers of business, and that they ran their trade with Syria and Egypt by sending out their slaves and their sons as their agents. The capital invested in the partnership is, for the period, relatively large; each partner bore

[31] For the great wealth of Syrian merchants, see Lapidus, p. 118.
[32] H. Inalcik, "Bursa and the Commerce of the Levant," in *JESHO,* III, no. 2 (1960), pp. 133-35.
[33] Inalcik, "Bursa," in *Belleten,* p. 78, doc. 14.
[34] Inalcik, "Bursa and the Commerce," p. 145.

an equal share of profit or loss. This example is interesting as illustrating the extensive trading ventures carried out between distant regions; but in Bursa, the transit center for Persian silk, it was the silk trade that produced most of the big fortunes and the big profits.

Each year several silk caravans came to Bursa. In 1513 a single caravan brought 400 *yük* (i.e., 24,600 kg.) of silk, worth about 220, 000 ducats. Most of the merchants coming from Persia were Muslim, from Gīlān, Shirwān, Tebrīz, and Nahjiwān (at this time the Armenians were still in a minority in this trade). Many of these merchants had made heavy investments in the trade (thus in 1467 *khoja* ᶜAbd al-Rahīm of Shamākha brought a consignment of silk worth 4400 ducats). Persian merchants would also bring silk belonging to others and sell it as agents. From early times, the rulers of Persia had had a share in this profitable trade: Silk to the value of 5700 ducats was sold in Bursa in 1513 on behalf of Shah Ismaᶜil. Shah ʿAbbās (1578-1628), mainly for political reasons, made the export of silk from Persia a state monopoly, but his successor canceled this measure, and in both Turkey and Persia it was a matter of satisfaction that the silk trade was once more in private hands.[35] At the same time, Turkish merchants of Bursa imported silk direct by sending their agents to Persia; a note in a *sijill*-register records that in 1576 the silk merchant of Bursa, Hājjī Ali, sent an agent to Persia to buy silk, giving him 100,000 *akches* (1660 ducats). The Bursa merchants who traveled to the East were numerous. In the same *sijill*-registers we find references to Ṣun ʿAllāh, who went to Egypt to trade (and who, at his death, had 1190 ducats on his person); to Ali, who went to India in 1525; and to the Bursa merchant Ömer, who died in Persia in 1555.[36]

Silk, being so much in demand, was one of the most important commodities for the production of high profits and for the encouragement of commercial capitalism. On the Bursa market the price of Astarābādī silk (*Setta stravai*) was always rising, so that one *lidre* (150 gr.), worth 60 *akches* in 1467, in 1478 sold for 67 *akches*. The price of silk varied greatly from district to district, so that there was scope for large profits: The Bursa representative of a Florentine firm, J. Maringhi, recorded in 1501 that one *fardello* (= Turkish *yük*, 61,5 kg.) of silk bought in Bursa had realized a profit of 70 to

[35] Inalcik, "Türkiye'nin Iktisadî," pp. 665-74.
[36] F. Dalsar, *Bursa'da Ipecilik* (Istanbul, 1960), pp. 218-19.

80 ducats in Florence;[37] and in 1506 one *lidre* of silk, bought at Bursa for 80 *akches,* sold at Kilia on the Danube for 100 *akches.*[38]

Maringhi portrays vividly how impatiently the agents of Italian firms at Bursa and the Jewish merchants waited for the arrival of caravans from Persia, and how fiercely they competed to buy the goods and dispatch them to Italy without delay.[39] Some Persian merchants were able to sell their wares direct to these Europeans; but the local Turkish merchants also acted as intermediaries. The Europeans at Bursa would either exchange for the silk the fine woolen cloth of Europe, which was much in demand in the Ottoman Empire, Persia, and Central Asia, or else pay for it in gold. The Florentine and Genoese merchants sold much of their cloth at Bursa on credit. Thus the Florentine Piero Alessio, who died in 1478 at Bursa, appointed the Genoese Sangiacomi as executor to collect his debts from various people in the city;[40] and the Bursa merchant Mustafa, resident in Istanbul, caused to be recorded in the *sijill*-register of Bursa the debt of 1252 *akches* which he owed to the Florentine Kerpid (?) Zenibio and the Florentine Banadid (Benedetto ?) for woolen cloth he had bought.[41] There are many such entries in the Bursa registers. The customs registers of the Danube and Black Sea show that Bursa merchants sold to these harbors European woolens, Persian silks, pepper, spices and dyes from India, and products of Anatolia (especially mohair cloth of Ankara, and the cotton goods exported in great quantities from western Anatolia).[42] In 1490, of 157 merchants entering Caffa by sea, 16 were Greeks, 4 Italians, 2 Armenians, 3 Jews, 1 Russian, and 1 Moldavian; the remaining 130 were Muslim. The Muslim rarely penetrated inland from these ports; the goods were transported into Poland, the Crimean Khanate, the Desht-i Kipchak, and Russia by local merchants or by Armenians, Jews, and Greeks (mainly Ottoman subjects).

Yet it is not true to say that Muslims never went to Europe or traded directly with Europe; rather than undertake these long and dangerous journeys themselves, they sent agents, their slaves or their

[37] G. R. B. Richards, *Florentine Merchants in the Age of the Medici* (Cambridge: Harvard University Press, 1932), p. 122.
[38] Inalcik, "15.asir," p. 13, n. 31.
[39] Richards, *Florentine Merchants,* p. 127.
[40] Inalcik, "Bursa," in *Belleten,* p. 70, docs. 4 and 13.
[41] *Ibid.,* p. 72, doc. 7.
[42] Inalcik, "Bursa and the Commerce," pp. 139-40.

converted and manumitted slaves. In 1554, the merchant Sejim sent from Bursa to Poland his Muslim slave named Ferhād, with a "capital" of 450 ducats (but Ferhād decided to revert to his former faith and stay there—with the money). There is a record in the registers concerning the estate of a Bursa merchant named Rejeb who, in 1537, went to "the country of Moskof" to trade, and there died;[43] there must have been many others who went but whose travels, as no occasion arose, were not mentioned in the records. Again, as our investigations proceed, we find that Muslim merchants formed an active element in the commercial life of such cities as Venice and Ancona.[44]

Having considered the activities of Bursa merchants engaged in long-distance trade, we turn to consider capitalist tendencies among the members of the guilds, an entirely distinct economic and social class. We have seen that the guild system is fundamentally opposed

[43] Dalsar, *Bursa,* doc. 72; for merchants traveling to Muscovy, doc. 77.

[44] The trade route, Bursa-Edirne-Raguza-Ancona-Florence, became increasingly important from the second half of the fifteenth century onward. "In 1514 Ancona was forced to grant special privileges to Ottoman merchants"; see T. Stoianovich, "The Conquering Balkan Merchant," JOURNAL OF ECONOMIC HISTORY, XX (1960), pp. 236-37; and the Palatio delle Farine became a fondaco for the Turkish and other Muslim merchants. In the middle of the sixteenth century there were here 200 houses of Greek merchants who were Ottoman subjects (Stoianovich, *ibid.*). Turkish and Persian (*Azemini*) merchants attending fairs in central Italy began to be so numerous as to threaten Venice's Levant trade. Commercial links between Ansona and Ragusa, the transit center for Ottoman trade, became so close that each city abolished customs dues on citizens of the other, and there were even rumors that Ancona was prepared to accept Ottoman suzerainty. It may be noted that the Ottoman registers too refer to Muslim merchants going to Ancona: in 1559 a merchant from Shirvān entrusted to his servant 'Alī b. 'Abdallah 200 lidre of silk which he had brought with him and 1000 ducats and sent him "to the city named Ankona to exchange them for cloth" (Dalsar, *Bursa,* doc. 47). As for Venice in the sixteenth century, Muslim merchants of Turkey and Persia begin to be mentioned among the other foreign merchants; see D. Possot, *Le Voyage de la Terre Sainte* (Paris, 1890), p. 80. At this period they were already working in close cooperation with the Jews. A decree of the Senate of 15 September 1537 ordered the arrest of Turks and Jews and others who were Turkish subjects in Venice and its dependencies and the seizure of their goods (the content of this document was communicated to me by Mahmud Sakir, who found it in the course of his research in Archives of Venice: Senato Mar. Regesti 24, 69r, 15 Settembre 1537). Turkish merchants in Venice lived at Rialto. The explosion which destroyed a part of the fleet at the arsenal on the eve of the Turkish invasion of Cyprus in 1570 was believed to be a plot engineered by the Turkish spies in Venice (G. Hill, *A History of Cyprus,* III, 1948, p. 883). In 1574, after the peace settlement, attempts were made to provide a building in which all the Turkish merchants could live together, and five years later a building was found. The Palazzo of the Duke of Ferrara, however, the well-known *Fondaco dei Turchi* of today, was given to them only later, in 1621. Permission was granted that this building should be occupied by Turks from Istanbul and "Asia" (i.e., Anatolia), by other Ottoman subjects from Bosnia and Albania, and by Persians and Armenians.

to the capitalist mentality; but since the silk industry at Bursa was engaged to a large extent in production for external markets, we find that in this city the guild system developed considerably.

In the Bursa silk industry, there was much differentiation within the guild, a pronounced distinction arising between, on the one hand, the masters of looms with much capital invested and, on the other, the journeymen and workmen employed by them, so that a labor market came into existence. By the government's investigation of the crisis which occurred in 1586, when silk supplies from Persia were cut off with the outbreak of war, the following situation was revealed: Of 25 persons owning 483 looms,

7 owned a total of 41 looms (between 4 and 9 each)
10 owned a total of 136 looms (between 10 and 20 each)
6 owned a total of 200 looms (between 21 and 40 each).

The biggest owners were Mahmud with 46 looms and Mehemmed with 60. Since a loom for brocade was worth 50 to 60 ducats and the cost of raw materials (silk, silver, gold) and laborers' wages must also be considered, Mehemmed's 60 looms represented a total investment of at least 5000 ducats. With the cutting off of silk imports and the steep rise in the cost of silk, 5 of the 25 persons disappeared, 4 went bankrupt, 5 died, while each of the others was left with only one to 5 looms working.

The woven silk stuffs were sold directly on behalf of the master weavers in specified shops in the city market. Various stuffs required for the palace were bought direct from the masters, from whom too the merchants trading far afield bought direct.[45]

The weavers bought their raw materials from the *hāmjis*, merchants engaged in the trade in raw silk. Silk coming by caravan from Persia was unloaded at the *bedestan*, where each *hāmji* bought his share. The *hāmji* would pass this silk to the guild of *dolabjis* to be wound and spun, then to the guild of *boyajis* to be dyed. These guilds worked for the *hāmjis* for pay; and their subordinate status appears from their being called *yamak*, or "assistant," guilds. The *hāmji* would then sell the skeins, prepared for weaving, to the weavers (*dokumajis*). The entrepreneurs of the industry were thus the *hāmjis* and the *dokumajis*.

The weavers were divided into various guilds according to the type of material they made. Each guild had a governing council:

[45] See Dalsar, *Bursa*, p. 132, doc. 176; p. 226, doc. 161; p. 229, doc. 168.

thus the velvet weavers had a council of six persons, known as "the six" (*altilar*), who were chosen from wealthy former masters to supervise the guild regulations, and who effectively controlled this branch of the industry. One of their chief duties was to prevent competition for labor among the masters. Those working in the industry fell into three groups: slaves (*kul*), apprentices (*shāgird*), and workpeople engaged for pay in the open market (*ejīr*). Every Saturday the masters and this third group of workpeople would collect at an appointed place in the city, and the two experienced members of the six known as *ehl-i hibre* would select suitable workpeople for a master who needed labor. The objects in this were to prevent competition between masters (and hence a rise in wages) and to select skilled workmen. The pay was fixed in accordance with the value of the material woven (10 percent for thick silk stuffs and 12 percent for gold-laced velvet). The workman was paid weekly in advance. The *ehl-i hibre* were responsible for overseeing the workmen, for ensuring that they worked in accordance with the regulations of the guild, and that they did not leave their work unfinished in order to take service with another master.[46] Thus the council of the guild had the power to ensure that the employees worked as they wished them to.

The purchase of slaves as workpeople was another important type of investment in the industry. In Islamic law, by the agreement known as *mukātaba*, the slave might be granted his freedom if he performed within a stipulated time a stipulated task—such as the weaving of a certain quantity of cloth. The large number of such *mukātabas* recorded in the registers, together with the fact that masters, small or great, owned one or several slaves, show that this type of labor was employed on a large scale. The price of slaves was fairly high (30 to 120 ducats), and Bursa had a busy slave market.

As for the apprentices (*shāgird*), these were boys and youths entrusted to masters by their legal guardians to learn the craft. A contract of apprenticeship was drawn up between master and guardian, the master undertaking to teach the craft within a stipulated time (usually 1001 days), and often paying the guardian a small wage in advance. The apprentice owed absolute obedience to his master. There was a small convent (*zāviye*) in which apprentices and workmen belonging to the guild were taught its rules and

[46] See *Encyclopaedia of Islam*, new ed., art., "Harīr," pp. 211-18.

customs. These rules, deriving from the *futuwwa* morality of the Middle Ages, had been codified in a traditional form observed by all guilds; they instilled into apprentices and workmen the principles of mutual assistance, absolute obedience to the master, and contentment with one's lot.

The work was usually carried on at looms installed in dwelling-houses, although sometimes masters of several looms would install them altogether in a *kārhāne,* or workshop (in 1487 a *kārhāne* was estimated to be worth 80 ducats). In the cotton industry of Manisa, the products of house looms were more highly esteemed and costlier than the products of workshop looms.

This silk industry of Bursa, so organized, can from one viewpoint be called "capitalist production." It worked mainly to supply the external market, and was dependent on merchants engaged in interregional trade. The first customer for silk stuffs produced at Bursa was the Imperial Palace, which, through the Sultan's purchasing agent, made heavy bulk purchases every month. Then came the merchants engaged in interregional trade, Turks and foreigners (including some Poles, Russians, Moldavians, and Ragusans, but mostly Persians, Arabs, and Italians). The important master weavers—our "capitalists"—did not engage in export themselves; for the export of their products, as for the acquisition of their raw materials, they were dependent upon the merchants.

The *tereke*-registers do not reveal the existence of any master weavers whose wealth could compare with that of the money changers and the merchants. In the the second half of the century the *cadi* records of Bursa show few weavers whose estates exceeded 500 ducats in value, although in the sixteenth century many of them were worth over 1000 ducats. It should be emphasized that these silk weavers were among the wealthiest of all the Ottoman guildsmen.

An extending market, ever-increasing demand, and an ever-rising profit led some Bursans to ignore the guild regulations based on controlled production. The master weavers endeavored, under cover of the guild regulations, to monopolize the profits of the industry and to make themselves ever richer. In principle, the number of master weavers was limited by the regulations of the guild. New masters could indeed open new shops with the guild's permission, by a license, or *ijāzet-nāme,* which the guild issued; but the former rich masters, looking to their own interests, tried always to limit the guild to its old membership, however much the market might expand; thus the number of masters remained the same and ambitious journeymen were forced to work for a wage, at a master's loom. The masters seem to have found methods to increase the number of their own looms. Newly trained workmen were unable to open "independent" (*bashka*) shops for themselves, in an industry which anyway demanded a substantial initial investment of capital (one loom and the necessary materials would require at least 80 to 100 ducats). The established masters fought bitterly against so-called "rebels"—those who opened shops without a license or who stimulated demand by producing new types of wares. On the ground that the rebels were infringing the *hisba*-regulations, they would try to bring the government into action against them, alleging that they were lowering the quality of the guild's wares, disturbing the functioning of the market, and so exposing the populace to loss. By and large, the state did intervene to support the claims of the established masters. From the end of the sixteenth century onward licenses for masters were granted with increasing reluctance, and finally the status of master was conferred only by occupancy of a recognized place of business (*gedik*), and hence was passed down by inheritance within the family. The result of all this was that the masters came to form, in effect, a quasi-caste, and the guild members were divided into capital-owning employers and wage-earning journeyman-laborers. Yet in the Ottoman guild system we do not find the journeymen organizing themselves to fight against this tendency, as they did in western Europe. All that happened was that, just as the former masters exploited the rules of the guild in their own interests, so the journeymen-workpeople and would-be new masters sought to turn the rules to their own advantage; those who opened new places of business in the outlying quarters of large cities without the guild's license would band together, elect a council of management, and set up a new guild. In spite of the opposition of the original guild, the new masters (called pejoratively *hām-dest,* that is, tyros, by the established masters) often persuaded the authorities to grant them recognition. We also find that the ancillary (*yamak*) guilds, which worked on behalf of the guilds of entrepreneurs, sometimes obliged the main guilds to grant their demands over rates of payment and so on by resolving to refuse to work for them—which in some sense amounts to a "strike," although admittedly this occurred only in the developed industries.

In Ottoman industrial activity we find some other developments, outside the guild framework, which are related to "merchant capitalism." The merchants themselves would organize the production of some wares for which there was a strong demand in external markets. They would distribute raw materials direct to weavers working at home, in the city or in adjacent villages, who worked for them for a wage, calculated by the piece or by the measure; then the merchants would collect the manufactured goods for export. This system prevailed in western Anatolia, as well as around Merzifon, Erzinjan and Erzurum, and in Diyarbekir with regard to the manufacture of various types of cotton cloth and thread. From the fifteenth century onward, these products were exported in large quantities to the Balkans, to the countries of the northern coasts of the Black Sea, and to Europe.

Another development which encouraged large-scale investment and paved the way for a capitalistic type of production was the ever-increasing demands of the state, especially to equip the army. We refer here, of course, not to the state arsenals, foundries, etc., organized as *kārhāne,*[47] but to private enterprises working for the state. One of the clearest examples of this is the woolen cloth industry of Salonika, which, from the end of the fifteenth century onward, greatly developed with a large annual production, particularly to provide uniforms for the Janissaries. A large proportion of the Sephardic Jews, skilled in the weaving of woolens, who had been settled in this city by the Ottomans in the last decade of the fifteenth century, were engaged in this industry. This Salonika cloth (*chuha-i Selānik*) was exported in great quantities to the Balkans and to the lands north of the Danube,[48] but a large proportion went to Istanbul for the Janissaries. Hence the state established a certain supervision over the industry to ensure that production was maintained and was sufficient in quantity and quality. These Jewish weavers were assisted by the state to procure, cheaply, the necessary fleeces in Macedonia. It is worth noting that in 1664, on the suggestion of

[47] See R. Mantran, *Istanbul dans la seconde moitie du XVII*e *siècle* (Paris, 1962), pp. 398-412.

[48] Inalcik, "Bursa and the Commerce," p. 139; Ö. L. Barkan, "Edirne," pp. 120, 125, 207, 217, etc.

the weavers that it would facilitate production, many of the looms were concentrated in a "factory."[49]

All these developments might well have formed the first steps toward an "industrial capitalism," but, for reasons which we will consider later, they went no further.

ISTANBUL

In Istanbul, which with its population of over half a million represented a vast market, commercial capitalism also developed in a special direction. The elements whom we may call "capitalist entrepreneurs" are, here as elsewhere, found among the merchants trading between distant regions. As the capital, Istanbul became at the same time the center for large-scale financial speculation in connection with the state's borrowing and tax farming and the vast demands of the palace and the army. The same individual or partnership would engage simultaneously in the exploitation of commercial concessions, in banking, and in the farming of taxes. The state provided fields of investment for capital and for speculative profits not only through its system of farming taxes but also by granting commercial concessions.

The state placed in the hands of privileged concessionnaires trade in certain commodities, the essential foodstuffs, and various raw materials needed by the guilds (cereals, cotton, wool, wax, and hides). Free trade in cereals and their export were forbidden, in order to prevent profiteers from speculating in them and to prevent their diversion to foreign markets. Only individuals licensed by the state could deal in them. These individuals were selected from wealthy and respected merchants and shipmasters. At the same time, the state fixed the prices, and the local authorities in the exporting areas helped the merchant to collect and transport the commodities. But the state had, unconsciously, created a situation favorable to speculation; although it tried to keep the fixed prices of sale (*narkh*) as low as possible, the restrictions of monopoly and state control led to a rise in prices. The prices offered by European merchants were artificially high, and this situation encouraged stockpiling and contraband dealings. The licensed merchants were therefore most closely supervised (thus, for example, a ship carrying grain had an inspector on board until it reached its appointed

[49] I. H. Uzunçarşili, *Kapilulu Ocaklari*, I (Istanbul, 1943), pp. 272-74.

destination), but even so it was not possible to prevent altogether the sale of cargoes at places offering higher prices.

To provision Istanbul, great quantities of wheat, rice, salt, meat, oil, fish, honey, wax, etc., were imported by sea, and those engaged in this trade were among the city's wealthiest merchants, who were organized in various associations. In the midseventeenth century, the first of these were the shipmasters transporting cargoes in their own ships. According to Evliyā Chelebī they were divided into the "captains of the Black Sea" (*Karadeniz reʾisleri*), numbering 2000, and the "captains of the Mediterranean" (*Akdeniz reʾisleri*), numbering 3000. They were Muslims or Greeks. The second group were shipowners, based on the *bedestan,* who equipped ships for overseas trade and who, again according to Evliyā, were very rich, some owning seven to ten large ships (*kalyon*) and fortunes of 4 to 5 million *akches* (20,000 to 25,000 ducats). "Each has several partners, in India, Yemen, Arabia, Persia and Europe; they dress as sumptuously as viziers; their patron is the Prophet." There was a third group who chartered ships for the import of cereals. These, according to Evliyā,[50] were wicked profiteers, who would buy cheaply the grain which the captains brought, store it, and then at a time of shortage would release it onto the market little by little and so make huge profits. Profiteering and contraband deals were common, especially when the central government was weak. The coasts and islands of the Aegean were alive with smugglers, and here many Greek shipmasters made fortunes. In order to prevent smuggling, the government was occasionally obliged to permit producer and merchant to settle a price by free negotiation.[51]

Another group enriching themselves from the trade in essential commodities were influential members of the ruling class attached to the Palace. They would elicit from the Sultan permission to export the great quantities of cereals grown on their *tīmār-* or *arpalik-*estates or their private estates or the estates of *wakfs* which they had founded, and make vast profits from the wide discrepancy between prices inside and outside the Empire: Thus in 1550 the Sultan's Jewish physician Moses Hamon was granted permission to sell to foreigners 600 *mud* (308 tons) of wheat grown on his *arpalik*-estate.[52]

50 Evliyā Chelebī, *Seyahatname,* I (Istanbul, 1314 H.), p. 551.

51 L. Güçer, *XV.-XVI. asirlarda Osmanli Imparatorlugunda Húbutat Meselesi ve Hububattan Alinan Vergiler* (Istanbul, 1964).

52 The copy of a document in the Munshéat, British Museum Manuscript No. 9503.

In any discussion of capital formation in the Ottoman Empire, special consideration must be given to the activities of the Marranos in the second half of the sixteenth century. Thanks to their great personal fortunes and skills and their extensive commercial network of agents in Europe, they appear to have played the principal role in Istanbul, as merchants, bankers, and tax farmers.

Ever since the fifteenth century the Jews had held a prominent place in trade between the Ottoman Empire and western Europe and in the farming of state taxes. In the middle of the sixteenth century, before the arrival of the Marranos, Nicolas de Nicolay wrote of the Jews[53]: "They have in their hands the most and greatest traffic of merchandise and ready money that is in the Levant." The Ottoman authorities, in accordance with the pragmatic principles so long observed in Near East states, regarded attracting wealthy merchants to their cities as one of the most effective methods of enriching the country and hence of filling the treasury. Thus even under Mehemmed II, and especially after the expulsion of the Jews from Spain in 1494, thousands of Jews were welcomed by the Ottoman government, and they settled in the principal ports of the Empire. So too the Ottoman authorities were eager to encourage the Marrano family of the Mendes, great bankers who controlled the spice trade in Europe, to settle in the Empire. The family's wealth was estimated in the 1530's to be three to four hundred thousand ducats. In 1553, thanks to the Sultan's personal interest and patronage, the family finally settled in Istanbul. The government used its political and diplomatic influence to enable them to transfer a part of their wealth from Europe. The family's operations were carried on through a network of agents in the principal towns of Europe. It is of some significance that the Mendes family settled in Istanbul in the very years that European trade was gaining an increasing importance for the empire. They were encouraged to move not only by the extensive scope for their operations promised in Turkey, but also by the religious toleration which prevailed there (whereas from 1536 the Marranos had been persecuted by the Inquisition). In 1555, when Pope Paul IV accused the Marranos of Ancona, who had close commercial links with the Ottoman lands, of being clandestine Jews, and when he began to arrest and burn them and confiscate their possessions, the Ottoman government intervened vigorously on their behalf, for many Jews

[53] *Quatre premiers livres des navigations et peregrinations orientales* (Lyons, 1567).

of Salonika and Istanbul whose capital was invested at Ancona had gone bankrupt and so were unable to pay to the Ottoman treasury the sums which they owed in connection with taxes they had farmed. In his letters to the Pope, the Sultan informed him that the treasury had lost 400,000 ducats and asked that the arrested Marranos be released. (Some of these Jews under arrest were in the service of Turkish merchants settled at Ancona.) Doña Gracia, then the head of the Mendes family, controlled a large proportion of the commerce between the Ottoman Empire and Europe (an exchange of European woolens for wheat, pepper, and raw wool). The business consortium (*dolāb*) which she had set up attracted deposits from rich Jews and Muslims, and the funds were employed in external trade and in tax farming. It was she, principally, of course, who had prompted the Ottoman intervention in the Ancona affair, and, with the Sultan's approval, she attempted to get the Jews of the Ottoman Empire to declare a boycott against Ancona.

It has been suggested by Professor E. Rivkin that the Marranos brought with them from Europe the methods and techniques of the modern capitalist entrepreneur and bestowed on the Ottoman economy a mercantilist character.[54] We do not know all the details of their activities in the Ottoman domains, but some idea of these can be gained from the study of the career of Don Joseph Nasi, Doña Gracia's nephew, who first succeeded in gaining the *entrée* to the palace and to the leading statesmen and in winning their confidence —which was, in the Ottoman state, the most important step in a prosperous business career. He acquired the monopoly of the wine trade, a trade which was shunned by Muslims but which brought great profits to Venice (at the beginning of the sixteenth century the wine trade between the Aegean and the countries of the Danube and eastern Europe was worth 6000 ducats a year in customs' revenues alone); a document shows that Joseph Nasi bought 1000 barrels of wine from Crete alone, and it was estimated that he made

[54] For the Marranos, see C. Roth, *The House of Nasi: Dona Gracia* (Philadelphia, 1947); *idem., The House of Nasi: The Duke of Naxos* (Philadelphia, 1948); E. V. Rivkin, "Marrano-Jewish Entrepreneurship and the Ottoman Mercantilist Probe in the Sixteenth Century" (paper submitted to the Third International Congress on Economic History, which will be published in its *Proceedings*). Professor Rivkin has most kindly permitted me to read this paper before its publication. When the material on the Marranos which he has collected from European and the Ragusan archives has been fully assessed, we shall be much more thoroughly informed on the whole question. Some Ottoman documents on the Marranos' activities were published by Safvet, "Yūsuf Nasi," *Tarih-i 'Osmāni Encümeni Mejmu'asi*, III (1330 H.), pp. 982-93 and pp. 1158-60.

from the trade some 15,000 ducats a year.[55] The Sultan, again with financial considerations in mind, removed from the hands of the Italians and granted to Joseph the administration of Naxos and the surrounding islands; this area was one of the chief centers of wine production in the Aegean. Joseph's commercial activities in Poland become so extensive as to produce anxiety among the local merchants of Lwów. The great loans which he made to the King of Poland (amounting, it is said, to 150,000 ducats) procured for him various commercial concessions. He gained the monopoly of beeswax, a valuable export commodity. He probably had a part also in the financial relations between France and the Ottoman Empire. In 1555, Henri II, pressed for money, floated a loan in France with the interest increased from 12 to 16 percent, and at this time many Turks, pashas among them, found it profitable to invest in this loan. Between 1562 and 1565 the Sultan sent several *firmans* to the King of France ordering him to pay without delay a debt of 150,000 *scudos* due to Joseph Nasi, and when the debt was not paid he caused the sum to be raised for Nasi by ordering the confiscation of French merchant ships calling at Levant ports. This question, which dragged on until 1569, seriously impaired the good relations between the two powers.[56]

Another noteworthy example is the Jewess Esther Kyra, who amassed a great capital from commerce and tax farming by putting to account the influence she had in the Palace.[57] She procured for herself and her sons the contract for the collection of the customs and, through the women and the eunuchs of the harem, the farms of the poll tax on non-Muslims, and collection of the sheep tax; she also made heavy investments in overseas trade. In 1600 the mounted regiments of the Porte mutinied, alleging that the underweight coin in which they had received their pay had been paid into the Treasury by Esther Kyra as collector of customs. They murdered her and one of her sons. Her fortune was confiscated, and was found to amount, in ready cash and commercial commodities alone, to 50 million *akches* (about 400,000 ducats)—not counting her real estate in 42 localities, goods actually in transit, and sums invested.[58]

55 Safvet, Yūsuf Nosi," p. 991.

56 Document, published by Safvet, pp. 992-93.

57 See J. H. Mordtmann, *Die jüdischen Kira im Serai der Sultane*, *MSOS*, XXXII (1929), pp. 1-38. Of the Ottoman chroniclers the most important is Mustafa Selānikī who was then a high official at the finance department.

58 Selānikī.

There is no question that since the fifteenth century Jews had had a large share in the farming of taxes of all sorts at Bursa and at Istanbul, but Greek and Turkish capitalists too do not seem to have been less active in this business. Thus in 1476, when a five-man consortium of Greeks bid 11 million *akches* (about 245,000 ducats) for the farm of the Istanbul customs for three years, a four-man consortium of Muslims outbid them by 2 million and gained the contract. Next year a Muslim Turk of Edirne and a Jew jointly put in a higher bid, but were outbid by a consortium of Greeks.[59] From the middle of the sixteenth century, with the coming of the Marranos, Jewish influence and control of the money market appear to have increased. But there is no clear evidence that they introduced a new mercantilist tendency in the Ottoman economy; it seems that they brought rather their own activities into conformity with the already existing pattern. The Ottoman government, realizing that the encouragement and protection of these great capitalists would help to meet its ever-growing need for ready money and so serve its own interests, was merely continuing its traditional policy.

EDIRNE

By considering the capital-owning classes and the formation of capital in Edirne (Adrianople), the principal city of the Balkans, we shall take a further step in formulating our generalizations on the Ottoman Empire. Of the estates of 3128 persons, mostly belonging to the "military" (*'askerī*)[60] class, who died at Edirne between the middle of the sixteenth and the middle of the seventeenth centuries, Professor O. L. Barkan has recently published ninety-three. An analysis of these estates, which amounted in total to more than 300,000 *akches,* discloses that the average value is half a million *akches;* a quarter of the total number amount to a million. Before 1605 five men died whose wealth, calculated in ducats, was between 10,000 and 18,000; three of these were merchants, while two belonged to the military class. The richest of them was a *sanjak-beg,* governor (Yūnus Beg).

The average estate among the rich in the sixteenth century was between 8,000 and 9,000 ducats, and, after the depreciation of 1584,

[59] H. Inalcik, "Notes on N. Beldiceanu's Translation of the *Kānūnnāme,*" *Der Islam,* XLIII/1-2 (1967), pp. 154-55.

[60] Under the term of "military" were included the administrators, the troops, and the men of religion in the Ottoman Empire.

between 5,000 and 6,000 and when this is compared with the fortunes of the Marranos or of the higher-ranking members of the ruling class in Istanbul, it is not so very impressive. For example, the annual income of a *sanjak-beg* from his *khāṣṣ*-estates was 200 to 600,000 *akches* (which represented, at the end of the fifteenth century, 4,000 to 12,000 ducats and after the depreciation, 1,650 to 5,000 ducats); and a *beglerbeg*'s (governor general) annual income was twice as much. Thus at all periods the military class ranked high, economically speaking, in Ottoman society.

The way in which the fortunes of the rich men of Edirne were composed is also of interest. When all the estates are considered we find that over this century the fields of investment for 49 million *akches* belonging to 175 persons are (in percent) as follows:[61]

Household goods and clothing	14.6	
Houses and shops	13.7	
Ready money	19.1	(usually in gold, but also in European silver coins)
Moneys due	21.2	(usually for goods sold on credit; money at interest and invested by *muḍaraba* is also included)
Agricultural (land and livestock)	16.6	
Stocks of industrial products	11.9	
Slaves	2.9	

Outstanding debts due on the estates amounted to 15 percent. If we except the first two items, we find that three-quarters of these fortunes can justly be called "capital."

The "capitalists" may be divided into four main groups: (1) Money changers/jewelers; (2) merchants trading with distant regions (especially in textiles, flax, gumlac, coffee, copper, iron and tin); (3) landowners growing wheat or raising stock for sale; and (4) "investors" making money by lending it at interest, renting out shops, milling, or investing it in various industries. As in the case of Bursa, the largest fortunes were owned by the money changers and the dealers in textiles, but among the greatest owners of capital, in this military base, were members of the military class.

(1) The money changers and jewelers left the greatest fortunes, which consisted mainly of gold and silver coin, silver ingots, and

[61] Barkan, "Edirne," pp. 471-73.

jewelry. They engaged largely in moneylending. Typical examples were Sünbül Hasan (d. 1604)[62] and Abū Bekir (d. 1624).[63] The former's fortune amounted at his death to 940,000 *akches* (7,833 ducats), of which 354,000 *akches* consisted of jewelry and goods in his house and shop and 466,000 in jewelry left with him in pledge for money which he had lent. The interest due to him was calculated at 100,000 *akches,* Abū Bekir left a fortune over 2,000,000 *akches,* of which 1,200,000 consisted of silver ingots and gold and silver coin; it is clear that he indulged in large financial operations with rich Jews and with the mint. At his death he was owed 220,000 by the Jew Abraham and 450,000 by the mint. He possessed ingot silver worth 399,000. Memi Beg b. 'Abd Allah (d. 1624) (presumably the son of a converted "slave of the Port"), who left 760,000 *akches,* was a banker, lending large sums at interest; at his death he was owed 160,000 by a Jewish tax farmer and 163,000 by another Jew. He used also to make small loans (e.g., 1600 *akches* to the gardener Niko).

(2) The textile dealers (*chuhaji and bezzāz*) of Edirne carried out extensive trade both in imported European cloth (particularly from Florence and London) and in home products (of Salonika, Istanbul, and Ragusa). The textile dealer Ḥajjī's estate (d. 1553) included Florentine cloth worth 2600 ducats. These dealers imported direct from Venice, to which, by their agents, they exported Ankara mohair, fleeces, wax, and coined gold (the rate of gold against silver being higher in Europe). The dealers in cottons (*bezzāz*) imported their wares mainly from western Anatolia and to a smaller extent, from Egypt, Yemen, and India.[64] Some of these goods were sold in Edirne itself, but an important proportion was sold in various regions of the Balkans. Hajji sold large quantities of cloth to the prince of Wallachia, but also to the governor of Syria (Shām) and to governors in eastern Anatolia.[65] When the *bezzāz* 'Abd al-Ḳādir died (1569) he was owed 97,000 *akches* in Edirne, 74,000 in Dobruja, and 63,000 in Belgrade for cottons and textiles which he had sold; he had also

62 *Ibid.,* p. 193, No. 29.

63 *Ibid.,* p. 429, No. 92.

64 For a caravan with the Indian merchants who in 1610 brought textiles on the route Basra-Baghdad-Aleppo, see H. Sahillioglu, "Bir Kervan," in *Belgelerle Türk Tarihi Dergisi,* No. 9 (1968); for the import of the Indian textiles into the Ottoman Empire in the fifteenth century, see H. Inalcik, "Bursa," *Belleten,* XXIV (1960), p. 75, doc. 12.

65 Barkan, p. 120, No. 11.

made investments in the cotton-producing regions of western Anatolia. The money he had invested as *muḍāraba* amounted to 148,000 *akches*. The *bezzāz* Mūsa (d. 1596),[66] worth 13,000 ducats, had sold cotton stuffs, wool stuffs, and silk stuffs in various parts of Rumeli-Belgrade, Ruscuk, and Pravadi. Saddler Ahmet[67] (d. 1649) traded with the northern countries, to which he sent spices, Indian cloth and thread, and cotton stuffs of Anatolia in exchange for furs and hides. Ahmet, who had begun life as a palace saddler, had presumably begun his business career by dealing in hides; when he died, it may be noted an Armenian merchant in Poland was owing him 600 riyals. Ahmed Chelebī (d. 1639), who imported flax, coffee, henna and cottons from Egypt ran this business by means of agents there. When he died the sums due to him for goods sold in various parts of Rumeli amounted to 208,000 *akches* (3466 ducats). Kapiji Mehemmed[68] (d. 1607) should also be noted; he transported iron from Samakov (near Sofia, an important center for iron production) to Istanbul and other parts of Rumeli and had dealings with the smiths' guild. The important point to notice in all this is that these wealthy merchants were all engaged in interregional trade. Unlike the money changers and the members of the military class, the merchants held relatively little ready cash; their wealth consisted mainly of stock and money due for goods sold on credit. But in about 1596, i.e., at a time when the exchange rate was very unsettled, the millionaire *bezzāz* Mūsa turned one-fifth of his fortune into gold coin. At Edirne, as at Bursa, sale on credit was evidently a widespread and indispensable commercial measure. A large proportion of the Edirne merchants' wealth, sometimes more than half, consisted of money due to them. That merchants tended to specialize is clear; yet there were some who spread their investments over varying fields. Khoja Ishak[69] (d. 1548), a wealthy textile merchant, had 59,000 *akches* lent out to a "Frank" (? Italian) named Jerino and 90,000 invested in Edirne in the shop of the Jew Mordecai. Merchants also lent at interest,[70] while some invested in mills or shops in Edirne. Most of them also had small land holdings and orchards to supply their families.

(3) Persons engaged in agriculture and stock raising also must be included among the "capitalists" of Edirne. These usually belonged

66 *Ibid.*, "Edirne," p. 335, No. 66.
67 *Ibid.*, p. 325, No. 65.
68 *Ibid.*, p. 170, No. 26.
69 *Ibid.*, p. 91, No. 4.
70 See *Tarih Vesikalari*, No. 9, p. 174.

to the governmental class, i.e., they were mainly *begs* and *sipāhīs* holding *khāṣṣ-* or *timar*-estates, "servants of the Porte," or *ulema*. The fortune of Bayram Beg b. Sevik (d. 1604),[71] who left 352,000 *akches,* consisted mainly of investment in his land and his stock. On his farm were 2 mills, 15 cattle, 3 dwelling houses, and 5 male and 3 female slaves; the slaves were doubtless laborers. He also employed laborers for wage (*irgad*). He engaged in large dealings in stock; at his death, he had sheep at pasture worth 53,000 *akches* and was owed 215,000 *akches* for animals sold and money out at interest. He was owed 6,000 *akches* by the villagers of Bilagon, Kozluja, and Sultan-yeri in respect of their sheep tax, which he had paid; he had also lent 6,000 *akches* to the villagers of Kestanlik to enable them to pay their poll tax.

Memi Beg b. ʿAbd Allah[72] (d. 1624) owned a large farm and two orchards. The grain in his barns was worth 96,000 *akches,* and his whole estate came to 760,000. He was engaged in dealing in wheat and in moneylending, an important part of his wealth consisting of moneys due—160,000 from the Jewish tax farmer Haydar and 163,000 from two other Jews. He was therefore both an agriculturalist and a moneylender.

The wealthy estate of 1,217,000 *akches* left by *Bostanji-Bashi* Süleymān *Agha*[73] (d. 1605), a high dignitary at the Seraglio, was made up of great flocks of livestock (2,651 sheep) and his farm (the farm itself 50,000 *akches,* stocks of grain 82,000). He had a large amount of coin (2,350 gold pieces and 35,000 *akches*) and of rich garments. The total money due to him from sales of beasts and grain and from money out at interest was some 180,000 *akches.* His debtors were mainly peasants, who had bought grain and animals from him. Although the retired, *Bostanji-bashi* Hasan *Agha*[74] (d. 1659) did not leave so wealthy an estate, he evidently made his money (583,000) by the same methods. Mehemmed *Agha* had 2 large farms (worth 72,000), 1 mountain pasture, several herds of animals (1,400 sheep, 93 cattle), large amount of grain, both harvested and sown (55, 000), and 3 mills; he also had 396 gold pieces. He himself lived in a fine house (worth 100,000) in Edirne.

Mahmūd Beg's son Mustafa Chelebī[75] (d. 1608), who held a

71 Barkan, "Edirne," p. 216, No. 33.
72 *Ibid.*, p. 425, No. 90.
73 *Ibid.*, p. 224, No. 35.
74 *Ibid.*, p. 414, No. 87.
75 *Ibid.*, p. 180, No. 28.

tīmār worth 25,000 *akches* a year, left 742,000 *akches;* much of this he may have inherited from his father. His basic fortune consisted of 48 cattle, 1500 sheep (worth 105,000 *akches*), 4 mills, and stocks of grain. At his death he had 196,000 *akches* out "on trust" (*emanet*) with 2 persons. It is stated that 70,000 of this came from the *tīmār.* The money "on trust" was probably invested. Mustafa Chelebī, who lived in his own village, owned 2 houses there, 4 stables, and 2 barns. That he was owed 71,000 *akches* by various people for grain and animals shows that he dealt in these commodities. He left stocks of grain and cheese worth over 20,000 *akches.*

Some *ulema,* like other members of the *'askerī* class, grew wealthy by growing wheat and raising stock for sale and by lending money. Thus Muslih al-Dīn, administrator of the Ergene *wakfs,* left at his death in 1548 a substantial fortune (338,000 *akches*),[76] half of it consisting of his animals (3,010 sheep and goats) and his pasture lands. He also engaged in moneylending, the debts due to him from guildsmen in Edirne amounting to 53,000 *akches.*

Sheykh Karamānī Muslih al-Dīn (d. 1598)[77]—a "sheykh" in the true dervish sense, for he had "*murīds*"—engaged in stock raising (840 sheep, 155 buffaloes and cattle, 34 horses) on his large farm near Edirne and he produced large amounts of butter in his dairy. He had 4 slaves, and left 352,000 *akches.*

In the early seventeenth century, when, as a result of the Jelālī disturbances in Anatolia, peasants abandoned their land to find safety in distant cities and in districts that were more secure, members of the military class, particularly Janissaries, occupied these deserted lands and made them into ranch-style grazing grounds for stock raising. A document describes the position in these words: "Powerful people among the population of the province have occupied the villages from which the original peasantry have fled and treat them as if they were inherited property. They have built houses and stables in the places abandoned by the peasantry and brought in oxen, slaves, servants, sheep and cattle, and set up independent farms; the former peasantry of these lands are too afraid of them to return to their old holdings."[78] Although the government took strong measures to procure the return of these lands to the

[76] *Ibid.*, p. 100, No. 7.

[77] *Ibid.*, p. 339, No. 67.

[78] H. Inalcik, "Adaletnâmeler," in *Belgeler,* II, Nos. 3-4, pp. 126, 128.

former owners, many of them certainly remained in the hands of members of the military class as ranches and farms. It is noteworthy that in the seventeenth century and later such estates held by the "military" were much more numerous than before. The important point which concerns us here is that such large farms and ranches, especially those situated near the sea or near large cities (so that transportation was no problem) and run in order to supply the market, became a new field for investment and exploitation and led to the formation of substantial fortunes. There is evidence that in later years such fortunes, invested in long-range trade or credit transactions, formed the nucleus of still larger fortunes.[79]

(4) It was a general tendency with the Ottomans not to leave idle any capital in their possession, however small. We often find that members of the military class and pious foundations put their ready money out at interest or bought properties to rent. Also the monetary fortunes in trust for orphans were widely loaned at interest or invested in *muḍāraba* enterprises. Some examples are: In Edirne Hüseyin Beg[80] (d. 1622) lived on the interest from the capital which was loaned to several shopkeepers in the city, and from the rents received from investments in shops and an oil press. The total value of the capital used in this way was about 1100 gold ducats. Hüseyin Beg had also advanced loans to the villagers which amounted to 44 thousand *akches* (260 gold ducats at that time). As for Mehemmed Beg (d. 1656),[81] he had made loans to 151 persons which amounted to 364 thousand *akches* (approximately 2000 gold ducats since 1 gold ducat had risen to 180 *akches* at the time). Among his debtors were villagers and small shopkeepers, including many Jews of Edirne. The rate of interest which he usually charged was 25 percent. Another Mehemmed Beg (d. 1648)[82] lived on the rents he received from his properties, namely 9 shops, 2 *bozahāne* (a kind of drinking house), 2 depots, and 1 slaughterhouse in Edirne. The case of an *imām* (Muslim priest) of a small district is particularly interesting. Though himself living a very modest life, Imām Abdī, when he died, was found to be the creditor of 92 persons who owed him altogether over 100 thousand *akches* (then worth 1700 ducats). The rate of interest was again 25 percent. Among his

[79] Barkan, "Edirne," p. 216 (Bayram Beg), p. 274 (Ahmed Beg), p. 293 (Ahmed Chelebī).
[80] *Ibid.*, p. 419, No. 88.
[81] *Ibid.*, p. 382, No. 78.
[82] *Ibid.*, p. 322, No. 64.

debtors were members of the military class, Jews, and Gypsies. In the *tereke*-registers there are many other examples of creditors who lived in Edirne and made loans to villagers to enable them to meet their tax obligations to the treasury. Besides this type of small moneylender, who was to be found in almost every Ottoman city, there were, as seen above, wealthy money changers engaged in large-scale credit operations in the big cities.[83]

Finally, the principal guilds represented in the main Ottoman cities developed in a special fashion in Edirne, for it was the capital of Rumeli and the mobilization center and base for campaigns into Europe. Leatherwork and the making of boots and shoes and of all types of harness developed in Edirne, and the products of these trades were distributed all over the Balkans. In these guilds which supplied external markets (as among the silk weavers of Bursa), wealthy masters were to be found, as the following examples show. The tanner Hajji Mehemmed[84] (d. 1606), who prepared and sold hides, left a shop containing unworked Morocco leather worth 45,000 *akches,* his total estate was 141,000 *akches* (1,175 ducats). He had received capital sums from various *wakfs,* which at his death totaled 19,000 *akches;* he had 14 cattle, a small farm, and 2 male and 2 female slaves. He lived in a house which was—for Edirne—expensive (316 ducats). Hajji Yūnus (d. 1549),[85] who made and sold all types of hair cloth wares, left the substantial fortune of 286,000 *akches* (4,766 ducats). In his guild's quarter he had 4 shops and 1 workshop (*kārhāne*). When he died he had stocks of goods worth 69,000 *akches* in his store and goods worth 18,000 in his shop. Forty-nine people owed him a total of 75,000 *akches*—an indication that guildsmen, like merchants, engaged in business on credit. At his death he left, in ready cash, 200 gold pieces and 57,000 *akches,* which for a tradesman represents substantial savings. The entry shows that he was a businessman on a large scale, selling hair cloth products to the government (on one occasion, sacks worth 12,000 *akches*). There were among the guildsmen some local mer-

83 In 1745 the villagers around Damascus sent a petition to the Porte saying that "since 1150 H. (1737) some of the usurers living in the city of Damascus loaned them money with interest to enable them to pay their tax obligations, but as the interest of each year had to be added to the following year's payments the villagers were reduced to a position in which they could never pay their debts." (The Başvekâlet Archives, Istanbul, Şam ahkâm defterleri, No. 1, p. 102).

84 Barkan, "Edirne," p. 228, No. 36.

85 *Ibid.,* p. 107, No. 9.

chants who bought for sale products made by others. An example is Ahmed Beshe,[86] a former Janissary, who sold sacks, horse cloth, rope, and all kinds of wares relating to animals; his estate was estimated at 114,000 *akches,* most of this consisting of the stock in his shop. These examples have been chosen from the wealthiest guildsmen and tradespeople of Edirne. Their fortunes are very moderate when compared with those of the money changers and the merchants—a confirmation of the conclusions drawn from seventeenth-century Bursa.

THE *wakf* (ISLAMIC PIOUS ENDOWMENT)

When the *wakf* is considered from the viewpoint of the extensive enterprises to which it gave rise, it is seen to occupy a special place in the question of capital formation in Muslim society.

The object of the Muslim *wakf* is to establish a charitable foundation; but the essence of the *wakf* is a thing "restrained" to God which produces an income, the income being expended only upon the defined charitable purpose. The *wakf* therefore is an institution closely related to an impersonal and perpetual fund of capital.[87] The *wakf* is set up by means of a *wakfiyya,* a kind of charter, in which are laid down the object of the *wakf,* its sources of income, the way this income is to be employed, and the way it is to be protected and increased. The fact that it is enregistered by the *cadi* and especially that, as found in the Ottoman Empire, it becomes legally valid after confirmation by the ruler, reveals still more clearly its character as a charter. Nevertheless, no one, even the ruler, can change or annul the conditions of the *wakf,* which are upheld by a religious and divine sanction on the principle that "the condition laid down by the founder of a *wakf* is like the text laid down by the legislator (of God's law.)" Although the aim of a *wakf* was to support a charitable object pleasing to God, in practice most *wakfs* benefited individuals; family *wakfs* particularly (*evlādiyye*) were founded with the deliberate object of protecting the interests of a specific family. Similarly, since the existence of the *wakf* was bound

[86] *Ibid.,* p. 375, No. 76.

[87] It is generally stated that Islamic law did not recognize the concept of legal personality. Nevertheless it has been persuasively argued that the institution of the *wakf* reposed, from the legal point of view, on the same basis as the trust or uses which appears in England in the thirteenth century. (See M. Khadduri and H. J. Liebesney (eds.), *Law in the Middle East* (Washington, D.C., 1955), pp. 212-18.

up with the preservation of the source of income, the administrators of the *wakf* concentrated their activity upon the protection and increase of the "capital"; many endowers of *wakfs* laid it down as a duty of the administrators to increase the income and extend the *wakf*.

Wakfs comprised two groups of institutions: On the one hand were establishments set aside for pious objects—mosques, colleges, hospitals, hospices, fountains, bridges, dervish-convents, etc.; on the other were foundations created to supply the expenses of such establishments. These latter were investments, created with the aim of showing a profit and made in a true spirit of economic enterprise; they might consist of agricultural activity or of property let for a rent; they might comprise slaves set to profitable work or simply cash put out at interest.

The administration of a *wakf* may be compared with a trust. The endower appointed an administrator (*mutawallī*) and, for a large *wakf*, a supervisor (*nāzir*) over him. The *mutawallī* is responsible for the maintenance of the *wakf*, for fulfilling the conditions of the *wakfiyya* and for guarding and increasing the sources of income. To achieve this, he may indulge in economic enterprises, by investing surplus income. The employees who, at a lower level, have responsibility for the administration of the *wakf*, meet the *mutawallī* once a year and check his activities and his accounts for the past year; they can apply to the *cadi* for his dismissal. *Wakf* accounts were also checked, under the Ottomans, by a representative of the state, according to the principle of public trusteeship. Thus the *wakf* obtained in Islamic society, from the aspects of both its foundation and its activity, the character of an economic enterprise with a special organization similar to a trust.

In the Ottoman Empire most of the large *wakfs* were founded by the members of the higher ruling class. Vizier Sokollu Mehemmed's project with the cooperation of Feridun Beg is an interesting example of how such *wakfs* gave rise to real economic enterprises. They proposed to the Sultan to grant them the proprietorship of the wasteland around Eskishehir on the important caravan route from Iran to Bursa and Istanbul. They promised to create a pious endowment there by investing capital to construct a dam and canals and turn this land into rice fields. The peasants in the neighborhood could use the water on condition they gave half of their crops to the *wakf*. The revenue would be spent for the construction of caravansaries, bridges, and fountains to serve the passing caravans.[88] This is an outstanding example of the hundreds of *wakf* estates in the Empire which initially had the character of a genuine economic enterprise: the founder played the role of an entrepreneur setting up the initial project, investing the capital for the profit-bringing establishments, usually bringing the land and slave labor together and disposing of the income.

A great number of founders of *wakfs* invested their "capital" partly or totally in erecting buildings (*musaḳḳafāt*) in the cities, such as Turkish baths, bazaars, shops, tenements, depots, workshops, bakeries, oil presses, mills, slaughterhouses, tanneries, tile factories, etc. These were believed to be the ideal *wakfs,* for they were long-enduring and secured a steady rent. It was such *wakfs* that were mainly responsible for the development of economic life in the cities.[89] The erection of a *bedestan* (*bezzāzistān;* in Arabic countries, *Ḳaiṣariyya*), a fortress-like building in the heart of the city, was especially significant, since it constituted a center for the money changers and big merchants engaged in international trade where important commercial transactions were carried out through brokers and the fortunes of the well-to-do citizens were preserved in special safes or invested in *muḍāraba* (*commenda*) enterprises.

In many cases cash money made up a part or the whole of the funds, the interest from which was the annual income of the *wakf.* For example in Edirne a certain Merjān Khoja founded a *wakf* for a children's school, the funds of which consisted of 200,000 *akches.* This sum would be put out at interest at 10 percent, and the yield would be spent for the current expenses of the school. The family *wakf* of Süleymān *Agha,* commander of the Sultan's gardeners in Edirne, is interesting. He made a *wakf* of 1 million *akches* cash (approximately 8333 ducats) to be put out on loan at 15 percent. The income from the interest was assigned to his wife and offspring. Only when his race was extinct was the income to be assigned to the building and maintenance of a college for the readers of the Koran. This type of money *wakfs* was quite widespread in the Empire. In 1561 the total sum of cash endowments made by the

88 The document is published by Ö. L. Barkan, *Kolonizatör Türk Dervisleri,* Vakiflar Dergisi, II (1942), p. 358.

89 For the Ottoman city, see Ö. L. Barkan, "Quelques observations sur l'organisation économique et sociale des villes ottomanes," in *La Ville,* Vol. VII (Société Jean Bodin, Brussels, 1955), pp. 289-311. For comparison, see Lapidus, *Muslim Cities,* and the bibliography, pp. 239-41.

people in the city of Bursa alone was estimated at 54,000 gold ducats (3,250,000 *akches*).[90]

CONCLUSIONS

The investigation into conditions in Bursa, Istanbul, and Edirne, the three principal centers of the heartlands of the Empire, have shown that the economic structure of the Ottoman Empire was typical of the traditional system in the empires of the Near East.[91] The Ottoman state endeavored to exercise close control over production and distribution, as having a close bearing on its own financial and political ambitions. As regards industrial production, the state remained loyal to the guild system only, and hence also to *hisba* and its traditional principles. Before the increasing demands of the great cities and external markets, economic laws began to make their pressure felt, so that as a natural consequence a few interesting developments occurred in some guilds, but the state still sought to solve the new problems within the old guild framework; it never considered moving in the direction of a system of mercantilist economy as Europe did.

The richest guildsmen who engaged in large-scale production, even the velvet weavers, did not possess large capital sums; they were unable to create expanding enterprises calling for ever-increasing investment and failed to win support in external markets through a state policy of protection and encouragement. The government, conscious of the necessity to increase the Empire's stocks of gold and silver, did, it is true, exempt precious metals and foreign currency from customs dues, encouraging their import and forbidding their export; but it never accepted—or perceived—the connection between the attraction of precious metals on the one hand and a capitalistic system of production and a protective policy of export on the other. The clearest proof that the Ottomans were interested only in imports is the readiness with which they granted capitula-

90 Barkan, "Edirne," pp. 34-35.

91 For the close connection between the Ottoman and Abbasid economic and financial institutions and practices, see, in addition to the introductory remarks in this article, A. Mez, *Die Renaissance des Islams* (Heidelberg, 1922); A. al-Dūrī, *Studies on the Economic Life of Mesopotamia in the 10th Century* (in Arabic), (Baghdad, 1948); W. Björkman, "Kapitalentstehung und -anlage im Islam," in *Mitteilungen des Seminars für orientalische Sprachen,* 32 (1929), 2. Abt., pp. 80-98; C. Cahen, "Les facteurs économiques et sociaux dans l'ankylose culturelle de l'Islam," in *Classicisme et déclin culturel dans l'histoire de l'Islam* (Paris, 1957), pp. 195-207.

tions to the states of western Europe in the sixteenth century.[92] Right up to the reform period in the nineteenth century, the Ottoman state remained loyal to the guild system and opposed to developments which might lead to a sort of industrial capitalism. This policy of the state and the traditional cultural attitude which were dominant forbade even a modest development in the direction taken by western Europe.

The principal fields of investment for the formation of capital were interregional trade and the lending of money at interest. In Ottoman society people engaged in these activities and the higher ranks of the ruling class could make vast fortunes. The fortunes of those members of the military-administrative class who, from the viewpoint of their wealth, formed the higher ranks in the society in general came, basically, from incomes from *tīmār*-estates, pay in cash, and the farms which they had organized as agricultural enterprises. The wealth gained from these sources they invested in long-distance trade, usually on a *commenda* basis, or on a larger scale in moneylending at high interest rates. The fortunes of this class, many of whom were of slave origin and whose wealth derived originally from state payments, were particularly exposed to confiscation by the state; thus many of them invested their wealth in *wakf* foundations—profit-bearing establishments such as shops, caravansaries, and baths—as being the best protected and most permanent source of income. Although the *wakf* provided one of the most important fields of investment in Ottoman society, yet because *wakfs* were fundamentally consuming institutions, they never assumed the characteristics of a really capitalistic enterprise. Moreover, the state extended its control over *wakfs* as well, and found means to divert superfluous *wakf* income, which might have been invested, into the treasury. This too should be added, that from the second half of the sixteenth century onward the members of the "military" class developed more and more into being really businessmen—merchants, landowners running large estates, and moneylending bankers.

The only elements in Ottoman society who can properly be called

[92] Drawing attention to the unfavorable balance of commerce of the Ottoman Empire, Naīmā (*History*, IV, p. 293), an enlightened Ottoman historian of the eighteenth century, said that only goods not needed in the internal market such as fleeces of wool, nut-gull, or potash were to be exported.

"capitalistic entrepreneurs" are the merchants and the money changers. They were in a position to accumulate, by any method they chose, as much wealth as they desired, and the state protected them and encouraged them as they did it. It is they who owned the large capital necessary to finance the exchange of goods between distant regions, who organized the despatch of caravans and ships (sometimes their own ships), who stationed their commercial agents in various cities abroad, who employed the method of *muḍāraba,*[93] who made investments in the producing areas, and who collected the products for distribution elsewhere. At every stage of these enterprises, they made extensive use of credit. Through *muḍāraba* they brought together great and small sums from all sides and endeavored to increase these sums by their various ventures; they invested in trade and moneylending; they contracted for tax farms; they sold their merchandise on credit in different parts of the Empire, and, in return for it, exacted interest.

But where wealth was concerned, it was only the *ṣarrāfs* who could stand comparison with the members of the ruling class. Engaged in trade in precious metals and jewelry and in the money market, they increased their wealth by giving credit to merchants and guildsmen, by contracting for tax farms, or by financing other tax farmers on credit, and thus amassed really large fortunes. At the same time they had their part in interregional trade. It should be noticed that the *ṣarrāfs* who made the greatest fortunes were those who undertook transactions connected with the government Finance Department. In order to find the finances for large state tax farms, they often banded together in partnerships, and it fre-

[93] Various forms of *muḍāraba* (*commenda*) are found in the Ottoman Empire. Some examples are: In 1614 Osman and Allahkulu, two merchants of Ibril (a place near Baghdad), made a *muḍāraba* contract, each contributing 1540 *riyal* (1026 gold ducats in value). Allahkulu took up the whole responsibility of the enterprise and was active in the Baghdad-Aleppo-Bursa caravan trade. The profit made was to be divided between them equally. All this was recorded in the register of the *cadi* of Bursa (Dalsar, p. 222). In 1605 Mustafa *Agha* (apparently from the military class), a merchant in Edirne, made a partnership with Hajjī Ridvān to import flax from Egypt and as the capital of a *muḍāraba* Ridvān put a capital of 12,500 *akches* (104 ducats) into the enterprise. Mustafa took the trip to Egypt to buy and transport the flax to Edirne. These are examples of the contract of *muḍāraba* between the merchants in interregional trade. A different kind of *muḍāraba* is found in the textile manufacturing trade. 'Abd al-Kādir, a merchant of cotton goods in Edirne, distributed "in the way of *muḍāraba*" a large sum of money to a number of people in the towns producing cotton goods in Anatolia. It appears that the money was used as a capital invested in making cotton goods for 'abd al-Kādir.

quently happened that they too fell victim to confiscation or other punishments as a result of their speculative ventures or their tax-farming activities.

This is the place to correct the mistaken view that these merchants and bankers were non-Muslims, and that Muslims entered only the profession of arms and the administration. This error is the result of projecting back into earlier centuries a development which occurred only after the eighteenth century. It can be said quite definitely that until the eighteenth century Muslims were as numerous and as active as non-Muslims in these fields—indeed until the seventeenth century the Muslims predominated among the merchants. In the sixteenth and seventeenth centuries Muslim merchants also engaged, without intermediaries, in commercial dealings in Europe, though it is true that in contacts with the West, Jews, Armenians, and other non-Muslims were, not unnaturally, more numerous and more active. That these later gained the upper hand in the economy of the Empire may well be related to the fact that the Empire's trade with the East declined and trade with the West gained in importance.

The dominant role played by the traditional view of the state and society in the Near East was mentioned above. Another aspect to be considered is the rigid forms imposed by the religious law. There was no legal principle permitting the establishment of permanent institutions possessing legal personality (except *wakfs*). Also the law of inheritance must be given weight: A large proportion of the deceased's estate went in gifts and bequests to *wakfs,* wives, and slave girls; then there were the various dues, which amounted to a twentieth of the estate; and the balance had to be divided among the heirs in the proportions prescribed by the religious law. Thus, accumulated wealth was destined to be dispersed in every generation, so that we look in vain in Ottoman society for long-established partnerships and firms which remained from generation to generation in the hands of a single family.

Also it must be remembered that credit facilities remained at a primitive stage and credit was obtainable only on harsh conditions. In the Ottoman Empire the merchant, shopkeeper, and peasant could not survive without credit. The use of credit was surprisingly widespread. The shortage of currency in circulation could be the main reason for it. This shortage was always acutely felt in the Empire, even after 1584, when the invasion of European silver coins started in the Ottoman markets.[94] Obviously the increasingly higher rate of interest was connected with this.

The religious law and the *hisba* based on it recognized the normal rate of profit as 10 percent, or in special cases as high as a maximum of 20 percent.[95] In the documents of *wakf* and the regulations of *hisba* we find that rates never exceeded this level. But the *tereke*-registers of Edirne between 1550-1650 testify that the rate of interest between individuals was usually 25 percent or higher. In the provinces, especially in the rural areas, the rate often exceeded 50 percent and this was denounced by the government as flagrant usury. In the famous *firman* of the Declaration of Justice (*'adāletnāme*)[96] of 1609, the Sultan himself exposed cases in which 50 percent of interest was charged. The local authorities were ordered to punish the usurers and to deduct for the debts the payments of interest made over 15 percent. In the critical period of 1596-1610, an outcry reached the central government that the members of the military class in the provinces were charging the peasants an interest three or four times the money lent. Usury was indeed one of the main sources of capital accumulation in the Ottoman Empire. For example, in 1571 an usurer named Osman had made a fortune estimated at 50,000 gold ducats in Larenda, a provincial town in central Anatolia, another 30,000 in Amasya in 1584. Avoiding outright confiscation, the government forced these usurers with massive capital to be suppliers of meat at fixed prices for Istanbul and the army, which was indeed a very risky business.[97]

In addition to the shortage of currency and the widespread practice of usury, credit instruments embodied in the *Sharī'a*, a religious law, were not adequately developed in the Ottoman Empire. In the *sijill*-registers the Ottoman *cadis* were to be found applying

94 See H. Inalcik, "Türkiye'nin Iktisadî Vaziyeti," pp. 656-61. During the second half of the sixteenth century the new conditions called for the growing use of currency in paying soldiers, taxes, and making *wakfs*. Then one might speak of a development of the Ottoman economy into a money economy. See the chapter which I wrote for the *Cambridge History of Islam* (in press).

95 In the regulations of *hisba* of Edirne in 1502 we read: "Merchants (*bāzirgān*), dealers in textiles (*bezzāz*), makers of caps, or merchants of silk cloths shall not take more than 20 per cent when they loan money at interest." (*Tarih Vesikalari*, No. 9 (1942), p. 174.)

96 H. Inalcik, "Adâletnâmeler," in *Belgeler*, II, Nos. 3-4 (1965), p. 130.

97 M. Akdag, "Türkiye'nin Iktisadî Vaziyeti," in *Belleten* No. 55, p. 367. For the capitalistic nature of this business, see B. Cvetkova, "Le service des *celep* et le ravitaillement en bétail dans l'empire Ottoman," in *Etudes Historiques*, III (1966), pp. 145-72. The wealthy members of the military class were interested in this business too.

extensively, according to the *Sharī'a,* the form of contracts known as *selem,* that is, a sale by immediate payment against future delivery, or *mu'ajjal* sale, that is, a sale on credit with an interest charge which was usually recorded in the registers in such a way as to conceal its true nature.[98] The great majority of the sale contracts fell in the second category. As a rule witnesses and sureties were required for these contracts. In the *sijill*-registers we also find the use of transfer, *hawāla,* of credits and debts to a third party, and examples of an agency in all kinds of dealings.[99] In the fifteenth-century registers we find Italian merchants having the Ottoman *cadi* apply the same procedures in their dealings with the Muslims as in their dealings with their Christian compatriots.[100] Thus the principle of the letter of credit was not unknown to the Ottomans through the Islamic *hawāla,*[101] which was the payment of a debt through the transfer of a claim. In public finances *hawāla* was extensively used to make payments to people through assignations on the tax farmer. The reasons why *hawāla* did not give rise in the Ottoman world of business to improved credit instruments similar to those found in the West may be the same general conditions which hampered economic development in the Middle East. It is indicative of those conditions that, instead, the pledging of valuables and of land became the most widely used security for loans and for sales on credit in the Ottoman Empire.

[98] For examples see H. Inalcik, "Bursa," *Belleten,* XXIV, docs. 13, 15, 16, 17, 18, 19, 21, 22, 32, 34.

[99] *Ibid.,* docs. 8, 13, 34.

[100] *Ibid.,* docs. 6, 7, 8, 10, 13, 16.

[101] See "hawāla," in *Encyclopaedia of Islam,* new ed., III, pp. 283-85.

OTTOMAN DECLINE AND REFORM

XIII

THE OTTOMAN DECLINE AND ITS EFFECTS UPON THE *REAYA*

I. THE SEEDS OF DECLINE IN THE OTTOMAN REGIME

The circumstances in which the villager lived during the final period of Byzantine rule and under the feudal regimes of the Balkans cannot be said to have been better than they were after the arrival of the Ottomans. Before the Ottoman conquest villagers who lived on *pronija* lands, those belonging to monasteries or feudal lords, were subjected to a variety of burdensome demands upon their labor. The so-called *paroikos* was obliged to render to his *seigneur* one wagonload each of wood, hay, and straw every year and was bound also to do wagon service and work for the *seigneur* two or three days every week. Even before the Ottoman period there was a tendency in maritime zones where a cash economy had developed or in the zones surrounding larger towns, towards the acceptance of a cash tax of a certain amount in place of these services, resulting, just as in Western Europe, in a loosening of the personal bonds which tied the villager to his *seigneur*. In general this tendency was welcome not only to the *seigneur*, who had a need for cash, but also to the villager, provided that he was in a position where he could obtain cash. This development was accelerated with the establishment of the Ottoman centralized regime. Although the older labor services were allowed to survive in certain areas, the Ottomans generally eliminated the labor services and replaced them with a single clearly-defined tax of 22 *akçes*, called the *çift resmi* or 'yoke tax', which was a specific sum paid by each villager once a year in place of the eliminated labor services. There is no doubt that this taxation policy eased the way for the Ottoman takeover.

In harmony with the traditional view of the state throughout the Middle East, the land and those who worked it were regarded by the Ottomans as belonging to the sultan himself. This direct control was regarded as one of the great principles upon which the state was based. With it in mind the Ottomans abrogated every sort of personal feudal bond and kept under vigilant control, subject to law, every sort of local military and legal authority and everything which might be exacted from the villager. Those to whom the *padişah* delegated his authority, primarily the provincial *beys* and their local lieutenants as well as the judges whose duty it was to oversee and guarantee enforcement of the law, kept each other under control as countervailing forces and stayed in continuous written contact with the central authority. The PRIME DUTY of the central government was to protect the subject from abuses of authority by local figures. Nonetheless, in every period there was evidence pointing to abuses of authority by those to whom it was delegated. We can see that when the central authority was weak and financial crises were endemic, these abuses widened and worsened to the point that they threatened the very constitution of the Empire. Nor can we overlook the fact that, under the *timar* system, certain rights over the lands and villagers were reserved to the military personnel to whom they were assigned and that in spite of all the intended limitations and attempts at control, these delegated rights were liable to abuse. As a start, let us take a glance at the labor services which were imposed upon the *reaya*, the term used for villagers, be they Christian or Moslem.

According to a law dating from the end of the 15th century, the *reaya* were obliged to transport the tithe belonging to the *sipahi*, the cavalryman set over them, to a granary or a fortress garrison. Moreover, if the cavalryman wished it, villagers had to transport this tithe to the nearest market. But in no instance were villagers supposed to carry produce more then a distance of one day. The *reaya* had to reap hay for the *sipahis* but were not obliged to transport it. But in spite of these limitations, there often were complaints that *sipahis* assigned to the land were using the *reaya* animals and wagons for their own benefit. One more labor service recognized by law was the *reaya*'s obligation to build a granary for the village cavalryman. Apart from this, however, *reaya* were not supposed to be forced to build a house or do anything else for the *sipahi*. One of the more onerous labor services was, of course, the *reaya*'s obligation to work on land reserved for the *sipahi*'s own profit. The *sipahi* of each *timar* had his own special fields, called *hâssa çiftlik* or his own *hâssa* orchard and vegetable garden which had to be worked by the peasants. Ottoman law limited this sort of service to three days in a year.

Subsequently this form of labor service was usually commuted into a cash tax of three *akçe* annually per villager, and the fields reserved for the cavalrymen were rented by him to the villagers. When Cyprus was taken by the Ottomans, they converted the two days of service per week by the *paroikos*, or serf, into one day of service per week in the sugar refineries belonging to the government. But it was not long before this was completely eliminated. Also in force was a custom surviving from older times by which one out of every fifty herders was supposed to render service to a *sanjak bey* (governor) for a period of six months. However, this service was also completely eliminated in 1536. The State serfs, called *ortakçı kullar*, who in the 15th century were drawn in limited numbers from war prisoners, merged completely with the regular *reaya* in the 16th century. Thus those forms of service which were at variance with the principles of the Ottoman system died out.

Another matter which always resulted in complaints by the *reaya* was the practice of obliging the villagers to feed without compensation the soldiers and officials who happened to visit their village along with their animals and all those who accompanied them. To combat this, the State came to place a limit of three days upon the length of time which a *sipahi* might alight in a village within his *timar*. The Ottomans tried to ease the situation of the villager by requiring that these visits be as infrequent as possible, that the visitor take as few people as possible with him and that he pay for everything received from the villager.

A worse form of abuse was the illegal requisition of the villager's grain, livestock, and cash reserves, a practice called *salma* or *salgun*. Normally it was resorted to by high ranking officials and military officers and involved a request for a certain amount of the goods in question from each village household. For this sort of thing, the expression *tekâlîf-i şâkka*, or 'onerous levies', was used. We know too that the central government sometimes issued special orders which permitted a general or commander to resort to this sort of requisition. Those who carried out unauthorized requisitions were severely punished in periods when the central authority was strong, but in the period of decline these arbitrary requisitions came at the head of the list of the abuses which stripped the villagers and ruined the country.

One more field for abuses lay in the widespread application of the practice by which the Ottoman administration allowed government officials to collect various forms of income directly from the *reaya* to make up their salary. In order to prevent abuses, the Ottomans carefully specified in their laws the kind and the amount of tax to be gathered, and the time of gathering. The practice found its widest application in the *timar* system, in which the *sipahi* collected for himself dues and taxes established by law. Each such *timar* had a known income. So that this income would neither diminish nor be lost, the government granted the *sipahi* a right to use part of the land himself, and also a number of means to control the lands worked by the *reaya*. Naturally, *sipahis* did not shrink from abusing the exercise of this delegated authority. Income from the larger *timars*, called *hâss*, which were assigned to commanders and governors, was either gathered by farming it out to individuals or by means of agents or collectors (*voyvodas*).

Apart from the *timar* system, the law permitted the collection of certain taxes from all *reaya* in return for services which officials performed directly for them. A tax collector, for instance, took for himself a certain fee from each household. Judges took standard fees for legal documents prepared for the *reaya* or when they made judgements on inheritance matters. Only when the central government effectively operated its system of controls was it able to keep at a minimum the abuses arising from this sort of delegated authority.

Finally, we must touch upon those abuses which arose from the operation of the tax farming system (*iltizam*) which existed from the earliest times of the Ottoman empire. This system operated through the sale of state income sources, such as those coming from *timar* or *hâss* lands, to private persons at ever higher prices. The state contracted to turn over such collections to the tax farmers, who each time promised to deliver more; it thus was able to increase indefinitely the tax revenues to be collected. The activities of tax farmers were controlled by a state appointed commissioner, called *emin*. But despite this, most of them managed to get out of the *reaya* just as much as they could, and it must not be forgotten that the State's own military forces assisted the tax farmer in making his collections. The Ottomans knew of the shortcomings of this system, and to the extent that it was possible endeavored to limit its operation and prevent its abuse; but starting from the latter half of the 16th century it both expanded and degenerated, due largely to the concurrent decay of the *timar* system. No better method other than the tax farming system remained for the collection of these revenues once the *timar* holdings, instead of being in the hands of *sipahis* living in their assigned villages, passed into the hands of influential parties living in Istanbul or other cities, or on the other hand, once they were attached directly to the treasury. The tax farming system spread so far that even judges began to lease to substitutes the courts within their jurisdiction, with each court being a means of income through the dues collected in the judge's name. Anyone leasing a court for its proceeds was of course bound to get involved in bribery. In similar fashion all state positions, all instruments exercising state-delegated authority, came to be means for personal gain. As the central government fell into an embarrasing financial position, it began to sell posts and delegate authority to the highest bidders regardless of qualifications. At the same time one must not forget that bribes were also received by those who vouched for appointees. In all cases, it was the *reaya* who in the end paid for these ever pyramiding bribes.

So here we have the seeds of ruination which the Ottoman State carried within it. According to the traditional view of the state in the Middle East, chief among the factors which kept a government viable was its success in protecting *reaya* from abuse and tyranny, since the impoverishment or dispersion of the *reaya* masses would result in the diminution of a State's sources of income, and a State without income could not survive. Imbued with this belief, the early Ottoman statesmen endeavored to prevent abuses and to make these measures work. But from the 1570's onward, as central authority weakened, they were no longer capable of doing this and the entire system declined.

II. EFFORTS TO ELIMINATE GOVERNMENT CORRUPTIONS: THE JUSTICE DECREES (ADALETNAMELER)

The 'justice decrees' are undoubtedly the Ottoman sources which reflect most authoritatively the administrative corruption which developed during the period of decline. A 'justice decree', or *adaletname*, is a decree of the *padishah* in the form of a manifesto which strongly forbids behavior contrary to law and justice, or any misuse of authority affecting the *reaya* by those who exercised authority in the name of the state.

The 'justice decree' sent to the commander-in-chief of Anatolia and to the district commanders and judges in 1595 on the occasion of the accession of the Sultan Mehmed III describes with an unprecedented explicitness the confusion which then for the first time prevailed within the Empire and the widespread abuses which accompanied it. After making clear that laws and regulations originating in the period of Süleyman the Lawgiver were being trampled underfoot and that dues and taxes extracted from the *reaya* had swollen by virtue of a host of unlawful innovations, it goes on to list the principal abuses of the day as follows: (1) *Vizir*, commanders-in-chief, and their agents in the provinces — the collectors, the other commanders, the bailiffs (*subaşıs*), the property administrators and private trustees, as well as supervisors (*kâhyas*) in villages (positions which had been given to palace favorites), state collectors and tax farmers, and judges' substitutes — had all been making rounds in the provinces, frequently accompanied by ten or fifteen cavalrymen, and after alighting in the villages they would oblige the *reaya* to feed them and their animals free of charge, and by misusing their authority would collect money in an unwarranted fashion. (2) *Sancak Beys*, district commanders, and *subaşıs*, bailiffs responsible for the peace and security of their zones, were collaborating with brigands instead of catching them. (3) Individuals from the various regular forces maintained by the central government *kapı-kulu*, or at least individuals who pretended to be such, had been going around in groups to villages and towns to rob the *reaya* causing the *reaya* to flee and scatter. The 'justice decree' adds that because of this oppression the *reaya* were abandoning their villages and scattering. This decree was published on the eve of Mehmet III's major expedition against the Hapsburgs.

Here we must pause for a moment to give attention to the *kapı-kulu* groups calling themselves government regulars who descended upon the people at that time. The beginning of all this dates to the last years of Süleyman's reign. At that time, because of the competition for the throne which was going on, worrisome pockets of resistance had arisen *vis-a-vis* the central government. One contender for the throne, Prince Bayezid, attracted freebooters coming mostly from the villages of Anatolia, and from them he founded a personal army, promising that if he acceded to the throne he would take them into the regular forces, or *arkapı kullar*. After Bayezid passed from the scene, the Ottoman government put this Anatolian soldiery on the payroll because of their skill with firearms, and used them during the wars in Iran (1578-1590) and Hungary (1593-1606), increasing their numbers steadily. These forces, which bore the name of *Sarıca* or *Sekban*, got into the habit of living off the people of Anatolia during periods when the government was not paying their wages by means of requisitions of their own invention, burning, plundering and killing in villages and towns which did not give in to their demands. To these the Ottoman statesmen gave the name *jelâli*, *eşkiya*, or 'rebels'. Most of them purported to be janissaries or regular army men and appropriated for themselves the privileges that went along with such status. On the other hand, the real janissaries and regular army men who had settled in cities and towns used what authority they had to intimidate and exploit the people around them, thus making themselves into a privileged socio-economic group. This situation thrust Anatolia into anarchy. Some of the people fled to Rumeli and to other surrounding regions. After 1603, when Iran became the aggressor and the Ottoman forces in Azerbaijan were withdrawn to Anatolia, the situation took on the proportions of a catastrophe. The confused scattering of the masses of villagers who fled Anatolia to save themselves from the *celalîs*, was called the *Büyük kaçgun*, the 'Great Flight'.

The 'justice decree' published by Ahmet I in 1609 reflects the grave circumstances of the time. The Anatolian and Rumelian commanders-in-chief and district commanders and judges are told:

You are not making the rounds of your provinces doing your duties. Instead you are going around taking money from the people unlawfully. And it has been brought to my attention that during these so-called 'patrols' which you are making for this purpose accompanied by unnecessary numbers of cavalrymen you are committing the following abuses: If somebody falls out of a tree you make this out to be a murder, you go to a village, settle down, and in order to rout out the supposed killer you harrass the people by putting them in irons and beating them. Finally besides taking hundreds of gold or silver pieces as 'blood money', you collect from the villager free of charge as a so-called 'requisition' horses, mules, slaves, barley, straw, wood, hay, sheep, lambs, chickens, oil, honey and other things to eat. You lease out your incomes to collectors at excessive rates. They on their part go out to collect with far too many horsemen and instead of satisfying themselves with collecting your incomes according to law and as is prescribed in the record, try to get as much money as they please. And besides the normal villages, they go onto imperial holdings, which are immune, under the pretense of following criminals and demand thirty or forty extra gold or silver pieces per month. And because you, you commanders and bailiffs, have been taking money from brigands and letting them off rather than giving them their just deserts, brigands have been getting hold and have been descending upon the people in groups. This is the sort of tyrannizing that I have been hearing about.

The decree continues:

The object in appointing you commanders-in-chief and district commanders and in giving you incomes is not to have you go around collecting goods and ruining the country. Rather, it is so that the holy law and the government's laws be respected, so that no one be allowed to tyrannize, so that individuals who cause trouble will be taken in hand and if necessary imprisoned and handed over to the government, or if necessary to get punishment executed according to the decision of the local justice and in this way to protect the country by every means and to make it prosper and flourish. To take from the *reaya* a tithe of blood money belonging to the victim's relatives, calling it 'blood tithe', is contrary to law and forbidden. Commanders who descend on a village with two or three hundred horsemen in order to get a blood tithe are causing the ruination of that village.

In the same justice decree we find information on abuses by judges:

Judges and judges' surrogates have been going around from village to village together with bailiffs on the pretext of judging wrongdoers in the villages or seeing to other legal work and have been taking sheep, chickens, oil, honey, barley, straw and wood from the *reaya* without paying for them.

Judges had the authority to take a fee of fifteen or twenty parts in a thousand in inheritance cases, but instead, they had been interfering into inheritance matters without being invited and without its being necessary and had made it a rule that people must get permission from them before the dead could be buried.

They have been denying permission for the burial of non-Muslims unless they get some money. When they make the rounds of the villages they have been going around to the graveyards, counting graves and fining those who have buried their dead without permission. And they have been committing various abuses in the settlement of inheritances. They have been raising appraisals of the value of goods in order to raise the tax they take, or have been making inheritance settlements a second time claiming that the first settlement was unjust. In this way the majority of inheritance goods have been adjudged two or three times and as a result a large part of these goods end up in the judges' hands in the form of a fee.

From time to time the central government appointed judges as inspectors in order to establish the reasons for confusion in this or that district or in order to hear the complaints of the *reaya.* Judges abused these missions for the purpose of robbing the people: they went around from village to village judging people who were innocent of any wrongdoing and then taking bribes for crimes which did not exist.

Judges have not hesitated to interpret the decrees of His Majesty the Sultan according to their own advantage. If anyone tries to find out how the decree actually runs, they accuse him of the crime of opposing that decree and thus get money out of him.

Again according to the aforesaid justice decree, judges who were in the process of making up tax registers deliberately overstated the number of those who were liable to taxes to extort bribes from them. Judges were taking fees higher than the law allowed on documents and copies of documents which the *reaya* received from the courts. Also judges had been ignoring clear instructions contained in imperial decrees with regard to *timars* or religious posts by issuing documents awarding them to whichever claimant gave the most bribe money. Judges, who had the right to appoint surrogate judges in their own jurisdictions, were dispensing these positions to whoever gave the most money. These in turn went out to harrass the *reaya* in order to collect various taxes and on those visits they forced the villagers to feed their numerous companions free of charge.

The same justic decree touches upon abuses by hoodlums, both military and non-military. This sort of individual would dispense some little thing to the *reaya* as a so-called gift — a knife, a skullcap, or a bar of soap — and afterwards would demand in return from each village family a sheep, a beehive, or two or three measures of wheat. In general soldiers did this sort of thing in order to fulfill their needs. Others of these strong arm soldiers would buy goods cheaply as they went into a town and then sell the same goods at a high price inside the town and in that way exploit the people.

Finally this justice decree depicts what a social blight the usurers had become for the villager. The *reaya,* left penniless by the lawless extortions of the military, were obliged to take money from usurers, the rate of usury going up to fifty percent. The *reaya,* unable to pay off this ever increasing debt load, were obliged to work for the usurer and become little more than his slaves. It was always easy for the usurer to have anyone opposing him thrown into jail.

III. THE FUNDAMENTAL CAUSES OF CORRUPTION

The deterioration of order in the Empire was already being cited by historians of the late 16th century such as Selânikî and Âlî. In the 17th century, Koçi Bey laid out the reasons for the Ottoman decline in sharp clear lines in his representations to Sultan Murad IV (1623-1640). And already in the 1610's an Ottoman author who concealed his identity dwelled on the same points in his *Kitab-i Mustatab.* Both writers assert that the authority of the sultan had weakened and broken down. In olden times, the grand vezir, acting as the sultan's right hand, secured order and unity in administration and maintained the state's interests above all other considerations. Now, they said, palace favorites and irresponsible individuals were interfering in the use of this authority, thrusting the administration into confusion and using their influence to fill their own pockets. Bribery was widespread. Palace favorites were handing out leases and posts as they pleased and taking money for it. Also very important, these favorites were having *timar* and *hâss* lands assigned as their own farms and as a result the *sipahi* forces living on the land were greatly reduced. For this reason it had been necessary to increase the other regular forces, especially the janissaries, and because these got their wages from the central treasury, the load on it had become excessive. Therefore the state was obliged to lay heavier taxes upon the shoulders of the *reaya*. One result of the increase in the remaining regular forces was that the latter was becoming rebellious and unmanageable both in the capitol and in the provinces. Both writers considered the decline to be a consequence of the degeneration and abandonment of the classic laws and regulations of the Ottoman State. According to them, in order to straighten out the situation, it would be necessary for the sultan's authority to be concentrated in the hands of the grand vezir, for the *reaya* to be protected from abuses, for the *timar* system to be reformed, for the number of janissaries to be reduced and discipline restored in the army, and for the practice of taking bribes to be eliminated absolutely.

The similarity between these views and the kind of thinking we see in the justice decrees is striking. No doubt there is a lot of truth in this thinking, which conforms to a traditional view of state and society by attributing decline to corruption. But the modern historian sees more in the Ottoman decline than administrative failings and corruption. Population increase accompanied by economic stagnation, and the destructive financial and political consequences of long years of war with Iran and in Hungary are accepted among the valid deep-running causes. Here we shall pause to discuss them.

It has been established that the population of the Ottoman Empire increased two-fold during the 16th century just as was the case in other Mediterranean lands. The Ottoman government was not able to send this excess population into conquered territories as in the past when compulsory deportations, called *sürgün*, played a large role in the Turkicization of certain parts of the Balkans. The last time this kind of deportation had been resorted to as a systematic effort had been following the conquest of Cyprus when landless villagers from central Anatolia were sent to the island. But now the great conquests in Europe had come to a halt.

At the same time the Ottoman economic system was not suitable to the task of securing new economic resources at a rate even with the population increase, a condition which I have attempted to demonstrate in a study on capital formation in the Ottoman Empire (see Bibliography). The Ottoman State was intrinsically bound to the corporation system typical of the Middle Ages. Here the principles found their place in the religious law of pre-Ottoman Islamic states under the name of *ihtisab* or *hisba.* Under this system, an industrial development capable of utilizing the increasing masses of workers in the cities was impossible. The concept then current among the mercantilist elite of West Europe held that industrial development and the exportation of goods enriched a country, but this concept was utterly foreign to the Ottomans. In the Ottoman economic system only in commerce was there any encouragement for the investment of capital. There did indeed exist a capitalist-minded class of traders in the 16th century, but changes in world trade routes at the end of that century and the beginning of the 17th began to take their toll on the Ottoman market with the result that the mercantilist states of the West were enabled to surbordinate the Levant to their own economic systems. Moreover, due to the fact that the English and the Dutch gained a supremacy in the Mediterranean, the Ottomans lost the upper hand at sea even in their own waters. Thus the advantages which could have been obtained by the Ottomans from the East-West or North-South trade were lost.

One more development of greatest significance can be seen in the great financial and economic crisis which befell the Ottomans following the 1580's. In Western Europe silver fell in value with reference to gold and it began to infiltrate the markets of the Levant. In the Ottoman markets now it was not the Ottoman *akçe* but the Spanish *reale* and the Dutch *rixdal* which prevailed. All the consequences which the 'price revolution' had brought in its train in Europe were experienced equally in the Ottoman Empire. The loss in value of silver money caused prices to jump to twice what they were. Counterfeit money flooded the market while speculation and soaring interest rates turned the finances and the economic existence of the state upside down. All of this upset the state's old establishments and institutions./ The new circumstances opened the way for unpleasant incidents and frequent revolts by groups with fixed incomes, particularly the janissaries and other standing forces who subsisted on a small daily wage. This financial chaos had to be counted as one of the basic reasons for the confusion and slippage which became apparent after the 1580's.

The situation was not only the underlying cause of the military rebellions at the center but also of the attempts by military groups in the provinces to squeeze more money out of the *reaya. Timar* holders whose incomes had been cut in half were so impoverished that they were unable to make their way to the battlefields of the Hungarian and Iranian wars and were instead robbing the *reaya*, avoiding campaigns and abandoning their holdings. Commanders and judges were resorting to bribes and abuses in order to hold their incomes level in the face of ever more costly living conditions.

The central government too was sharply aware of the insufficiency of its older fixed income. The continuous need for meeting the heavy expenses of long wars made its financial crisis ever more severe. Lowering the amount of silver contained in the *akçe* as a counter measure simply opened the way to more confusion. The government often was forced to resort to collecting extraordinary levies for the treasury (*âvâriz-i divâniyye*) a practice which formerly had been saved for only the most unusual circumstances. These levies became a regular cash tax collected year in and year out from villager and townsman alike. Gradually the amount of the tax rose. It was about 250 *akçe* per household in 1590 while the usual taxes were maintained. The principal traditional taxes were: *Ispenje*, 25 *akçe* for an adult male; tithes of usually one-eighth from each kind of crop, garden and orchard; 2 *akçe* for each one thousand square meters; pig-tax and sheep-tax, one *akçe* for each two; and fines and occasional dues grouped under the names of *badihava* and *niyabet*. Our calculation based on the *defters*, Ottoman surveys, showed that the average tax burden per household was about 250 *akçe*, which was equal to four gold florins by 1580 and only two florins in the early 17th century. Thus an increase of a hundred per cent in the amount of taxes was not real in value. The same was true for *jizye*, poll-tax. It was usually one gold florin which the Christian *reaya* had been bound to pay yearly but now it was raised to conform to the new value of the *akçe*. In the middle of the 16th century, when the gold florin exchanged for sixty *akçe*, the polltax varied between 40-60 *akçe*, whereas by the beginning of the 17th century the tax amounted to 140 *akçe*. About the same time the government announced that the official exchange value of a gold florin was 120 silver *akçe*. But the rate for gold was always 10-20% higher on the free market. At any rate in the countryside where the effects of the monetary changes were slow and incomplete the new *avâriz-i divâniyye* taxation was felt as a heavy burden by the *reaya*. And, as we have already pointed out there were many other abuses committed in the collection of these taxes. Under these conditions the situation of the Balkan villagers became drastically worse.

IV. THE VILLAGER AND THE LAND: THE ADVENT OF LARGE ESTATES

When a villager had become saddled with an impossible tax burden his only choice was to abandon his land and move. Such villagers, wandering on the loose, show up in the records as *haymana* or '*reaya* left out of the record' (*defter harici reaya*); often their trails were lost and they settled in other regions altogether. Naturally some of them turned to brigandage which constituted one of the chief headaches of government. The passive resistance by the villagers was a most effective factor in forcing the central government to condemn abuses and to take measures to lighten taxes. Now influential people among the military were appropriating lands abandoned by the villagers and settling on them by bringing slaves and hirelings to work them, thus converting them into their own estates. Because of the general shortage of labor, lands of this sort were generally used for livestock raising, thus becoming veritable ranches. After the confusion died down, the *reaya*, dreading these soldiers, found it impossible to return to their old villages. Although the sultan often demanded that the houses and stables of these military interlopers be torn down and that these soldiers quit their holdings immediately, such orders were rarely obeyed.

There were three main modes by which the great estates of Rumeli came into being in the 16th and 17th centuries:

1. *Estates established on unused land*

Rich and influential individuals would buy for cash land which was not officially registered in the tax registers or which was not being worked, then would settle slaves on it and make it into their own estate. In the records, one notices that private estates were generally established on lands to which the state had not previously laid claim and that they utilized slave labor instead of *reaya* labor. *Reaya*, working for wages on these estates as farm laborers, called *irgad*, are those who had fled their own lands and were left out of the tax surveys. Starting from the 17th century this kind of *reaya* constantly increased. Because of the confused way in which tax registers were maintained at this time it became easier to get state land through bribery and add it to a private estate or for the *reaya* to sell their fields and enter the service of the estate owners. According to citations from the Edirne region dating from the 16th and 17th centuries, a large part of the estates there were established in this manner and were generally turned over to animal raising. The animals were sold to the villagers while the grain which was raised was sold either directly or by circuitous routes to European merchants who paid good prices in return. Under these conditions, large estates developed and became numerous. Most of the estate owners were military men by origin. They often lent money to villagers, who then lost their fields because they were unable to pay these debts. With some local differences the same conditions can be identified in other parts of Rumeli.

2. *Trust estates (vakf) founded by turning State Land into Property*

Influential figures from the palace or close to palace circles got hold of state lands in the form of property grants and subsequently turned them into trusts, thus giving rise to plantation-like establishments. This sort of trust-estate was not unknown in the older periods, but to the extent that central authority and control loosened in the decline period this style of converting state land into property and *vakf* increased proportionally. There was no great difference between these trust estates and the other big estates just described from the point of view either of their management or even their basic purpose. A large part of their rent went either to the trust founder personally or to his family. Slave labor and animal raising were widespread. Estates and trust establishments in the hands of the powerful were generally free from the interference of local governors and for this reason it is understandable why fugitive *reaya* generally settled on them. But once they did that, the *reaya* were bound tightly to the trust or the estate.

3. *Estates Founded by Renting State Lands*

Because the treasury rented out on a rent-lease basis (*mukataa*) the *timar* and *hǎss* lands belonging to the state, rich and influential individuals were enabled to take control of many villages and farms. Owing to the treasury's difficulties in the era of decline, rent-lease contracts began to be made out on a life-term basis, sometimes even on a hereditary basis, so that they became virtually like private property. Originally the lessor was the villager who now was regarded as leasing the land hereditarily and eternally from the holder of the *timar* or *hâss*. Under this arrangement the villager paid taxes and dues fixed by law to the *timar* or *hâss* holder and in theory was not obliged to pay anything else. Under the new system, where a whole class of rich and influential landlords intervened between state and *reaya* and obtained the rights to the usufruct of the soil, the villager was obliged to pay a separate rent to them in ADDITION to the taxes due to the state. The majority of the new lease-holders were again of military origins. Landlords who had succeeded in obtaining lease rights to extensive holdings were eventually entrusted with a number of functions, such as gathering taxes, raising troops, and keeping order, thus ushering in the era of the *âyâns*. But this era only reached its full development in the second half of the 18th century. Thus the state allowed its control, even its sovereign rights over the *reaya*, to grow weaker, demonstrating that the classic regime associated with the Ottomans had completely broken down and that the Empire had become feudalized.

There is one other important development which took place at the same time in which the great landlords and notables (âyâns) were making their appearance: This came about as the state left to communities of villagers and townsmen the collection of certain taxes and their delivery to the treasury; or to put it another way the communities took on the task of farming taxes. As a result, an individual who headed such a community gained some control over it. At the same time the community took on an organization which began to function in ways other than the collection of taxes. The Ottoman government used this method in many districts both to defend the interests of the treasury and of the *reaya* from the rapacity of the officials and tax farmers. And in fact the *reaya* would promise more than the tax farmer precisely in order to secure the application of this other system, which was called *maktûa bağlamak* or *maktû 'iyyet*. This *maktû 'iyyet* system was applied especially in Balkan Christian zones for the collection of the poll tax (*jizye*). By giving the Christian communities an opportunity for some kind of organization this system actually provided a means and prepared the ground for future action on their part against the Ottoman regime.

For all these reasons, we can verify that, starting from the 1590's, the *reaya* under Ottoman rule, including the Christian *reaya* of the Balkans, fell into far worse circumstances than had formerly prevailed. As a result, dissatisfaction spread among the *reaya*, and brigandage increased. This situation contributed to the rebellion of Michael, Prince of Wallachia, starting in 1594, the first large scale reaction to the Ottoman regime in the Balkans; and to the resulting reverberations which this created south of the Danube. Nor can one forget the upsurge of rebellious activity in the mountainous parts of Albania in the same period nor the fact that the

Serbs, Greeks and Albanians were making contact with foreign powers in opposition to the Ottomans.

Systematic archival research to uncover the precise forms which the Ottoman decline took in the Balkans is still in its beginning stages. To this end there is a great need for detailed studies on changes within the framework of village life, the spread of brigandage and its causes, migrations and the reasons for them, the circumstances leading to the formation of landed estates, and changes taking place in town life.

On the other hand it should not be forgotten that in the beginning years of the period of decline Rumeli was not as deeply affected as Anatolia. Recent studies have suggested that an acceleration in trade relations between Rumeli and Europe had a positive effect upon the circumstances of the *reaya.*

BIBLIOGRAPHY

Barkan, Ömer Lütfi, *XV. ve XVI. asırlarda Osmanli Imparatorluğunda ziraî ekonominin hukukî ve malî esasları*, vol. I, *Kanunlar* (Istanbul, 1945).

——, "Les déportations comme méthode de peuplement et de colonisation dans l'Empire Ottoman", *Revue de la Faculté des Sciences Économiques de l'Université d'Istanbul* XI (1953), pp. 67-131.

Beldiceanu, L., tr., *Les Actes des premiers sultans conservés dans les manuscrits turcs de la bibliothèque Nationale à Paris; I. Actes de Mehmed II et de Bayezid II du MS fonds turc ancien 39* (Paris and The Hague, 1960).

Braudel, F., *La méditerranée et le monde méditerranéen à l'époque de Philippe II*, 2nd ed., 2 vols. (Paris, 1967).

Gibb, H. A. R. and Harold Bowen, *Islamic Society and the West*, vol. I (in 2 parts) (London, 1950-1957).

İnalcık, Halil, "Timariotes chrétiens en Albanie au XVe siècle d'après un registre de timar ottoman", *Mitteilungen des Oesterreichischen Staatsarchive*, IV (1951), pp. 118-138.

——, "Osmanlı Imparatorluğunun kuruluş ve inkişafı devrinde Türkiye'nin iktisadî vaziyeti üzerinde bir tetkik münasebetiyle", *Belleten*, XV (1951), pp. 626-990.

——, "Land problems in Turkish history", *Muslim World*, XLV (1955), pp. 221-228.

——, "Ottoman methods of conquest", *Studia Islamica*, II (1954), pp. 103-129.

——, "Osmanlı hukukuna giriş: örfi-sultanî hukuk ve fatihin kanunları", *Siyasal Bilgiler Fakültesi Dergisi*, XIII (1958), pp. 1-25.

——, "Osmanlılarda Raiyyet Rüsûmu", *Belleten*, XXIII (1959), pp. 575-610.

——, "Osmanlılarda Saltanate Veraseti Usulü ve Türk Hâkimiyet Telâkkisi ile Ilgisi", *Siyasal Bilgiler Fakültesi Dergisi*, XIV (1959), pp. 69-94.

——, "Bursa; XV. asır sanayi ve ticaret tarihine dair vesikalar", *Belleten*, XXIV (1960), pp. 45-102.

——, "Adâletnâmeler", *Belgeler. Türk Tarih Belgeleri Dergisi*, II (1955), pp. 49-145.

——, "Notes on N. Beldiceanu's translation of the Kanunname, fonds Turc ancien 39, Bibliothèque Nationale, Paris", *Der Islam*, XLIII (1967), pp. 139-157.

——, "Capital Formation in the Ottoman Empire", *Journal of Economic History*, XXIX (1969), pp. 97-140.

Ostrogorsky, George, "Agrarian Conditions in the Byzantine Empire in the Middle Ages", *Cambridge Economic History of Europe*, vol. I (1942), pp. 194-223, 579-583.

——, *Pour l'histoire de la féodalité byzantine*, tr. H. Grégoire and P. Lemerle (Brussels, 1954).

Tuncer, Hadiye, *Osmanli Imparatorluğu Arazi Kanunlari* (Ankara, 1963).

XIV

The Socio-Political Effects of the Diffusion of Fire-arms in the Middle East

I. THE DIFFUSION OF FIRE-ARMS IN THE OTTOMAN EMPIRE

IT was a strict rule in the Ottoman Empire not to allow the *reāya*, both the Muslim and the non-Muslim subjects, to bear weapons of any kind. In this respect special measures were taken over fire-arms, since their superiority to conventional arms was soon recognized. Even the *derbendci reāya*, appointed by a special charter to guard bridges and routes at dangerous points, were not allowed in principle to use arms other than the conventional ones. In 1576 the *derbendcis* near Yalova applied to the Porte, saying that it was not possible for them to perform their duties properly, unless they were permitted to bear the *tüfeng* (musket), for highway robbers were armed with this weapon. Even now, the government allowed only twelve of the *derbendcis* to get muskets.[1]

In peacetime all kinds of arms were stored in special depots under the control of the *cebeci-başı*, the head of the *cebecis*, who were charged with storing and repairing the arms. Besides the chief *cebe-hāne* (depot of arms) in the capital, every fortress had its own *cebe-hāne* under the care of a local *cebeci-başı*. Arms were distributed to the military on receipt of a special order from the sultan.[2]

It would appear that the prohibition of the bearing of arms became very important when, in the first half of the sixteenth century, the Kızılbaş of Asia Minor were co-operating with the Safawids. The frequent searches for arms showed that the use of the musket had become quite widespread among the Kızılbaş around the middle of that century. It became afterwards a routine matter for the government to make periodical searches for *tüfeng* among the *reāya* in general, because now *levend* bands of *reāya* origin, armed with the *tüfeng*, were roaming about the countryside in Asia Minor. The reason given, in the contemporary Ottoman documents, for the prohibition of the *tüfeng* was that it encouraged disorders and banditry in the provinces. 'It was an old regulation from early times', a document of the year 1607[3] declares, 'to search and collect *tüfeng* from the *reāya*, as it is known that most

[1] Cf. Cengiz Orhonlu, *Osmanlı Imparatorluğunda Derbend Teşkilâtı* (Istanbul, 1967), 64.

[2] It is possible to give a detailed description of the organization of registers preserved in the Başvekâlet Archives at Istanbul (see Appendix I of this paper).

[3] Cf. I. H. Uzunçarşılı, *Kapukulu Ocakları*, ii (Ankara, 1944), 28.

of them get possession of it.' It must be noted, however, that this remark was made during the high time of the *celālī* disorders in Asia Minor.

The punishment inflicted on those who transgressed against the prohibition was particularly severe, as the *kānūn-nāme* of Egypt reveals already in 1524:[1] the manufacturing of and trade in *tüfeng* was prohibited; those who violated the law would be punished by *siyāset*, i.e., by mutilation or by capital punishment; those who had *tüfeng* in their possession and failed to hand them over to the local authorities were to be hanged.

The manufacture and the import of fire-arms were a state monopoly. The same *kānūn-nāme* of 1524 reads: 'the *tüfeng* is to be manufactured or repaired only in a workshop set up and supervised by the state.' In 1607 this old regulation was called to mind in an order of the sultan to the Qadi of Istanbul[2] in these words:

formerly the *tüfeng* was manufactured and sold only in the state workshop at Istanbul and nowhere else. Whenever there was an expedition, soldiers received their *tüfeng* and powder through the hands of the *cebeci-başı* . . . It was an old regulation to confiscate those *tüfeng* made outside and to punish those who traded in them.

It is generally assumed that the rebellion of Prince Bāyezīd in 1559 was responsible for the spread of the use of *tüfeng* among the *reāya* and for the increase in the soldiers of *reāya* origin.[3] It is true that the majority of the soldiers whom Bāyezīd gathered around himself were *çift-bozan reāya* or *gharīb yiğids* (*yiğits*), workless or landless peasant youths, who sought to gain a livelihood and a career in the use of arms. But we must emphasize the fact that such people always existed in the Ottoman Empire. When needed, they were called up to serve, under the names of *gönüllü*, *'azeb*, *levend*, or *sekban*, as guardians of the fortresses or as raiders on the borderland or else as marines in the imperial fleet. Also for military expeditions the sultan often called up, by promises of reward, whoever was desirous to make *ghazā'* (*ghazāya sefālu*)[4] and there was always a large group of irregular militia with the imperial armies. On the other hand, whenever a civil war or an insurrection broke out, these restless elements made up an important part of the forces serving the contenders. The point is that the central importance which the *levends* and the *sekbans* assumed in the second half of the sixteenth century was connected not so much with the fact that changing economic and social conditions caused an increase of the landless elements in the countryside,[5]

[1] Cf. Ö. L. Barkan, *Osmanlı Imparatorluğunda Ziraî Ekonominin Hukukî ve Malî Esasları* (Istanbul, 1943), 356.

[2] Cf. Uzunçarşılı, loc. cit.

[3] See Şerâfettin Turan, *Şehzâde Bayezid Vak'ası* (Ankara, 1961), 83–96; M. Cezzar, *Levendler* (Istanbul, 1965), 37.

[4] An early example is to be found in a *firmān* preserved in the records of the Qadi of Bursa and issued originally just before the expedition of 1484 against Moldavia.

[5] This is the theory defended by Mustafa Akdağ (cf. M. Akdağ, *Celâli İsyanları* (Ankara, 1963), 13–57).

as with the spread of the use of the *tüfeng* amongst the *reāya*. The peasant youths and the nomads who, in return for a small pay, joined Prince Bāyezīd in 1559 were in great part armed with the *tüfeng*. Both Bāyezīd and his rival Prince Selīm enrolled *çift-bozan reāya*, i.e., peasants who had left their lands, in the *tīmārs* for this or that reason, and promised to make them Janissaries.[1] Being soldiers no less efficient with their *tüfeng* than the Janissaries, they wanted to enjoy the same privileges as the members of that corps. Briefly speaking, the civil wars under Süleymān I encouraged large numbers of peasant youths to become professional soldiers armed with the *tüfeng*. On the evidence of the contemporary *Mühimme* documents we can assert that by 1570 the use of the *tüfeng* had become widespread among various groups of *reāya*, despite the government's prohibition and confiscation of arms. Free from the prejudices of the established military class and aware of the advantages inherent in the new weapon, the populace of the country-side became eager, more than ever before, to possess it. The documents of the period between 1560 and 1570[2] describe as armed with the *tüfeng* such rebellious elements as *sūkhte's* (*softa*), i.e., *medrese* students turned into brigands, and *levends*, i.e., jobless peasant youths roaming about or bands of highwaymen. In order to fight against them, the government tried on one occasion to furnish the timariot *sipāhīs* with the same weapon and, at times, even permitted the *reāya* to arm themselves for defence.[3] The fact that, during the expedition to Cyprus in 1570, nomadic groups from eastern Asia Minor were armed with the *tüfeng* demonstrates how widely this weapon had spread over the country.[4]

Of course one prerequisite essential to this development was the easy availability of the *tüfeng* to the *reāya*. In the *firmān* of 1607[5] re-establishing the prohibition against the use of the *tüfeng* by the *reāya* it was admitted that, for some time past, the state monopoly had been relaxed: '*tüfeng* and powder were made and sold by anybody anywhere. Thus, the *tüfeng* being available to people of evil intention, its spread became the main source of the disorders and banditry in the empire.' It seems that the pressing demand for fire-arms and the government's inability to maintain control encouraged, on the one hand, the import of *tüfeng* smuggled from Western Europe, from Ragusa,[6] and from Algiers and, on the other hand, the growth of local private enterprise seeking to manufacture the weapon. In a list of arms (dated 1009/1600),[7]

[1] Cf. Turan, op. cit. 158–69.

[2] Cf. the document in A. Refik, *XVI asırda Rafizîlik* (Istanbul, 1932), no. 27; also M. Akdağ, 'Türkiye Tarihinde Içtimaî Buhranlar Serisinden: Medreseli İsyanları', *İst. Üniv. Iktisat Fakültesi Mecmuası*, xi, no. 14, 361–87.

[3] Cf. A. Refik, op. cit., no. 23.

[4] Cf. A. Refik, 'Kıbrıs ve Tunus Seferlerine Ait Vesikalar', *Edebiyat Fakültesi Mecmuası*, v/1–2, document no. 10.

[5] Cf. Uzunçarşılı, loc. cit.

[6] See P. Djurdjitsa Petrović, 'O vatrenom oružju Dubrovnika u XIV Veku' *Vesnik Vojnog Muzeja*, xv) (Beograd, 1969).

[7] Cf. Başvekâlet Archives, Maliye Defterleri, no. 1612.

from a Vizier's *cebe-hāne*, we find, amongst 75 *tüfeng*, the following types: *Cezāyirī* (from Algiers), *Frengi* (from Western Europe), *Rūmī* (Ottoman), *Istanbulī* (from Istanbul), *Macārī* (from Hungary), *Alaman* (from Germany), *Macārī zenberekli*, and *kār-i Moton* (made in Modena or Modon?). The *Cezāyirī* was a heavy musket (with shot of 25 *dirhems*), the *kār-i Moton* a lighter musket (with shot of 7 *dirhems*). The price of a *tüfeng* was quite low during this period. In the last decades of the sixteenth century an ordinary type of *tüfeng* cost between 300 and 600 *akçes*, while the price of an average horse was twice as much. It was a profitable investment for a peasant youth to buy a *tüfeng* and offer his services to anybody who would pay him, a pasha or a beg. If there were no one to hire him, he might join a band of adventurers seeking to live on what they could extract from the villagers. Such bands were known as *celālī*.[1] It was chiefly the state itself which was responsible, during the last two decades of the sixteenth century, for the rapid increase in soldiers armed with the *tüfeng* and drawn from the *reāya*.

Under the impact of the German infantry, 'modernization' of the Ottoman army, through a more extended use of fire-arms, had made headway especially in the reign of Süleymān I (1520–66). Already in 1531 A. Venier, the bailo of Venice at Istanbul, reported that 'to his usual troops [Süleymān] has added fifty thousand [five thousand?] infantry with permanent pay, which must proceed from Sultan Süleymān's having become aware that infantry are needed to oppose the Christian soldiery'.[2] By this remark Venier obviously meant the increase of the Janissaries equipped with *tüfeng*. Süleymān was reported also to be responsible for the expanding of the state factories making guns and ammunition.[3] Koca Nişancı, a contemporary Ottoman historian and statesman, confessed that the German infantry caused great losses to the Ottoman soldiery by the efficient fire of their guns and muskets during the campaigns of 1529 and later. In the naval warfare of the Mediterranean, too, the *tüfeng-endāz* soldiers were badly needed: in 1538, before the battle of Preveza, Barbarossa's fleet was reinforced by three thousand *tüfeng-endāz* Janissaries.[4]

In 1555 Busbecq tells us how Ottoman raiders were routed by comparatively small groups of Christian arquebusiers and adds: 'our pistols and carbines, which are used on horseback, are a great terror to the Turks, as I hear they are to the Persians also.'[5] Apparently during the campaign of 1548 against Persia, the Grand Vizier Rüstem attempted, so Busbecq relates, to arm with pistols 200 horsemen at his Porte, but soon he had to give up the idea. The reasons Busbecq gave for this failure are interesting enough to show why

[1] On the *celālīs* cf. M. Akdağ, *Celâlî İsyanları* (Ankara, 1963).

[2] See H. İnalcık, 'Türkiye'nin İktisadî Vaziyeti', *Belleten* xv/60 (1954), 654.

[3] Cf. Uzunçarşılı, *Kapukulu Ocakları*, ii. 39.

[4] Cf. M. Cezzar, op. cit. 160.

[5] Cf. *The Turkish Letters of Ogier Ghiselin de Busbecq*, trans. E. S. Forster, Oxford, 1927, 123–4.

'modernization' could not include the Ottoman cavalry and was restricted to the Janissary corps at that time. 'The Turks', he said, 'were also against this armature, because it was slovenly (the Turks, you must know, are much for cleanliness in war), for the troopers' hands were black and sooty, their clothes full of spots and their case-boxes, that hung by their sides, made them ridiculous to their fellow-soldiers, who therefore jeered at them, with the title *medicamentarii.*' But later on, at a critical moment during the siege of Szigetvar in 1566, all the soldiers at the sultan's Porte as well as the retinues of the pashas, Selānikī writes, used the *tüfeng* against the enemy.[1] Outside the standing army at the Porte, the timariot cavalry in the provinces, which made up the greater part of the Ottoman army during this period, persisted in using their conventional arms. We do not know whether there was any attempt to make them use fire-arms, if we except some instances in the naval expeditions, when the timariots appear to have been equipped with the *tüfeng*.[2] The only provincial regular soldiers who were armed with the *tüfeng* were the *tüfengcis*, the *mustahfız*, and the *'azebs* in the fortresses.[3] The *tüfengcis* were horsemen, the other two corps consisting of infantry. When in need of more arquebusiers in expeditions on land or sea the sultan called up a part of these garrison troops. It must be pointed out that these *tüfeng-endāz* soldiers were originally from the *reāya* class.

Again under the impact of the German infantry, revolutionary developments in the use of *tüfeng-endāz reāya* took place during the long war against the Hapsburgs between 1593 and 1606, when the Janissaries and the other sources of manpower failed to meet the growing need for musketeers. This war brought surprises for the Ottomans, who were now faced with large imperial armies, wholly equipped with fire-arms of new types. The Ottomans experienced their first surprise in Wallachia at the hands of Prince Mihal and the Cossacks. The Ottoman army under the Grand Vizir Sinān was compelled to retreat since, as Selānikī observed,[4] 'it could not withstand the musketeers from Transylvania, though the Ottoman general-in-chief brought into action all the forces at his command.' In the course of the battle, the Ottoman light cavalry were slaughtered. Later on, in 1011/1602, Mehmed Pasha, in a report to the sultan,[5] confessed to the same experience at the hands of the German infantry:

> in the field or during a siege we are in a distressed position, because the greater part of the enemy forces are infantry armed with muskets, while the majority of our forces are horsemen and we have very few specialists skilled in the musket . . . so the *tüfeng-endāz* Janissaries, under their *agha*, must join the imperial army promptly.

[1] MS. in the Library of the Dil ve Tarih-Coğrafya Fakültesi, University of Ankara (fol. 37).
[2] Cf. A. Refik, 'Kıbrıs ve Tunus', 84.
[3] See the *kānūn-nāme* of Egypt, in Ö. L. Barkan, op. cit. 356–8.
[4] Cf. Selānikī, *Tā'rīkh* (unpublished section: MS. cit. above, note 1, 131ᵛ).
[5] Cf. C. Orhonlu, *Telhîsler 1597–1607* (Istanbul, 1970), document no. 81.

Under pressing need the Ottoman government took all kinds of measures to cope with the situation. In 1010/1601, 10,000 soldiers armed with the *tüfeng* being required for the defence of Buda and Pest, the Christian Pandurs and Eflāk, militias used for local security purposes, were hastily called to the imperial army.[1] During the course of this war (1593–1606) even small Ragusa was asked to send musketeers to the Ottoman army.[2] The regions best known in Rūmeli as sources of *tüfeng-endāz* soldiers of *reāya* origin were Bosnia and Albania. Foot-soldiers, armed with the *tüfeng*, were hired in these two regions by the Ottoman government to serve for a certain period of time each year in the imperial army or as guards along the frontiers.[3] That the Christian *reāya* in Rūmeli learned to use the *tüfeng* and that the tributary prince of Wallachia exploited this weapon with success against his Ottoman suzerain were developments most significant for the future. But the most important region of hired *tüfeng-endāz* soldiers was Asia Minor. We have described earlier the origin of these soldiers, who were best known under the name of *sekbān*, and how, using the *tüfeng*, they became indispensable to the Ottoman army. The war of 1593–1606, by making their role unusually significant, was to bring about fundamental changes not only in the military, but also in the social and political structure of the empire. The usual procedure in enrolling the *sekbān* was as follows:[4] the sultan sent an order to the local authorities and a special commissioner was appointed to supervise the whole operation and to lead the assembled troops to their destination. The sultan also sent standards, as many as the number of the companies to be formed. Under each standard a *bölük*, i.e., a company of fifty or sometimes of one hundred *sekbān*, would be assembled. The moment a standard was taken back the *bölük* under it was considered to be legally dissolved and, from then on, their activities as a group were held to be illegal. Before the enrolment started, the local authorities chose the *bölük baṣı*s, the heads of the *bölüks* to be set up, and then a *baş bölük-başı*, a commander over them. The *sekbān*, armed in general with the *tüfeng*, acted either as foot-soldier or as horseman. Each *sekbān* received a 'bonus' (*bakhşīş*) to prepare himself for the expedition and also his salary in advance for the months he was going to serve. All this was to be distributed through the *baş bölük-başı* and the *bolük-başıs*. They were real masters and organizers of these soldiers, comparable to the *condottieri* of medieval Europe. The *sekbān* had the reputation of being good marksmen. In 1601, at the battle of Istolni Belghrād, it was the *tüfeng-endāz sekbān* who saved the army from complete rout.[5] But, on the other

[1] C. Orhonlu, *Telhîsler 1597–1607*, document no. 60.

[2] Cf. N. H. Biegman, *The Turco-Ragusan Relationship* (The Hague, Paris, 1967), 78.

[3] L. F. Marsigli, *L'État militaire de l'Empire Ottoman* (La Haye, 1732): '*Serhad-Kulu*'.

[4] Cf. Na'īmā, *Tā'rīkh* (Istanbul, A.H. 1283), i. 257. See also the documents in Çağatay Uluçay, *Saruhan'da Eşkiyalık ve Halk Hareketleri* (Istanbul, 1944), 464–7; and M. Cezzar, op. cit. 383, 399.

[5] Cf. Na'īmā, *Tā'rīkh*, i. 257.

hand, the *sekbān*—through their *tüfeng* superior now to the timariot *sipāhīs* in the provinces—became a factor of disorder.

After their contract of service had expired, the *sekbān*, usually under the same *bölük-başı*, looked for new employment in the service of the pashas or the begs. If none was available, they roamed about the countryside, exacting money and provisions from villages and towns without defence.[1] In this case the *sekbān* were pursued by the government forces as *celālīs*, unlawful bands. Many a powerful *celālī* leader emerged from amongst the *bölük-başıs*. This was the actual origin of the *celālī* disorders of 1595–1610, which ruined Asia Minor and at times paralysed the government. Later, the *celālī* disorders recurred, especially during periods of war, because the sultan always needed *sekbān* as *tüfeng-endāz* soldiers. Thus, despite attempts to suppress them, the *sekbān* continued to be the most important auxiliary force of the Ottoman army, until the time of radical reform. Moreover, the pashas and the begs governing the provinces were encouraged by the central government to bring to the imperial army, in their household forces, as many *sekbān* as they could. Nasūh Pasha, the *beglerbegi* of Diyarbekr, was known to have one thousand of them, all armed with the *tüfeng*, under his direct command in 1607.[2] Many pashas, needing to feed their *sekbān*, often had recourse to exactions from the *reāya* and, when dismissed from office, became *celālī* themselves.[3] This, too, was an unfamiliar development in Ottoman history. Now, pashas might turn easily into rebels at the head of their *sekbān*, whereas it was impossible for them to do the same with the *sipāhīs* subject to the control of the central government and living on their distant *tīmār* lands. It must be remembered that these *sekbān*, with their *tüfeng*, were fully able to resist the sultan's Janissaries. This new situation can be considered as one of the decisive factors leading to the decentralization and feudalization of the empire. For, later on, in the seventeenth and the eighteenth centuries, it was the *aʿyān*, the local magnates, who were to be authorized to entrol *sekbān* for the sultan's army or for themselves.[4]

The use of the *tüfeng* spread not only among the Turks of Asia Minor, but also among the subject peoples, such as the Christians in Rūmeli, the Dürzīs (Druzes) in the Lebanon, the Kurds, Arabs, Georgians, and Lazi, apparently from the last decades of the sixteenth century onward. Brigandage became widespread in Rūmeli, especially in Albania, in Macedonia, and in other mountainous parts of the peninsula. This situation was undoubtedly connected with the spread of the *tüfeng*, over and above the deterioration of economic and financial conditions in the Balkans during this period. Again, in the Lebanon, the Druzes became rebellious at this same time and we know

[1] Details are available in the works here cited of Ç. Uluçay, M. Akdağ, and M. Cezzar.

[2] Cf. M. Cezzar, op. cit. 296.

[3] Cf. the examples given in Ç. Uluçay, op. cit. 20–49.

[4] Cf. Ç. Uluçay, loc. cit., and also Ç. Uluçay, *18. ve 19. asırda Saruhan'da Eskiyalık ve Halk Hareketleri* (Istanbul, 1955).

that in 993/1585 the Pasha of Egypt captured from their lands thousands of *tüfeng* in the course of a punitive expedition against them.[1] Maʿn-oghlu's men were armed with the *tüfeng*; and Ewliyā Çelebī was later to observe that 50,000 *tüfeng-endāz* could be gathered from amongst the Druze and Yazīdī villages and that taxes could be collected there only under threat of arms.[2] In another distant part of the Arab world, in Tunis, the native Arabs, armed with the *tüfeng*, were collaborating with the Christian invaders against the Ottomans already in the 1570s.[3] In 1009–10/1600–1, during the rebellion of the Imām Kāsim in the Yemen, the Arabs and some of the Turkish soldiers who had settled there under the name of *Rūmlū* rose up and captured the arms in the state depot under a certain Jaʿfer Rūmlū, who was reported to be one of the *celālī* chiefs formerly associated with Kara Yazıcı in Asia Minor.[4]

In the middle of the seventeenth century Ewiliyā Çelebī gave an estimate—obviously exaggerated—of 200,000 for the *tüfeng-endāz* in eastern Asia Minor. This estimate indicates how extensive the use of the *tüfeng* was in this mountainous area. He also noted on one occasion that the *tüfeng-endāz reāya* among the Laz had assembled against the Cossacks who made a surprise attack on Günye in 1057/1647.[4]

II. THE OTTOMAN ROLE AND POLICY IN THE DIFFUSION OF FIRE-ARMS IN ASIA AND AFRICA

The Ottomans seem to have played an important role in the introduction of fire-arms into various Asian countries, either as the direct suppliers or as causing their rivals in the East to obtain them from the Europeans. In the first category can be mentioned the Khānates in Turkistān, the Crimean Khānate, the Gujerātīs in India, the Sultan of Atche in Sumatra, and Sultan Ahmed Grañ in Abyssinia. The Ak Koyūnlū and the Ṣafawids in Iran and the Mamlūks in Egypt can be included in the second category.

Also it must be emphasized that the Ottoman government tried to exploit its privileged position in respect of fire-arms to pursue a policy of universal power. For not only did that position bestow on the Ottoman government a definite superiority in battle over its rivals in the Middle East—it gave it also an incomparable prestige in the countries which were threatened by the Portuguese, the Russians, and the Iranians in Asia.

Paradoxically enough, it was the Mamlūk Sultanate, a powerful rival of the Ottomans and the leading Muslim state in the world of that time, which first appealed to the Ottomans for military aid. In 1509, defeated near Diu, the Mamlūk Sultan, Ḳanṣawh al-Ghawrī, asked the Ottomans for materials to build a navy able to withstand the Portuguese in the Red Sea and the

[1] Cf. Selānikī, *Tāʾrīkh* (Istanbul, A.H. 1281), 68v.
[2] Cf. Ewliyā Çelebī, *Seyāḥatnāme* (Istanbul A.H. 1314–18). iii 105.
[3] Cf. A. Refik, 'Kibris ve Tunus', 88.
[4] Cf. Çelebī, op. cit. iv. 25, 68.

Indian Ocean.[1] Obviously the demand included fire-arms. For at the beginning of the year 1511, the Ottoman sultan sent, so Ibn Iyās reports,[2] 300 *makāḥil sebkīyāt*, which should be interpreted here as arquebuses, and forty *kantars* of powder, besides soldiers and also material to build ships. About 1512 Mehmed b. ʿAbdallāh, an Ottoman, was appointed captain of the fleet to be built at Suez.[3] Three years later the Mamlūk fleet at Suez was placed under the command of another Ottoman sea captain, Selmān Re'īs.

The dependence of the Mamlūks on Ottoman aid would appear to have enhanced the prestige of the Ottomans throughout the Muslim world at the expense of the Mamlūks. Thanks, definitely, to their superiority in fire-arms and to their tactical use of these weapons the Ottomans destroyed Mamlūk rule over Syria and Egypt in two decisive battles only a few years later. The attitude of the Sharīf of Mecca and of the Arabs in the Hijāz is particularly interesting as an illustration of our present theme. The sacred places of Islam, Mecca and Medina, were then in imminent danger of a Portuguese attack and the Sharīf, as Selmān reported to the Ottoman government in 1517, was panic-stricken and planned to take refuge with his family and treasure in the mountains. The people of Jidda begged Selmān not to leave the country, when he was ordered by Sultan Selīm to come to Cairo. The Sharīf Barakat II soon submitted to the Ottoman Sultan. Thanks to the gunfire from his ships Selmān was able to repulse a Portuguese attack against Jidda during the same year.[4]

In the following years Selmān sought actively to establish Ottoman rule in the Red Sea and in the Yemen. The fleet which was built at this time in Suez had quite a powerful artillery—7 *bacalūṣka*, 13 *yān-top*, 20 *zarbūzan*, 29 *ṣāyka*, 95 iron pieces, and 97 *prangī*.[5] In 1526 the plan which he submitted to the Ottoman government[6] on how to supplant the Portuguese in the Indian Ocean revealed him as possessed of great confidence in the forces under his command.

The Ottoman–Portuguese rivalry in the Indian Ocean soon extended to Abyssinia. Sultan Ahmed Grañ, the Abyssinian Muslim leader, received aid in the form of fire-arms from the Ottoman Pasha of the Yemen and proclaimed a *jihād* in 1527 against the Christian King of Abyssinia, whom the Portuguese were supporting. In 1541 the King of Abyssinia obtained an auxiliary force of 400 Portuguese, armed with fire-arms, which enabled him

[1] See H. İnalcık, *Belleten*, xx/83 (1959), 504–5; also Y. Mughal, 'Portekizlilerle Kızıldeniz'de Mücadele ve Hicaz'da Osmanlı Hakimiyetinin Yerleşmesi Hakkında Bir Vesika', *Belgeler*, ii/3–4 (1967), 38.

[2] Cf. Ibn Iyās, *Badā'iʿ al-Zuhūr fī Waḳā'iʿ al-Duhūr*, ed. M. Mustafa, iv (Cairo, 1960), 201; see also D. Ayalon, *Gunpowder and Fire-arms in the Mamluk Kingdom* (London, 1956): mukḥula.

[3] Cf. İnalcık, in *Belleten*, xx/83 (1959), 504.

[4] Cf. Y. Mughal, loc. cit.

[5] The report of Selmān is available in Fevzi Kurtoğlu, 'Selman Reis Layıhası', in *Deniz Mecmuası*, xlvii (1943), 67.

[6] Cf. Fevzi Kurtoğlu, loc. cit.

to halt the onslaught of his rival. But the following year, supported by a larger Ottoman reinforcement of 900 musketeers and gunners with 10 pieces of artillery, Ahmed inflicted a complete defeat on the King, most of the Portuguese in his army falling in the battle. After this victory 200 men of the Ottoman contingent remained with Ahmed.[1]

Ahmed Grañ was killed two years later and the Muslim offensive brought to a halt until the mid sixteenth century, when the Ottomans themselves took the initiative on this front and created there, eventually, a Beglerbeglik of Habeş.[2]

Before the beginning, in 1517, of Ottoman rule in the Yemen, we find there, and in India, a number of soldiers, seamen, and gunners or specialists in fire-arms bearing the name of *Rūmī* or *Rūmlū*.[3] At that time, in the East outside the Ottoman Empire, this designation had the sense, unequivocally, of 'Ottoman'. The *Rūmīs* included apparently not only those Ottomans who were sent by Bāyezīd II to the Mamlūks from 1509[4] onward, but also adventurers who left the Ottoman lands, especially Western Asia Minor and Karamān. Bābūr,[5] the founder of the Mughal Empire in India, knew well how much he owed his victories to the two specialists in fire-arms, Ustād 'Alī-Kulu and Mustafa Rūmī, and emphasized it in his memoirs. 'Alī-Kulu cast large guns for him. Mustafa Rūmī, with his guns and his *tüfengcis*, did great service in the battles of Bābūr. On one occasion, at the battle against Sanka, Mustafa made for Bābūr wagons in the *Rūmī* style, thus enabling him to apply the tactics of *destūr-i Rūmī*. Those Ottoman tactics, employed under the supervision of the two specialists, were responsible for Bābūr's victory at Panipat in 1526 and for his success in expeditions against the Afghans in India. Bābūr himself compares his *tüfeng-endāz* soldiers to the 'Rūm Ghāzīleri'.[6] In applying the *destūr-i Rūmī*, which the Ottomans themselves called *ṭābūr cengi*, heavy wagons were chained to each other and reinforced with guns and arquebuses ranged around the main part of the army, like a fortress. The Ottomans learned this procedure during the campaigns against John Hunyadi between 1441 and 1444.[7] This order of battle was actually not unfamiliar to the Turco-Mongols in the steppes—they called it *küriyen* or *küren* in Mongol and *çapar* or *çeper* in Turkish.[8] But what was new for the Ottomans was the reinforcement of this formation with fire-arms. It was not merely his possession of fire-arms, but his skilful use of them, in accordance with the *destūr-i Rūmī*, which gave to Bābūr a marked superiority over his

[1] Cf. *The Portuguese Expedition to Abyssinia in 1541–1543 as related by Castanhoso and Bermudaz*, trans. and ed. R. S. Whiteway, London, 1902, 69 (mentioned in C. Orhonlu, 'XVI asrın ilk yarısında Kızıldeniz sahillerinde Osmanlılar', *Tarih Dergisi*, xii/16 (1962), 22.

[2] Cf. C. Orhonlu, 'Osmanlıların Habeşistan Siyaseti', *Tarih Dergisi*, xv/20 (1965), 39–54.

[3] Cf. Y. Mughal, *Osmanlı Imparatorluğu ve Hindistan Münasebetleri* (Doctoral thesis, Dil ve Tarih-Coğrafya Fakültesi, University of Ankara).

[4] Cf. H. İnalcık, in *Belleten*, xxi/83 (1959), 504.

[5] Cf. Babur, *Vekayi*, trans. R. R. Arat, Ankara, 1943–6.

[6] Ibid. ii. 362.

[7] Cf. İnalcık, in *Belleten*, xx/83 (1959), 510.

[8] Ibid.

rivals. Bābūr himself criticized the Bengalis for their careless, haphazard fire.[1] The *Rūmīs* continued, later, to be in high esteem with the successors of Bābūr and it is interesting to note that Shāh Jihān had his miniature portraits made with his *silahdār* carrying a *tüfeng*, instead of a sword.[2] As late as the mid sixteenth century the comparative backwardness in fire-arms of the Indian states can be seen through the memoirs of Seydī 'Alī Re'īs. With a company of less than 150 *tüfeng-endāz* he was able to overcome all the attempts of the local rulers and governors to stop him in his journey. The Gujerātī Sultan Ahmad and then 'Isā Turhān Shāh in Sind urged him to take part in their expeditions as a most appreciated servant. Once, on his way to Afghanistan, 1,000 Rajputs encircled him, but his *tüfeng-endāz*, entrenching themselves behind kneeling camels, made them give up the idea of attacking him. On another occasion, by the fire of his *tüfeng-endāz*, he forced a large group of Afghans to retreat.[3]

In 1538, during the expedition against the Portuguese at Diu, the Ottoman vizier Süleymān Pasha had indeed in his fleet a powerful artillery of over 110 pieces[4] and a strong company of *tüfeng-endāz*, but he failed in his enterprise, mainly because he did not get from the Gujerātī Sultan the co-operation which he had expected to receive. The Sultan was not mistaken in his belief that the Ottomans had come to Diu with a powerful fleet more to establish their own rule than to support his own. In 1554 Seydī 'Alī Re'īs expressed this Ottoman aspiration yet again in his memoirs.[5] But the Ottomans discovered that the whole adventure in the Indian Ocean was beyond their means in the face of the more urgent responsibilities confronting them in Central Europe, in the Mediterranean, in the Yemen, and in Iran. The expeditions in the Indian Ocean were restricted essentially to the resources of Egypt and of Iraq. This situation became apparent in the period between 1550 and 1570, when the Portuguese–Ottoman struggle for domination in the Indian Ocean flared up once more.

The Ottomans attempted in 1551 to draw off the Portuguese from the Persian Gulf altogether. But they showed themselves unable to achieve their goal because of the superior naval forces of the Portuguese and the alignment of some of the local rulers with them. Fire-power played a major role in all these clashes, which Seydī 'Alī Re'īs called 'battles of artillery and tüfeng'.[6] Now, the Portuguese control of the routes in the Indian Ocean tightened more than ever before. The Muslims in India and in remote Indonesia, accustomed to come to Basra or to Mecca as traders or pilgrims,

[1] Cf. Babur, *Vekayi*, ii. 421.

[2] Cf. *Oriental Art in Rumania* (Bucarest, 1963), fig. 100, and also '*Hunar u Mardum*', no. 79.

[3] Cf. Mir'āt al-Mamālik, ed. Necib Asim, Istanbul, A.H. 1313, 60. On Seydī 'Alī see now C. Orhonlu, 'Seydi Ali Reis', *Istanbul Üniversitesi Edebiyat Fakültesi Tarih Enstitüsü Dergisi*, i (1970), 39–56.

[4] Cf. Y. Mughal, op. cit.

[5] Ibid. 28.

[6] Ibid. 17, 19, 36.

were now in real distress and alarm. The Sultan of Gujerat, the rulers of Calicut and Ceylon, and the Sultan of Atche in Sumatra asked the Ottoman Sultan to send a strong fleet to those waters in order to keep the routes open for trade and pilgrimage. He accepted readily the role of protector of all Muslims in the world, but was unable to fulfil his promises. A letter (dated November 1565) of the Sultan of Atche has a particular interest,[1] since it shows how the eastern governments believed that success against the Portuguese depended ultimately on the possession of fire-arms:

> The Portuguese have taken under their control all the passages between the islands in this region and, in these passages, capture the ships with the pilgrims and merchants in them or sink them by gun-fire.

And he added that

> if an Ottoman fleet with a sufficient number of arms is sent, I can guarantee to draw these infidels out of the region altogether. It is requested that you send us artillery of the types *bacalişka*, *hawāī*, and *ṣāyka* to demolish the Portuguese fortresses and allow us to buy horses, copper and all kinds of arms in such provinces of yours as Egypt, the Yemen, Jidda and Aden in all seasons . . . The eight artillerymen whom you have sent previously arrived here and are as precious as mountains of jewels to us . . . Also we beg you to send us specialists in the building of fortresses and galleys.

He made it clear, in the same letter, that the Sultan of Gujerat and the rulers of Calicut and Ceylon had a great number of Muslims among their subjects and wanted to co-operate with him against the Portuguese; and when they received the aid which they expected from the Ottoman Sultan, all the population under them would convert to Islam. The Sultan of Atche stated also that the Friday prayer (*khutba*) in the islands under his rule was read in the name of the Ottoman Sultan. The Ottoman government decided to send from Egypt, under the command of Kurd-oghlu Hızır, fifteen galleys and two *barca* with artillerymen and arquebusiers. But, a little later, the envoy of the Sultan of Atche was told that, because of the rebellion in the Yemen, the expedition was adjourned to the next year.[2] Thereafter, the expedition to Cyprus and the critical situation following it made it impossible for the Ottomans to realize the Atche project, though the promise of aid was in fact repeated. However, the small number of Ottoman artillerymen in Sumatra made for the Sultan of Atche 200 bronze cannon, with which he attacked the Portuguese at Malacca.[3]

Always with the idea of finding allies against the Ottomans, the Portuguese established diplomatic relations and sent fire-arms to the Safawids in Iran also. Shāh Tahmasp received twenty pieces of artillery from them for use against Sultan Süleymān, when he invaded Iran in 1548.[4] Under the impact

[1] Cf. Razaulhak Şah, 'Açı Padışahi Sultan Alâeddin' in Kanuni Sultan Sulëyman'a Mektubu', *Tarih Araştırmaları Dergisi*, v/8–9, 1967 (1970), 373–410.

[2] Ibid. 395. [3] Cf. F. C. Danvers, *The Portuguese in India* (London, 1894), i. 535.

[4] Cf. *EI*², s.v. *Bārūd* (Ṣafawids: R. M. Savory).

of Ottoman superiority in fire-arms the successive dynasties in Iran, beginning with the Ak Koyūnlū and their chieftain Uzūn Hasan, tried to get such weapons from the Europeans. In 1471 Uzūn Hasan made an agreement with the Venetians, who were to send a force equipped with fire-arms to Gorigos, a port on the south coast of 'Caramania'. He himself would gather an army of 30,000 men to join them there and then invade the Ottoman territory. This plan failed because Uzūn Hasan's army did not arrive, though the Venetians brought the aid, as agreed, to Gorigos in 1472. In the following year the Venetian envoy Barbaro brought with him, for Uzūn Hasan, some pieces of artillery and a number of specialists.[1] It should be noted that the battle of Başkent (Terjān) between Uzūn Hasan and Mehmed the Conqueror in 1473 was decided by Ottoman fire-arms. And at Çaldirān, waged between the Ottomans and the Safawids in 1514, the victory—as attested in the accounts from both sides—was decided by the Ottoman gunfire. The Safawids learned their lesson there. In 1528 Shāh Tahmasp owed his crushing victory over the Uzbeks to his imitating the Ottoman tactics of *ṭābūr cengi.*[2] For the Safawids a new route for the acquiring of fire-arms from Europe was to be opened, when the Russians captured Astrakhan and Terek in 1556 and the Englishman Anthony Jenkinson visited the Shāh's capital in order to establish a trade route to Iran via Moscow.[3] Furthermore, the Tsar, being in rivalry with the Ottomans, soon entered into diplomatic relations with the Shāh and sent him aid in the form of fire-arms. But, paradoxically, Iran—before the time of Shāh 'Abbās the Great (1587–1629)—obtained fire-arms and also the materials and specialists to make them, more, it would seem, from the Ottoman Empire than from any other state.

We know that in 1528 Shāh Tahmasp had 'Rūmlū Tufangcīs'[4] in his army; and most of the terms connected with fire-arms in Persian come from Ottoman Turkish—e.g., *tūb*, *tūbcī*, *tūbcī-bāshī*, *tufang*, *tufangcī*, *darbzan*, *ḳazḳan*. We also know that a great number of Kızılbaş from Asia Minor took refuge in the Shāh's territory; that the rebellious Ottoman Prince Bāyezīd came to Iran as a refugee in 1559, bringing with him thirty pieces of artillery and many soldiers;[5] and that, later on, many *celālī* bands armed with the *tüfeng* fled to Iran and served in the Shāh's army.[6] On the other hand, there was also an active caravan trade between the two countries; and, despite the prohibitions laid down by the Ottomans, arms and strategic materials were smuggled from the Ottoman territories into Iran. Later, Shāh 'Abbās the Great founded Bandar-'Abbās chiefly with the purpose of saving Iran from this dependence on the Ottomans and of establishing a direct contact

[1] Cf. *EI*², loc. cit.
[2] Cf. Babur, *Vekayi*, ii. 394.
[3] Cf. W. Foster, *England's Quest of Eastern Trade* (London, 1933), 15–21.
[4] Cf. *EI*², loc. cit.
[5] Cf. *EI*², loc. cit.
[6] Cf. Iskandar Munşī, *Tā'rīh-i 'Ālem-Ārāy-i 'Abbāsī* (Tehran, A.H. 1313), 539.

with the Western nations.[1] One Ottoman Grand Vizier of that time said, in a report to the sultan, that it needed no great thought to realize what danger this establishment of direct relations might bring about for the Ottoman Empire.[2] It was undoubtedly under ʿAbbās the Great that Iran became really a power able to compete with the Ottoman Empire, thanks to his 12,000 *tüfengcīs*, and his 10,000 *ghilāmān-i khāṣṣa*, armed with the *tüfeng*, foot and horse respectively—a replica of the Ottoman Janissaries and the *Sipāhīs* of the Porte.[3] Shāh ʿAbbās tested his army with great success against the Uzbeks in 1598, thus depriving the Ottomans of a valuable ally in his rear. He passed over to a counter-attack against the Ottomans in 1603 and recovered, without great difficulty, the Ottoman conquests in Adharbayjān, including many fortresses which were built there by the Ottomans and equipped with artillery and *tüfeng-endāz*.[4] This blow threw the Ottoman Empire into an unparalleled confusion and became one of the causes accelerating its decline.

The successors of Shāh ʿAbbās were not able to maintain his reforms. First, his successor had to give up the monopoly of the silk trade and thus lose a great source of revenue, which had enabled ʿAbbās to realize his reforms.[5] Nevertheless, the use of hand-guns appears now to have spread among the warlike peoples in Iran. The Shāh had to renounce the services of the Māzandarānī musketeers in the middle of the seventeenth century.[6] In this period the office of '*tūbcī-bāshī*' was already abolished.[7]

We have mentioned the fact that the Iranian success over the Uzbeks at the battle of Mashhad in 1528 was ascribed to the *destūr-i Rūmī*, i.e., to the Ottoman tactics of *ṭābūr cengi*. The Safawid superiority in fire-arms caused the Uzbeks to ask insistently for these weapons and also for specialists from the Ottomans; and Süleymān I sent to Barak Nawrūz Khān (1540–59) an 'auxiliary force of 300 Janissaries armed with the *tüfeng* and some artillery of the kind known as *zarbüzan*'.[8]

The Ottoman interest in making the Central Asian states her allies goes back to the time of Mehmed the Conqueror who, in 1478, invited Sultan Baykarā of the Tīmūrid house to make a joint attack on Uzūn Hasan in Iran. Now, in the mid sixteenth century, the Uzbeks of Çingiz Khān's descendance, who had replaced the Tīmūrids in Central Asia, and the grandsons of Tīmūr Beg in Afghanistān were addressing the Ottoman sultan in their letters, asking for help in the style of a vassal ruler to his suzerain. One can see, between the lines of Seydī ʿAlī Re'īs, that Süleymān I then enjoyed a great prestige at the courts of the rulers in India and in Central Asia.[9] The same

[1] See H. İnalcık, 'Türkiye'nin İktisadî Vaziyeti', *Belleten*, xv/60 (1951), 664–74.

[2] Cf. C. Orhonlu, *Telhîsler*, 86.

[3] *EI*², s.v. *Bārūd* (Safawids: R. M. Savory).

[4] See B. Kütükoğlu, *Osmanlı-İran Siyâsî Münâsebetleri* (Istanbul, 1962), i. 135–41.

[5] Cf. İnalcık, in *Belleten*, xv/60, 674.

[6] Cf. Ewliyā Çelebī, *Seyāhat-Nāme*, ii (Istanbul, A.H. 1314), 228.

[7] Cf. *EI*², s.v. *Bārūd* (Ṣafawids: R. M. Savory).

[8] Cf. Seydī ʿAlī, op. cit. 88.

[9] Ibid. 28, 69.

author gives details indicating how the military aid that Süleymān sent to Barak Khān played an unusual role in Turkistān. The commander of the Ottoman force was killed during the civil war which broke out after the death of 'Abd al-Latīf Khān. In 1556 some of the Janissaries sent to Barak Khān left Turkistān to return home. The Ottoman soldiers left the country in two groups, one via Tashkent and the Daşt-i Kıpçak, the other via Bukhāra and Khwārazm. The latter group, during their journey, had to fight against a force of Russians, Moscow having recently captured Astrakhan and thus cut off the route between Central Asia and the Crimea. The Janissaries who remained in Transoxania entered the service of Seyyīd Burhān, the Khān of Bukhāra, and also the service of the sons of Barak Khān. Barak Khān himself, it seems, had taken the larger part of the Janissaries into his own service. He urged Seydī 'Alī Re'īs and his arquebusiers to join his army, for a company of *tüfeng-endāz*, however small, was then considered to be a vital element in the wars between the rival princes in Transoxania. Seydī 'Alī had then about forty *tüfeng-endāz* with him. Wherever he went in Transoxania, the local ruler insisted that he remain there or else hand over the *tüfeng* in the possession of his men. Determined to return to the Ottoman Empire, Seydī 'Alī resisted all promises and threats. 'Ali Beg, who was then fighting against the Khān of Bukhāra, seized ten of his arquebuses—*mıltık*, in Çagatai Turkish. The Khān of Bukhāra, in turn, forced Seydī 'Alī to surrender the remaining *tüfeng*, which were made of iron, giving him in exchange forty *tüfeng* fashioned from copper. This story is of some interest as revealing how Ottoman fire-arms played an important role in the internal struggle within Turkistān at this time. The Uzbek Khāns of a later time made new demands for fire-arms to Istanbul. The reaction to the request of 'Abd al-Bākī, the Khān of Bukhāra in 1103/1690 is interesting: in his report to the Ottoman sultan[1] the Grand Vizier expressed the opinion that twenty muskets would be sufficient and that a number of cannon called *zarbūzan* (*ḍarbzan*) should be sent from Shirvān via the Caspian Sea. He added that it was always a good policy to support the Khāns of Transoxania with fire-arms against Iran, even though the Ottoman Empire might be at peace with that country.

Z. V. Toğan[2] thought that the Uzbeks also received Portuguese muskets via India and that the Russians perhaps smuggled muskets into Transoxania for sale to the Uzbeks. In the seventeenth century the Uzbek Khāns continued to have small units of musketeers in their armies. Abu'l-Ghāzī Bahādūr, the Khān of Khwārazm (1643–63), had twenty musketeers, a resource which gave him a superiority in his conflicts with the Kalmuk and the Türkmen, who had none. Fire-arms were better appreciated, when the Russian Cossacks armed with them became a threat to the Uzbeks during the

[1] Cf. C. Orhonlu, *Telhîsler*, 80; also the *firmān* sent out to the Khān: cf. Ferīdūn, *Munşa'āt al-Salātīn*, ii (Istanbul, A.H. 1265), 73–4.

[2] Cf. Z. V. Toğan, *Bugünkü Türkistan* (Cairo, 1929–39), 95–6.

first years of the seventeenth century. In 1011/1602 a Cossack band made a surprise attack and looted Urgenj in Khwārazm. Pursued by the Khān in their retreat, they defended themselves behind their wagons with their muskets.[1]

With the Cossacks we come to the Russian penetration into Eurasia during the sixteenth century. It is generally assumed[2] that their use of fire-arms was again chiefly responsible for the spectacular developments in this region. As with the Portuguese in the Indian Ocean, so now, in the present case, the Ottoman Empire, as the one Muslim state able to halt the bewildering Russian expansion,[3] received appeals for protection from the Muslim peoples living in the area between the Crimea and Turkistān. Here, too, the Ottoman reaction followed the same pattern, placing under the direct command of the Crimean Khān, who was the champion of the resistance against the Russian expansion in Eastern Europe, a small force of Janissaries and a few artillerymen, but in fact exploiting the situation essentially for the strengthening and enlarging of Ottoman control in that region and embarking, in due course, on great projects of military expeditions, as in 1569.[4]

To conclude, some general observations can be made as follows:

1. It was under the impact of the fire-arms used by the European nations in their expansion into Asia and the Indian Ocean that peoples in this part of the world became anxious to acquire these formidable new weapons; and they obtained them for the first time through the Ottomans—in the Indian Ocean against the Portuguese, and in Eurasia against the Russians. The Ottomans themselves used fire-arms extensively and developed their formations, again under the impact of Europe, first of all during the wars with John Hunyadi in 1441–4 and then in the face of the German infantry encountered during the wars against the Habsburgs in the sixteenth century. It seems that the turning point in this respect was the 'Long War' of 1593–1606, during which the Ottomans were overcome by the Imperialist armies now fully equipped with up-to-date fire-arms. The traditional military organization of the Ottoman Empire, furnished with conventional arms, proved to be obsolescent at this time and, thereafter, underwent fundamental changes.

2. Being the most advanced Muslim nation in respect of fire-arms the Ottomans benefited from their privileged position to expand their rule over other Middle Eastern countries and, later on, to exploit that position in order to support their claim to be the protector of all the Muslims in the world. It is also to be noted that Ottoman aid to the other Muslim countries consisted usually of a small unit of artillerymen and musketeers,

1 Cf. Abu'l-Ghāzī Bahādūr Khān, *Şecere-i Turk*, ed. Riza Nur, Istanbul, 1929, 289–90.

2 See Z. V. Toğan, *Bugünkü Türkistan* (Cairo, 1929–39), 115.

3 Cf. H. İnalcık, 'The Origin of the Ottoman–Russian Rivalry and the Don–Volga Canal (1569)', *Annales de l'Université d'Ankara*, i. (1947), 47–110. See also W. E. D. Allen, *Problems of Turkish Power in the Sixteenth Century* (London, 1963); and A. N. Kurat, *Türkiye ve Idil Boyu* (Ankara, 1966).

4 Cf. the references listed in the preceding note.

sometimes with a few specialists capable of making cannon. The states which received this aid were, in general, not able to utilize it well enough to create for themselves units employing fire-arms—partly because of the traditional and feudal organization of these states and partly because of the Ottoman policy not to facilitate such a development. At any rate, except for the Ottoman Empire and Iran for a short time under ʿAbbās the Great, the other eastern governments could never create an army effectively equipped with fire-arms. But, on the other hand, the soldiers with fire-arms, however small in number, played in India, in Turkistān, and in the Crimean Khānate a major role in regional warfare.

3. The use of fire-arms was considered, in these traditional societies, to be something 'common' and not compatible with the traditional ethics and symbolism of the established military class or with feudal and tribal organization. But when, under the necessity to adopt these arms, the state created or expanded a corps of slave or popular origin, with pay, as was the case with the Ottomans in the fifteenth and with the Safawids and the Crimean Khāns in the sixteenth century, the new corps, equipped with these superior weapons and subject to the direct command of the ruler, became—at least for a time—a basis allowing the state to follow a centralizing policy within its territories. This development, leading to an alienation of the state from the feudal and tribal troops, was carried almost to completion in the Ottoman Empire, whereas in Iran and in the Khānates of Turkistān and the Crimea it was the latter elements which continued to be the basic force.

4. In studying the history of fire-arms, a distinction must be made between hand-guns and artillery. From the last decades of the sixteenth century onward the use of *tüfeng* (a name given to all kinds of hand-guns) spread widely among the common people in the countryside. Not only in the Ottoman Empire among the *reāya* as well as the nomads—Türkmen, Arabs, Kurds—but also in the adjacent countries among the Cossacks, Çerkes and Georgians the spread of the *tüfeng* brought about, in the course of time, revolutionary social and political consequences. It caused the spread of brigandage, the formation of mercenary companies and the growth both of local resistances and of decentralizing forces.

APPENDIX I

Ottoman Collections of Documents Concerning Fire-Arms in the Ottoman Archives

The most important series are:

1. The books of accounts for the Top-Hāne and for the Bārūt-Hāne (the Cannon Foundry and the Powder Factory).

   Examples: Maliyeden Müdevver Defterler No. 18523 is a book of accounts (dated

Ṣaʿbān 1102) listing the purchases and wages for the casting of forty pieces of artillery at the Top-Hāne (the Imperial Cannon Foundry). It contains data on the material and tools, also on the specialists and workers, with exact information as to quantities and prices.

There exist many such *defters* in this series, as well as in the collections classified by Cevdet. The oldest *defter* of this series thus far discovered is dated 934/1527 (No. 7668). Most of the *defters* belong to the seventeenth and eighteenth centuries. Maliyeden Müdevver Defterler No. 683 is a book of accounts (dated 1095/1684) for the production of iron cannon-balls at the factory and mine of 'Banaluka' in Bosnia. A résumé of its contents is given below in Appendix II.

2. The books of survey and inventory of the fortresses.

Example: Maliyeden Müdevver Defterler No. 610 (dated 1113/1701) is a book of inventory of the fire-arms, tools, and ammunition in the fortresses of the empire.

It contains details on the number, type, and dimensions of the artillery and the *tüfeng* found in each fortress; the quantities of powder, lead and other materials are also included. Sometimes the number of the garrison is given. A list of the fortresses, with the number of cannon and *tüfeng* is given below in Appendix III.

Some of these *defters* give an inventory only for one single fortress or for a few fortresses.

3. The books of the *mevācib*, i.e., the salaries of the *cebecis*.

Examples: Maliyeden Müdevver Defterler No. 19650 (dated 1101/1689) is a roll of the *cebecis* at the Porte. It is the main source for data on the organization and number of the *cebecis*, whose function it was to store and repair fire-arms and also to supervise their manufacture. Each fortress had its own *cebe-hāne*, i.e., a depot of arms and ammunition under the care of the *cebecis*. Thus we have a separate book for each fortress or group of fortresses. Also available is the roll of the *topcıs* and *top-arabacıs* (*Defter* No. 16453).

4. The books containing copies of the orders given at the Porte concerning the Top-Hāne, the Cebe-Hāne, and the Bārūt-Hāne.

Example: A book of this class bearing the title '*Kuyūd-i Mühimmāt-i Ṭophāne-i ʿĀmire*' (Maliyeden Müdevver Defterler No. 2811), dated 1098/1687, contains all kinds of orders concerning the casting of guns, the materials needed, the salaries and wages, the transportation of guns and material, etc.

This series is most useful for circumstances affecting the manufacture, prices, personnel, and distribution of fire-arms as well as for government policy and administrative measures.

APPENDIX II

As an example of a foundry making iron cannon-balls, I give here a résumé of a book of account relating to 'Banaluka' in Bosnia and dating from 1095/1684 (on this book cf. the reference included above in Appendix I).

The workers were drawn from the Christian *reāya* of the area. They worked for six months in the foundry, with pay. In return for this obligation, they were exempted from all other extraordinary services or dues. Their wages were assessed according to the kind of work they did—a *kālci* (foundry worker) got 16 *akçes* per *ḳanṭār* (fifty *vukīyye*), while an *ocakcı* (worker in the iron pit) received 10 *akçes* a day. The various groups of workers are listed as follows:

woodcutters (*baltacı*)	240 persons
coal-heavers (*kömürcü*)	180 persons
extractors of iron ore (*cevher-keşān*)	40 persons
dam-makers (*bendciyān*)	35 persons
soil-carriers (*toprakciyān*)	18 persons
shovellers (*kürekciyān*)	2 persons
ordinary workmen	50 persons
pit-workers	as many as needed

In three foundries the iron (*helun*) produced in six months amounted to 162,000 *vukīyye*, 100,000 *vukīyye* of which was used to make iron cannon-balls in a separate foundry. The men were at work day and night for six months. The expenses, in all, amounted to 203,000 *akçes*.

APPENDIX III

A List of the Artillery and Muskets in the Principal Fortresses of the Ottoman Empire according to a Survey Book of 1113/1701 (See Appendix I)

Name	*Artillery pieces*	*Musket pieces*	*Garrison*
Sedd al-Bahr (Dardanelles)			
Sultan Hisarı	52	292	
Alaiye (Alanya)	53	20	208
Eski Foça	63		
Yeni Foça	20	48	
Bodrum	32	35	80
Meis	14	120	
Sancak-Burnu	30	150	116
Sığacık	16		106
Yılan-Başlık	19	45	
Yenice-i Çandarlı	9	7	18
Marmaros (island)	22		28
Izmir Limān Kalesi	8	200	16

Name	Artillery pieces	Musket pieces	Garrison
Biçin	3		12
Ayasolug	4		24
Antalya	31	407	240
Kuşada	33	50	
Güzelhisar		20	90
Rum-Kale	26	30*	
Kahta	8	18	
Külek	4	20	
Temruk	12	21	
Birecik	32	23	
Ayıntab	25	56	
Ayas	17	60	
Tarsus	5	62	
Payas	34	78	
Adana	12	66	
Merkez-Kale	6	5	
Maraş	17	1076	
Ruha (Urfa)	32	4	
Rakka	2		
Amasra 1	4	22	
Amasra 2	17	21	
Erzurum	97	52	
Kars	43	47	
Kecvan	6	9	
Ozgur (?)	5	29	
Magazberd	1	5	
Kagızman	1	15	
Hartus	9	28	
Bardiz	4	11	
Avnik	18	24	
Hasan Kale	108	36	
Büyük Ardıhan	7	26†	
Mecinkerd	3	9	
Ahsiha	20	87	
Kutais	8		
Giresun	31		
Sinop	156	36	
Tirebolu	6		
Ünye	10	14	
Samsun	28	7	
Günye	25	7	
Görele	12		
Trabzon	48	358	
Rize	5		
Inebolu	4		
Halep	135	81	
Midilli	1	432	

* Plus 400,000 ***vukiyye*** of iron and 5,000 *vukiyye* of powder.
† Plus 6,000 ***vukiyye*** of powder.

Name	Artillery pieces	Musket pieces	Garrison
Sakız	10		
Sivas	36	380	
Granbosa (Crete)	45		
Soğucak	15		
Sohum	5		
Faş	35		
Hotin	157		

There are some pages missing at the end of this survey book. According to the list of names on the first page, this volume included also other fortresses on the northern shore of the Black Sea, on the river Danube, and in south-eastern Asia Minor.

APPENDIX IV

Lists of Arms and Ammunition at the Fortress of Bodrum on 16 Ṣafer 929/4 January 1523 (the Date of its Conquest) and in 1113/1701

In 929/1523

Tūc Bāş Ṭop (bronze baş ṭop)	2 pieces
Tīmūr Ṭop (iron piece)	1 piece
Büyük Tūc Zarbūzan (big bronze zarbūzan)	12 pieces
Küçük Tūc Zarbūzan (small bronze zarbūzan)	4 pieces
İkişer ot-evlu tīmūr bāş ṭop (bāş ṭop with two powder magazines)	22 pieces
Büyük Tīmūr Zarbūzan	1 piece
İkişer ot-evlu tīmūr Prangı (iron pranga with two magazines)	2 pieces
Büyük Tūc Şakaloz (large bronze şakaloz)	12 pieces
Küçük Tūc Şakaloz (small bronze şakaloz)	8 pieces
Total Number of Artillery pieces	— 64

In the Storehouse:

Tūc Tüfeng (bronze musket)	46
Zenberek (crossbow)	12
Cevşen (armour)	69
Tolga (helmet)	14
Kalkan (shield)	44
Ḥarbe (halberd)	65
Cevşen-i Köhne (worn out armour)	20
Zenberek Oku (arrows for crossbow)	1 chest
Könder (lances)	300
Katranlı Çölmek (jars filled with tar)	200
Külçe Kurşun (pig lead)	20
A Workshop (Kār-Hāne) with all the tools ready for work	
Kükürt (sulphur)	3 barrels
Ṭop Otu (powder for cannon)	2 barrels
Ṭop Otu (again)	7 barrels
Ṭop Taşı (stone balls)	7000
Iron Cannonballs	400
Stone Balls for Zarbūzan	400
Tīmūr Butrak (iron caltrops)	1 barrel

In 1113/1701

Tūc Şāhī Ṭop (bronze, 12 *karış* long, firing stone shot 1 *okka* in weight)	4 pieces
Tuc Şāhī Ṭop (bronze, 17 *karış* long, firing stone shot 4 *okka* in weight)	1 piece
Tīmūr Saçma Ṭop (iron, firing small shot)	4 pieces
Tīmūr Ingiliz Ṭop (iron, of English provenance, 11 *karış* long, firing stone shot 4 *okka* in weight)	5 pieces
Tūc Ṭop (bronze, 13 *karış* long, firing stone shot 4 *okka* in weight)	3 pieces
Tūc Ṭop (bronze, 16 *karış*, long, firing stone shot 3 *okka* in weight)	2 pieces
Ingiliz Ṭop (of English provenance, 11 *karış* long, firing stone shot 2 *okka* in weight)	4 pieces
Tūc Ṭop (bronze, firing stone shot 1 *okka* in weight)	2 pieces
Ingiliz Tīmūr Ṭop (iron, of English provenance, firing stone shot 1 *okka* in weight, 11 *karış* long)	2 pieces
Tīmūr Ṭop Ḥavan (iron, a mortar, 9 *karış* long, firing stone shot 11 *okka* in weight)	1 piece
Tuc Saçma Ṭop (bronze, firing small shot)	4 pieces
Total Number of Artillery Pieces	32

In the Storehouse:

Zarbūzan Tüfeng (musket)	20
Tüfeng	15
Ṭop Keçesi (felt for cannon)	20
Könder (lances)	10
Ḥarbe (halberds)	21
Cannon-balls	1500
Lead	10 ḳantār
Iron	15 ḳantār
Powder	90 ḳantār
Ḳazma (hoes)	30
Kürek (shovels)	18
Powder (not good for use)	15 ḳantār
Garrison: (40 with salary, 40 with *tīmār*)	80

APPENDIX V

Résumé of a Book of Account (dated 1107–1109/1695–1697) Concerning the Bārūt-Hāne (the Powder–Mill) at Gallipoli

The raw material bought:

Vukīyye		*Price (in akçes)*
45,485	Pure saltpetre	2,560,775
8,000	Sulphur	12,000
8,000	Charcoal	24,000
1,000	Barrels	36,000
1,130 *çeki*	Wood (one *çeki* = 180 vukīyye)	40,000

20,000 *vukīyye* of saltpetre was bought in the *Sancaks* of Gallipoli, Biga, Karesı, and Midilli and the rest from merchants at 40 *akçes* and 69 *akçes* per *vukīyye* respectively (1 *vukīyye* or *okka* = 1·2828 kg.). The saltpetre of poorer quality bought in the *Sancaks* had to be melted a second time at the Bārūt-Hāne.

In addition, wages paid: 745,875 *akçes*.

102,645 *akçes* were paid for the tools, for repair work at the Bārūt-Hāne and for transportation.

Other expenses paid for the preparation of gunpowder: 49,725 *akçes*. The production of black powder for the year 1107/1695: 1,130 *ḳanṭār* (one *ḳanṭar* = 56·443 kg.).

Deliveries made therefrom to the Imperial Fleet and elsewhere: 1,090 *ḳanṭār*.

Note. According to Ewliyā Çelebī (I, 564) there were five powder-mills at Istanbul. The two largest ones were the mill at Kağıt-Hāne and that near Macuncu Çarşısı. The latter was under the Bārūt-Emīni, the Commissioner for Gunpowder, and had 30 mortars at work. The other three were the mill working for the Janissary Corps in the At-Meydanı, that of the Tüfeng-Hāne at the Un-Kapanı, and the mill of the Cebe-Hāne, under the care of the *cebecis*, at Ayasofya.

The powder produced in these mills was stored under the domes in the walls of Istanbul from Silvri-Kapı to Yeni-Kapı.

Ewliyā gives quite a detailed description of the powder-mill at Kağıt-Hāne. The founder of the mill, he declares, was Bāyezīd II. Sultan Süleymān rebuilt it, with extensions. There were in employment there two hundred Acemi-Oghlanı as workmen operating under the Bārūtcu-Başı, the Ketkhudā, and the Çāvūş from the corps of *cebecis*. In making the powder *deste-zens*, pestles weighing 40 or 50 *vukīyye* and driven by water-power from the river, pounded the mixture, while the workmen stirred it continuously with wooden poles.

The Bārūt-Hāne of Gallipoli was the chief powder-mill before the conquest of Istanbul.

XV

THE NATURE OF TRADITIONAL SOCIETY: TURKEY

We can best describe the original features of the Ottoman-Turkish traditional society by going back to the time of Süleyman I (1520-1566). In the period immediately before the political modernization of the nineteenth century, we find only more or less degenerate forms of the original Ottoman institutions, and new social and political developments threatening the basis of those institutions. The generation of reformers confronting the period of decline after the sixteenth century avowedly sought to restore the Golden Age of Süleyman I. Under the impact of the defeats in Hungary between 1683 and 1699 the Ottoman Turks first became aware of the superiority of the West; the reforms thereafter increasingly acknowledged Western influences, first in the military field and then, in the nineteenth century, in administration. The decisive modernization movement, accompanied by a basic change in the concept of state and society, began with the national revolution after the First World War.

The hesitations and delays in the Turkish modernization process were due to the fact that, until the twentieth century, Turkey was an empire comprising nations of different cultures and that the dynasty became at a certain time the only focus of common loyalty. On the other hand, the political and social superstructure of the empire was still based on the *sharīʿah* (Turkish: *şeriat*), the unalterable religious law of Islam, and this politico-religious structure culminated in the office of the sultan-caliph.

The position of this Ottoman ruler and the developments which reduced his power and ultimately led to modernization will constitute the main theme of this essay.

I. The Ottoman Ruler and Ottoman Society

Tursun Beg, Ottoman statesman and historian of the late fifteenth century, stressed that harmony among men living in society was achieved only by statecraft, which kept each individual in his proper place as determined by his ability. As the instrument of social order, statecraft possessed two aspects or sanctions: the authority and power of the ruler and the divine reason or *sharīʿah*. Insofar as the rules instituted by the ruler did not have a perpetual character, he should always be present in a human society. He should have absolute power to determine the place of each man in the social scheme. Always seeking to strengthen his position by expanding his revenues and his armies, he should serve society as a whole by consolidating public security and order. Tursun Beg's rational arguments were manifestly designed to prove that every society must have one ruler with absolute power and with the authority of issuing regulations and laws outside the religious law. The values which this ruler was to conserve were social order and security under justice. These ideas constituted the basic political philosophy of the Ottomans.

The absolute power of the Ottoman ruler found further support in the old Oriental maxim that a ruler can have no power without soldiers, no soldiers without money, no money without the well-being of his subjects, and no popular well-being without justice. Repeated in Turkish political literature from *Kutadgu Bilik* in the eleventh century to the Gülhane Rescript of 1839, this formula was regarded as the summation of practical statesmanship. Kâtib Çelebi in the seventeenth century particularly stressed the central position of the sultan in the state. Though absolute power was ascribed to the caliph in the Islamic community, the theorists stressed that absolute power was simply a means of implementing the religious law.

The Ottoman rulers first made this theoretical absolutism a reality by establishing a type of administration that concentrated power in their persons. This they achieved notably by eliminating all kinds of aristocracies in the conquered lands, by entrusting executive functions only to slaves trained in the court (*kuls*), and by enlisting the *ulema* in their service. The sultan's slaves were entrusted with executive power and the *ulema* with the administration of law, including the supervision of all legal and financial matters. Both of these branches of administration were attached to the central government but each was independent of the other. A governor had no authority to give orders to a local judge (*kadı*) appointed by the sultan. If a conflict arose between the branches, it was appealed directly to the central government. The same judges administered both the *sharīʿah* and the subsidiary laws and regulations directly issued by the sultan. On the other hand, the *şeyhülislâm*, the highest authority in formulating opinions on points concerning the *sharīʿah*, had no right to interfere directly in the government or in legal administration. Once, when *Şeyhülislâm* Ali Cemali came over to the seat of the government to protest against a decision of Sultan Selim I (1512-1520) which he thought contrary to the *sharīʿah,* the sultan denounced him as interfering in state affairs. But in the eighteenth century it became established practice to seek the *şeyhülislâm*'s opinion on every governmental matter of importance. The limitations so imposed on the government by the *sharīʿah* and by religious authority in the period of decline made the application of reforms especially difficult. The all-embracing *sharīʿah* became the stronghold of traditionalism in Ottoman government and society—introducing, as we may note in passing, a major difference between the Turkish and the Japanese modernization processes.

Ottoman social policy conformed closely to the traditional view that for the sake of social peace and order the state should keep each man in his appropriate social position. In the first place, Ottoman society was divided into two major classes. The first one, called *askerî,* literally the "military," included those to whom the sultan had delegated religious or executive power through an imperial diploma, namely, officers of the court and the army, civil servants, and *ulema.* The second included the *reaya,* comprising all Muslim and non-Muslim subjects who paid taxes but who had no part in the government. It was a fundamental rule of the empire to exclude its subjects from the privileges of the "military." Only those among them who were actual fighters on the frontiers and those who had entered the *ulema* class after a regular course of study in a religious seminary could obtain the sultan's diploma and thus become members of the "military" class. It was, in fine, the sultan's will alone that decided a man's status in society. In the period of decline, Koçi Beg and others asserted that a major cause of the disorganization of the empire was the abandonment of this fundamental rule in favor of letting subjects become Janissaries or fief (*tımar*) holders.

The subjects in turn were divided into Muslims and non-Muslims, townspeople and peasants, sedentaries and nomads, each with a different status, as reflected in their tax obligations. Taxation was indeed the most important factor in determining the subject's status. Those who were granted certain tax immunities in return for public service actually constituted an intermediate group between the simple subjects and the "military," who were wholly tax-exempt. Living for the most part on state-owned lands as tenants, the peasantry were subject to special taxes and were divided into groups according to the taxes they paid, the status of each being individually recorded at regular intervals. Peasants were not allowed to leave their lands, nor could they settle in towns.

These laws reflect a rigid social organization imposed by the will of the Ottoman ruler. But in the late sixteenth century a profound transformation took place which may be attributed ultimately to economic and military changes in Western Europe. During this period, for example, in order to resist German infantrymen, the Ottomans discarded their *timar* cavalry in the provinces and increased the force of Janissaries, who were by this time equipped with firearms. This neglect of the fief holders within the army was followed by the disorganization of the land and taxation system upon which their status had been based. Simultaneously, the shift of international trade routes to the Atlantic Ocean and the invasion of the markets of the Levant by American silver resulted in the disorganization of the rigid Ottoman fiscal and economic structure.

Already during this period of decline, the sultan and his bureaucracy, who sensed immediate danger to the state from outside, adopted the idea of reform, although they thought of it as a reform along traditional lines. The Japanese, at a much later date, experienced the same challenge from outside and their emperor too personified the idea of reform. But the Japanese reform movement found national support at least among some leading classes in the society, while in the Ottoman Empire the major ruling classes took a reactionary stance. In the Ottoman Empire reform remained a concern of the sultan and his immediate collaborators alone. *Ulema* and a rising semi-feudal landed aristocracy in the provinces, called the *âyan*, resisted any innovation that might disturb their vested interests.

II. The Decline of the Sultan's Power; The Janissaries, the Ulema, *and the Rise of the* Âyan

In the capital of the empire the politically influential groups were the military corps at the sultan's Porte, particularly the Janissaries, constituting the "military" proper, and the *ulema*, the learned in Islamic sciences, who were vested with authority to express and apply the commands of the *sharī'ah*. In the provinces, too, the *ulema* and the Janissaries at one time possessed commanding power, but in the eighteenth century the *âyan*, a group of provincial magnates, came to be the most powerful class throughout the empire.

The Janissary corps constituted the original foundation of the centralist government and the principal support of the sultan's absolute power. It formed a standing army at the Porte, which was directly attached to the person of the sultan and which he could use at any time to strike at an internal or external foe. In addition, Janissary garrisons were stationed in the main strongholds in the provinces. In the large cities they occupied the forts, which no one else, not even a governor, was allowed to enter. In the period when central authority grew weaker, these Janissaries took over the actual control of the government in such distant parts of the empire as North Africa, Baghdad, and Belgrade. In the capital they determined who would wield control. As early as 1446, Murad II had accepted the throne only after obtaining their consent in a public meeting. In the first half of the seventeenth century they strengthened their grip on the government. In 1628 for the first time a former commander of the Janissary corps was appointed Grand Vezir with the support of the *şeyhül-islâm*, the head of the *ulema*. In the 1630's Koçi Beg complained that the balance established earlier between the power of the Janissaries and that of the provincial forces was gone and that the Janissaries invaded all sectors of the empire. The vezirs, courtiers, and heirs to the throne all sought their aid to attain power. The Janissaries furthermore obtained for themselves additional privileges, among them that of engaging in trade. Hence many of them joined the class of small shopkeepers and were thus affected by the government's financial policy as was the rest of the Istanbul population.

Let us observe also how the *âyan*, a powerful class of magnates, rose in the provinces. Traditionally the Ottomans granted the craftsmen and merchants in the towns a distinct and honorable status and recognized the most influential and wealthy among them as their natural leaders. Organized in so-called *ahi* unions, the craftsmen had played a major social and political role in Anatolia from the thirteenth century onward; their leaders, the *ahi*'s, acquired control of the administration in many Anatolian towns. Under the centralist government of the Ottomans, they were gradually reduced to simple guilds, but each guild continued to elect its own master, called *kâhya*, to supervise the application of the guild's rules and to act as its representative before the authorities.

Above the guildmasters were the *âyan* (notables) and the *eşraf*, the most influential residents of the city whom the government always addressed on matters directly concerning the town population. We find these *âyan* and *eşraf* present even in fourteenth-century Ottoman cities. Whenever an imperial order was to be communicated to the townsmen, the local judge convoked the *âyan*, *eşraf*, guildmasters, and *imams* (district clerics) of the town, because "these were," our source adds, "the agents and representatives of the people, who did what they said to do." Among the population, *kâhya*'s were elected as representatives of each district of the town and, from very early times, a mayor or town *kâhya*, representing the whole municipality. The local *eşraf* included the head of the descendants of the Prophet in the town, the head of the local *ulema*, and the mufti, the local agent of the *şeyhülislâm*. Though their influence derived originally from religious services, the *eşraf* were usually among the well-to-do citizens.

The *âyan* were the most influential and wealthy citizens in a town except for the *eşraf*. Most of them came from humble origins, many being minor local officials or Janissary officers who had risen by exploiting their official position.

As pointed out earlier, the tax and land-tenure system of the empire underwent a transformation during the upheavals between 1595 and 1610. The new conditions enabled the *âyan* to become feudal lords in the provinces, replacing the fief holders in the state-owned lands as lessees or tax collectors. In the meetings of *âyan* and *eşraf* under the judge, the most important issue was usually the distribution among the people of the total tax assessment of the district. After the decline of the earlier army, the central government, in increasing need of money to support the enlarged Janissary army, resorted more and more to extraordinary assessments, which were allotted to the counties. These special taxes and the assessments for local expenses were farmed out to individual persons by the council of *âyan* and *eşraf*, who often used these responsibilities to increase their own wealth and influence. They usually added to the assessment books items for themselves, or collected additional dues for their services. They often neglected to send the assessment books to the central government for inspection, and thus levied taxes without government control. In 1705 in Manisa, a city in western Anatolia, the populace became outraged by such abuses, and invaded the judge's court where the *âyan* and *eşraf* were sitting.

But usually the *âyan* managed to show themselves to the people as their protectors. They occasionally sent the sultan petitions for tax exemptions, which bore their own signatures though they were confirmed by the judge. They contended with oppressive government officials sent by the sultan. They were so influential in their areas, all in all, that the sultan's governor and judge often became simple tools in their hands. Without their cooperation, the authorities could not collect taxes, levy troops, or maintain public security.

The *âyan* gained their wealth and power through leasing state-owned lands as well as by tax farming. The larger part of such lands ceased to be assigned to fief holders and were leased by the state to local notables, *âyan* and *ağa's* (*âyan* usually had the title of *ağa*'s, but *ağa*'s mentioned together with *âyan* meant lesser *âyan* in the provinces), and more than fifty per cent of agricultural lands in the empire were state-owned leaseholds. Large areas of endowed land and land assigned to officials and favorites were similarly exploited. The *âyan*'s influence on, and close cooperation with, local authorities favored them in these leasing operations. Later, in the eighteenth century, the leases were made for lifetime and prior rights to the leases were granted to the sons of lessees.

Tax farming, too, was extended after the dissolution of the old *tımar* system near the end of the sixteenth century, and local notables benefited from their involvement in this profitable business.

In the period of decline, the sultan's governors themselves employed the *âyan* as their local agents in financial and administrative matters under such various titles as *mütesellim, voyvoda,* and *subaşı.* Increasingly in need of new troops for its prolonged wars, furthermore, the state encouraged the *âyan* to equip at their own expense the forces under their direct command. Thus in the eighteenth century the ground work had been laid for the rise of a powerful semi-feudal aristocracy in the provinces of Anatolia and in the Balkans. Many of the *âyan* families were able to maintain their position for several generations and founded local dynasties. Actual clashes sometimes occurred among rival *âyan* seeking to extend the area of their leasehold. Some of the most powerful among them even forced the government to confer upon them the official titles of vezir or pasha, thereby consolidating their control of the provinces in which they held their estates and becoming able in time to challenge the sultan's authority. The latter tried in his weakness to play one *âyan* against another, but often only with the result of making his ally excessively powerful. Tepedelenli Ali Pasha, actual ruler of southern Albania and northern Greece, was the most famous example of a pasha of *âyan* origin.

III. The Revolutions of 1807 and 1808: The Struggle for Power Among Janissaries, Ulema, *and* Âyan

A brief account of the revolutions of 1807 and 1808 will illustrate the part which the Janissaries, *ulema,* and *âyan* played in political developments in the Ottoman Empire at the turn of the nineteenth century.

Selim III (1789-1807) has been regarded as the father of Ottoman-Turkish Westernization and as an exponent of general reform in the state. He was indeed interested in Western civilization in its various aspects. Ebu Bekir Ratib, his envoy to Vienna in 1791, brought him a detailed report not only of the military and administrative establishments but also of technology and social advances as embodied in such institutions as postal systems and hospitals. Selim gave positive instructions to his newly appointed ambassadors to Western capitals to study the administrative as well as the military institutions of those states and encouraged the staffs at the embassies to learn Western languages and observe all the things that they considered useful. At home before he began his reform he invited the principal officials in his service, among whom was a French officer in the Ottoman army, to submit appropriate reform proposals. But Selim's main motive for reform was his determination to restore the military power of the empire and throw back the Russians, who had recently conquered the Muslim-inhabited land north of the Black Sea and now threatened Istanbul itself. His state philosophy was not very different from that of his predecessors. He reasoned, that is, that there could be no power without an army, no army without sufficient sources of revenue, and no revenue without justice and prosperity among his subjects. In his decrees introducing military reforms he pointed out that his ancestors had given him an example and that the *sharīʿah* permitted Muslims to use "the enemies' tricks to overcome them." What was new and anti-traditional in his measures was the introduction not only of European weapons but also of the sciences, training procedures and uniforms of Europe. For Western scientific thought challenged traditional Muslim thought, and the European uniforms challenged traditional symbols.

He also issued reform decrees on governorship, *âyan* leases of the domains, currency, and the status of the *ulema,* but all these followed absolutely traditional lines.

Despite his personal conservatism, Selim III created in Ottoman society a trend toward Westernization and a sense of the necessity for rapid and progressive change. The *ulema*, representing religiously sanctioned traditions, opposed him for the most part. The reforms found support only among some of the higher *ulema* who either sought the favor of the sultan or considered the reforms necessary to the ultimate interests of Islam and caliphate. These supporters too appealed to the *sharīʿah* to justify their position.

The true reasons for the opposition to Selim were to be found in the social situation. His efforts to create a regular army under his direct command threatened the dominant position in the state of the Janissaries, on the one hand, and of the *âyan*, on the other. In addition, his financial measures created widespread discontent in the country and turned public opinion and the *ulema* against him.

To finance the new army, Selim created a treasury of the "New Order" and allotted to it the revenues of an important part of the domain leaseholds. To find additional resources he also raised the rates of the various dues. Since the dues paid for the imperial diplomas conferring an office, immunity, or fief were among these, he thereby alienated a number of influential people. The first reaction came from the *âyan*. When the sultan in 1806 planned to extend the military reform to the Balkans by a transfer of "new troops" from Anatolia, the *âyan* in the Balkans gathered together in Edirne and opposed his further advance. Selim retreated, and this marked the beginning of his fall. The conservatives at once seized power under the leadership of Hilmi Pasha, the new Grand Vezir who had once been the commander of the Janissaries, and *Şeyhülislâm* Ata'ullah, a fanatic supported by the reactionaries. The opposition of the Janissaries to the New Order was understandable enough: it was no less than an instrument of their own destruction. They also rallied the populace of Istanbul, who were afflicted by the new taxes and by the inflation following Selim's debasing of the currency. The sultan's price-fixing and terrible threats against profiteers had proved useless. The abolition of Janissary pensions in the possession of non-military persons had also affected a number of people in the capital. Finally, Selim had let a group of favorites draw up his reform plans and control their application. Exploiting his ambition to restore the power of the sultanate, many of these favorites in fact set out to gain wealth and power for themselves. The responsible government officials hated them and in time turned against the sultan himself. In their eyes the reformist sultan had merely brought back the arbitrary rule of a handful of favorites. Under his successors the same accusation was made.

In brief, the population of Istanbul was, as our analyst says, split into two camps, partisans of the New Order, and its enemies. Finally in 1807 the Janissary *yamak*'s rose against the reformist sultan. All the Janissaries, *ulema*, and the populace of Istanbul joined them, seeking the abolition of the New Order and of the treasury created for it, and the execution of the favorites. The head of the *ulema*, Ata'ullah, gave a formal opinion (*fetva*) for the deposition of Selim III, in which he said that Selim was unfit for the caliphate because he had let irresponsible men usurp power and use it against the Muslim population. The rebels made an agreement with the new sultan, Mustafa IV, providing that they would not be prosecuted for their past actions; in return they themselves promised not to interfere in state affairs any more. Our analyst notes that such a pledge on the part of the sultan was unheard of in Ottoman history. The Janissaries and their conservative allies were now in control of the whole government and busy with the purge of Selim's partisans. Mustafa's authority was not heeded outside the walls of his court.

The *âyan* were quick to seize power from the hands of the Janissaries. The *âyan* of Rumelia under the leadership of Alemdar Mustafa Pasha, formerly an *âyan* of Rusçuk (Russe), marched against the capital together with the imperial army then on the Danube. Alemdar seized Istanbul, suppressed the Janissary leaders, and demanded Selim's restoration to the throne. When it turned out that Selim had been put to death in the meantime, Alemdar made Mahmud II sultan and became himself Grand Vezir and dictator. In his diploma of appointment to the Grand Vezirate it was stressed that he should be most careful to act in accordance with the *sharīʿah* in all state affairs, to cooperate with the Janissary corps and *ulema*, and enforce the ancient laws of the Ottoman sultans. Under Alemdar, nevertheless, there was a violent reaction against the enemies of the New Order, about one thousand of whom were executed in two months.

Previously the *âyan* had not made a united front against the Janissary corps. In 1806 those in Rumelia had cooperated with the Janissaries while some powerful *âyan* in Anatolia supported Selim's New Order. But now the *âyan* of Rumelia and Anatolia united against the reactionaries, less out of sympathy for the reforms than from a desire to control the central government and guarantee their position in the provinces. Soon the joint forces of the *âyan* flocked into the capital with their armies, terrifying the Janissaries and the court.

Following the example of the Janissaries, they too made the sultan sign an agreement called *Sened-i Ittifak* (Covenant of Union). In the introduction of this document, it was emphasized that the division and conflicts within the government and among the *âyan* in the provinces were the main causes of the desperate situation of the empire and that this covenant proposed to revive it. The main provisions were as follows: Vezirs, *ulema,* high officials, "dynasties" of major *âyan* in the provinces, and military corps in the capital promised always to respect the sovereign authority of the sultan and the orders of the Grand Vezir, who represented in his person the sultan's absolute power, and to take united action against any rebellion. The important article 5 declared that, just as the signatories promised collectively to safeguard the person and authority of the sultan and the order and security of the state, so the security of the provincial "dynasties" was to be protected by joint action of the signatories in the event that any law-abiding "dynasty" was assailed by the "state" or by vezirs in the provinces. The "dynasties" further undertook not to punish any lesser *âyan* under their own authority without first consulting the central government. Each "dynasty" was to respect the boundaries of the other's area of control, and all were to take joint action against any transgressor. In article 2, the "dynasties" and lesser provincial notables sanctioned a state army and promised to conscript soldiers for it in the face of any opposition, including opposition from the military corps in the capital. In the same article, they promised to cooperate in the collection of state taxes for the sultan in the provinces. They further pledged themselves to protect the population under their authority and observe carefully the tax regulations agreed upon among the state, ministers, and provincial *âyan* (article 7).

The document was drawn up in the form of a regular contract according to the *sharīʿah,* the parties being the state and its officials, *ulema,* generals of the military corps in the capital, and representatives of the provincial "dynasties." It will be noted that the "state" but not the sultan himself was mentioned as a party in the document. He took no oath as the others did, but for confirmation put his imperial seal upon the covenant, even though he had been warned by his closest advisers that it would severely limit his absolute power. The several "dynasties" stood surety for each other. In the postscript it was made clear that the covenant was to be the perpetual and unalterable basis for the regeneration of the empire. As such it was to be signed by every Grand Vezir and *şeyhülislâm* upon his accession to office, and these were to see that it was observed in every detail. A copy of it was also to be deposited with the sultan, who would see in person that it remained in force forever.

This important document has been interpreted in very different ways, often without sufficient recognition of its historical meaning and background. Like Magna Carta, it was a limitation upon the king's power imposed by local magnates; it was not, like Magna Carta of popular conception, a preparation for liberal-democratic development. It clearly indicates the diminution of the sultan's power and the rise of the provincial magnates. In it the "dynasties" acknowledged many traditional rights of the sultanate: the supreme authority of the sultan, the independence of his government, and the rights of the state to conscript soldiers and collect taxes directly in the provinces (articles 1-4). At the same time it clearly stated that as long as the "dynasties" did not infringe upon the central authority, the government had to respect their status and their established rights. The "dynasties" and grandees of the empire, furthermore, were arrogating the right to take common action against anyone, including members of the sultan's government, who violated the provisions of the document. Article 4 provided that if the Grand Vezir violated the laws and fell into corrupt practices, it was the duty of all to sue him and check the abuses. But the document did not constitute any special organization which might carry out such a suit. What the "dynasties" wanted, in fact, was precisely to assure themselves of a degree of autonomy incompatible with a centralist and progressive government.

IV. The Restoration of the Sultan's Power in the Empire: His Bureaucracy Takes the Lead in Modernizing the State

The rule of the *âyan* did not last long. The court and members of Ottoman bureaucracy as well as the population of Istanbul were in a state of terror and rather welcomed the counter-attack of the Janissaries which put an end to *âyan* rule. To reestablish his authority in the provinces, Mahmud II (1808-1839) could only rely on the Janissaries, who now became more disobedient than ever. In 1812, nevertheless, immediately after the conclusion of the peace treaty with Russia, Mahmud began to suppress the principal *âyan* in the provinces. He crushed some of those who resisted him by sending into their territories troops commanded by the neighboring governors. Others he was able directly to deprive of their titles and leases so that they themselves were forced to submit and their sons to accept humbler positions. But in 1821 Tepedelenli Ali Pasha, the most powerful among the pashas of *âyan* origin, raised truly massive resistance. The Greek insurrection followed his revolt.

Mahmud's war against the refractory *âyan* resulted in the dispossession of many of them and restored much of the sultan's authority in the provinces. Yet hundreds of these notables remained at the head of local administrations and in possession of large leaseholds. Still constituting the most influential class in the provinces, they often appeared to the passive local populations in the guise of protectors against oppressive governors and an arbitrary central authority. Later, when the masses were given the opportunity to participate in political life, men of this class were to play a major part in political leadership.

In 1826, during the most critical period of the Greek insurrection, Mahmud II at last made the fateful decision to get rid of the Janissaries. Having done away with these as well as the rebellious *âyan* in the provinces, he would then possess unlimited power to reorganize the empire as the conditions of the time required.

Before the destruction of the Janissaries, Hâlet Efendi, a favorite whom they had supported, had been virtual master of the state. Thereafter, Hüsrev, a reformer left over from Selim's time, was given the task of creating a new army and became the major force in the empire for fifteen years. He was a product of the old Ottoman *kul* (imperial slave) system. This institution, established to provide wholly reliable instruments for the exercise of the sultan's absolute power, had been clearly defined by Kemal Pasha-zâde at the beginning of the sixteenth century. Hüsrev, its last great representative, had himself trained many slaves who became generals and governors of the empire. It would remain, of course, for westernized diplomat-bureaucrats to introduce truly modern reforms in the Ottoman state.

Muhammad Ali, who had become pasha of Egypt in the manner of pashas of *âyan* origin, proved more dangerous than Tepedelenli. From 1833 on, he threatened to extend his power to all Asiatic provinces of the empire. His influence was felt even in Anatolia, where the *âyan* and conservative masses hostile to Mahmud's reforms were sympathetic to him. He defeated Mahmud's new armies in 1833 and 1839. It was during this critical period that a new generation of reformers, of whom Mustafa Reşid Pasha was typical, emerged to save the empire from total destruction. Differing wholly from the military reformers like Hüsrev, these men were chiefly diplomats who had become acquainted with international conditions and with the structure of Western states during service in European capitals. They came out of the age-old bureaucracy which formed the third class of Ottoman state functionaries, the other classes being the *ulema* and the military. Their training was a practical one in the state bureaus, differing from that of the military, who were mostly trained under the *kul* system, and more markedly still from that of the *ulema*, who came from the rigidly formal religious seminaries. Thanks to their services in diplomacy and finance, the bureaucrats gained an increasing influence in the administration from the eighteenth century on. Devoted exclusively to the secular interests of the state and free from formalism and the bonds of tradition, they were ready to become faithful instruments of radical administrative reform. In 1821 when the Ottoman government had to replace the Greek interpreters with Turks, a Translation Office was created at the Sublime Porte, and Western languages were taught there, the first teacher being a professor from the military engineering school. This Translation Office, like the embassies which Selim III had established in Western capitals, became an educational center for a new generation of Westernized administrators and intellectuals. Âli Pasha, future Grand Vezir and reformer, and Fuad Pasha, collaborator of Reşid, received their first education in these centers.

Confronted with the disaster at Navarino in 1827 and Muhammad Ali's startling successes, Mahmud II heeded the advice of his reformist diplomats who saw the necessity of gaining the sympathy and confidence of Western powers and modernizing the Ottoman administration. Accordingly he introduced, between 1831 and 1838, some administrative and social reforms which can be regarded as the first decisive steps toward Westernization. Principal among these were the creation of state departments and of a council of ministers with a prime minister, the establishment of two high councils for military and civil reform, the use in the administration of civil servants with fixed salaries, the founding of a modern postal service and of secular professional schools, and modernization in clothing and state protocol. But Mahmud's most significant achievement remained the restoration of the sultan's power in the provinces and in all branches of administration.

After his success on a diplomatic mission to London in 1838, when war was pending with Muhammad Ali of Egypt, Reşid Pasha gained an increasing influence over Mahmud II and was able to persuade him that the disposition of Egypt would finally be decided in Western capitals. The very survival of the Ottoman state, in his view, was dependent on a modernization of its administration which would enable it to enter the concert of European states. The Ottoman defeat at Nezib in 1839 was followed by the death of Mahmud II, and thereafter everyone, including his great opponent Hüsrev, looked to Reşid for salvation and became receptive to his reform projects. The most radical Turkish decisions to reform, we observe, were almost always made in time of crisis.

On November 3, 1839, an imperial rescript, read by Reşid Pasha at Gülhane, initiated the era of reform called Tanzimat in Turkish history. That document said in summary: The empire had been declining for one hundred and fifty years because the religious law and imperial laws had been disregarded. In order to restore its prosperity and strength, new legislation was required which should be based on the principle of securing the life, honor, and property of all subjects. Taxation and conscription laws would be revised in accordance with the demands of justice. The tax farming system would be abolished and each citizen taxed in proportion to his means. Every accused person should be publicly judged. These guarantees should be extended to all subjects of whatever religion or sect.

A high council of reforms (*Meclis-i Vâlâ-yı Ahkâm-ı Adliye*) would devise, after free debate, bills fulfilling the purposes agreed upon, and those in turn would be submitted to the sultan to be confirmed and published. Since all the bills would be drawn up for the sake of resuscitating Islam, the state, and the empire, the sultan promised to take an oath not to disregard them. The *ulema* and grandees of the empire were to take oaths to the same effect, and those who broke their word were to be punished without respect of rank and position according to the provisions of a penal code. These dispositions, finally, were to be made public throughout the empire and communicated officially to all the ambassadors of friendly powers resident at Istanbul.

In this rescript the main features of the European constitutions of the 1830's are quite skillfully combined with traditional Ottoman institutions and with practical necessities. A number of references to the *sharīʿah* obscured from conservatives the revolutionary content of the document, and indeed the traditional state philosophy was genuinely apparent in it: The rescript said that the state needed armed forces which in turn required money, that state finances could remain in good order only if the subjects were protected against injustices, and so on. The basic principle of legislation, also, was discovered not in natural rights but in the practical necessity of resuscitating the empire. In brief, state power remained the ultimate goal as before; the people were still regarded as mere subjects of the state.

It should be remembered that in classical Islamic thought no principles of law could exist apart from the *sharīʿah*. But with the Ottomans there had always in fact been an independent category of laws called imperial laws or *kanun*'s which were derived directly from the sovereign will of the ruler. For their justification it was asserted that, though applying to situations not covered by the *sharīʿah*, they were necessary for the well-being of the Islamic community. The Ottoman sultans had promulgated hundreds of such *kanun*'s concerning public law, state finances, taxation, economic life, and criminal law. The Gülhane rescript was promulgated on the same principle, the legislation which it envisaged being thought necessary to regenerate the state. The document itself was rendered in the form of a decree.

When all this is said, it remains nevertheless clear that the rescript introduced revolutionary ideas and institutions into Ottoman society. Among them was the sultan's promise, confirmed by an oath, to respect the laws to be made pursuant to its principles and the establishment of a council for legislative activities with the guarantee of freedom of debate.

When he composed the decree, Reşid had intended to impose limits on the despotic power of the sultan. In his letter to Palmerston, dated August 12, 1839, he confessed this intention: "Les puissances de l'Europe," he wrote, "savent à quel dégré était progressivement parvenue la tyrannie des Empereurs ottomans depuis la destruction des Janissaires. . . . Lorsque malgré la considération, si forte du voisinage, l'Autriche et la Russie, quelqu'en soit le motif, permettent à la Walachie et à la Servie, d'adopter une constitution, aucune puissance ne saurait-elle jamais vouloir empêcher que les populations musulmans obtiennent rien que de simples sûretés pour leur [sic] vies et pour leur fortune."[1]

A further revolutionary element in the document was the extension of the guarantees in it to all subjects. Later, in 1846, the sultan could confirm these principles in a speech saying: "The differences of religion and sect among the subjects is something concerning only their

[1] F. E. Bailey, *British Policy and the Turkish Reform Movement*, Cambridge, Mass., 1942, p. 275.

persons and not affecting their rights of citizenship. As we are living all in the same country under the same government, it is wrong to make discriminations among us." The revolt of the Greeks and the European crusade for Greek independence had taught a severe lesson to the Ottomans. Now, possessing equality before the law, the non-Muslim subjects would, it was expected, no longer feel that they were a segregated and oppressed element in the state and would no longer strive for independence from it. The Western powers, too, would appreciate this change in favor of the Christians in the empire. It must be noted that with their demands for equality, freedom, home rule, reforms in taxation, and land ownership the non-Muslim subjects were contributing to the Westernization of the Ottoman-Turkish state. Perceiving their peculiar position and the intervention of the West on their behalf, the sultan was moved increasingly to secularize public institutions. As sultan-caliph, he began to distinguish as best he could between his offices as ruler of all Ottoman citizens equally and his office as caliph of only the Muslims in accordance with the *sharī'ah*. The significant concession to the non-Muslims caused apprehensions among the Muslims in general, who regarded it as the destruction of the caliphate and denounced the Westernization movement as a whole. The fanatical ones stigmatized it as apostasy. The division thereby brought into focus between Westernizers with chiefly secular views and conservatives attached to the rule of the *sharī'ah* remained for many years the principal schism in Turkish political life.

In brief, equality before the law and the securing of life, honor, and property for all subjects were the revolutionary ideas in the rescript. Reşid himself asserted that the Tanzimat, the reforms introduced with the rescript, would change the imperial regime completely. The change in the concept of the state was further visible in the various decrees in which the sultan announced that the laws were made solely for the subjects' benefit.

We can ascertain the sincerity of Reşid's professions when we study the measures by which he undertook to put into effect the principles proclaimed in the rescript. Reşid showed his zeal to make the rule of law a reality by the haste with which he published a penal code.

In the provinces, administrative councils were established, the members of which were the governor, his two secretaries, the local judge, the mufti, the local military commander, four notables, and, if there was a Christian community in the province, the *metropolit* and two Christian notables. The notables were to be elected by the people.

The provincial councils and smaller councils in the dependent towns were freely to discuss all administrative matters and were to sit as criminal courts. The High Council of Reforms in the capital constituted a court of appeal for them. With the establishment of the provincial councils, Ottoman subjects, non-Muslims in particular, may be said to have received for the first time a voice in the local administration, though in actual fact these councils were composed of the local high officials, *ulema*, and notables, and differed little from the old councils of notables under the judge. Sometimes, paradoxically enough, the local *âyan* and *eşraf* used their new positions in local administration to obstruct the Tanzimat and incite the conservative masses against it.

Introduced with the intention of protecting both the peasants and the public treasury, financial reforms followed hard upon the proclamation of the rescript. To secure greater justice in taxation Reşid abolished the tax immunities and exemptions affecting such influential groups as *âyan*, *ağa*'s, *ulema*, and the military, as well as the exemptions connected with religious endowments. The affected groups started an intense propaganda campaign against the reforms. The survey and census embarked upon for purposes of the reform gave them an opportunity to incite the conservative masses, and they spread rumors variously that the government had determined to double the taxes or to abolish them altogether. The abolition of tax farming affected the large group of tax farmers and credit agents and the substantial number of officials profiting from it in dubious ways. It must be recalled that most of the tax farmers were local notables who had gained wealth and influence through this activity. Again in order to extend the state's protection over the peasantry, Reşid abolished forced labor and usury. One of the first decisions of the High Council of Reforms read: "In the Balkans most of the notables used to think that the peasants were their serfs, and employed them for their own services without any compensation. Also they did not permit them to leave their estates to work elsewhere and they interfered even in their marriages. Now the sultan has never accepted such abuses, and those who oppose this order [abolishing them] will be punished according to the provisions of the penal code recently published." Another decree pointed out that the usurers were getting twenty per cent per month for the money they lent to the peasants. Never able to pay their debts, these were eventually deprived of all their possessions. The usurers also used to appropriate the peasants' crops at below market prices. Now the government reduced the rates of interest and permitted the peasantry to pay their accumulated debts in installments.

The government had ordered the officials in the provinces to explain to the people in mass meetings the principles embodied in the Rescript of Gülhane. In some areas in the Balkans the peasants became so impatient to see the results of the reforms that they attempted desperate actions. Seeing that the Tanzimat had not brought any immediate relief in their tax burden, for example, and that they were still subject to forced labor, the Bulgarian peasants around Nish rose up under their own lesser notables. Further uprisings in 1849 and 1850 in the Vidin area were even more serious. Most of the agricultural lands in this area were originally state-owned. But local Muslim *ağa*'s had the exclusive rights to lease them and in fact possessed them as their own estates. Rejecting the popular demands and organizing a local militia (*başıbozuk*'s), the *ağa*'s fell upon the rebels, and it required regular government forces to end the struggle. The High Council of Reforms in Istanbul decided first to abolish the existing administrative council and granted the Christian peasants the right to lease the state-owned lands themselves. These radical decisions proved impracticable, however, and the situation did not change much subsequently. Similar reactions occurred in Anatolia. The *âyan* of Bala near Ankara, for example, was prosecuted before the High Council of Reforms for evading tax payments, subjecting the peasants to forced labor, inciting people to rise against the government. The difference here was that the Muslim population, under the influence of the local *ulema* and *âyan*, were extremely conservative, whereas the Christian subjects in the Balkans, under the influence of nationalist leaders, were in a mood to rebel.

These examples indicate how difficult it was for Reşid to effect his reforms and how various were the social forces arrayed against him. The privileged classes of the old regime, especially *ağa*'s in collaboration with the *ulema*, were asserting that the grant of civil equality to the non-Muslims and the "infidel" disregard of the *sharīʿah* would ruin the state and religion. To control them, Reşid had hastily published his penal code so that he might legally prosecute offenders against the government's reform measures. Many reactionaries in the capital as well as in the provinces, including even old Hüsrev, were punished. In Ankara a mufti, a member of the administrative council, was condemned for inciting people to rebel against the reforms.

In line with his efforts to introduce a Western system of administration, Reşid decided to entrust public service in the provinces exclusively to salaried civil servants appointed by the central government and to abolish all the forms of dues and bribes which the *âyan* and officials of all degrees had been accustomed to accept. In seeking to create a corps of civil servants to implement the reforms, Reşid was directly threatening the position of the provincial *âyan* who, as agents of the governors-general, then occupied most of the local administrative posts in Anatolia. Reşid was intent on changing those features of the organization of the empire which were inherited from feudalism. His administrative reform meant, in the last analysis, profound social reform. One of his radical measures after the abolition of tax farming was to appoint revenue collectors (*muhassıl*'s) in the provinces who were attached directly to the central government. But he failed to find enough civil servants trained for the job and was forced after all to employ local notables, who often followed the old practices.

It was later decided to found special secular schools to supply the civil servants so urgently needed. In these schools and in the military academies a body of Westernized officials were trained who were destined to play a decisive part in the modernization of Turkey. The resistance to Reşid's reforms caused his fall in 1841 (he was then foreign minister). The newly introduced institutions had not worked well; the new system of tax collection in especial was a failure. Reşid had relied solely on the sultan's favor, which he had gained through his services in solving the Egyptian question. His successor in power was Rıza Pasha, the Minister of War, who like many old-type reformers believed chiefly in military reorganization as a means of resuscitating the empire. Tax farming came back with him, and radical reforms in the administration generally were judged ill-timed. When in 1845 Reşid came back to power he gave priority to training the bureaucrats needed to implement his reforms; to this end he created a High Council of Public Education and projected the foundation of a university.

In the same year the government took the bold step of asking each province to elect two delegates and send them to Istanbul to consult on the reforms to be undertaken. These delegates were "elected from among the prominent and respected people." The assembly seemed in concert to be simply an extension of the provincial administrative councils. Yet it remains the first representative assembly ever convoked in the Ottoman capital. Though the *âyan* who appeared at the sultan's Porte were timid enough and soon returned home, the conservatives were appalled. Serasker Said Pasha went so far as to denounce Reşid for intending to proclaim a republic. Perhaps more significant in its consequence was the promulgation of a commercial code borrowed from France which established tribunals of commerce, the first secular tribunals of the Ottoman state.

For two principal reasons the bold steps taken by Reşid remained without effect. In the first place, the current severe economic depression was identified in the popular mind with the West and its ways—not improperly, since the cheap and plentiful products of Western industry, invading the Turkish market under the capitulary regime, were ruining the native industries. Of these happenings the contemporary consular reports give us vivid descriptions. In the second place, disgruntled persons were accusing the reformist Sultan Abdülmecid (1839-1861) of letting Reşid abuse the power of the sultanate. The highly centralist and authoritarian system of government espoused by Reşid and his followers became the particular target of the rising Ottoman-Turkish intelligentsia, who saw in it a despotism harmful to the empire. Organized as the secret society of the Young Ottomans in 1867, these intellectuals embraced the romantic nationalism then prevalent in Europe and advocated a constitutional regime which would introduce elements of Western civilization while preserving traditional Islamic-Turkish culture. For the first time we find a group of progressives acting independently of the government and opposing the official reform program. The Young Ottomans were the real forerunners of the nationalist and democratic movement in Turkey.

The major characteristics of modernization in this early period can be succinctly summarized.

A program of modernization was first adopted by the state as a measure of self-defense against an aggressive and imperialistic Europe. The superiority of European military techniques and organization was recognized as early as the end of the seventeenth century. This perception was a necessary psychological preparation for the later cultural borrowings from the West.

Second, systematic modernization started with military reforms in the eighteenth century, especially under Selim III. From 1830 on, the process was extended to administration and public institutions, a trend which culminated in the proclamation of the Ottoman constitution of 1876.

Third, in the modernization movement the state was the initiator, and changes were imposed from above, the sultan using his absolute power to create the bureaucratic machinery necessary to effect changes.

Fourth, the masses, the great majority of whom were living in a closed rural economy, were generally dependent on the *âyan*, *ağa's*, and clerics, who were vitally interested in keeping them attached to the traditional institutions. Even in the period between 1800 and 1850 these groups actively resisted the reforms imposed by the state; the Turkish-Muslim population of the empire remained in general indifferent or even refractory in the face of change.

Fifth, a desire to satisfy non-Muslim subjects and the Western powers definitely encouraged the Ottoman state to adopt secular laws and institutions. The Western powers were interested in furnishing the empire with liberal institutions, which they thought would guarantee at once the integrity of that state and their own economic interests in it.

Sixth, around 1860 a small group of Turkish patriots with Western outlook emerged and carried out, in the newly introduced press and in a number of literary periodicals, a vigorous campaign against the sultan's absolutism. His reform measures were, they believed, both arbitrary and contrary to the real interests of the Turkish-Muslim population.

In the Turkish modernization movement, finally, the principal difficulties stemmed from the religious basis of the traditional society and state. In general, the Tanzimat reformers and intellectuals, though wanting to Westernize the administration and to borrow modern techniques, believed it desirable to preserve such basic traditional institutions as the *sharī'ah*, the religious courts, and the religious schools. It was thought that these might be taken out of public affairs and relegated to their own sphere. Later, radicals who wanted wholesale Westernization and a national sovereignty like that of European states were to blame the failure of the Tanzimat upon this dualism. But no concept of the nation-state was in fact realized until Atatürk called the Turkish republic into being after the dissolution of the empire in 1919.

XVI

Application of the Tanzimat and its Social Effects

One week after its announcement in the *Takvîm-i Vekâyi*, the official newspaper of the State, the *Gülhâne Hatt-i Hümâyûnu* (Gülhane Imperial Rescript) was communicated, in the form of a *fermân* (edict),[1] to the *vâlis*, governor-generals of every province (*eyâlet*), and to the deputy-governors of every *sancak* (county), notifying them to await further orders which would be sent to them concerning taxes and military service, but to start immediately with the execution of all other articles of the *Hatt-i Hümâyûn*. According to the same *fermân*, the *Hatt-i Hümâyûn* was to be made public first by being read to the people in the public square of the capital city of each *sancak* amidst an impressive ceremony in the presence of all the notables, and was then to be sent to the sub-counties (*kazâs*) and townships (*kasabas*) one by one and thoroughly explained to all the people, great and small, to both city and rural population. The government had feared that the announcement of the *Hat* might, through mistaken interpretations or abuse of its contents, lead to confusion. Therefore the Sultan, as he had done previously when the accession edict[2] was read, issued a firm warning stating that, "Should people misbehave and start rumors by mistakenly saying, 'See, our Padishah has lifted all duties and taxes' or by proclaiming that 'Such and such things will take place', or else should there be some people so carried away by the security, prosperity, and honours our imperial grace has granted to them and be so bold as to show even the least disobedience toward any of our public officials and officers, from the highest to the

* Revised English version of my article "Tanzimat'ın uygulanması ve sosyal tepkileri", *Belleten* 28 (1964), pp. 623-649.

[1] One copy in *Bursa şer'îye sicilleri*, No. C 540, ff. 20^v-21^r; also in *Takvîm-i Vekâyi*, No. 187; and in R. Kaynar, *Mustafa Reşit Paşa ve Tanzimat*, Ankara, 1954, pp. 180-184.

[2] One copy in *Bursa şer'îye sicilleri*, No. C 540, f. 3; *see* also H. İnalcık, "Tanzimat'ın uygulanması ve sosyal tepkileri", *Belleten* 28, pp. 650-653, doc. no. 1.

lowest and humblest", such people will be punished in the most severe manner. It was also made clear that the *Tanzimat* meant only the beginning of "further beneficial and advantageous measures to make certain the execution of orders insuring the well-being of the people, rich and poor, whose happy state is a necessary pre-condition for the reinvigoration of religion and state and the prosperity of country and nation".

The government made an all out effort to promote the *Gülhâne Hattı* as the beginning of a new era, and, indeed, elaborate ceremonies were everywhere arranged.

The announcement of the *Hat* caused strong repercussions among the population throughout the Empire. Just as the government had feared, every group started to give the reforms its own interpretation. The Muslim subjects in general did not like the concessions granted to the non-Muslims. Religious leaders, notables, and even some governors were active in inciting the Muslim population, while on the other hand the non-Muslim *râya*s, carried away by high hopes, created unrest and upheavals.

C. Hamlin,[3] who was an eyewitness to these events, gave the following account of his impressions :

> It [the *Hat*] was both praised and ridiculed. The old Mussulmans cursed it as a flagrant sacrificing of the divine law it so much praised, and the Christian subjects looked upon it as the introduction of a new era. It was an open confession, before all the world, of the miserable condition of the empire, and that nothing but reform could save it. ... It went through the empire. It woke up the slumbering East. It was the first voice that announced to the people the true object of government, and legitimate ends to be attained. ... While this imperial rescript was, in general, a disappointing failure, it can not be denied that it accomplished some good in the administration. ... It gave the rayahs courage to contend for their rights.

For instance, in Filibe, where the news that the corvée was to be lifted caused extreme excitement, and the *râya*s, urged on by their leaders, demanded their freedom as soon as the *Hat* was announced. But those holding the land objected to this vehemently. In Bulgaria in particular, and among the Bulgarian *râya*s in Macedonia, the *Hat* gave added impetus to the growing nationalistic sentiments.[4]

Later on in this article, when examining in the light of pertinent documents in the Ottoman archives the uprisings that took place among

[3] C. Hamlin, *Among the Turks*, New York, 1877, pp. 55-56.

[4] Hamlin, *op. cit.*, pp. 266-268.

the *râya*s in Bulgaria following the announcement of the *Hat*, it will become evident that these uprisings were more of the nature of social outbursts against the Muslim landowners (*ağa*s) and the *gospodar*s than of rebellions against the state. Far from remaining a dead letter, the *Gülhâne Hattı* led to unrest and large scale movements in many parts of the Empire, which shook to the roots the traditional social make-up prevailing in those areas.

Before delving more deeply into an analysis of these outbursts, I would like first to give a description of those administrative and financial measures which were carried out immediately in accordance with the basic ideas of the *Hat*.[5]

The changes ordered in the administrative setup were aimed at reducing the great authority of the governors of the provinces. Henceforth, only matters of security were to remain in their hands, and financial matters were to be handled by *muhassıl-i emvâl*s, officials with wide-ranging power and appointed directly by the central government. And, so as to enable the people to participate in administration at various levels, new local administrative councils were ordered to be set up everywhere.

As explained in the document, in a place where a *muhassıl* was appointed,[6] if it was a province, it was the *müşîr* pasha, and if it was *sancak*, it was the *ferîk* pasha who, with the regular army units, was to take care of all gendarmery, security, and disciplinary matters; also, a number of these soldiers were to be assigned to the *muhassıl* to aid him in his tax-collecting duties. In places where was no regular army, reserve soldiers (*redîf*) were to be used for this purpose.

[5] An important document giving all these enactments collectively is the *fermân* which was sent to the provinces toward the end of *zilkâde* 1255. A copy of it can be found in *Bursa şer'îye sicilleri*, No. C 540, ff. 31^{r}-32^{v}. The copy given in Lûtfi's *Tarih*, vi, Istanbul, pp. 152-156, is somewhat different. The copy published by Kaynar in Latin characters (*op. cit.*, pp. 226-234), which had been sent to the *müşîr* of Ankara and which Kaynar found in one of the *Tanzimat* registers, seems to be defective in some parts. The document is given in full, as it appears in the *Bursa şer'îye sicilleri*, in İnalcık, *op. cit.*, pp. 660-671, doc. no. 4. For the formal memorandum dated 15 *safer* 1256 and complementing this *fermân*, *see* A. Vefik, *Tekâlif kavâidi*, ii, Istanbul, 1330, pp. 39-42.

[6] Enactements of the *Tanzimat* pertinent to fiscal matters were implemented first in the provinces nearest to the capital : for instance, at the island of Thasos these measures were introduced in *rebiyülevvel* 1256, and in Albania (Yanya, Avlonya Delvine) only in 1257 (*see*, *Başvekâlet* Archives, *Maliye yeni seri*, No. 13663). Nonetheless, upon proclamation of the *Tanzimat* compliance with the general principles of the *Hat* was expected everywhere.

6

Certain of the changes involving provincial administration were to result in closer central authority over the local *kadı*s. Though the former ties of the *kadı*s to the *Bâb-i Meşîhat* (Office of the *Şeyhülislâm*) were not severed, their deputies (*nâib*s) now received monthly salaries like all the other state employees and were forbidden to collect remunerations, such as dues on inheritance taxes or fees for judicial deeds and licences, for services forming part of their duties. Their monthly salaries were henceforth to be paid by the office of the *muhassıl*, and the legal fees were to be collected directly by the same office of the *muhassıl* and treated as court revenue.[7]

As to the councils,[8] upper councils (*büyük meclis*es) were formed in the capital cities of the *sancak*s and in the sub-counties to which *muhassıl*s were appointed. These upper councils consisted of thirteen members : six of them were officials, that is, the *muhassıl* himself with his two clerks, the local *kadı*, the *müftü*, and the security chief (*umûr-i zabtiyye âmiri*). The rest was made up of local Muslim notables (*vücûh-i memleket*), and in the case of a non-Muslim population the metropolitan and two of the village elders (*kocabaşı*s) were to be made part of it. The non-officeholding members of the council had to be elected representatives of the community, and regulations concerning their election were soon to follow.[9] The *müşîr* pasha became the natural head of the council in the provincial capital of his seat. As for the *sancak* capitals, the *ferîk* pasha, if any were seated there, could be appointed head of the council by the Sultan. Later regulations stated that, in case the *ferîk* pasha was a person not capable of filling this position, the head of the council should be elected by a drawing of lots from among the *muhassıl*, the *kadı*, and the security chief. Literacy was made a sine qua non for the head of the council.

In the counties and townships without a *muhassıl*, so-called lower councils (*küçük meclis*es) consisting of five members were to be established. At first no specifications were given concerning the make-up of these lower councils; it was stipulated simply that they be set up "according to prevailing circumstances". Only later on were regulations formulated prescribing that the lower council be made up of the *kadı* of the place, the security chief, the deputy *muhassıl*, and two local notables. And if there were Christians in the community, one of the

[7] *Bursa şer'iye sicilleri*, No. C 540; concerning orders affecting the tax status of the *ulemâ*, *see* Vefik, *op. cit.*, ii, pp. 39-42.

[8] *See* İnalcık, *op. cit.*, pp. 660-671, doc. no. 4.

[9] *See* Kaynar, *op. cit.*, pp. 254-258, facsimile.

notables had to be a Christian village elder. (For instance in Bulgaria, in the Belgradcık *nâhiye* (sub-county) which belonged to Vidin, the lower council in 1850 consisted of the security chief, the deputy *muhassıl*, the deputy *kadı*, an *ağa* representing the Muslim population, and a Christian village elder.) The lower councils were to meet two or three times a week and were to discuss civil and administrative matters and implement decisions in accordance with regulations which were to be issued later on. In the meetings, members were to express their opinions freely and without interference. It was also ordered that the lower councils submit their decisions for approval to the upper councils of the *sancak*s to which they belonged. The upper councils had the authority to consider and decide on civil, judicial, and financial matters. They also had the authority to prosecute those who committed tax fraud or other offenses in obvious disregard of the stipulations of the *Tanzimat*, and to sentence them according to the *Şerî'at*; only cases of murder or robbery had to be brought to the attention of the central administration. According to a register of the High Council in Istanbul (*Meclis-i Vâlâ-i Ahkâm-i Adliye*),[10] cases of killing, of assault, of robbery, and others which called for punishment by hard labor in chains were to be referred to that court; and so were cases where the local upper council was in doubt as to the solution. Furthermore, the weightier cases dealt with by a local council were to be heard in the presence of the notables of the community involved, in other words a quasi-jury was to be formed of the prominent people of that community.[11]

Abdülmecid, in his New Year's speech to the High Council, dwelt with great emphasis on this change in administrative practices.[12] And Ubicini,[13] comparing these councils to the French department councils, observed that this institution was the most liberal among the institutions introduced by the *Gülhâne Hattı* : it guaranteed equal rights before the law to all subjects of the Empire regardless of their religion and creed.

Mention should also be made here of an edict, dated May, 1840, which stipulated that the notables from the provinces be called to an assembly in the capital so that the government could obtain their views on the envisaged and needed reforms. Five years later such a consultative assembly consisting of provincial notables gathered in Istanbul.[14]

[10] *Bâb-i Âsafî* registers, No. 370, *Başvekâlet* Archives.
[11] *Bâb-i Âsafî* registers, No. 370, f. 13.
[12] Lûtfi, *op. cit.*, vi, p. 93.
[13] *Letters on Turkey*, tr. from the French by Lady Easthope, London, 1856, p. 31.
[14] *See* B. Lewis, *The Emergence of Modern Turkey*, London, 1961, pp. 110-111.

Apparently imperial finances were the main concern of the *Tanzimat* in 1839, and the prescribed administrative innovations were mostly designed to realize a substantial increase in state revenues by means of a more centralized revenue system. The result was the appointment by the central government of *muhassıl*s with broad authority, an act aimed at taking tax collection out of the hands of the governors and notables in order to put an end to fraudulent tax practices and other abuses made possible by and committed under the old, established system.

Yet there was a basic idea behind the innovations of the *Tanzimat*, the idea of a modern revenue and budget system; all state revenues were to be collected directly by and go into the Central Treasury and all state expenses were to be paid from and by the same Treasury. The old revenue system was to be reorganized accordingly.

To make way for the new order it was decided that the system of farming out state-revenue collection (*iltizâm*) should be abolished altogether, as had been promised in the *Hat*. In particular, the farming out of tithe collection and the system of state leases (*mukâtaa*s)[15] were ordered discontinued immediately. The farming out of custom dues had been abolished even before the proclamation of the *Hat*.[16] At the same time a new institution, the institution of the *muhassıl*, was established for the collection in the name of the Central Treasury of dues and fees and certain newly installed taxes. As was acknowledged by the government itself, malpractices made possible by the system of farming out tithe collection often led to exactions, collectors demanding multiple the amount the taxpayers really owed to the state. It also was made known that in order to put an end to this situatian, the old practice of farming out and leasing of the right of collecting public revenues in return for lump sum (*maktû*) was to be halted and immediately abolished.

In 1838 and after the proclamation of the *Tanzimat*, many sessions were held in the High Council to discuss how best to apply the new taxation policies and to determine what measures should be taken to assure that each taxpayer paid taxes in proportion to his means. It was con-

[15] *Mukâtaa* means in its broader sense that the amount of a given state income in a given area is established for a given period of time and, based on that amount, the revenue is then farmed out through open bidding to tax gatherers (*mültezim*s or, in earlier times, *âmil*s). *Emânet*, the other method used to gather state revenues, meant the collection of taxes by way of government employees, so-called *emîn*s. Concerning the tithe-ratio, etc., *see* Vefik, *op. cit.*, ii, pp. 39-42; concerning the Council of Accountancy (*Meclis-i Muhâsebe*), *see* Lûtfi, *op. cit.*, vi, p. 125.

[16] *Bursa şer'îye sicilleri*, No. 540, f. 46.

cluded that, first of all, a census and survey of properties would have to be carried out, and the feasibility of this plan was to be further discussed in an assembly of the provincial notables to be held in the capital.[17] Since all this was a long process, the new revenue system could not be put into effect all at once. In the meantime, in order not to lose state revenues, it was decided in 1839 that, as a temporary measure, advance payment of given amounts fitting local conditions should be collected from each district, and that it should be the duty of the *sancak* councils to establish the amount of taxes due from each inhabitant of the areas of their jurisdiction. Overpayments resulting from this temporary arrangement should then be refunded as soon as the regular tax to be paid by each individual was established. To summarize it, it was decided that since the system of farming out state-revenue collection was now abolished : 1) the activities of all *voyvoda*s and tax-farmers in the provinces should come to an end; 2) taxes should henceforth be collected only by the *muhassıl*s and the councils; and 3) the taking of fees and remunerations by state officials and employees under various titles (mainly *tayyârât* and *cerâ'im*, that is, fees for incidental services and fines for minor offenses) should cease at once. According to the old laws and practices, fees and remunerations called *tayyârât*, *bâdıhavâ*, or *resm-i niyâbet* formed a regular part of the income of a *tımar*-holder, a circumstance which — with the deterioration of the *tımar*-system — had opened the way for many and varied abuses on the part of state officials. Next in line as a source of abuse were the various fees and remunerations collected by the governors and the various agents of the central government. These customary dues had become open doors to arbitrary and unscrupulous exactions by officials for their services, and all previous efforts of the central government to abolish or at least curtail these practices[18] had been in vain. Third on the line as a source

[17] These reforms were already planned in 1838 (*see* H. İnalcık, "Sened-i İttifak ve Gülhâne Hattı", *Belleten* 28, pp. 611-622). Large scale implementation of some of the reforms laid down in the Blessed *Tanzimat* had already begun in the last years of the reign of Mahmud II. Valuable information concerning these reforms can be obtained from the *Mühimme* register No. 253, year 1254 (*Başvekâlet* Archives), such as the regulations on the quarantine, the abolition of confiscation practices, a number of administrative and finance measures aimed at protecting the *râya* population, in particular the measures against usury, and the measures intended to stimulate the economy, as for instance the abolition of monopolies, just to mention a few. At the same time, a new penal code was also being worked on.

[18] Beginning with the sixteenth century, it became customary that the Sultan, when ascending the throne, issue a rescript (*adâletnâme*) forbidding abuses in administration

of abuse were the remunerations which notables and special government employees had customarily exacted from the population for their services and expenditures while assigning and collecting *avârız* taxes in the country for the Central Treasury.[19] For the population perhaps the most irksome of these practices was the custom whereby a government employee, upon arrival in a city, town or village demanded that lodging and sustenance be provided by the inhabitants for him, his attendants, and his animals, or be substituted for by a cash equivalent. In addition there was the obligation to provide horses for the couriers (*ulak*s). And whenever the central authority weakened, these old established customs could create immeasurable hardships, especially for village inhabitants. In the accession edict of Abdülmecid as well as in the above-mentioned edict dealing with the implementation of the *Tanzimat*,[20] it was ordered that these practices be halted and the new regulations adopted in their place. It was stated in particular that "starting with the lowest attendant and courier up to the grand vizier, full payment should be made by them for all the provisions they get and for the animals they use on their tours in the country-side. Henceforth not a single penny, not even a single kernel of grain should be demanded from the inhabitants."

Reşid Pasha, promotor of the *Hat*, was most concerned with the full application of these decisions. As soon as the *Tanzimat* was proclaimed he gave careful attention to the complaints and petitions submitted to the High Council on these matters, and he did not hesitate to demote, or to fine, or even to imprison governors, *muhassıl*s, and other officials as prescribed by the newly established penal code if they were found to be unlawfully collecting fees, demanding services and taking bribes as before. According to the registers in the archives, especially those dated 1256/1840 and 1257/1841,[21] punishments for this kind of offense were aboundant. It is interesting to see the great number of newly appointed

---

and finances and promising a new era of just rule. For more on *adâletnâmes*, *see* İnalcık, "Adâletnâmeler", *Belgeler* 2, pp. 49-145.

[19] For more on this *see* M. Ç. Uluçay, *Saruhan'da eşkıyalık ve halk hareketleri*, Istanbul, 1944, pp. 110-139 as well as index entries on dues; *see* also Uluçay, *18. ve 19. yüzyıllarda Saruhan'da eşkıyalık ve halk hareketleri*, Istanbul, 1955, pp. 36-55. Notwithstanding the mistakes which occur in the given texts, the Uluçay editions are the first publications offering a large collection of material rich in information about social conditions and movements of the population in Anatolia.

[20] *See* İnalcık, *op. cit.*, pp. 653-658 and 660-671, doc. no. 2 and 4.

[21] *Mühimme* registers, No. 254 (years 1256-1258), *Başvekâlet* Archives; and also *Maliye yeni seri*, No. 13663, *Başvekâlet* Archives.

muhassıls among those dismissed. One should not forget that the majority of them were old-time officials who, it seems, could not forego their old habits. Indeed, one of the main reasons for the failure of Reşid Pasha is to be sought in the fact that he had no personnel available to carry out the reforms in their true spirit.

Upon declaration of the *Tanzimat*, the first of its resolutions to be carried out almost immediately was the abolishing of the corvée. Dated August 1838, a *fermân* which was sent to the governors of Rumelia dealt in particular with the question of the corvée as a major cause of most of the unrest among the *râya*s. The document stated that notables in many parts of Rumelia treated the *râya*s on their land as if they were their personal slaves, forcing them to work without pay on the fields of their *çiftlik*s (farm estates) and exacting scores of other personal services from them. They did not allow the *râya* to move from one piece of land or one place of work to another, and they interfered even with their marriage arrangements. These and similar abuses seem to have been common practice with them. The document then concluded with the statement that such practices being now strictly forbidden, those who did not comply with the present orders would be duly punished in accordance with the new penal code.[22]

Later on in this article, while analyzing more closely the uprisings in Nish and Vidin, we will see what a critical role the question of forced labor played in all these events.

The *cizye* (Islamic poll-tax) was another matter of great concern to the *râya*s. In accordance with the Islamic Law this head-tax was collected only from non-Muslim subjects. Though it was decided to effect considerable changes in the method of the collection of this Islamic tax too, since the changes were to involve a canonical matter, a *fetvâ* had first to be obtained from the *Şeyhülislâm* before any action could be taken.

The poll-tax, once collected only by official gatherers called *cizyedâr*s, was now the subject of many abuses and misuses. The *cizyedâr*s had been allowed to collect not only the tax itself but also fees and remunerations for themselves, such as *maîşet*, *resm-i kitâbet*, *zahîre*, *sarrâfiye*, and *kolcu akçesi*, but the total of these was never to exceed one twenty-fifth of the amount of the tax collected.[23]

[22] *Fermân* from the first part of *cemaziyelâhir* 1254 (*Mühimme* registers, No. 253, f. 10); for text *see* also İnalcık, *op. cit.*, pp. 650-653, doc. no. 1.

[23] *See*, *EI*², i, p. 565 : *s. v.*, *Djizya*.

In the course of the last few centuries already, in certain particular areas and instances, the government had left the lump-sum collection of the poll-tax to the local population as a community, and had permitted that this be carried out and the sum be forwarded to the Treasury by their village elders. In many instances the *râyas*, if they wanted to do so, were able to obtain the privilege of lump-sum taxation by offering to pay more to the Treasury then the amount officially laid down. In some places the *râyas* were prompted to such demands by their village elders who, like the Muslim notables, stood to gain personally from such a method of tax collection. Upon the announcement of the *Tanzimat* a new *maktu* system was introduced over all the Empire. To this end it was ordered by the already mentioned *fermân*, dated January, 1840,[24] that a register showing the total of the poll-tax paid by a *sancak* or a *kazâ* had to be presented to the government appointed *muhassıl*. On the basis of these registers the *muhassıl* had to establish on the spot the portion of the total amount collected that a given village had been paying in the past. He then had to call in the village elders and notify them of the sum he had arrived at. To collect the prescribed amount of the poll-tax established for their area, the village elders had to portion it out among the inhabitants according to their standing in three categories; that is to say, they had to set different rates for the wealthy (*alâ*), for the poor (*ednâ*), and for those of medium means (*evsat*). Since the poll-tax was a tax collected only from non-Muslim subjects, the *râyas* interpreted it to be a measure contradictory to the principle of equal taxation proclaimed by the *Tanzimat*. And, when the European press in its criticism of the *Tanzimat* maintained that the proclamation of equal rights was nothing but an empty promise, its criticism was based particularly on these objections. Yet it is easily understood why the government of the Ottoman Empire, a Muslim state, could not abolish the existing poll-tax system at one stroke. Nevertheless, the Sublime Porte was keenly intent on lifting the poll-tax by 1851 and converting it into a kind of capitation levied equally on every subject. But it was only in 1856, with the *Islâhat Fermânı*, that the principle was finally fully adopted and the *cizye* converted to the *bedel-i askerî* (military service exemption tax).

We will elaborate upon the difficult problems and the confusion brought about by the changes in the taxation system and the abolition

[24] *See* İnalcık, *op. cit.*, pp. 660-671, doc. no. 4; on directions given to the *muhassıls*, *see* Vefik, *op. cit.*, ii, pp. 7-32; and Kaynar, *op. cit.*, pp. 224-245.

of forced labor later on while studying the uprisings in the Nish and Vidin areas. The downfall of Reşid Pasha was caused mainly by his obvious failure to put into practice his intended measures concerning state finances. The abolishment of the system of farming out state revenues was in its effects the most far-reaching and the most radical among all the reforms the High Council had initiated. But owing to lack of means and personnel the new system, which through a revolutionary decision had taken the place of a centuries-old institution, resulted in complete chaos and anarchy in revenue matters. In addition there was the fact that a rather good-sized group of people, consisting mainly of tax-farmers, *voyvoda*s, and bankers (*sarrâf*s) with all their affiliates, now suddenly realized that their means for earlier easy gains had been cut off. It has to be added immediately that many of the notables and *ağa*s in the provinces also made their money as small-scale provincial tax-farmers. To aggravate matters, provincial notables and *ağa*s in general now found that, as a result of the new system of gradual taxation, taxation according to financial standing, on the one hand they would have to pay considerably higher taxes, and on the other they would be deprived of the benefits they had previously realized from the inhabitants through forced labor and other customary practices and the abuses thereof.[25] The principle of equal taxation and the ensuing abolition of all exemptions and privileges were strongly objected to by the Christian notables (*çorbacıs*) as well, who until then had been paying very little or no taxes at all. But the levying of taxes on the Christian religious endowments, and the resulting decrease in their sources of income turned even the clergy, whose influence over the people was very great, against the reforms.[26]

Reşid Pasha faced almost insurmountable difficulties in the execution of the various reforms aimed at improving administrative and financial conditions. The reforms introduced on paper had, in most cases, ended in the continuation of old customs under new names or, at best, in the mixing of the new with the old.

Now let us take a closer look at the actual situation of the administrative reforms. Until the *Tanzimat* the existing councils, made up of urban notables (*âyân* and *eşrâf*) and headed by local *kadı*s, had the

[25] *See* below pp. 124-128.

[26] On the survey of the land income of the Aynaroz (Athos) monasteries prepared so as to secure duly proportionate state revenues, *see*, *Maliye yeni seri*, No. 13663, ff. 93-94, *fermân* dated 22 *zilkâde* 1257.

authority to levy and collect taxes and to decide on local administrative expenditures. As a rule, cases involving local administrative financial matters were handled by the local *kadı*s; yet it is evident that in certain instances the decisions were brought in by local *divân*s headed by local notables. One might say that the main difference between the old and the new councils as prescribed by the *Tanzimat* was that the chairmanships were now taken from the hands of the *kadı*s, that is from the *ulemâ*, and given to the governors, *muhassıl*s, and *kazâ* directors (*müdür*s), that is, to government employees. Furthermore, through their clergy and their village elders, non-Muslim subjects were granted some voice in the administration. Nor was the latter a complete innovation since, as we have seen, already in the eighteenth century Christian village elders had been given a semi-official role as go-betweens in tax matters between the *râya*s and the government. Still, the official admittance of the non-Muslim village elders into the formerly closed ranks of Muslim notables in these rather influential councils must be seen as an important innovation brought about by the *Tanzimat* and intended to lead to a policy of equality toward all subjects of the Empire. As to vesting the council-chairmanship in government officials, it was aimed at bringing provincial administration under more stringent control by the central government by freeing it somewhat from the power of the local *ulemâ* and notables. Yet the statements claiming that this change provided greater possibilities to the people to participate in local administrative matters cannot be taken at face value. The membership of the new councils consisted mainly of government employees responsible to the governors and, though these councils were to represent the people of their respective areas, Muslim members in them were in the overwhelming majority even in places where the population consisted mainly of Christians. Furthermore, the members of the new councils were not selected from the ranks of the common people but from the *vücûh*, the leading men of the place, in other words the notables and, in the case of the Christians, from the *kocabaşı*s and the *çorbacı*s. (Following the repression of the rebellious *âyân* under the reign of Mahmud II, the word *âyân* had eventually given place to such terms as *vücûh*, *müte'ayyinân*, or *erbâb-i iktidâr*.) The election of new council members was carried out in a mixed process as follows :[27] 1) The candidate, who had to be from the local community and a man whose ability and honesty was in good repute there, had to have his name registered with the local court; 2) To form

[27] *See* Kaynar, *op. cit.*, pp. 254-256, copy of election bylaws.

an election committee, every village had to select from its community, by lot, five representatives who were then sent to the center of their *kazâ* to participate in a meeting with the landowners and influential citizens of the area. At the meeting an election committee of these representatives (consisting of twenty to fifty members depending on the size of the area) was selected; 3) The candidates had to appear in front of this committee in the sequence in which their names had been drawn. In each case those who favored the candidate had to stand on one side and those who were against him on the other, in order to be counted. Attempts to interfere and to influence electors were to be punished in accordance with the new penal code.

Twenty years later the French traveller Perrot[28] gave the following interesting account of these councils :

The election of the members is disorganized and arbitrary. Whether a council does or does not meet depends entirely on those who have an interest in obstructing its function. Anyhow, since it never was clearly stipulated, the authority of these councils is a matter of interpretation. ... In places where the members work together and have the benefit of an able and active chairman, the council will have great authority; and on the contrary, in places where the council has fallen into the hands of some *beys* (notables) backed by the administrator of the *nâhiye* and the *kadı*, and where the council members are at odds with each other, the council is unable to function properly or at all, and its role diminishes to close to nothing. I have asked many a Turkish and many a Christian council member : "Under what condition do the decisions of a council carry the weight of law, and when are they expressing only suggestions and ideas?" or "In which case does the council have the authority to formulate court decisions, and when does it act simply as an advisory body?" But I could get no clear answer from them. It seems to me that the council members themselves have no clear idea on the matter. ... For instance, in Ankara the situation is about as follows : the Turkish council members are selected by the Pasha of Yozgat, that is, the governor of the province, and the chairman, who has to be a Turk, is also appointed by him. Members representing the other communities are appointed by the religious heads of their communities. ... One can say in general that a non-Muslim member sent to the council is usually not someone from among their notables but rather someone from the bourgeoisie, from the second rank. I heard this with amazement and could not restrain myself from telling the Catholic bishop who gave me this information that "In my opinion, if the representative sent to the council were to be one of the notables who have wealth and influence, as let us say a farmer of revenues would, he could speak up more freely and more authoritatively and could make his words and suggestions better listened to". Upon which the bishop answered : "A representative sent to the council does not

[28] G. Perrot, *Souvenirs d'un voyage en Asie Mineure*, Paris, 1867, pp. 343-346.

speak in his own name but in the name of his community. And when it comes to speaking up in the council, a notable might be more hesitant to do so because of fear of putting himself and his position into jeopardy by falling out with any of the Turkish officials whose good graces his well-being depends on." ... The situation is obviously confused. When there is a matter of emphasized importance to be discussed and decided upon, the *Büyük Meclis* is convened with a considerably enlarged number of participants. To such meetings the religious leaders and the notables are, as a rule, invited. Basically speaking, there is no general meeting of the community or elections in the European sense when it comes to the selection of the representatives to be sent to the council or to giving them instructions once elected. There is no representation of the community in the true sense of the word in these councils, just as there is no trace of any real home-rule. There is no order, no system to be found in any of these things. Instead, one relies on common sense, on common practice and tradition, and one considers it natural that authority should be in the hands of the wealthy and the most able.

In many places, especially in small cities and towns, the councils had fallen into the hands of *ağa*s and earlier established local notables, now called *vücûh-i memleket*. For instance, in the case of the 1850 Vidin uprising it came out from the ensuing government investigation that it was the *ağa*s and notables who, having gained command over the council and having reduced the power of the governor to close to nothing by forcing the other government employees, as well as the local *kadı* and the *müftü* to side with them, were actually running affairs there.[29]

As Ziya Pasha said :[30]

Though the privileges of the *âyân*, the control of the Janissaries, and bad practices such as placing government agents into governorships have been abolished on paper by the Blessed *Tanzimat* ... in the provinces feudal lords still flourish but under different names now, one group of them consisting of the foreign consuls and the other of influential and rich local people, such as council members and other urban notables.

The proclamation of the *Tanzimat* did not bring about considerable changes on this line : the old local notables still prevailed not only in the councils but also in the lower-echelon government positions. Just as in the old order, in the new system too the administrator of the *nâhiye* and the deputies (*mütesellim*s) were selected by the governor from among the prominent, most influential *ağa*s of the area, and the only thing the

[29] *See* İnalcık, *Tanzimat ve Bulgar meselesi*, Ankara, 1943, p. 76, doc. no. VI and VII.

[30] Ziya Pasha, *Arzıhâl*, Istanbul, 1372.

government did was to ratify their appointment.[31] In a *fermân* dated 1850 we find strong criticism of the administrator of the Vidin *nâhiye*. As stated in the *fermân*, actions taken by the administrator as well as actions of the notables in the councils there were often flagrant violations of the principles of the *Tanzimat*.[32] Obviously the central government was aware of the problems, but the number of personnel schooled and trained for administrative work was far too small to replace those who ignored the new regulations.

There were strong objections to and in many cases rejection of the stipulations of the *Tanzimat* among the *ulemâ* too. Indeed, they were often not content just to express their defiance by siding with the reactionary *ağa*s in the councils, but even went so far as to openly incite the population to rise up. One can find various archive entries from this time which show that on more than one occasion the High Council had to take measures against some of the *ulemâ* who obviously went too far in their subversive activities.[33] For instance, in Amasya a group of the inhabitants, a number of council members among them, had, upon the instigation of the *ulemâ* there, killed the quarantining doctor in a protest against a government-enforced quarantine.[34] In Midilli, Abdülkadir Efendi who was head of the *Mevlevî*s, and Mustafa, the *müderris* (a rank in the *ulemâ*), were tried by the High Council for inciting the population and were afterwards reprimanded by the *Şeyhülislâm* himself.[35]

There are other instances where *ağa*s, who persisted in treating the peasant population in the old autocratic way in open defiance of the *Tanzimat*, were tried by the Upper Council of their province or by the High Council in Istanbul and sentenced in accordance with the newly introduced penal code. Then again there were those who stirred up the population by citing the increased taxes as their reason for protest.[36]

[31] In documents of that time the administrator of the *nâhiye* was called *kaymakâm*.

[32] *See* Lûtfi, *op. cit.*, volume ix of the manuscript in the TTK Library.

[33] *See* İnalcık, *op. cit.*, pp. 684-685, doc. no. 12.

[34] *Bâb-i Âsafî* registers, No. 370, doc. dated 20 *safer* 1257; *see* also İnalcık, *op. cit.*, pp. 680-681, doc. no. 9.

[35] *Bâb-i Âsafî* registers, No. 370, doc. dated 16 *safer* 1257.

[36] *Bâb-i Âsafî* registers, No. 370, doc. dated 4 *rebiyülâhir* 1257 : "There are some among the inhabitants of the Yalvaç *nâhiye* whose names are well known and who, so as not to have to pay the taxes designated as their proper share in accordance with the benevolent measures of the Blessed *Tanzimat*, were found inciting the population to resistance", and doc. dated 20 *safer* 1257, according to which even the *müftü* of Adapazar was "inciting the people by telling the inhabitants of Söğütlü, 'See, though

One of the more interesting cases of this sort was that of İbrahim Ağa, a notable of Bâlâ. Investigation made into the case had shown that İbrahim Ağa, who came from the village of Şeyh in Bâlâ and had soon become the chief notable of that district, "made it his habit to demand of the people the rendering of all kinds of corvée, but he himself had not payed a single penny in taxes up until then". Realizing that the *Tanzimat*'s abolition of tax exemptions meant that he had to pay taxes on the large state properties in his hands, he now wanted to obstruct tax collection. To this end he aroused the population in his own and in surrounding villages and was able to gather some 400 men from the poor of the villages in the vicinity of Ankara. But after a stern admonishing the gathering was dispersed and İbrahim Ağa arrested. In the ensuing inquiry held by the High Council in Istanbul, he stated that in comparison to the 1,500 piastres in taxes the previous year, he now had to pay 2,400 piastres, and that even a poor villager with but two donkeys had now to pay 150 piastres instead of the 60 piastres of the previous year.[37]

It is obvious from the above that the various reactionary groups had decided to fight against Reşid Pasha and the reforms in every way and by every means possible. It is thus easily understood why, during the transition period following the proclamation of the reforms, a time of anarchy ensued, caused mainly by the confusion that reigned in the tithe-collection and by the undermining efforts of the old tax-farmers and provincial notables, and therefore the major part of the government taxes for the year 1839-1840 could not be collected. The Treasury was already in great difficulties owing to the unfortunate war against Mehmed Ali of Egypt. When Reşid Pasha came to power he was faced with a tremendous state deficit and, in order to cover part of the state salaries and other expenditures, was forced to issue government bonds called *eshâm kavâ'imi*.[38] It was this precarious financial situation

---

you were unable to meet your present obligations in taxes, you are already being asked for more' ", and many other documents on similar incidents.

[37] *See* İnalcık, *op. cit.*, pp. 682-684, doc. no. 11.

[38] *See* İnalcık, *op. cit.*, pp. 671-672, doc. no. 5; on the loan efforts *see* Kaynar, *op. cit.*, pp. 283-291; *see* also *Mühimme* register, No. 254. In the same register there also are documents dealing with various economic innovations and measures for commerce introduced by the *Tanzimat* (customs, application of the 1838 trade agreements, the Feshâne and other factories, the coal works in Ereğli, money and credit, etc.); *see* also F. E. Bailey, *British Policy and the Turkish Reform Movement*, Cambridge, Mass., 1942. Having been forced to pay for the growing trade deficits in gold, the Sublime Porte not only started to issue paper money but also undertook serious efforts to increase national production by furthering improvements in agriculture and mining.

in particular which was used by Reşid Pasha's enemies in the capital to bring about his downfall. In the Palace it was the two son-in-laws, Rıza and Mehmed Ali, who did their utmost to turn the Sultan against Reşid.[39]

Finally, on March 31, 1841, Reşid Pasha was dismissed.[40] With his dismissal the conservatives had come to power, and Rıza Pasha, whose main concern was military development, became the leading figure of the time.

In an effort to appease the conservative Muslim elements, one of the first measures taken by the new government was to send a *fermân*[41] to all governors outlining a more moderate government policy. In this *fermân* the Caliph-Sultan declared that "execution of the religious law is obligatory" and warned that those who for no serious reason should fail to comply with the Islamic rule of the prescribed five daily prayers would be strictly punished. Furthermore, the office of the *muhassıl*, the government tax-collector, was abolished almost immediately, and the governors were once again entrusted with the authority to deal with both the security and the financial matters of their provinces, just as before the proclamation of the *Tanzimat*. "The execution of financial and security matters was combined into one and entrusted by the government to the *müşîr* of the area."[42] All tax registers were now to be sent to the *müşîr*s and they, in turn, were requested to provide the government with their signed letters of guarantee declaring their readiness to forward to the government without delay all taxes collected as established in the registers. Consequently governors who, because of negligence, had collected less than the amount prescribed in the registers had to make up the difference from their own means. All government-appointed provincial directors and clerks for financial matters were placed under the

---

It was during this period that Sadık Rifat Pasha and Reşid Pasha had imported various European economic concepts. Reşid Pasha firmly believed that more liberal economic and commercial policies would bring about a general material prosperity in the Empire. A comprehensive monograph on the economic history of this period, so vital to the better understanding of the economic conditions of present-day Turkey, is yet to be written. The works by Z. F. Fındıkoğlu and S. Ülgener, however, can be considered as first steps taken in the direction of such a study.

[39] *See* Cevdet Pasha, *Tezâkir*, i-xii, C. Baysun ed., Ankara, 1953, pp. 6-9.

[40] On the role the Egyptian question and its tendency to turn once again into open discord played in Reşid Pasha's dismissal, *see* Cevdet, *op. cit.*, i-xii, pp. 8-9; *see* also Kaynar, *op. cit.*, pp. 382-386; *see* also Lûtfi, *op. cit.*, vii, pp. 6-7.

[41] *Mühimme* register, No. 255, doc. dated *rebiyülevvel* 1258.

[42] *Maliye yeni seri*, No. 13663, doc. dated 10 *ramazan* 1257.

order of the governors. A second *fermân*,[43] addressed to Mehmed Sadık Rifat Pasha (former cabinet minister for foreign affairs) in particular and to the province administrators in general, was issued in mid-August, 1842 (*evâil-i receb*, 1258 of *Hijra*). Although the *fermân* claimed to uphold the basic principles of the *Tanzimat*, it in fact abolished the seemingly more radical reforms of Reşid Pasha as having caused mounting problems to state and population, and reinstated the old institutions instead. As the Sultan stated in this *fermân*, he had instituted the Blessed *Tanzimat* in order to further the welfare of the country and the prosperity and security of his subjects. But now, in view of the difficulties which had arisen from their application and so as to overcome these difficulties, some of its provisions were changed by a unanimous decision of the Cabinet (*vükelâ*). The *fermân* then continued with the enumeration of the difficulties and the measures taken to counteract them, as follows:

1) There are some among the people who "in the hope of furthering their own cause" try to obstruct rightful taxation. To this end they incite the population to resistance, causing by their misconduct delays for the government in the collection of taxes. Such mischief-makers shall be sought out by the governors and given their due punishment.

2) Government losses have been suffered by the direct method of using government agents for the collection of tithes.[44] To avoid further losses of this nature, and at the same time to provide business and income for the notables and the people in the provinces,[45] it has been decided that the collecting of tithes shall be given once again to local administrators and prominent men in return for a lump sum.[46]

It should be mentioned here that serious consideration was given to the possibility of reestablishing in full the previous method of farming

[43] *See* İnalcık, *op. cit.*, pp. 687-690, doc. no. 14.

[44] Tithes stored (*der-anbâr*) by the *muhassıl*s and their aids, that is, land-income tax collected in kind and by the government itself, often spoiled because, owing to the lack of transportation facilities, they could not be forwarded immediately to the market to be converted into cash, and there were no silos for keeping them. Such cases caused serious losses in one of the most important government revenue sources, and the full blame for it was, of course, placed on Reşid Pasha.

[45] "*Hem telafâtın önü kesdirilip ve hem de vücûh ve ahâli hakkında bir nevi temettü ve bâis-i ticâret olmak üzere*", meaning in fact to have tax farmers, notables, and *ağa*s once again share in state income as before.

[46] One has to remember that county *kaymakâm*s or *müdür*s were often of the old *âyân* class, only now they were called *vücûh-i ahali.* Also, instead of the word *iltizâm* (farming-out of state revenues) the expression *maktu'an ihâle* (contracted for a lump sum) was being used in the *fermân.*

out all state revenues. On the other hand, as early as the beginning of 1841, in more important areas the government had begun with the consolidation of the office of the *muhassıl* and the installing of newly appointed provincial *defterdârs*, finance officers with wider authority.[47] Then, as soon as Reşid Pasha was ousted, the *muhassıls* were replaced everywhere by these new *defterdârs*.

3) Steps were taken to end all abuse of office and maltreatment of the people by government employees in tax matters. At the same time orders were given that those who incite the population against rightful state taxation should be duly punished.

In the provinces the application of the new measures was entrusted to the *müşîrs* or military governors, who once again had great powers and authority bestowed upon them. To head it all, Rifat Pasha was appointed inspector general for Rumelia, and Mahmud Hasib Pasha, former head of the High Council, for Anatolia. One of the changes was aimed at pleasing the *ulemâ* in particular : the recently established salaried status of the deputy *kadıs*, that is, their receiving regular government pay through the offices of the *muhassıls*, was terminated as of Sept. 18, 1841. Also, *kadıs* were authorized once again to collect their legal fees directly in the courts. Only the taking of *âdet*, a fee previously customary and taken by the *kadıs* and their deputies for drawing up tax registers, remained forbidden.[48]

*

As already mentioned, the tax reforms introduced by Reşid Pasha brought in their wake serious social upheavals throughout the Empire. The uprisings in Rumelia particularly bring out this point clearly.

I. The Uprising in Nish (1841)

The Sultan, in his *fermân* notifying the governors of the adoption of the *Gülhâne Hatt-i Hümâyûnu*, had stated that the aim was first of all "to eliminate the general distress caused by malpractices in taxation and to alleviate the tax burden of the populace, so as to bring about a happy solution to this question".

In the district of Nish (then neighboring Serbia) the special *fermân* of the Sultan — proclaiming the adoption of the principle of equal

[47] About the creating of the *defterdârlık* in İzmir, *see*, *Maliye yeni seri* , No. 13663, f. 46.

[48] İnalcık, *op. cit.*, pp. 685-686, doc. no. 13.

taxation, that is, taxes measured to means, and the abolition of the system of farming out state revenues and the ending of forced labor — was presented to the population at a general meeting at which both Muslim and non-Muslim notables were present.[49] According to the *fermân*, from then on everyone was to pay 3 piastres and 12 paras (1) piastre equaled 40 paras) in taxes to the State for every 100 piastres value of their holdings, and no exemption was to be given from this tax either to Muslim subjects of the area or to those otherwise privileged; taxes from the *râya*s were to be collected by the *knez*es (chiefs) of their villages; no extra dues were to be collected in the future; government officials were not to collect any remunerations for themselves from the peasant population, whether in cash or in sustenance; furthermore, the *subaşı*s (farm magistrates) were to be removed from the villages;[50] only the rural policemen (*kır serdarı*s) were to remain, and they were to cover their personal expenses from their own pay.

The peasant population was greatly pleased with the reforms proclaimed. They interpreted them to suit their own desires expecting that, now that part of the tax burden of the area was to be placed on groups that up to now had been tax exempt, that is the Muslim inhabitants and the so-called *Avrupa tüccarı*s (non-Muslim merchants with special privileges to trade with Europe), the tax burden of the villagers would certainly be reduced to half of the previous amount.[51]

It is only natural that in order to prepare for the application of the tax reforms certain preliminary measures had to be taken. As a first step *muhassıl*s, newly appointed finance officers with broad authority, were assigned by the government everywhere with the immediate task of surveying all personal holdings of the inhabitants, a task which required more than nine months to be completed.

Then, as soon as the actual application of the reforms began, the government was everywhere faced with unexpected difficulties. First of

[49] Wealthy notables among the Bulgarians were called *çorbacı*. Eeach district (*mahalle*) had its own *çorbacı*. For additional information, *see* İnalcık, *Tanzimat ve Bulgar meselesi*, Ankara, 1943, pp. 53, 66, 78-89.

[50] On *subaşı*, *see* below, pp. 125-126; *see* also İnalcık, *Tanzimat ve Bulgar meselesi*, index.

[51] The taxes levied in Nish county and its villages do not show any considerable increase :

In 1253/1837 3 *yük*s and 30,400 piastres (*kuruş*)
In 1254/1838 3 *yük*s and 25,000 piastres (*kuruş*)
In 1255/1839 4 *yük*s
In 1256/1840 3 *yük*s and 79,000 piastres (*kuruş*)

all, there was increasing unrest among the peasant population, many claiming that in the survey their personal holdings had been entered at double their true value. Next, groups until then tax exempt turned against the reforms, "disclaiming the validity of the Blessed *Tanzimat*". Prominent among the latter were the Muslim inhabitants of the fortress of Nish. Having been granted their tax-exempt status by documents of exemption issued by previous sultans, the Muslim inhabitants of this frontier city considered it a great injustice to be subjected to taxation now. The Sultan, on his part, confirmed the reforms by a new *fermân*. Also aroused were the rich Christians, the *çorbacıs*, who up until the proclamation of the *Tanzimat* had paid taxes equal in amount to that of poor peasants, but who now had to pay taxes proportionate to their holdings. As one of the documents says : "Since the well-to-do now have to pay taxes in proportion to their financial means and business profits, they have to pay more than the poor and are upset by this fact", but, hiding their real reason under various complaints, they take it upon themselves to incite the peasant population to rise up against the government.

The main complaints of the *râyas* were formulated by two of the *çorbacıs* who claimed to be the representatives of the *râyas*, namely Nikola Četković from Leskovac and Stoyan Marinković, *pazarbaşı* in Nish, as follows :

1) Though it was first announced that the new ratio of taxation would be 3 piastres and 12 paras per 100 piastres, later on, when it came to the collection of the tax, the ratio of levying was found to be 8 piastres and 12 paras; 2) though the Sultan's *fermân* had proclaimed the abolishment of duties (*resim*) on wine (4 paras per oka) and raki (8 paras per oka), collection of these duties was still being continued; 3) the same as before, the collecting of *zecriyye*[52] was being continued; 4) in addition, unconfirmed reports were heard about the misbehavior of some of the Ottoman officials; one such complaint maintained that the Pasha of the area had come to a village, had had himself entertained at the expense of the inhabitants, and had behaved in general in an unfitting manner; 5) it was also claimed that Muslims often converted Christian women by force.

Ottoman authorities assented to the correctness of the first three of the claims, but rejected the last two as accusations without foundation.

The increase in the tax ratio from 3 to 8 piastres was explained to the

[52] Excise tax on wines and spirits; *see* Vefik, *op. cit.*, ii, p. 404.

people as follows : The total of the taxes to be collected from an area was projected by the government on the basis of previous years' taxes, in the case of the Nish area 3 *yük*s and 79,000 piastres (1 *yük* equaled 1 cargo or 100,000 piastres), and this total, when levied proportionally against the records in the survey book, resulted in the higher ratio. In other words, the government wanted not so much to reduce the total amount of the taxes as to establish a more balanced distribution of the tax burden by levying taxes proportionate to the means of each individual taxpayer. And now that the Muslims, the merchants trading with Europe, the Jews, and the Copts or Gypsies had also been made subject to taxation, the portion of taxes to be paid by the peasant population had, in fact, been reduced to half of the amount of the previous years. The *râya*s, in general, realized and accepted this. But the *çorbacı*s, owners of vineyards, and other rich Christian farmers continued to object to the taxes collected on wine and raki and, to agitate the peasants, threatened to destroy the vineyards, cease to hire the peasants, and cease to buy any of their grapes, rather than pay these taxes. The peasants, on their part, also resisted, saying that since the Sultan had abolished all dues on alcoholic beverages and on forestry, they would refuse to pay such taxes. Aroused by agitators, groups of peasants gathered around the stronghold of Nish. The Pasha there invited nine of the *çorbacı*s to discuss grievances and enjoined the rest of the gathering to disperse. Then, accusing the nine *çorbacı*s of being involved in subversive activities, he arrested them and sent them to Sofia. Only two months later were they set free, and even then, so they claimed, they had to pay the Pasha in order to obtain their release. The arrest of the nine *çorbacı*s only aggravated the already tense situation. Once again non-Muslim peasants, about 1,500 in number, gathered in Nish outside the fortress to voice their grievances and to demonstrate their unwillingness to pay more than a three per-cent ratio in taxes since, so they claimed, everything above that was indeed unlawfully taken, be it by the officials or be it by their own village elders. It is interesting to see that the peasant population of the area even turned against its own village elders if they sided with the Ottoman administrators.[53] To ease the growing tension the tax registers

[53] In the past the *kocabaşı*s, in their status as Christian notables, had often been put in charge by the government of dividing and collecting taxes from the Christian population and forwarding it to those responsible, and tax matters in such cases had been discussed in the court of the local *kadı* where the *kocabaşı*s met with the Muslim notables to confer on the issue. Even after the proclamation of the *Tanzimat*

were ordered brought to the churches for joint examination by the populace and the village-elder council representatives. After careful examination of the registers the *râya*s were given one month to make good on their tax obligations. But the deadline passed without the peasants showing even the slightest intention of paying their debts. On the contrary, they stiffened their resistance, gathering once again around the stronghold of Nish, this time armed with whatever weapons they could lay their hands on. They cut the road leading to Istanbul, seized the mills, and started to kill Muslims who had the misfortune to fall into their hands. Upon receiving this news, Kerim Bey, one of the council members and notables of Nish, taking action on his own, led an attack against the rebelling non-Muslim *râya*s and recaptured from them the Kotina Pass on the Nish–Istanbul road. In the meantime, the governor of Nish, attributing the rebellion to the instigation of the *çorbacı*s and wanting to frighten them with a show of strength, called in the Albanian soldiery from Kosova (according to one report some 200, according to another some 1,500 men), and sent them against the rebellious villages. Using canon, the Albanian troops then (April, 1841) captured the towers (*kule*s) in Kamaniça (Kamenitsa) and Mutafça (Matievats), two villages considered to be the chief rebel centers. The uprising finally ended by the village elder Miloe (Turkish : Milyo or Milyoye), leader of the rebels, being killed in a clash and the *râya*s slowly dispersing and returning to their villages. But this did not mean the end of the calamities for the area. Though the leaders of the Albanian irregulars had sworn that there will be no plundering, the soldiers did not keep this promise. According to a later report, some 205 of the villages in the Nish area were burned down by the Albanians, many of the villagers killed, women and children taken prisoner, and livestock everywhere taken away by force. The inhabitants of twenty-eight villages barely escaped by crossing over into Serbia with all their belongings.[54]

---

the *kocabaşı*s, though often members of the administrative councils, in general kept their former positions as tax collectors. Their frequent transgressions in this capacity aroused the *râya*s against them.

[54] J. A. Blanqui in his *Voyage en Bulgarie pendant l'année 1841* (Paris, 1845, pp. 175-177), though relating the course of events somewhat differently, ascribes the continuous unrest in this area mainly to the abuses of collectors as well as of local authorities in tax matters and to the growing antagonism between the Muslim *ağa*s and the Christian *râya*s. But he also points to the influence of the Serbs on the rebellious mood of the population in Bulgaria, the exaggerated news spread around about

Russia, anxious to use even the smallest incident to enhance her role as the protector of the Christian population in the Balkans, once again found a good excuse in this turmoil which had come about despite the good intentions of the Ottoman government. Count Nesselrode handed a note of protest to the Sublime Porte condemning the incident. It also was made known that the Czar's government had decided to send an observer to visit the places in question and to see what measures were to be taken to prevent the reoccurrence of similar unfortunate incidents and mistreatment of the population. The Sublime Porte was disturbed. At first efforts were made to prevent the visit by declaring the incident already closed. Then, however, consent was given that such an observer might pass through the dsitrict of Nish, but without doing any direct investigating there.[55] The other great powers did not want to be surpassed by Russia. France, who, after her defeat in Egypt, was now involved in the unrest in Lebanon, had also decided to take action by sending a note condemning the Nish incident and expressing her intention of making inquiries into the deplorable affair. As is known, M. Blanqui, a member of the French Academy was eventually sent to the area.[56] It should be added here that it was about this time that rebel agents made contact with the French consul in the area in an effort to secure some 40,000 guns to prepare for a general uprising.[57] Even Prince Metternich hastened to send a note deploring the unfortunate incident, pointing out that turbulence such as this could lead to general upheavals throughout the Ottoman Empire which, in turn, would have damaging effects on the efforts of those outside her boundaries who were sincerely trying to defend the cause of the Empire.[58]

---

the casualties of the Nish incident, the excesses of the Albanian irregulars against the *râyas*, and the unsuccessful or rather the distorted application of the reform measures in the area. Another important source of information on the Nish incident is C. Romanski, "The Austrian Documents", *Sbornik narodni umotvorenia* 26 (1910-1911). According to the Ottoman sources the rebels numbered about 1,500. Arif Hikmet reported that uprisings were simultaneous in the Nish, Leskovça and Şehirköy counties.

[55] Lûtfi, *op. cit.*, vii, pp. 109-113.

[56] *See* J. A. Blanqui, "Communication sur l'état social des population de la Turquie d'Europe", *Séance de l'Académie des sciences morales et politiques* 1, Paris, 1842, and his *Considérations sur l'état actuel de la Turquie d'Europe*, Paris, 1843.

[57] *İrâdeler*, Box 13, doc. No. 2420, *Başvekâlet* Archives. The râyas were forbidden to carry arms. The Bulgarian villagers shouted to Blanqui, "Poutschka! Poutschka!" meaning that they were helpless before the well-armed Muslims.

[58] *İrâdeler*, Box 13, doc. No. 2420.

The Sublime Porte made serious efforts to bring the unfortunate incident to a quick conclusion, hoping thus to foreclose the possibility of any further foreign interference. To expedite matters, Ahmed Tevfik Bey was sent to Nish to investigate and report on the event to the government. According to his findings, the incident was not an uprising brought about by the unjust treatment the population had suffered in tax and other matters, as earlier maintained, but rather an upheaval of a political nature. Ever since the time when the *râya*s of some six *nâhiye*s of this province had first been incited to rise up and demand the annexation of this region to Serbia, there had been a growing hope among the Christian peasants that the Muslim inhabitants, realizing their precarious situation, would eventually leave the area. It was this hope, fanned by the Christian notables, that had brought about the present incident. Indeed, when thirty-five non-Muslim emissaries of the peasant population of the area came to Nish to discuss questions in connection with the repatriation of the group of *râya*s who had fled to Serbia to escape the Albanian irregulars, in the course of the discussion they demanded the instituting of a special administrative system for Nish, a kind of home rule (*idâre-i istiklâliyet*), as they referred to it.

The fact that this region was in the immediate vicinity of autonomous Serbia had undoubtedly had a decisive influence on the events that had take place there. The *râya*s, whether rebels or non-rebels, found convenient refuge and support in Serbia. Not only did the Prince of Serbia take in the *râya*s of twenty-eight villages who fled with all their livestock and other belongings at the time of the turbulence, but he even went so far as to declare that should there be soldiers sent after them, he would consider it his duty to protect them. The rebels too had placed all their hopes in the Prince of Serbia. But while the Princess Liubitsa was all for direct interference on behalf of the rebels, Michael Obrenović, the Prince himself, or more exactly his ministers, were hesitant. And not without reason. The Sublime Porte sent Prince Michael a note of warning and demanded that the Bulgarian *râya*s who had fled there be returned without delay. In addition, Miloš Obrenović, the former Prince of Serbia, who had been expelled from Serbia and was then in Vienna, had established firm relations with the Bulgarian revolutionaries in Walachia, hoping that through a general uprising in Rumelia he could eventually gain leadership over all the South Slavs. The Ottoman authorities, on their part, were in serious doubt about the measures to be taken next, fearing that leniency toward the rebels might be interpreted by the *râya*s as a sign of weakness and encourage them to a general uprising which would set aflame the whole of Rumelia.[59]

The Sublime Porte ordered a deeper probe into the Nish incident. Arif Hikmet, who had been appointed general inspector of Rumelia and had been given the task of instituting the *Tanzimat* there, now hastened to Nish and, without much delay, submitted a report to the Sublime Porte on the findings of his investigation.[60]

In Istanbul the incident was discussed at length by the High Council in the light of the reports gathered from various sources, the Serbian Government being one of them. The Grand Vizier in a memorandum to the Sultan summarized the results of these discussions, stating: "It is apparent that the disorders which recently occurred in Rumelia and Anatolia were caused in most cases by the resentment of the *râya*s over their mistreatment by government officials, especially where tax matters were concerned." Thus it was concluded that immediate measures should be taken to pacify the *râya*s. First of all, a military unit under the command of Yakub Pasha and made up of regular soldiers (*asâkir-i nizâmiye*) was sent to Nish. Furthermore, ransom was paid to the Albanian irregulars in order to free from their hands the *râya*s they had captured and were holding prisoner, and to have livestock and other possessions taken by force from the population restored to their owners. The Sultan ordered the distribution of 150,000 piastres to the *râya*s as his imperial gift. Also, discussions were undertaken with the authorities involved to pave the way for the repatriation of the *râya*s who, during the turmoil, had escaped to Serbia. As a result, the refugees now slowly started returning and, by the end of June, 1841, as many as 400 families had come back and were re-settled in their villages.

The problems brought to light by the Nish uprising are illustrative

[59] On the Serbian policy during the Nish incident, *see* Lûtfi, *op. cit.*, vii, pp. 116-120; also V. Stojančević published some important studies on the Serbian interest in the area and the rebellious movements in Western Bulgaria between 1804 and 1840: "The First Serbian Uprising, Bulgaria and Bulgarians", *Istoriski Glasnik* 1 ii (1954), pp. 121-147; *The Prince Miloš and Eastern Serbia, 1838-1839*, Belgrade, 1957; "The Liberation Movement in the Region of Nish in 1833 and 1834/35", *Istoriski Časopis* 5 (1955), pp. 427-436; "Two Armed Incidents on the Turco–Serbian Frontier During the First Reign of Prince Miloš", *Istoriski Časopis* 4 (1954), pp. 129-145; "Prince Miloš and the Belogračik Revolt of 1836", *Istoriski Časopis* 3 (1952), pp. 131-140 (all in Serbian); *see* also V. J. Vučković, *The Serbian Crisis during the Eastern Question, 1842-1843*, Belgrade, 1957.

[60] *İrâdeler*, Box 13, doc. No. 2420.

of the conditions prevailing in Rumelia at the time the *Tanzimat* was introduced. The proclamation of the *Tanzimat* created high hopes among the non-Muslim population who had taken verbatim all the promises made in it by the Sultan. And then, because the realization of these promises was slow in forthcoming and the rights granted to them were not immediately recognized, the Christian *râya*s turned to force and resistance movements started to break out throughout the region. This open resistance clearly demonstrated that the *râya*s were determined to stand against any further government abuses, particularly in tax matters, and had decided to seek their rights by all available means. The determined attitude of the *râya*s and the subsequent interference by foreign powers caused deep apprehension at the Sublime Porte among the supporters of the *Tanzimat*. The conservatives on the other hand were satisfied that the event had proven them right in their predictions of the dangers hidden in the application of the *Tanzimat*. The Nish uprising, they maintained, confirmed their view that the *Tanzimat* catered too much to the *râya*s and that this was bound to create the danger of a general uprising and the disintegration of the entire Empire.

On the practical line, the confusion that resulted from disrupting the old system in order to institute the new tax policy of the *Tanzimat* greatly hindered the tax-gathering efforts of the government. An especially interesting feature of the Nish uprising is the prominent role the privileged class, members of the previously tax-exempt groups, played in it. Investigations showed that the leaders on the one side were the *çorbacı*s and *kocabaşı*s who had incited the *râya*s, and on the other side the *ağa*s who wanted to suppress the revolt of the *râya*s by force. Neither could accept the idea of losing their old privileged status and, "disclaiming the validity of the Blessed *Tanzimat*", made a stand against it. In addition, the notables of the Christian communities had obviously taken the leading role in the uprisings in the hope that, in the event Ottoman sovereignty faltered and the Muslim inhabitants left the area, they, being on hand, would take the place of the *ağa*s.

It becomes clear that in all this social turmoil local officials neither restrained themselves from taking sides, nor were they able to free themselves from the old practices of abusing office. Thus conservatives in general dismissed the acts of violence committed by the Albanian irregulars as excusable by the *Sherî'at* since, indeed, the lands of any non-Muslim who rebelled against the rule of the Caliph were regarded as *Dār al-Ḥarb* (The Land of War). Yet the reformists at the Sublime Porte were convinced that in the interest of the stability of the Empire it was more important to comply with the needs of the immediate situation than to adhere to the rules of the *Şerî'at*; the discussions in the High Council at that time show that the main concern of the central government was to save the Empire. Nevertheless, following as it did in the wake of the Nish insurrection, the Vidin uprising of 1850 made even more obvious the helplessness of the supporters of the *Tanzimat* in the face of the social clashes that aroused the masses to act with such vehemence and zeal.

II. The Uprising in Vidin (1850)

Nine years after the uprising in Nish, a new insurrection broke out in the northern section of the same area and this time on an even larger scale. In 1850, in the month of May, some 10,000 Bulgarian *râya*s revolted in the Vidin, Sahra, Belgradcık and Lom sub-counties; they began to rob and kill Muslims wherever they encountered them, in the villages as well as in the fields. Just as during the Nish uprising, they besieged the strongholds where Muslim inhabitants fled for safety, they cut the road leading from Vidin to Istanbul, and they tried to set aflame the whole of Bulgaria by sending agitators all over the territory. While the governor made desperate efforts to find a peaceful solution by sending an inspector to the area, the *ağa*s from Vidin brought together a few bands of irregulars, met force with force, and succeeded in dispersing the rebels. Some of the dispersed *râya*s then went back to their villages, but the majority of them took the road to the Serbian border. There they remained until the arrival of a regular military unit commanded by the inspector general, Ali Riza Pasha made it safe for them to return to their villages.[61]

Though the role of the numerous revolutionary committees acting mainly from Serbia cannot be denied, nor the impact of the general international situation on these events dismissed entirely,[62] the true reason behind this uprising, same as in the case of the Nish uprising, is to be sought partly in the prevailing land and tax systems but mainly in the worsening relations between the landless non-Muslim peasants

[61] The Vidin uprising is described in detail according to the Ottoman documents in İnalcık, *Tanzimat ve Bulgar meselesi*, pp. 45-111; *see* also K. Panov, *Belogradčiškoto Vstanie*, Belogradčik, 1937; *see* also D. Kosev, "Vstanieto na selianite v Severozapadna Bulgaria prez 1850 g.", *Istoričeski Pregled* 6 (1950), pp. 4-5.

[62] İnalcık, *Tanzimat ve Bulgar meselesi*, pp. 91-92; *see* also Kaynar, *op. cit.*, pp. 272-283.

and the landowner Muslim *ağa*s, holders of large estates. It was strain on the social relationships caused by the proclamation of the *Tanzimat* that led to this sudden outburst of violence.[63] This also was the conclusion the Ottoman authorities arrived at from their investigations.

In this frontier area, with the protection and safety of the territory in mind, "each village had been entrusted to an *ağa* by a title deed",[64] a privilege given only to Muslims. By dint of the *mukâtaa* system (leasing out of state properties), that is, through the down-payment of a lump sum (*icâre-i muaccele*) arrived at in open bidding, the more prominent *ağa*s of the area had gained control over extensive tracts of state lands; malpractice in these dealing was by no means an uncommon phenomenon.[65] Later on the *ağa*s who were given the use of these properties for life and who could pass their rights on to their sons tried to turn the slackening of central control to their advantage and started to act as if these lands were their private property. The *râya*s lived on these lands and cultivated them as tenants of the *ağa*s. They compensated for the use of the land by working for the *ağa* without pay for a period of one or two months. In addition, they had to furnish yearly one wagonload of firewood or pay to the *ağa* 12 piasters instead; and there was a grain tax (*hırızma zahiresi*) whereby each family had to provide yearly 25 okas (1 oka equaled 2. 8 pounds) of various grains, and a corn tax (*budarlık*) whereby 30 to 40 okas from each wagonload of corn had to be turned over to the *ağa*; they had to pay 12 paras for each grapevine in their vineyards and also a certain amount of cheese as a sheep-grazing tax. Beyond these they still had to pay to the *ağa* levies such as the hive tax and the cowshed tax. All in all, the yearly taxes a *râya* had to deliver to his *ağa* equalled by and large the amount of the head- and tithe taxes he had to pay yearly to the government. Furthermore, the *ağa*s who lived in towns or cities, left the administration of the villages on their estates to farm

[63] For full details on the system of land tenure called *gospodarlık*, *see* İnalcık, *Tanzimat ve Bulgar meselesi*, pp. 83-107; *see* also C. Dimitrov, "Pages de l'histoire du mouvement revolutionaire en 1850 dans le Vilayet de Nish", *Izvestia na Instituta za Istoria pri BAN* 16-17 (1966), pp. 407-422 (in Bulgarian); *see* also C. Gandev, "L'apparition des rapports capitalistes dans l'économie rurale de la Bulgarie du Nord-Ouest au cours du XVIIIe s.", *Etudes Historiques*, Sofia, 1960, pp. 207-220.

[64] *See* İnalcık, *Tanzimat ve Bulgar meselesi*, p. 91.

[65] After the proclamation of the *Tanzimat* relations between the big landowners and the peasants deteriorated everywhere in the Balkans, thus preparing the way for the violent insurrections in Bulgaria and Bosnia. For the latter *see* the bibliography in *Ten Years of Yugoslav Historiography, 1945-1955*, Beograd, 1955, pp. 450-462, and *Historiographie yougoslave, 1955-1965*, Beograd, 1965, pp. 366-378.

bailiffs, called *subaşıs*, who made their living at the expense of the *râya*s and, in addition, exacted from them about 1,400 to 1,500 piastres each year for travel- and similar expenditures. They even undertook to collect for themselves fines and dues which, earlier in the *tımar* system, the *sipahi*s had been entitled to. To summarize, the total perversion of Ottoman institutions had led to a situation in the Vidin area as elsewhere that could best be characterized the de facto rule by the Muslim *ağa*s.

As soon as the abolition of all forced labor was proclaimed by the *Gülhâne Hattı*, the *râya* population of Vidin, just as the *râya*s of the other areas did,[66] refused to render any of the services demanded by the *ağa*s as compensation for their land rent payments. The *ağa*s countered this by taking a stand on their rights as landlords, even going so far as to claim that the land did not belong to the state but was in fact their personal property. Tension grew, and the matter was presented to Istanbul. The government confirmed once again decisively that by the Sultan's *fermân* the corvée in Vidin, as elsewhere, had been abolished. But the Council of Vidin, which was the authority whose responsibility it was to implement these orders, was in the hands of the village *ağa*s. They protested the ruling and, resorting to the principles of the Sultan's *fermân*, retorted by saying that every citizen was the free owner and absolute master of his lands and properties, and no one was entitled to use land that belonged to somebody else except with just compensation.[67] The Sublime Porte, desirous that the landowner class should not suffer injustice either, declared that since the matter entailed a dispute between two parties, it was to be settled by the two parties coming to terms with each other. Upon this the *knez*es, as representatives of the *râya*s, met with the landowner *ağa*s to discuss the issues. As a result of their discussion, the rights of the *ağa*s as landowners and their due share from the produce were agreed upon; this agreement was then approved by the Sublime Porte as valid beginning with the year 1841.

Though forced labor services had been abolished, the main root of the problem, that is, the question of the *râya*s and the lands they cultivated, had not been touched upon. It is interesting to see how painstakingly the reformists, with all their adherence to Western liberalism, protected the ownership rights of the landlord *ağa*s without questioning

[66] On forced labor in Bosnia, *see* İnalcık, "Bosna'da Tanzimat'ın tatbikine ait vesikalar", *Tarih Vesikaları Dergisi* 5, p. 38.

[67] *See* İnalcık, *Tanzimat ve Bulgar meselesi*, pp. 95-96.

by what title the *ağa*s were holding these lands.[68] Naturally it would be unfair to blame the reformists for not having undertaken thorough land reforms which, in all probability, would have thrown the whole Empire into complete turmoil, not to mention that such a revolutionary measure would unavoidably have broken the authority and strength of the Muslim population in frontier territories and would have left the area in question, which the Serbs already had their eyes on, completely unprotected against such outside designs. After 1841 the *ağa*s, benefiting from the concept of ownership as expressed in the *Tanzimat*, were able to further strengthen their hold over state lands by the mere fact that they were in control of the *sancak* councils and in a position to implement the orders from Istanbul as they saw fit. In 1850, the High Council in Istanbul had come to the conclusion that these *ağa*s simply ignored the reforms and persisted in "making the *râya*s their personal slaves".

To sum it up, the main theme behind the resistance movements both in Rumelia and in Anatolia was the same : the application of the new principles of the taxation system. Yet we also find that by bringing about a radical change in the attitude of the *râya*s toward existing conditions and by undermining the privileges of the rural notables, Muslims and Christians alike, the *Tanzimat* set off a series of social reactions in the Ottoman Empire. Paradoxically enough, the leaders of these movements in most cases came from the privileged social groups of the ancien régime, Christian notables, *kocabaşı*s and *çorbacı*s in the Balkans, and Muslim *ağa*s, *âyân* and *eşrâf* in Anatolia. There was, however, a basic difference between the two. The Christian leaders in Rumelia were determined to extend the meaning of the reforms to give their endeavor the character of a nationalistic movement in close ranks with peasantry, the rising urban bourgeoisie, and the intelligentsia, since the elimination of the Muslim landlord *ağa*s would have been beneficial to all three of these groups. In contrast, the Muslim *ağa*s and *eşrâf* in Rumelia, as well as in Anatolia, were anxious to preserve the traditional social structure in which the institutions of the ancien régime were sanctioned by the *Şerî'at*. From then on, parallel to the growing social and national movements in the Balkan provinces, Turkish political life in the homeland was to become the scene of conflicts between the traditionalism of the powerful provincial *ağa*s and *eşrâf* and the modernization efforts of the central bureaucracy.

[68] One of the measures taken in 1847 under Western influence was the extension of inheritance rights to include daughters, an additional step toward full recognition of land leases as private properties (*idem*, p. 98).

[illegible] clearly [illegible] the [illegible] [illegible] not [illegible] Whatever [illegible] into complete turmoil. For convenience [illegible] have been [illegible] would have [illegible] already has [illegible] of the [illegible] and even [illegible] they were in control [illegible] and [illegible] [illegible] the [illegible] of the [illegible] and [illegible] the [illegible] of the [illegible] in 1839 [illegible] of the [illegible] the [illegible] period [illegible]

[illegible]

INDEX